The Shaw Mansion.

CONNECTICUT'S NAVAL OFFICE AT NEW LONDON DURING THE WAR OF THE AMERICAN REVOLUTION

VOLUME II OF COLLECTIONS OF THE NEW LONDON HISTORICAL SOCIETY

Ernest E. Rogers

HERITAGE BOOKS
2008

HERITAGE BOOKS
AN IMPRINT OF HERITAGE BOOKS, INC.

Books, CDs, and more—Worldwide

For our listing of thousands of titles see our website at

www.HeritageBooks.com

Published 2008 by
HERITAGE BOOKS, INC.
Publishing Division
100 Railroad Avenue #104
Westminster, Maryland 21157

Copyright © 1933 Ernest E. Rogers

All rights reserved. No part of this book may be reproduced or transmitted in any form or by any means, electronic or mechanical, including photocopying, recording or by any information storage and retrieval system without written permission from the author, except for the inclusion of brief quotations in a review.

International Standard Book Number: 978-0-7884-1239-4

*To my Wife
Fanny Gorton Rogers
With Affection*

Publication Committee

Howard Palmer
Elizabeth Gorton
John Edwin Wells
Ernest E. Rogers, *Chairman*

CONTENTS

	Page
Dedication	iii
Preface	xiii
Introduction	xv
I. The Early Port of New London, 1646-1763	1
Maps from the Faden Collection	5
II. Nathaniel Shaw, Jr., Merchant, 1763-1782	6
His Will	10
Letter written by Josiah Waters, Jr., to Thomas Shaw	12
Letter from John de Neufville & Son to Nathaniel Shaw, Jr.	14
Bill of Exchange by Thomas Turner to Thomas Burton, Trustee	15
Letter from Thomas Shaw to Mr. Texier	15
III. The Naval Office	16
Commissions as Naval Agent from the	
Continental Congress	18
Colony of Connecticut	19
State of Connecticut	19
Letter from Nathaniel Shaw, Jr., to Jonathan Trumbull	26
Letter from John Lawrence to Nathaniel Shaw, Jr.	27
Letter from Daniel Tillinghast to Nathaniel Shaw, Jr.	27
Receipt from John Keeney to Nathaniel Shaw, Jr.	28
Receipt from Colonel Ledyard to Nathaniel Shaw, Jr.	28
Flag of Truce Document	29
Letter from Brigadier General John Tyler to Brigadier General Arnold	29
Letter from David Sproat to Nathaniel Shaw	30
Petition for Provisions	30
Permission for Sloop *Queen of France* to return to New London	31
List of Naval Prisoners	32
Acknowledgment of Jeremiah Pemberton concerning Exchange of Prisoner	34
Seven Letters from the Marine Committee of the Continental Congress to Nathaniel Shaw, Jr.	34
Eleven Letters from the Board of Admiralty to Nathaniel Shaw, Jr.	38
New London Prison Ships	44
IV. The First Naval Expedition under the authority of Congress	45
Appointments of the First Officers of the Fleet	45
Letter from Esek Hopkins to John Hancock	47
Letter from Captain D. W. Knox, U. S. N. (Ret.)	49
Excerpts from the "Bahamas Handbook"	51
Excerpt from "Nassau Guardian"	52

CONTENTS

		Page
V.	The Ship *General Putnam*, New London Privateer..........	54
	The Dunmore Silver....................................	56
	Letter from Nathaniel Shaw, Jr., to Captain Deshon......	58
	Letter from Nathaniel Shaw and Company to Captain Nathaniel Saltonstall	58
	A List of the Officers and Men on Board the Ship *Putnam*	59
	Petition presented in Boston by Josiah Waters, Jr.	61
	Instructions from Congress concerning Capture of British Vessels	62
	Commission from Congress to Nathaniel Saltonstall......	64
VI.	The Shaw Mansion	66
VII.	The Shaw and the Perkins Families........................	77
	Genealogical Record	79
	Tombstone Inscriptions	82
VIII.	The Shaw Collection..	84
	Collection in New London...............................	84
	Collection at Yale.......................................	85
	Account Book No. 4 of Nathaniel Shaw, Jr., Merchant...	86
IX.	George Washington's Correspondence with Nathaniel Shaw, Jr.	88
	George Washington's Visits to New London.............	88
	Five Letters from George Washington to Nathaniel Shaw, Jr.	90
	Letter from George Washington to Major General Greene	95
	Fifteen Letters from Nathaniel Shaw, Jr., to George Washington	95
	Letter from F. Greene to George Washington............	105
	Invoice for Arms from Clark & Nightingale to Nathaniel Shaw, Jr.	105
	Invoice for Arms from Daniel Tillinghast to Nathaniel Shaw, Jr.	106
	Letter from Thomas Shaw and Others to Governor Trumbull	106
X.	John Hancock's Letters to Nathaniel Shaw, Jr.	110
	Two Letters	110
XI.	Esek Hopkins' Letters to Nathaniel Shaw, Jr.	111
	Six Letters from Esek Hopkins to Nathaniel Shaw, Jr. ...	112
	Receipt from Esek Hopkins to Henry Billings...........	115
	Receipt from Esek Hopkins to Nathaniel Shaw, Jr.	116
	Receipt from Samuel Lyon (Esek Hopkins' Secretary) to Nathaniel Shaw, Jr.	116
	Two Letters from Thomas Shaw to Esek Hopkins.....116,	118
	Letter from Esek Hopkins to Thomas Shaw............	117
	Receipt from Samuel Eddy to Thomas Shaw for Esek Hopkins	119
XII.	Benedict Arnold's Letters to Nathaniel Shaw, Jr.	120
	Four Letters	120
	One Bill of Sale from Captain Truxton to Benedict Arnold	124

CONTENTS

		Page
XIII.	Captain Charles Bulkeley	125
	His Manuscript Narrative of Personal Experiences in the War of the American Revolution	126
	The Inscriptions on his Monument	129
	The First American Ensign	130
XIV.	The New London Lighthouse	132
	Built with Funds from a Lottery	132
	The Harris Family	132
	Tax on Vessels to Maintain the Lighthouse	134
XV.	Marquis de Lafayette's Visit to New London	135
	Article by Nathaniel Shaw Perkins	135
	Receipt for Payment of Use of Horses by Lafayette, from his Aide-de-Camp	137
	Letter from William H. Jones to Ebenezer Way	138
	Letter from Frederick Lee to Ebenezer Way	138
	Address by Judge Elias Perkins to General Lafayette	139
XVI.	The New London Custom Houses	140
	The King's Custom House	140
	Change from Colonial to State Government	140
	The United States Custom House	141
	Letter from Alexander Hamilton to Jedediah Huntington	142
XVII.	The Later Port of New London, 1783-1933	143
	Warren, Survey in 1807	143
	Meyer, Survey in 1846	143
	Map by Theodore Barrell, 1820, including Wharves	143
	Map by Colfax and Holt, 1847, including Wharves	144
	City Map, about 1865 to 1871, including Wharves	144
	Whaling Industry	144
	United States Submarine Base	145
	United States Coast Guard	147
	Connecticut's State Pier	147
XVIII.	A Journey of Thirty-one Years in Retrospect	150
XIX.	Unveiling of Commemorative Tablet on the Shaw Mansion	163
	Program	164
	Presentation by Ernest E. Rogers	165
	Acceptance by Mrs. Minor	168
XX.	The Mercantile Letter Book of Nathaniel Shaw, Jr. (complete) December 27, 1765, to July 23, 1783	169
	Captains mentioned in the Letter Book	337
Bibliography		338
Index of Names		339
Index of Vessels		356

ILLUSTRATIONS

The Shaw Mansion	Frontispiece
	Facing Page
Map of the Early Port of New London	5
Thomas Shaw and his Mother, Temperance Harris Shaw	7
Davis Quadrant	9
Letter from John Hancock to Nathaniel Shaw, Jr.	17
Letter from Nathaniel Shaw, Jr., to Governor Jonathan Trumbull	47
Invoice of 34 Cannon from Nathaniel Shaw, Jr., to Governor Jonathan Trumbull	49
Old Fort Montagu, Nassau, New Providence, Bahama Islands	51
Type of Privateer Ship of 20 Guns	54
The Dunmore Silver	56
Cannon, 24-Pounder on U. S. S. *Constitution*	62
Elizabeth Gorton, when assuming the office of Secretary in 1901	66
The Summer House and Root Cellar	70
Jane Richards Perkins in the Summer House	72
The Shaw Mansion (rear view)	76
Lucretia Harris Rogers Shaw, Mary Shaw Woodbridge	78
Ellen Richards Perkins, Dr. Nathaniel Shaw Perkins, Joanna Burnham Perkins Caulkins, Nathaniel Shaw Perkins, Jr., Dr. Nathaniel Shaw Perkins	80
William W. Perkins, Benjamin R. Perkins (above)	82
The Washington Room	89
The New London Lighthouse	132
Judge Elias Perkins	135
Lucretia Shaw Woodbridge Perkins and son, Nathaniel Shaw Perkins	137
The New London Custom House	140
The Seal of the City of New London	143
Map of the Later Port of New London	144
Ernest E. Rogers, when assuming the office of President in 1900	150
Commemorative Tablet	163
Map of New London and Harbor	End Papers

PREFACE

THIS book is the outgrowth of a long-cherished dream. It had its inception thirty-seven years ago, February 22, 1896, on which date the late Nathaniel Shaw Perkins invited the author to the Shaw Mansion, showed him the rare documents, letters and manuscripts known as the "Shaw Collection," and unfolded to him the history of the house and its occupants, present and past, especially emphasizing the important rôle enacted by Nathaniel Shaw, Junior, as Naval and Marine Agent during the period of the American Revolution.

Among the immediate results of the call was my article of March 14, 1896, in a local newspaper, titled the "Shaw Mansion, Connecticut's Naval Office." This designation was used to show that while Lebanon possessed the War Office of Revolutionary fame, New London still retained the historic Naval Office.

The Lebanon War Office had been given to the Connecticut Society Sons of the American Revolution and restored by that organization in 1891. Patriotic pilgrimages were being made to Lebanon from many places in Connecticut and elsewhere. Since the Naval Office was a private home it could not be exploited publicly at that time. However, it is now a public institution, the mecca of tourists from all sections of our country, owned and occupied by the New London County Historical Society as a permanent home.

The contents of this book, gathered from original sources, reveal for the first time a wealth of local, important, and historic material heretofore unpublished. Much more could be written without completely covering this interesting field of research.

It is remarkable after the lapse of many years, with every member of the large family deceased, that not only the property should have passed to an organization devoted to its preservation, but also its story should be written by one who for nearly four decades hoped the opportunity would arise for performing this service.

E. E. R.

INTRODUCTION

THIS year completes the sesquicentennial of the end of the American Revolution, the Treaty of Peace having been signed at Paris on September 3, 1783. We of New London, a town whose career was almost blotted out by the ruthless hand of war, in the burning of many of its public buildings and residences, its storehouses and shipping, the wharves and stores, and the loss of life and of the business, should at this late day survey the causes and effects of those days "that tried men's souls" in no spirit of passion or prejudice, but with calm judgment and with accurate discrimination, especially since there is so much reliable historical material at hand.

Because, occasionally, that which was considered authentic history, eventually proved to be only tradition, modern historical scholarship now insists that in the writing of history the author should consult original sources of information as well as the existing publications upon the subject. Take for example Stuart's *Life* of Nathan Hale, our own citizen by adoption. It is highly gratifying that Stuart performed that excellent service to the memory of Hale at the particular period when information could be acquired first hand, and probably could not have been obtained later. Yet Stuart's work is only the foundation of Hale memorabilia, for certain items given to him as facts proved upon the investigation of later writers to be only tradition. Hale's own relatives passed away without acquaintance with the full details of his last days as known to us. The late historian, Professor Henry P. Johnston, of the College of the City of New York, upon consultation of the proper war records, both in this country and in England, eliminated certain statements made to Stuart and added several new facts with official proofs. Johnston's second history, *Nathan Hale, 1776*, was published in 1914, thirteen years after the first history, as the author had found new and authentic material in London and elsewhere which disproved several conclusions in his first edition of 1901.

The large number of accessions to the archives of the State Library in Hartford, and to those of historical societies, public libraries and private collections, should indicate the depletion of Americana in the attics, trunks and hiding places of old colonial homes. Nevertheless, there has come recently into the possession of the New London County Historical Society the Shaw Collection consisting of certain furniture, portraits and heirlooms by bequest of the late Jane R. Perkins; also, by agreement with Miss Perkins at the time of the purchase of the property, certain important papers of great value pertaining to the eminent services of Nathaniel Shaw, Jr., and family in connection with the American Revolution. Therefore it is possible to publish at this time this volume of original documents and letters including the Mercantile Letter Book, all of which remained in one family and in one house for a period of over one hundred and fifty years. The papers are now in a bank vault. In addition to the New London Collection a large section of papers was given to Yale College by Miss Perkins.

It is significant that both the Lebanon War Office and the New London Naval Office of the American Revolution should have been situated in New London County. The Trumbull papers of the War Office (now in the State Library) are the most valuable of that period of the County and of the State. The Shaw papers of the Naval Office are said to be the second in importance in New London County.

On the inside of the covers of this book appear exact illustrations from a photostatic copy of "A Sketch of New London and Groton with the attacks made on Forts Trumbull & Griswold by the British Troops under the Command of Brig[r] Gen[l] Arnold Sept 6th 1781." This is from the original manuscript drawing by the British engineers at the time, and is a part of the Faden Collection, as explained in the text. The reader will observe the original orthography is used in reproducing the manuscripts. Particularly noticeable will be long "s."

The contents of this volume have a direct correlation to the

Naval Office, its present and past owners and the period covered. They deal with family and individual patriotism, and they give an unusual color to the services of the persons concerned for the scenes were enacted at home and among relatives. It is hoped that this original material, here first published, will furnish theses for students of history, encourage the spirit of research and promote the publication of local history amplified along the manifold lines herein mentioned, so that men and ships sailing from New London in the American Revolution may receive their just recognition on the pages of history. Fascinating historical novels could be woven with the Shaw Mansion and family as a background in connection with the mercantile ships and the privateers.

The autograph letters of Benedict Arnold are an illustration of an added interpretation of his varied career, showing his local investments and, only a month previous to the public announcement of his treason, his request to Nathaniel Shaw, Jr., for an accounting of the voyage of the sloop *John*. Without doubt, at the time of his attack on New London, Arnold was better acquainted with the details of the shipping and the defenseless condition of the town because of the absence of most of the soldiers and seamen, than heretofore has been realized.

Acknowledgment is made to Miss Elizabeth Gorton, Executive Secretary of the New London County Historical Society, for reading the proof and preparing the index; to George S. Godard, State Librarian, for many courtesies; to Andrew Keogh, Librarian, and Miss Anne S. Pratt, Reference Librarian, of the Yale University Library; to Dr. John Edwin Wells of New London; to Howard Palmer of New London; to Hon. Hiram Bingham of Washington, D. C.; to Frederick W. Edgerton, Librarian of the Public Library of New London; to Mrs. Alverda S. Beck of Providence, R. I.; to Louis F. Middlebrook of Hartford; to the Misses Nevins of Waterford and to the Essex Institute, Salem, Mass.

ERNEST ELIAS ROGERS.

New London, Connecticut,
  September 3, 1933.

I

THE EARLY PORT OF NEW LONDON
1646-1763

WHEN that bright star of the great Puritan emigration to New England from the mother country, John Winthrop the Younger, sailed into this port to build his home and found a settlement, he chose a spot forming a crescent with a cove on the south and a cove at the north on the west bank of the "faire harbour" some three miles from the mouth of the river Pequot. He located his own home in the woodland glen at the head of the northern cove now bearing his name. Here he built his house of stone on a location which is now the southwest corner of Winthrop and Mill Streets, and nearby established the town mill which, with its picturesque surroundings and babbling brook, still endures in the heart of a city as an historic landmark visited by multitudes of tourists.

New London's natal day was May 6, 1646. On that date Winthrop received from the Massachusetts Bay Colony his commission for making a settlement in the conquered Pequot country. He was no ordinary adventurer. He came from a family distinguished in England and afterwards in America, his father having become the founder of Boston and the Governor of the Massachusetts Bay Colony. He became the founder of New London and the Governor of the Colony of Connecticut. Among the many contributions made to the advancement of the times in which he lived his supreme service was obtaining from King Charles II, in person, the royal charter (the only American colonial charter without power of kingly veto) making Connecticut free all but in name. This charter embodied the first written constitution of the colony (the fundamental orders of 1639) and was the basis of government until the adoption of the present constitution of

1818. The government of the Colony of Connecticut was the only continuous government among all the colonies, for the charter never was surrendered.

The settlers from the old world naturally located on the seacoast and its tributary rivers, for these rivers at first were the only thoroughfares for transportation. This settlement extended from Winthrop's home along the water front, and at the top of the hill at the west was the town plot with its meeting-house and cemetery. Where the cove joins the river were located the wharves and the shipping on the beach (now Water Street); and soon, on account of the prominence of her founder and her maritime interests, New London assumed a high place among the settlements of New England.

The inhabitants petitioned the General Court that their adopted home should bear the name of London; but the request was not granted at first, and it was only when Winthrop became Governor that the name was given.

"Whereas, it hath bene a comendable practice of ye inhabitants of all the Collonies of these parts, that as this Countrey hath its denomination from our deare natiue Countrey of England, and thence is called New England, soe the planters, in their first setling of most new Plantations haue giuen names to those Plantations of some Citties and Townes in England, thereby intending to keep vp and leaue to posterity the memoriall of seuerall places of note there, as Boston, Hartford, Windsor, York, Ipswitch, Brantree, Exeter,—This Court, considering that there hath yet noe place in any of the Collonies bene named in memory of ye Citty of London, there being a new plantation within this Jurisdiction of Conecticut setled vpon ye faire Riuer of Monhegin, in ye Pequot Countrey, it being an excellent harbour and a fit and convenient place for future trade, it being alsoe the only place wch ye English of these parts haue possessed by conquest, and y^t by a very iust war vpon y^t great and warlike people, ye Pequots, that therefore they might thereby leaue to posterity the memory of y^t renowned city of London, from whence we had our transportation, haue thought fit, in honour to that famous Citty, to cal ye said Plantation, New London."¹

In order to show the importance of the harbor of New London and the town as a prominent early trading port, two quotations from Miss Caulkins' *History of New London* are given here. She said: "New London was settled with the hope and prospect of making it a place of trade. Commerce was expected to become its presiding genius under whose fostering care it was to grow and prosper." She quoted from Hinman's *Antiquities* a letter from the colonial government to the King's commissioners in 1665: "Whereas this colony is at a very low ebb in respect to traffick, and although out of a respect to our relation to the English nation, and that we might be accounted a people under the Sovereignty and protection of his Majestie the King of England, we presumed to put the name or appellation of New-London, upon one of our towns, which nature hath furnished with a safe and commodious harbour, though but a poor people, and discapacitated in several respects to promote traffique; we humbly crave of our gracious Sovreigne, that he would be pleased out of his Princely bounty to grant it to be a place of free trade, for 7, 10, or 12 years, as his Royall heart shall encline to conferr, as a boon upon his poor yett loyal subjects."

A petition of the town on June 26, 1744, to the King, is a further proof of the prominence of New London as an early port.

"The humble representation and petition of the inhabitants of the town of New London, in the colony of Connecticut, in New England, to the king's most excellent majesty:

"May it please your majesty, we your very dutiful and obedient subjects being fully sensible that your majesty's royal ear is ever open and ready to hear, and your paternal care and goodness ever ready to diffuse itself even to your most remote subjects, beg leave with the greatest submission to represent

---

¹ *Colonial Records of Connecticut*, Vol. I, p. 313.

the consequence (importance) of this harbor and town, and its defenseless state.

"Our harbor is the principal one in this colony, and perhaps the best in North America, capable to receive the whole navy of Great Britain, being at least seven miles in length, and near one mile in breadth, six fathoms water, bold shore and excellent anchor-ground; all the navigation trading to this colony enter and clear at your majesty's custom-house in this port, and we shall probably have twenty, thirty, or perhaps forty vessels at a time, laden mostly with provisions, belonging to this and the neighboring governments, waiting for convoy, and have not any thing to defend such fleet from your majesty's enemies but a battery of seven guns, (some of which are very unfit for service,) and three other guns at the harbor's mouth, about three miles distant, and have no reason to question but an enemy on our coast will soon gain intelligence, when such number of vessels shall be here, and we fear make them a quick prey. With such large quantities of provisions, they will be enabled to fit out many more privateers, to the great annoyance of other your majesty's good subjects, and what renders such attempts from an enemy more to be expected, is the easy entrance to this harbor, it being very free and bold, and in three hours' sail they may be again without land in the open sea . . . ."

The above petition was drawn at the beginning of King George's War. Later came the French and Indian war with the conflicting claims of France and England to territory in America, when again trade, commerce and shipping in the colonies were greatly disrupted. Throughout these unfortunate conditions the business of New London had been depressed and stagnant. It was, however, not until the end of this war by the Treaty of Paris in 1763 declaring peace, that business revived as it always does under favorable conditions. The year 1763 was the turning point in British colonial policy toward imperialism that afterwards brought on the war of the American Revolution.

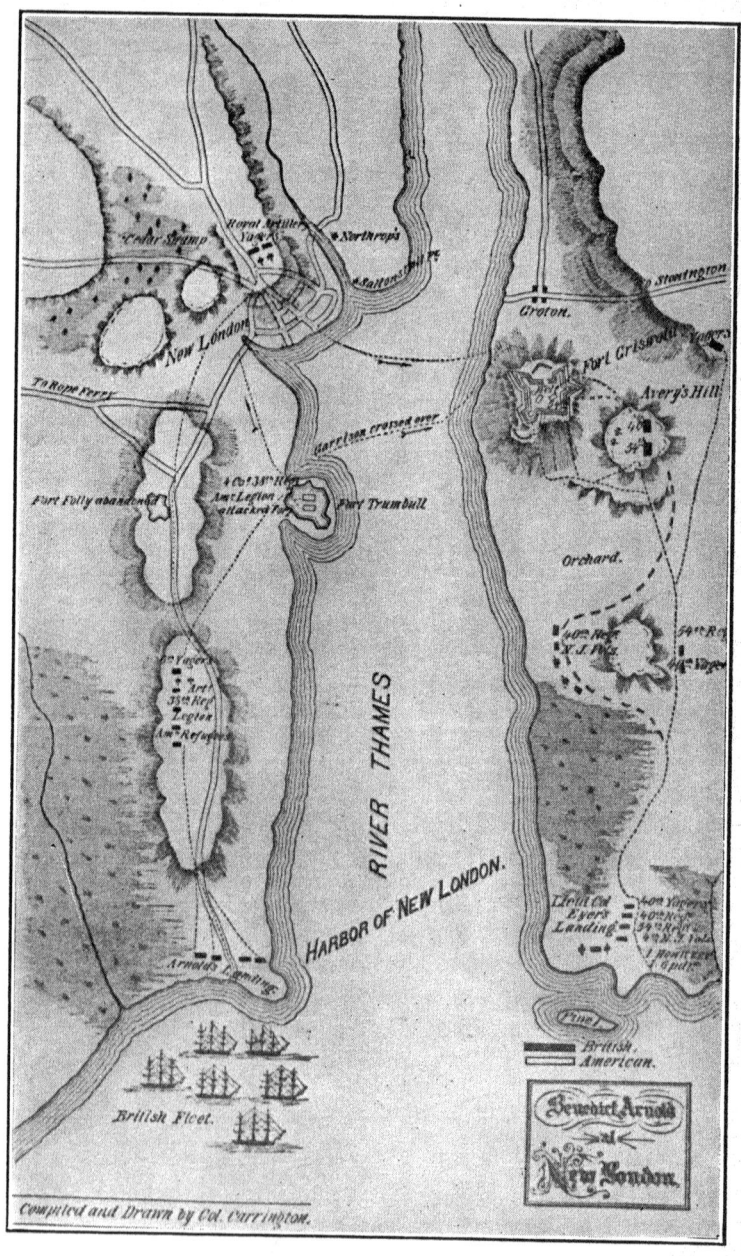

MAP OF THE EARLY PORT OF NEW LONDON.
(From the Faden Collection.)

Maps from the Faden Collection.

The outline map designated "Benedict Arnold at New London" shows the early port of New London with the addition of the forts of the revolutionary period. It is reproduced from the original in the Faden Collection[1] comprised of maps of military positions held in the old French and revolutionary wars, which are original manuscript maps drawn at the time by officers of the English Army. The Collection was formerly owned by Edward Everett Hale and was purchased from him by the United States.

There are four maps of military positions in Connecticut in the Faden Collection. Two, "Benedict Arnold at New London," and "A Sketch of New London and Groton with the attacks made on Forts Trumbull and Griswold by the British Troops under the command of Brig^r. Genl. Arnold Sept. 6, 1781," are reproduced in this volume, the former here and the latter as end papers. The remaining two are "Fort Griswold," and "Gov. Tryon's Expedition to Danbury in 1777."

---

[1] Phillips, *List of Maps of America.*

II

NATHANIEL SHAW, JR., MERCHANT,
1763 to 1782

WHEN shipping revived after the Treaty of Paris in 1763, there was a young merchant, native of New London, Nathaniel Shaw, Jr., about twenty-eight years old, who as a partner of his father, a sea captain, became "a wealthy and public spirited citizen, and was on intimate terms with Washington and other Revolutionary leaders."[1]

This chapter deals only with Shaw's mercantile career, the closing events of his life, and his tragic death; the following chapter narrates his activities as Continental, Colonial and State Naval Agent.

His experience (as business manager for his father's shipping interests and property), age, poise, judgment, remarkable executive ability, and, above all, his character, peculiarly fitted him for a successful career as a merchant dealing both locally and abroad. His name is intimately blended with the renown of New London. After a careful study of the prominent personages of New London during the Revolutionary period it should be conceded that Nathaniel Shaw, Jr., was NEW LONDON'S OUTSTANDING CIVILIAN PATRIOT.

At first the business was conducted under the name of Nathaniel Shaw & Son, but soon the father retired and the son, the eldest of eight children, continued under the name of Nathaniel Shaw, Jr., Merchant. All conditions at that time were in his favor, and he extended his business to Newport, Providence and Boston on the east; to New York, Philadelphia and Newbern on the west and south; occasionally to Mediterranean and European ports; but chiefly to the West Indies, to the ports of Hispaniola (now Haiti), Dominica, The Mount (Monte Cristi, Haiti), The Cape (Le Cap or Cape Haitien), The Mould (Le Moule, Guadeloupe), Dom-

---

[1] Paullin, *Out Letters of the Continental Marine Committee*, Vol. II, p. 1.

THOMAS SHAW AND HIS MOTHER, TEMPERANCE HARRIS SHAW.

inique (Dominica), St. Christopher, St. Pierre (Martinique), Turks Island, St. Croix, Cape François, Port au Prince (Haiti), St. Eustatia (St. Eustatius), St. Johns, Antigua, Pointe à Pitrie (Guadeloupe), and many others.

New London being the clearing port for the colony, young men imbued with the spirit of romance and adventure came here to engage in a seafaring life. Many of them died from fever in the West Indies and also from the elements. Three brothers of Nathaniel Shaw, Jr., were lost at sea before reaching twenty-two years of age.

The Shaws had extensive mercantile relations with the West Indies, and their vessels called at many of those ports.

The French merchants at Pointe à Pitrie, Guadeloupe, were the Constants; and the Gaignards lived at Le Cap (Cape Haitien), Haiti.

The Shaws sent vessels to both firms for many years, and very friendly relations existed between the Shaws and those families. Some members of both of the French families came to New London; and William Constant married a New London girl. Thomas Shaw speaks of her as a near neighbor whom he esteemed highly, but only states her name as Miss Lucy. Pierre Gaignard came to New London to live; Thomas Shaw was in charge of his trust estate.

Other mercantile names prominently mentioned are Goban, Pouquet, Charrier, Texier, Mase, Desmoulins, Delcasse and others, whose letters written in French are still extant. In one of the letters, the privateers of Nathaniel Shaw, Jr., are referred to as American Corsairs. Nathaniel Shaw, Jr., had a great faculty for details as well as management, which caused him in 1765 to start a record book for copying by hand all outgoing mercantile orders for goods. This he continued until his death in 1782, the letters often containing items of public interest. In addition to this letter book, there have been preserved to the present about 10,000 letters, account books, receipts, bills, etc., in the Shaw Collection alone, which show his indefatigable industry.

Although Shaw was fond of sailing and kept at his wharf

his private sloop, the *Queen of France*, for local business and pleasure trips, and though he journeyed to the camp at Cambridge for intelligence, to Lebanon to confer with Governor Trumbull, to Hartford continually as a member from New London to the General Assembly, to New York and Philadelphia on business, so far as yet noticed he did not make any business voyage in his own ships, but stuck to his office in New London actively engaged for himself and for his country. His business organization proved of incalculable assistance to his town, his state and his nation in their time of need, as is shown in these pages, and circumstances permitted him to perform the many duties placed upon him by the exigencies of war, while living in his own home town.

As prosperity came he invested in his own line of business, in shipping and wharves, and as the avenues of investment in that period were limited principally to real estate, he purchased numerous properties in his town, and farms in many of the towns of New London County. Descendants of the Shaw family are at present the largest landholders in the town of Salem, Connecticut, most of which property is ancestral land.

The particulars concerning the vessels owned and operated by Nathaniel Shaw, Jr., their names and voyages to distant ports, would add a touch of romance, but space forbids including them. Shaw's Mercantile Letter Book is illuminating in many ways. It shows not only the system of commercial dealings of that period, but also the necessity of nonconformity on the part of merchants to the British Acts of Parliament, especially the Sugar Act of 1764, unless they allowed their businesses to be ruined. It was the spirit of nonconformity against British authority that was an important factor in fostering the revolt of the colonies in the critical period of pre-Revolutionary days. Shaw's whole-hearted support of the colonial side of the controversy in a seaport town would in itself make a very interesting chapter. In addition to his mercantile affairs he carried on an extensive banking business in local and foreign exchange.

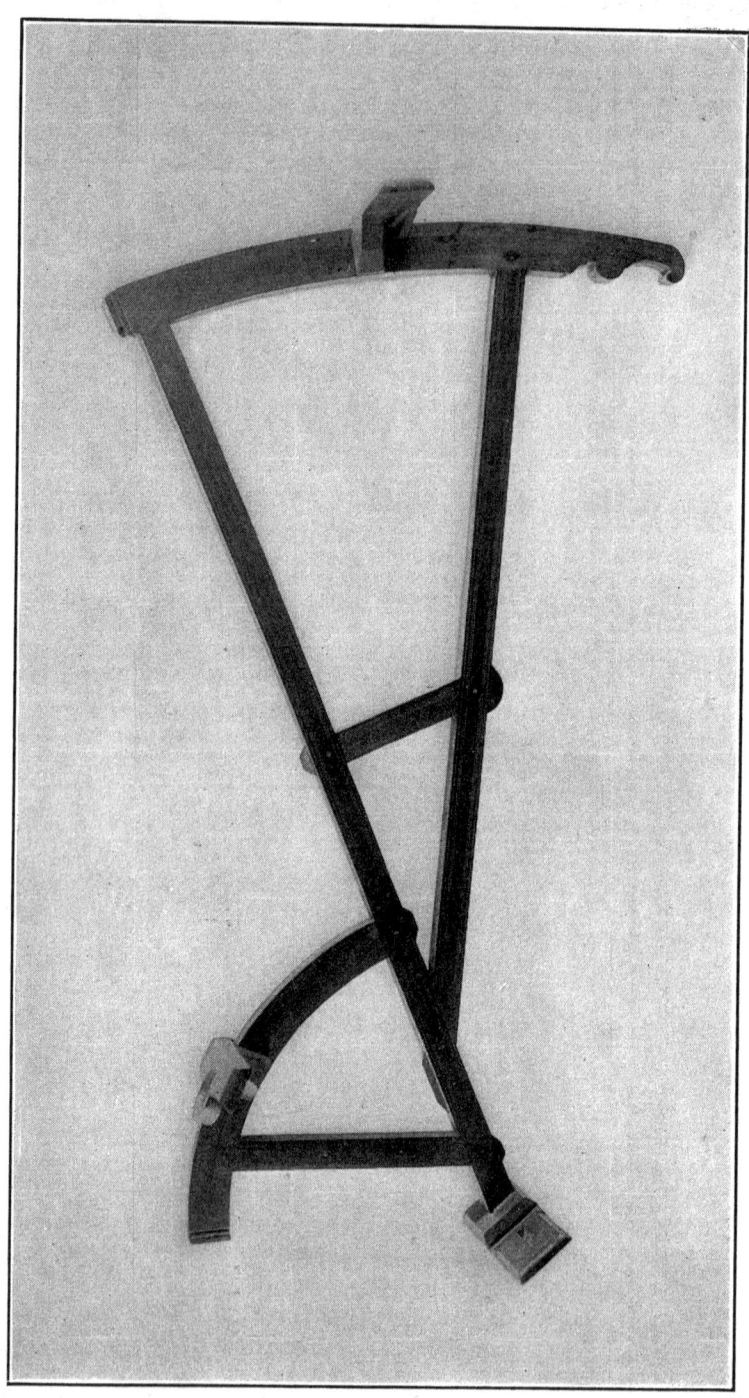

DAVIS QUADRANT.

Marked "Made by Clark Elliott in New London for Mr. Michael Melally, 1760." Now in the Collection of the New London County Historical Society, given in 1895 by Mrs. Mary A. Elliott of Walla Walla, Washington. Used by Captain Michael Melally on merchant vessels and privateers of Nathaniel Shaw, Jr.

An illustration of his public spirit was shown on April 8, 1767, when he ordered a fire engine from Philadelphia, had it brought to New London by Captain Harris, and presented it to the town (see Mercantile Letter Book).

At twenty-two, July 20, 1758, he married Lucretia Harris Rogers, the young widow of Captain Josiah Rogers. His stepson, Josiah, died in the Shaw Mansion on March 20, 1764, aged seven years and eight months. His wife, the New London *heroine* of the war, died in their home on December 11, 1781, from a malignant fever contracted from sick prisoners received into her home and nursed by her. His own pathetic death occurred in his home before the close of the war on April 15, 1782, from an unfortunate wound received while on a local hunting trip.

From all accounts, and from the voluminous records extant, the subject of this sketch evidently had a very agreeable personality. Unfortunately there is no known portrait of him in existence, consequently no information concerning his personal appearance can be obtained. He was a kind neighbor, a helpful citizen, a considerate employer, a successful merchant, an ardent patriot and Christian gentleman. There seems to have been a strong bond of friendship between him and Captain Michael Melally who had sailed his merchant vessels and privateers and been in his employ for many years. Apparently Captain Melally when not at sea assisted him in the headquarters at New London, for he was often in his employer's company and was with him on a ducking trip to the eastward when the fatal accident occurred. There were with him in the boat Captain Michael Melally, Captain James Angel, Ebenezer Way and William Clarke. It was Captain Melally who wrapped Shaw in his coat, held him in his arms until the shore was reached, accompanied him to his home, the Shaw Mansion, witnessed his will the day following and remained with him until his death two days later.

The description of the last hours of Nathaniel Shaw, Jr., by his brother Thomas Shaw, is fully described in a letter to Colonel Josiah Waters, Jr., Merchant, of Boston, dated April 25, 1782, and found near the end of the Mercantile Letter Book. There follow here the Will and Colonel Waters' reply to Thomas Shaw's letter. There have been added three letters taken at random from the quantity of his mercantile correspondence.

From a Copy, in the Shaw Collection, of the Last Will and Testament of Nathaniel Shaw, Jr., Made by Him on April 13, 1782, and Admitted to Probate in New London on May 3, 1782

At a Court of Probate held at New London 3^d May 1782.
Present the hon^l Gurdon Saltonstall Esqr. *Judge*

The last Will & Testament of Nathl. Shaw late of New London dec^d. was exhibited in this Court, proved, approved and ordered to be recorded.

In the Name of God Amen, the last Will & Testament of Nathl Shaw of New London in the County of New London Esquire being now confined to my Bed by an unfortunate wound and apprehending myself near the close of Life tho now of a found & disposing mind, recommending my Soul to almighty God through the merits of a bleeding Saviour my worldly Estate I dispose of in manner following. That is to say Imprimis, To my honoured Mother M^{rs}: Temperance Shaw I give three hundred pounds annually during her natural Life to be paid her in Silver or Gold Coin.

Item, To Thomas Shaw I give all my perfonal or moveable Estate and Debts not otherwise especially bequeathed to any other perfon he paying all my Debts, Legacies & funeral Charges. I also devise him Mamacock & Butler's Orchard being the Lands so called, as also the Barn on Hogneck with the Lot of Land adjoining, likewise my Stone houfe and Lands back of it with all my wharves in New London & Lands adjoining them.

Item, To Daniel Shaw I devise all my Farm at Jordan plain so called to be to him & the heirs of his Body, but if he should die without Ifsue then the fame is to go to Nathaniel Shaw Woodbridge & Lucretia Shaw Woodbridge to be divided between them in the fame proportion as the other Lands I devise them & to defcend to the furvivor of them in case either dies without Ifsue in the fame manner as the other Lands I devise them, & in case they both die without Ifsue then I devise the said Lands on the death of Daniel without Ifsue to Thomas Shaw.

Item, To Nathaniel Shaw Woodbridge & Lucretia Shaw Woodbridge I devise all my Real Estate Lands, Tenements & Heriditaments not otherwise

NATHANIEL SHAW, JR., MERCHANT

especially disposed of to receive & take pofsefsion of when they arrive of Age two thirds to said Nathaniel and one third to said Lucretia & to their heirs forever. And untill they arrive of age the fame is to remain in the Improvement & care of Thomas Shaw who is to have the whole benefit thereof and therewith is to fupport & educate said Nathaniel & Lucretia; and in case either of them die without Ifsue then the devised premifes is to go, and I do hereby devise the fame, to the Survivor, his heirs &c. And in case it so happen that they both die without Ifsue then the fame is to go to Thomas & Daniel Shaw, their heirs & Afsigns forever; or if either of them die without Ifsue then to the furvivor in manner aforesaid, his heirs & afsigns forever. Item, To Peter Rogers the houfe in which he lives & Garden Spot adjoining & all he is now indebted to me.

Item, To Peter Rogers Junr. the houfe in which he lives & garden Spot adjoining.

Item, To William Rogers the Sloop *Queen of France* when she arrives from the Havanna.

Item. To Harris Rogers the houfe lot formerly Leet's with two hundred pounds in Silver or Gold Coin to be paid him at my decease and all he is now indebted to me.

Item, To Doctor Simon Wolcott five hundred pounds to be paid him at my decease in Continental Certificates of so early a date as draw Interest in France.

Item, To Walter Beebe's Wife a Cow with the liberty of pasturing her every fummer in Butler's Orchard untill Nat^l. is of age.

Item, To William Clark my Boat and one hundred filver Dollars.

Item, To Sally Clark one hundred pounds in Silver or Gold Coin.

Item, To Grace Harris two hundred filver Dollars.

Item, To Amy Whipple a Cow.

Item, To Fanny Allen one hundred Silver Dollars.

Item, I do hereby emancipate & fet at liberty all my Negroe Slaves except Selah who is to be free at twenty one years of age.

Item, To Cofar ten pounds in Silver or gold Coin to be paid him annually during his Residence in this town—

Lastly I do hereby appoint my loving Brother Thomas Shaw fole Executor of this my last Will & Testament. In Testimony whereof I have hereunto fet my hand & feal April 13^h. 1782.

          Nat^l Shaw Seal

Signed, fealed and
pub^d by the Testator   Recorded from the Original
as his last Will & Test.   Joshua Coit Clerk
in prefence of
L. McClellan
Mich^l Melally
Marvin Wait

      A true Copy of Record
      Attest Joshua Coit Clerk

Letter Written by Josiah Waters, Jr., to Thomas Shaw

(From the original in the Shaw Collection)

Boston April 28. 1782

Dear Friend,

    Yours of the 25 Inst I have recived, with the particulars of the death of our dear deceased friend and although on the one hand there is indeed great cause for mourning, yet on the other their is great cause of thanksgiving and rejoicing of thanks to God for the manifestation of his love; of rejoicing at the triumphant departure of the man we so tenderly regarded—there is also reason to rejoice that his senses were allowed him and that so brightly, as not only to praise his redeemer, but also so judiciously to dispose of the abundance with which heaven blefsd him—if what I hear be true, his endeavor was that many should blefs his memory for his friendship and attention and that though they might sorrow At his departure yet they might rejoice in his benefactions, and that while God gave him riches he also gave him a disposition to do good not only in his life but also to close his days with deeds of kindnefs to men. The manner & cause of his death together with his resignation of life to the will of his divine master proves the propriety of the Poets observations when he saith

> Why should vain mortals tremble at the sight, of,
> Death and destruction in the field of Battle
> Where blood and carnage cloath the ground with crimson
>   Sounding with death groans.
> Death will invade us by the means appointed
> And we must all bow to the king of terrers
> Nor am I anxious if I am prepared
>   — What shape he comes in
> Infinite goodnefs teaches us submifsion
> Bids us be quiet under all his dealings
> Never repining but for ever praising
>   God our Creator

May we my dear friend, live the life, that so we may dye the death of the righteous and our last end be like his—

    Inclosed you have the letter which your brother sent me to forward Mifs de Neufville hous, as also Mr Mumfords receipt for £43.18.0/ in gold being for the bills of 180 dollars sold at 15 p^r Cent discount on the Livres—I have also deliverd to his care the Pall a bill of which will forward next week, as I cannot now afcertain the cost of every particular—I could not obtain any Cloth inferior, except such as I judged would not answer, have therefore compleated it according to my best judgment and hope twill be to full acceptance—

    I will enquire concerning the China & write thereupon next week—

    Respecting the Bills for which was to forward my note, upon hearing the death of your brother I pafsd them to his credit in account not knowing in whose name it might be most agreeable to make the Note in, and judging it might not make any material difference, and if it did I might afterwards do as you might think best to direct—You will indulge me in writing a little particularly respecting them of what paſsed betwixt your Brother & me on the subject it being pendant to set out right in every particular of buſineſs—The Bills I rec^d from your brother were as my receipt for them specifies Thirteen Hundred & two dollars at five Livres tournay p^r doll^r. which is Three hundred ſeventy two pounds being par for the Livres

    vis   1302 doll^rs. at 5 Livres Tournay
         5
       ──────
       6510
        20
    105/130200/1240   dollars which is £372 (and is
       105
       ───
       252   paſsed to the Credit of acc^t.) as your
       210
       ───
       420   Brother agreed and which was the
       420
       ...

reason of Livres tournay being mentioned in the receipt given him for them—My taking the Bills at par was a loſs of twelve or fifteen per Cent to me, but I was inclined to take them from an aſsurance that your Brother would loan them to me, I paying the Intrest Annually—he also aſsured me he would receive Money in greater or leſs sums as I might conveniently spare and at any time sooner or later as best suited me—these considerations together with what I had experienced of his kindneſs were inducements to me to take them; he offerd me as much more upon the same terms but as I did not like to run in debt I declined his offer, although at another time hereafter I might be glad of his or your friendship in such away—You will permit me to rely much on your kindneſs in giving me every opportunity that may be in my power to leſsin the debt—Your orders I shall hope for, for whatever you may need this way, and wish to be able to comply with them at all times; proving by every means the sincerity of my attachment to the family and connections of our friend—

I am with sentiments of real esteem my dear Sir your reciprocally bereaved

              Friend

                Josi Waters Junr

Mr Thomas Shaw

I intended to have mentioned my determination if buſineſs & providence permit, of paying you a short visit the ensuing season; when among other things we may be able to conclude upon matters of buſineſs to mutually advantageous—but what is the reason you cannot come to Boston it might be Very healthfull and I am sure I shall be glad to have you occupy the place of Our late friend—do think of it & come—The *firebrand* I expect will sail this week

Letter from John de Neufville and Son to Nathaniel Shaw, Jr.

(From the original in the Shaw Collection)

Nathan^l. Shaw Esqr Amsterdam 30 May 1781
New London

    Sir

        We Cannot but regret the being so long deprived of your much esteem'd favours and as we were ever ambitious to deserve them and equally desirous of giving you Satsfaction in the execution of your Commands. we flatter ourselves want of opportunities only hitherto, have been the reason of our being debar'd so long of the pleasure of your agreeable Letters. as none here have it more in their Power to Serve your Interest than we presume we have, so we Can also with Truth afsure you none Can have it more in their Inclination, we shall Continue to hope for their Continuance as should the War we are entered into with Eng^d. have been an obstacle from the dread the American Vefsels were exposed to in Coming in our Port. you must before this be Inform'd that hitherto we have had only the dread of the Common Enemy in our Coasts without experiencing any other evil, for as to Captures it can hardly be said that they have taken any thing since the Commencement of hostilities in the North Sea—tho 'tis of late that any Ship of war has sailed from our Ports and as a much greater number are preparing to follow, we doubt not we shall soon be able not only to keep the Enemy from our Coasts but act on the offensive and go in quest of their Cruizers wherever 'tis likely our trade May be affected by them. In short there is every reason to suppose the Contest will not be long and England be Compell'd to yeild Claims as Injurious as they were oppresfive to your States and ours. May we soon see that haughty and Iniquitous Power properly humbled, which the triumphant Liberty effected by the Superior virtue of the Inhabitants of your Continent is likely to Contribute most to, we flatter ourselves with some reason to see its Independance shortly hailed over all the world, tho we believe our States will be next in following the wise Steps of France in that respect.—The mutual advantage will result to both the Republicks from an advantageous Commerce is easily Conceiv'd, till then 'tis however with great Satisfaction we find that our Market preserves and rather Increases its advantages over all others by the Superior prices w^h. all West India & American Products obtain here and the moderate ones of all European Commodities and Articles which they are obtain'd at. In short we have these Latter without scarcely any acceptions better and Cheaper than any where else. We Inclose you the Prices Current of this day for your future Speculation, and In hopes of being favoured with your orders we remain with particular Esteem and regard.

                Sir

                      Yr^e M^t Ob^t hum^l Ser^t

                          John de Neufville & Son

Bill of Exchange for Antigua Currency Written by Thomas Turner to Thomas Burton, Trustee

(From the original in the Shaw Collection)

Exchange for L 100 Antigua Currency

At twenty days Sight of this my first bill of Exchange my Second and third of the same tenour and date not paid pay to Mr Nathaniel Shaw Junr or his Order One hundred pounds Antigua Currency (it being for my Annuity from the 1st September 1763 to ye 1st September 1764) Vallue Received and Charge the Acco^t of

Your hum^l Servant

New London December 12th 1764   Thomas Turner
To Mr Thomas Burton Trustee
for the Estate of Thomas Turner
In Antigua

Letter from Thomas Shaw to Mr. Texier

(From the original in the Shaw Collection)

New London June 15th 1784

Sir

I am informed that you are in good circumstances & happy, while I am poor and much reduced by the late war, my unfortunate brother Nathl Shaw's Estate has suffered much by the burning of this Town Sepr 6, 1781 by the British Savages.

You have doubtles heard of the Death of Mr Shaw & his Lady he died two years since, & has appointed me his Sole Executor.

Your Note in my hands is dated 12th Novr 1772. for 576 livers, & your Note & Receipt of the same Date for an Execution against Mr Castaignet for 3915.^{lb} 12.^{s}

I should be happy that you would inform me in what manner it would suit you to remit me the amount together with the Interest. If you pay it into the hands of Mr Doufset it will be agreeable.

In compliance herewith you will greatly oblige and relieve

Sir

Your Most Obedient
Hum^{bl} Servant
Thos Shaw

Mr Texier

III

THE NAVAL OFFICE

THE previous chapter alluded to the mercantile career of Nathaniel Shaw, Jr., who was invariably addressed by his patrons as "Nathaniel Shaw, Jr., Merchant." In his capacity as Naval Agent Shaw was occasionally and officially designated "Continental Agent at New London,"[1] "Naval Agent of the Port,"[2] "Agent for the Continental Fleet at New London,"[3] "Continental Agent,"[4] "Marine Agent for the State,"[5] usually, however, as "Naval Agent."

The term "Naval Officer" should not be confused with the Naval Agent who was in charge of Continental prizes, naval supplies for the colony, sick seamen sent on shore to his care, and, in the case of the Naval Agent at New London, also the oversight of all armed ships the property of the state. The Naval Officer had charge of the customs and the custom office.

When the outline of this volume was first planned, the thought arose, Were there Continental Naval Agents for the other colonies? About that time, the *Letter Book of Esek Hopkins* appeared, and an appeal was made to the editor, Mrs. Alverda S. Beck, who stated that Daniel Tillinghast was Naval Agent for Rhode Island, and suggested that the *Journals of the Continental Congress* be consulted for further information. This was done with the following result:

---

[1] Paullin, *Out Letters of the Continental Marine Committee*, Vol. II, p. 1.
[2] Caulkins, *History of New London*, p. 447.
[3] Esek Hopkins, *Letter to Nathaniel Shaw, Jr.*, Jan. 20, 1777.
[4] *Ibid.*, Feb. 4, 1777.
[5] *Records of the State of Connecticut*, Vol. II, p. 136.

The Delegates of the Thirteen United Colonies,

To Nathaniel Shaw Jr. Esq.

Greeting,

You being Appointed by Congress Agent for Continental Prizes in the Colony of Connecticut, I do hereby Authorize & Impower you to Act in said Office, and to Appoint one or more Deputies under you as you may judge necessary, & do Require you to be carefull in the Execution of said Trust, & strictly to Conform to the orders & Directions herewith Transmitted you, & to such further Directions as you shall from time to time Receive from Congress, or the Marine Board Touching your said Office———

Given under my hand at Philadelphia this Twenty third Day of April 1776

By order of Congress
John Hancock Presid^t

LETTER FROM JOHN HANCOCK TO NATHANIEL SHAW, JR.

From Journals of the Continental Congress

Vol. IV, p. 289, April 17, 1776

Resolved, That the Marine Committee recommend to Congress proper persons to be agents for prizes in the several colonies.

Vol. IV, p. 301, April 23, 1776

The Marine Committee having, agreeable to the orders of Congress, recommended gentlemen to be agents for prizes in the several colonies,
Resolved, That Captain John Bradford be appointed for the colony of Massachusetts bay, Daniel Tillinghast for Rhode Island, Nathaniel Shaw, Junr for Connecticut, Jacobus Vanzantz for New York, John Nixon, and John Maxwell Nesbit for Pennsylvania, William Lux for Maryland, John Tazewell for Virginia, Cornelius Harnet for Wilmington, Richard Ellis for Newbern, and Robert Smith for Edenton in North Carolina, with power to each, to appoint one or more deputies, if necessary.

Vol. V, p. 478, June 25, 1776

. . . . . . John Langdon Esq as Agent of prizes for the Colony of New Hampshire.

Nathaniel Shaw, Jr., received appointments as Naval Agent from the

>Continental Congress, April 23, 1776
>Colony of Connecticut, July 10, 1776
>State of Connecticut, October 21, 1778

Neither the commission given by the Council of Safety and sent by Captain Harding, nor the commission from the State of Connecticut, if sent, has been found in the Shaw Collection. Nevertheless, they are printed from the records as indicated below. All three follow.

Commission from the Continental Congress

(From the original in the Shaw Collection)

The Delegates of the Thirteen
United Colonies,

To Nathaniel Shaw Ju^r: Esqr.

Greeting,

You being Appointed by Congress Agent for Continental Prizes in the Colony of Connecticut, I do hereby Authorize & Impower you to Act in said Office, and to Appoint one or more Deputies under you as you may Judge necessary, & do Require you to be carefull in the Execution of said Trust, & strictly to Conform to the orders & Directions herewith Transmitted you, & to such further Directions as you shall from time to time Receive from Congress, or the Marine Board touching your said Office —

Given under my hand at Philadelphia this Twenty third Day of April 1776

By order of Congress
John Hancock Presid^t

The appointment of Shaw by the Continental Congress was soon followed by his appointment as Agent for the Colony of Connecticut.

Commission from the Colony of Connecticut
"Council of Safety of Connecticut"

"Mr. Nathaniel Shaw jun^r of N. London is appointed Agent for the Colony, for the purpose of naval supplies and for taking care of such sick seamen as may be sent on shore to his care. *Copy given, sent by Cap. Harding.*"[1]

The efforts of Shaw were so commendable that the State of Connecticut broadened his powers with appointment as Marine Agent as follows:

Commission from the State of Connecticut

Att A Genl Afsembly of the Govenor & Company of the state of Connecticut holden at Hartford by adjournment the 21st day of October A D 1778.

Resolved by this Assembly that Mr Nathl Shaw of New London be and he is hereby appointed Marine Agent for this State to take the Oversight & to give direction for the Management & Equipment of all armed Ships or Vefsels, which are the Property of and fitted out by this State when in Port, to direct & Order what Cruifes they shall go upon, to Receive & difpofe of the prifes that shall be taken by them.

Takeing the advife of the Govenor & the Council of Safety from time to time for his proceedings therein.

And it is further Refolved that his Exelency the Govenor & his Council of Safety be and they are hereby Impowered & authorifed to Settle the terms and Regulations upon which the Officers and Privates for the Armed Ships and Vefsells aforesaid shall be Engaged & Inlisted in refpect to their Wages, and the Shares & Proportions they shall have of the Prifes they shall take."[2]

A true Copy of Record
Examin^d
By George Wyllys Secret^y

---
[1] *Colonial Records of Connecticut*, Vol. XV, p. 474, July 10, 1776.
[2] From the *Trumbull Papers*, Connecticut State Library.

Naturally, it could be assumed that since Washington was the guest of Nathaniel Shaw, Jr., on April 9 and 10, 1776, and discussed with him the situation of the colony in those days of stress, and as Nathaniel Shaw, Jr., was commissioned on April 23, 1776, that he had recommended him to the Congress for the position of Naval Agent.

A letter in the Shaw Collection at Yale reveals that a friend of Nathaniel Shaw, Jr., Samuel Huntington of Norwich, Connecticut, President of the Continental Congress at Philadelphia, was the recommender. President Huntington's letter, in his own handwriting, to Shaw is very complimentary.

Philadelphia 4th May 1776

Sir
    I am favoured with yours of the 20th April, note the contents, but before it came to hand, I had the pleaſure of procuring you to be appointed Agent, being the most suitable person I could think of, the Resolution of Congreſs appointing you will doubtleſs come to hand before this reaches you: we have obtaind an order of Congreſs to exchange your powder in this City for continental powder in New London, the Committee will soon give you particular directions on that subject, hope the harbour of New London will soon be sufficiently fortified as I make no doubt Ships of force will soon be in there if it be not made secure.

                I am Sir your humble Serv't

                        Saml Huntington

So far reaching were the services of Nathaniel Shaw, Jr., that his name in addition to appearing in the Shaw Collection is mentioned 123 times in the *Trumbull Papers*; 18, in the *Huntington Papers*; 30, in the *Colonial Records of Connecticut*, Vols. XIV and XV; 62, in *Records of the State of Connecticut*, Vols. I and II; 38, (including family) in Caulkins, *History of New London*; 7, in the *Journals of the Continental Congress*; 30, in *Maritime Connecticut*; 20, in *Esek Hopkins' Letter Book*; and many times in other sources not here enumerated.

Shaw's appointment as Naval Agent by the Continental Congress on April 23, 1776, is recorded previously in this chapter. The other six items containing the mention of his name in the *Journals of the Continental Congress* are printed in full.

THE NAVAL OFFICE

May 4, 1776, Vol. IV, p. 327

A letter from Governor Trumbull, of the 27 of same month, enclosing a letter from N. Shaw, Junr with a list of the cannon left at New London.

March 14, 1777, Vol. VII, p. 177

Ordered, That the bill drawn by Governor Trumbull, for twenty-five thousand dollars, in favour of Nathaniel Shaw, be paid and charged to the State of Connecticut.

February 28, 1778, Vol. X, p. 207

Ordered, That a warrant issue on the treasurer in favour of the Marine Committee, for five thousand dollars, to be transmitted to Nathaniel Shaw, Esq. continental agent in Connecticut:

That a warrant issue on John Lawrence, Esq. commissioner of the continental loan office in the State of Connecticut, in favour of the Marine Committee, for thirty-five thousand dollars, to be transmitted to the said Nathaniel Shaw, for which two sums the said Committee is to be accountable.

July 15, 1778, Vol. XI, p. 689

That a warrant issue on John Gibson, Esqr auditor general for 80,000 dollars, in favour of the Marine Committee, to enable them to pay a bill drawn on them by the navy board of the eastern department, dated 11 May, in favour of Nathaniel Shaw, Esqr the said committee to be accountable.

July 15, 1778, Vol. XI, p. 690

That a warrant issue on John Gibson, Esq. auditor general, in favour of Mr. Joseph Nourse, pay master to the Board of War and Ordnance, for thirty thousand four hundred and ninety four and 15/90 dollars, upon the application of the Board of War, to answer a draught of Nathaniel Shaw, Jun. New London, in favour of Captain John Mitchel, dated 4 May, 1778, for duck and lead; the said Joseph Nourse to be accountable.

November 4, 1778, Vol. XII, p. 1101

Ordered, That a warrant issue on the treasurer in favour of Thomas Kennedy, for fifty thousand dollars, in discharge of a bill drawn by his Excellency Jonathan Trumbull, Esq. governor of the State of Connecticut, dated Hartford, October 24, 1778, in favour of Nathaniel Shaw, for that sum, on the president of Congress; the State of Connecticut to be accountable.

Nathaniel Shaw, Jr., used his own home for the storing of his most valuable *papers and letters*.[1] His *account books*[2]

---

[1] Statement to the author by Nathaniel Shaw Perkins, Jr., February 22, 1896.

[2] The Letter of Thomas Shaw to Robert Morris on May 14, 1782 (see Mercantile Letter Book), explicitly stated that settlement with the government of Nathaniel's account could not be made accurately, since the books containing this account were in a chest and burned in his office. Miss Caulkins obtained from Dr. Nathaniel Shaw Perkins (born 1792, died 1870) the information concerning the Shaws for her history of New London.

were kept next north on his house lot in "an ancient dwelling house of wood adjoining the stone Mansion," and used by Shaw as an office and storehouse. "This was burnt to the ground and in it a chest of valuable papers was consumed"[1] on September 6, 1781, when New London was burned by Arnold.

"The day ye enemy was at this place Mr Shaw was out of Town & his Books & Papers were huddled away by his Servents; except one chest w^c was left for a team y^t was sent for but was taken by ye enemy, by w^c means it was left & was burned in his office. The approach of ye enemy was so quick y^t it was w^t ye greatest difficulty y^t any of his B & P were saved."[2]

The books and papers were returned to the stone mansion and remained there through the succeeding generations. Therefore the Shaw Mansion is rightly designated as Connecticut's Naval Office.[3]

Of the Naval Agent, Caulkins' *History of New London*, p. 507, says:

> "Nathaniel Shaw, Jun., has been mentioned in a former chapter, as an enterprising merchant; we may add that he performed important service to the country during the Revolution, particularly in naval affairs. His judgment in that department was esteemed paramount to all others in the colony. He also acted as a general agent, or friend of the country, in various concerns, military and fiscal, as well as naval. His mercantile letters, though brief, and devoted to matters of business, contain allusions to passing events that are valuable as contemporaneous authority."

The war was achieved, so far as New London was concerned, by voluntary service as there was no organized community effort. This principle of public spirit on the part of

---

[1] Caulkins, *History of New London*, p. 555.
[2] *Mercantile Letter Book*.
[3] Jane Richards Perkins, *Chapter Sketches, D. A. R.*, p. 98.

the Colonists together with personal sacrifice and brave deeds, coupled with the determination and leadership of Washington, won the war.

Many of the inhabitants were loyal to the Mother Country which fact makes such names as Nathaniel Shaw, Jr., Captain John Deshon, Thomas Mumford, Richard Law and William Hillhouse stand out prominently as patriots.

Nathaniel Shaw, Jr., was early associated with the patriotic movements of the "Sons of Freedom."[1]

He was a member of the committee of fifteen appointed in 1767 upon the receipt of the circular letter of Samuel Adams calling upon the sister colonies of Massachusetts to unite in obtaining a redress of grievances.[2]

In 1770 he was one of the four delegates to the New Haven convention.[3]

He was a member of the original Committee of Correspondence in 1774 and was the only member to serve continuously during the war. "Other changes were made, but his name always remained as one of the committee."[4]

His letters show, before actual hostilities commenced, his forecast of war and his offer to the state government to procure powder from the French islands.

It is the belief that the contents of this book will demonstrate that NATHANIEL SHAW, JR., WAS NEW LONDON'S MOST VALUABLE CONTRIBUTION TO THE SUCCESS OF THE AMERICAN REVOLUTION.

After six years of devastating war, New London was almost depopulated of men of military age. Those remaining were exhausted with their sacrificial services. It was at sunrise on the morning of September 6, 1781, the alarm guns from Fort Griswold fired twice to warn the minute men of impending danger were nullified by a third shot from the

---

[1] Jane Richards Perkins, *Chapter Sketches, D. A. R.*, p. 93.
[2] Caulkins, *History of New London*, p. 502.
[3] *Ibid.*, p. 502.
[4] Jane Richards Perkins, *Chapter Sketches, D. A. R.*, pp. 93-94.

enemy in the harbor.¹ Amidst the confusion of the inhabitants Brigadier General Arnold landed about eight hundred men on the Groton side, captured Fort Griswold, and with about nine hundred men on the New London side partly burned the town.²

Various reasons have been given for the attack on New London. At the time of the recent Sesquicentennial it was generally conceded that the expedition was planned to destroy the vessels, shipyards, storehouses, and valuable naval supplies, European and West Indian goods stored in New London, and especially to retaliate for her naval victories and the recent capture of the ship *Hannah* containing the most valuable cargo of the war with invoice of £80,000 sterling. The ship *Hannah* lay at the wharf of Nathaniel Shaw, Jr., in Beach Street (now Water Street), later the location of Williams & Havens' wharf at the foot of Douglas Street. The ship was burned and drifted over toward Winthrop Neck and sank.³ The *Hannah* was captured by the *Minerva* privateer, Captain Dudley Saltonstall of New London.

The destruction of the ships, wharves and storehouses commenced at the northern end of the town and extended the whole length of Beach (Water) Street to the "Parade," for the most of the wharves and storehouses were situated there at that period. There were a few south of the "Parade" on the "Bank," but the greater part of Bank Street had no wharves until a later period.

---

[1] Two shots were an alarm; three denoted the arrival of a prize ship.

[2] "The loss of New London from this predatory visit, can only be given in its main items: sixty-five dwelling-houses were burnt, occupied by ninety-seven families; thirty-one mercantile stores and warehouses, eighteen mechanic's shops, twenty barns, and nine other buildings for public use, including the Episcopal church, court-house, jail, market, custom-house, &c. Nearly all the wharfing of the town was destroyed, and all the shipping in port, except sixteen sloops and schooners which escaped up the river." Caulkins, *History of New London*, p. 569.

[3] The old hull of the *Hannah* was dragged out in 1815 by Amasa Miller to whose shipyard it was an obstruction. Caulkins, *History of New London*, p. 553.

Referring to the property on the water front near the Shaw mansion, Miss Caulkins records:

"In this part of the harbor were the spar and shipyards and a considerable number of unemployed vessels, which were all given to the flames. Old hulls half sunk in the water, or grounded on the flats here and there, are remembered by persons who were then children, as having been left for years afterward lying about the shores. A privateer sloop, fitted for a cruise and in fine order, that lay swinging from a cable fastened to a ring in the projecting rock where is now Brown's wharf, was set on fire, and her cable burning off, she drifted across the harbor a mass of flame. Through the whole of Bank Street, where were some of the best mercantile stands and the most valuable dwelling-houses in the town, the torch of vengeance made a clean sweep. No building of any importance was left on either side of the street; all combustible property of every description was consumed."[1]

It is probable that Nathaniel Shaw, Jr., had no more than a boat landing on his homestead property up to this time, for rocks were situated just north, and wharves on Bank Street except near the "Parade" were built later. His will reads, "To Thomas Shaw I give . . . . . my Stone houſe and Lands back of it with all my wharves in New London and Lands adjoining them," whereas Thomas Shaw's will probated October 3, 1795, thirteen years afterwards, reads explicitly, "I also give and devise to my said niece and nephew, Elias & Lucretia Perkins, the house and land adjoining it in which I now live, and the land wharf and building on the opposite side of the highway." Therefore the conclusion is reached that the wharf and building were built subsequent to the death of Nathaniel.

From all records consulted there was little or no shipping

---
[1] Caulkins, *History of New London*, p. 555.

from the south end of the Bank during the war period, although the author formerly supposed Nathaniel Shaw, Jr., conducted his extensive maritime enterprises from his waterfront property at the Shaw Mansion.

Unfortunately, Nathaniel Shaw, Jr., wearied from his incessant duties, had left just previous to September 6 with Dr. Simon Wolcott on a fishing excursion[1] to Fishers Island. He was the highest town official at that time by reason of being First Selectman. Beyond doubt, if he had been present more of the shipping would have been saved and some definite leadership planned, the lack of which was sadly felt in New London on that fateful day.

Herewith are letters and other papers taken at random from the important correspondence on naval affairs.

Letter from Nathaniel Shaw, Jr., to Jonathan Trumbull

(From the original in the Shaw Collection)

New London April 25th, 1775

Sir

Agreable to your Defire I have Sent up Eighty Three Barrels of Powder to Col°. Jed. Huntington Contain^g about 108 Each the Remainder is in this Town I hourly Expect Thirty Two Barrels more that I have Account of the Capt having it on bord the Remainder of what Moneys was in My hands Capt Packwood left with Capt Jn° W Thibbin who is in One of my Vefsels in the West Indies to Lay out in the first Powder that Arives, he says that a large Quantity was Daly Expected he purchafed all that Could be had and thought it best to push home with this Rather than Tarry Longer—this Quantity he Obtain'd through the Influence of the Famous Palankey (who was an Old Commander of a Private Tear the Warr before Last who Prevailed with the Governour of the Cape to take it out of the Kings Store)—In Short Packwood Says the French Seem to be Dispofed in the Islands to Afsist in this way as Much as in their power, I Intend he Shall Sail Again for the Cape Next Week and I Don't Imagine he will be Gone More than Six weeks If you Intend to have Any more Money Laid out in that way it will be a good Opportunity Tomorrow by the Post I Expect to hear from Phil^a.—Relative to Lead I Am Sir Your Very Hum Servt

Nathan^l. Shaw Junr

To the Honb^{le} Jon^a Trumbull

---

[1] Caulkins, *History of New London*, p. 548.

Letter Written by John Lawrence, Treasurer of the Colony, to Nathaniel Shaw, Jr.

(From the original in the Shaw Collection)

Hartford May 11th 1775

Mr Nathl Shaw
   Sir

      The Governor, and Council have ordered me to purchase, Three Hundred Barrells, Or Six Hundred Half Barrells of Gun Powder. Am adviſed to Apply to you. Admit you will Undertake it according to the former Agreement, please to let me hear from you; the first Opportunity. It is proposed to keep our own Council

                       I am
                             Your Humble Servant
                                   John Lawrence[1]

P. S. If you do undertake let there be no Delay.—

---

[1] John Lawrence for twenty years was Treasurer of the Colony and State of Connecticut. When Treasurer of the State of Connecticut, the author had Lawrence's portrait placed in a conspicuous position in the State Treasurer's office in the Capitol. Lawrence's son William married Alice Adams Ripley, the betrothed of Nathan Hale.

Letter Written by Daniel Tillinghast to Nathaniel Shaw, Jr.

(From the original in the Shaw Collection)

Providence 17th: July 1776

Sir
      I wrote you 12th: Inst: by Willm: Brown & by which Oppertunity forwarded you 3 Cases Arms, S A No 1 a 3 (together with 6 & 7 a Barrell & Cag Gun Flints from Meſsrs: Clark & Nightingale) wch: I hope according to my Request you Immediately forwarded his Excellency General Washington at New York.—With this Pr Mr Jos: Bradford now goes S A No 8 & 9—2 Cases more Scotch Arms as Pr Invoice herewith; with this Team I likewise ſend No 4 & 5 a Chest & barrell qt: Arms & Flints as Pr: Invoice herewith from Thos: Green Esqr: all of which I wish safe to your hands & that you will not miſs the first Oppertunity of forwarding the

same to the General as they are greatly wanted at this critical Juncture & I wrote his Excellency by yesterdays Post I had forwarded them to your Care at New London to be sent him Immediately—I am Sir

Y^r: very hble Servant
Danl Tillinghast Cont^l. Agent

N B the Carter receives his pay of me on producing a Rec^t: from you for the delivery of the Goods to you—

Nathl: Shaw Esqr:

The Letter herewith you will please to forward his Excellency Gen Washington together with the Packages you herewith Receive
        Danl Tillinghast   Agent

Receipt Made by John Keeney to Nathaniel Shaw, Jr.

(From the original in the Shaw Collection)

Received of Nathaniel Shaw Junr. Three Chests of Arms N 9-8-4 and One Barrell of Gun Flints wich I Promise the Danger of the seas Excepted to Deliver to his Excellency General Washington or his order in New York, Paying Customary Freight having Sign'd Two Receits

                            John Keeney

New London July 22, 1776

Receipt Written by Col. Ledyard to Nathaniel Shaw, Jr.

(From the original in the Shaw Collection)

Receiv^d New London 1th Jan^y, 1781 of Nathl Shaw Esqr One hundred & thirty three pounds hard Bread for twenty three British N Prifoners Bound to New York also Recieved Seven hundred & fifty two pounds of hard Bread for a Number of German Prifoners Bound to New York in the Cartiels *Pinguin* & *Peace* for Account of the Public which Bread we are to se replaced to Said Nathl Shaw as Soon as we can Obtain it from the Public

                      Wm Ledyard Lt Colo
                           Command^t
                    Guy Richards Junr A. C.

rec^d Col Ledyard 75^{lb} Bread for a Flag Jan. 22 1781

Copy of Flag of Truce Document

(From the copy in the Shaw Collection)

New London County

Be it known that we the Justices of Peace for New London County resident in the Towns of New London & Groton in said County do hereby authorize & impower Mr Nathaniel Shaw of New London and Ebenezer Ledyard of Groton to pafs as Flag Officers in the Sloop *Queen of France* to the Fleet carrying Troops under the Command of Brig^r General Arnold in the Service of his Britannic Majesty and these on the Authority & Behalf of the Civil Authority of said County to negociate the Liberation or Enlargement of Prisoners taken by the Troops under the Command of General Arnold at New London & Groton on the 6th Day of September 1781. And we do hereby agree that the Negociations of said Nathaniel Shaw & Ebenezer Ledyard respecting the Prisoners aforesaid shall be binding on Us & our Succefsors—Dated Sept 9th 1781—

        Win^a Saltonstall ⎫ Justices of Peace for
        Tim^o Green
        Jo^s Harris   ⎬ New London
        William Williams ⎪ Justices of Peace for
        William Avery ⎭ Groton

We the Selectmen of New London do hereby ratify the foregoing Appointment for the Purpose aforesaid to be binding on us & our Succefsors. Sept. 9. 1781

        Joseph Packwood ⎫
        Guy Richards J^r ⎬ Select Men
        Joseph Harris J^r ⎭

We the Select Men of Groton do hereby ratify the foregoing Appointment for the purposes aforesaid to be binding on Us & our Succefsors Sept 9. 1781

        John Magant ⎫
        Peter Avery ⎬ Select men
        Robert Allyn ⎭

New York 14th Septr 1781 I do Certify the within to be a true Copy— Jos^a. Loring Com. Genl Pris^{rs}.

Letter Written by Brigadier General John Tyler to Brigadier General Arnold

(From the original in the Shaw Collection)

                      New London Sepr. 9th: 1781

Permifsion is hereby granted to Nathl. Shaw to Procede to the Brittish Fleet (now in Long Island Sound) and Negotiate an Exchange of Prifoners, and for that Purpose he is to take on Board the Sloop *Queen of France* Brittish Subjects to Exchange for Subjects of the United States and any Obligations he Enters into for that Purpose Shall be Strictly Complied with

John Tyler: B: Genl
militia

To Brigadier General Arnold

Copy of Letter from David Sproat to Nathaniel Shaw

(From the original in the Shaw Collection)

New York 14th September 1781

Sir

Mr Ledyard delivered me your letter informing me of the death of his Brother Commeſsary of Prisoners at New London for which I am very sorrie indeed.

I have sent up to go by the Schooner *Mifflin* Seventy one Naval Prisoners chiefly belonging to Your Port in exchange for those she brought here, and those whom you say still remains at Norwich whom Mr Ledyard has aſsured me will be sent here immediately on the return of the Flag.

I wish how soon the Schooner may be dispatched as many of them has been lately discharged from the Hospital Ship, and yet appear to be in a Convalecence State I am with offers of my best services here

Sir
Your mo. obed^t hum^l Servt
David Sproat
Commeſsary General N. P.

P. S. Mr Loring delivered me a list of Six Naval Prs. received p^r the Sloop *Queen*—whom I have placed to the Credit of Connecticut in Acco^t of Prisoners

D S

Nathaniel Shaw
Master of the Cartel Sloop *Queen* [of France]
   laying off White Stone
     in the Sound

Petition for Provisions

(From a copy in the Shaw Collection)

To His Excellency the Governor and Council of Safety,

The Owners and Concerned in the Prize Brig *Hope*, captured by the Letter of Marque Brigantine *Navarre* of Philadelphia and brought into this Port. Laden with Flour, Beef, Pork, Butter, Candles, Soap, Porter, and other

Articles of Provision which the Inhabitants in consequence of the late conflagration in this Town are in immediate want of, Petition your Excellency & Council for Liberty to sell the same Immediately at Auction as they imagine it will be a happy and speedy means of releiveing their present necefsities, and cannot justify themselves to the other concerned by selling at private sale, We being at a great distance from Home, the concerned living in Philadelphia.

    In complyance to the above Petition you will greatly
        oblidge you humble Servants
            Hood & Clarkson in behalf of the Owners.

New London Sept 12th 1781

    We the Civel Authority & Select Men
    Join in the Above Petition

            Wint Saltonstall }
            Timo Green   } Justices of Peace

            Nathl Shaw
            Guy Richards Junr } Select Men
            Jos Harris Junr

Order Signed by Samuel Birch, Giving Permission for Sloop Queen of France to Return to New London

(From the original in the Shaw Collection)

            By Samuel Birch, Efquire,
            Brigadier-General and Commandant of
            New-York.

Permission is given to the Sloop *Queen of France*, a Flag Sloop—from New London to return to there, having landed the British Prisoners here, which She brought from there.

            GIVEN under my Hand and Seal. in the City
            of New-York, the Fourteenth Day of
out of dat.   September in the Year of our Lord, One
            Thoufand Seven Hundred and Eighty. One.
                        S. Birch

To all whom it may concern.

List of Naval Prisoners

(From the original in the Shaw Collection)

List of Naval Prisoners sent p^r the return Flag of Truce Schooner *Miflin* William Willis Master addrefsed to Comm^y of Prisoners at New London - - - Viz^t:

Number	Names	Rank	Vefsel taken in
	Christopher Whipple	Captain	B^g *Mariamne*
	Abel Willis	Prize Master	"
	William Pierson	1st Lieutenant	Ship *Aurora*
	Alexander Sampson	Seaman	
5	James Codnir	"	
	James Rogers	"	
	Benj^a James	"	
	Philip Craw	"	
	Samuel Craw	"	
10	Jonathan Cushing	"	
	Joshua Joy	"	
	John Tod	"	
	Joshua Bruster	"	
	Frederick Willis	"	
15	George Milzard	"	
	Arnos Pike	"	
	John Ruth	"	
	Elisha Stoddard	"	
	Elisha Rich	"	
20	John Rogers	"	
	William Chapple	"	
	Thomas Gardner	"	
	Samuel Rufsel	"	
	Benjamin Tompkins	"	
25	Danl Whyat	"	
	John Clark	"	
	Elisha Guard	"	
	John White	"	
	Elisha Green	"	
30	Paul Gurrish	"	
	Daniel Marston	"	
	Robert Fry	"	
	Samuel Medcalf	"	
	Joseph Hamsdill	"	
35	Edward Target	"	Carried forward

THE NAVAL OFFICE

List Continued

Number	Names	Rank	Vefsel taken in
(35)	Bro. forward		
	Thomas Tobin	Seaman	
	Robert Mathew	"	
	──── Jarvis	"	
	Henry Small	"	
40	James Collins	"	
	James Jackson	"	
	William Rofs	"	
	Mich¹ Beekman	"	
	Silas Atkins	"	
45	John Currier	"	
	Christʳ Sloakum	"	
	Lem¹ Anthony	"	
	Thomas Smally	"	
	Sam¹ Gooding	"	
50	John Fairfield	"	
	Gideon Rose	"	
	Jonas Grafs	"	
	Benjamin Berry	"	
	Joshua Woodward	"	
55	Jonathan Ellis	"	
	Samuel Shaw	"	
	Jonathan Saunders	"	
	Christopher Baker	"	
	Nath¹ Baker	"	
60	Brazilla Crowell	"	
	Benjamin Bullock	"	
	Samuel Cox	"	
	Richard Akerson	"	
	Thomas Felton	"	
65	Robert Taylor	"	
	Thomas Shearman	"	
	Samuel Dagget	"	
	Paul Butler	"	
	Thomas Terrill	"	
71	John Gill	"	
72	Wᵐ Perkins	"	

New York 14ᵗʰ. September 1781

Seventy Two

David Sproat
Commifsary General N. P.

Acknowledgment of Jeremiah Pemberton (British Subject) Concerning Exchange of Prisoner John Clay

(From the original in the Shaw Collection)

I Jeremiah Pemberton Subject of his Britannic Majesty acknowledge myself to be a Prisoner of War to the United States of America. Having obtained this my Parole of Thomas Shaw Dep. Com^r Nav. Pris. to go into New York to endeavour the exchange of John Clay late of the Schooner *Young Cromwel* now prisoner there. And in case said exchange does not take place, & said Clay is not Liberated & sent out into the State of Connecticut, then I the said Pemberton do promise to return to New London & deliver up myself to said Com^r Shaw, within the Term of Twenty Days from this date. And that I will not Act, Say or Write any thing prejudicial to, or against the United States of America, During said term & untill I am exchanged. For the faithful performance of which I do hereby pledge my most Sacred Faith and Honor. Dated at New London this Third Day of April 1782.

Jeremiah Pemberton

In Presence of
Stephen Jos. Bouget
Saml McClellan Ju^r

Seven Out-Letters of the Marine Committee of the Continental Congress

(From copies in the Library of Congress)

[To Nathaniel Shaw, Jr.[1]]

Philadelphia Augt 22d 1776

Sir

Commodore [Esek] Hopkins recommends the purchase of the armed Schooner his Fleet lately carried into New London as an adviseable measure for this committee to adopt and in hopes to promote the Public Service thereby, we now request you will purchase said Schooner on the best terms in your power and assist the Commodore to fit equipp and man her with all possible expedition as a Continental Cruizer, he is ordered to offer the command to Captain Chew of New London and we hope he may accept it as he is so well recommended by your Committee. You will supply this Vessel with all necessary Provisions and Stores for a Six Months Cruize providing the whole on the best terms and in due Time rendering us an account thereof. If you have not money sufficient for this purpose your drafts on us will be duely honored by Sir

Your very hble servants

---

[1] Shaw was the Continental agent at New London, Connecticut. He was a wealthy and public-spirited citizen, and was on intimate terms with Washington and other Revolutionary leaders. (Paullin)

[To Nathaniel Shaw, Jr.]

August 22nd 1776

Sir

The Secret Committee[1] have directed Mr. Barnabas Deane[2] of Whethersfeild Connecticut to deliver you sundry articles he has imported on Continental account which you are to receive for the use of the American Navy, granting Mr. Deane a receipt for the whole in order to answer the accounts of said Secret Committee, but as Mr. Deane is in want of some of those very articles as well as others for the Frigate built under his direction, you are to supply any of these and assist him in procuring any other articles wanted for that Ship charging the same to his account or to the Ships as you shall judge most proper. You are hereafter to render us an account of the expenditure of all Stores you receive or buy on account of the Continent. The Salt you will keep for the purpose of putting up Pork the ensuing Season for the use of the Navy.

We are sir
Your hble servants

[Circular Letter to the Continental Agents in New England]

Circular
To Nathl Shaw junr. eqr.
Danl. Tillinghast. esq
John Bradford esq
John Langdon eqr.

October 13th. 1776.

Sir

This will be delivered to you by Nathaniel Falconer esqr. a Gentleman in our service and who has in charge to execute some business for us in yours or the neighbouring States. Should he stand in need of your assistance we hope it will be readily afforded him, and if he wants money you may depend that his drafts will be paid. We recommend this Gentleman to your friendly attention and are sir

Your very hble servants.

[Circular Letter to the Continental Agents]

October 18th 1776

Sir

Herein you will find two Resolves of the Continental Congress of which we have the honor to be members, whereby you'l observe you are ordered to account with us from time to time for the Continental Share of all Prizes

---

[1] The Secret Committee of the Continental Congress was engaged in exporting colonial products and in importing supplies.

[2] A brother of Silas Deane.

received and sold by you as Agent and to pay the amount thereof to our order. In obedience to this Resolve we think proper to lay it down as a Rule, that you State your accounts every three Months crediting therein the Continental Share of every Prize whose accounts can be settled and included within that quarter of a year, and that you add thereto a Schedule containing an exact account of all the prizes that then remain in your care whose accounts are unsettled, and we desire that you will constantly remit us undoubted good bills on this place as you can meet with them which will save the trouble and risque of sending money, in taking drafts prefer those of the Continental Agents, Paymasters & Commissarys to any other provided they are drawn on the President of Congress, this Committee or any other public Board for public Service— Next to these [are] undoubted good private Bills but none others. When neither One or the Other can be met with, inform us and of the sums you have, that we may give particular orders respecting the Remittance or application thereof.

By the other Resolve you will find yourself under orders of Congress to make a just distribution amongst the officers and men concerned in taking each Prize as soon after the sales as possible agreeable to the Rules and Regulations made by Congress in this respect, and it is our duty to see this punctually complied with as the Service has already suffered by delay— therefore you will always make the said distributions as soon as can be after the Sale and transmit us duplicates of the accounts and your proceedings therein. We shall allow all your just expenditures on account of the Continent to be charged against their share of Prize Money but those charges must be supported by vouchers.

We are Sir
Your very hble servants

To

John Langdon Esqr. Continental Agent	.....	Portsmouth New Hampshire
John Bradford Esqr.	Do.......	Boston Massachusets
Daniel Tillinghast Esqr.	do.	Providence Rhode Island
Nathl. .Shaw jr. Esqr.	do.	New London Connecticut
Jacobus Vantzantz[1] Esqr.	do.	New York
John Nixon & John Maxwell Nesbitt Esqrs.		Philada. Pennsylvania
William Lux Esqr.		Baltimore Maryland
John Teazwell[2] Esqr.		Williamsburg Virginia
Robert Smith Esqr.		Edenton
Richard Ellis esqr.		Newbern } No. Carolina
Cornelius Harnet esqr.	do.	Wilmington
Livinus Clarkson & John Dorsius esqrs.	.....	Chs. Town So Carolina
John Wereat Esqr.		Savannah Georgia

---

[1] Jacobus Van Zant.
[2] John Tazewell.

THE NAVAL OFFICE

[To Nathaniel Shaw, Jr.[1]]

June 17th 1777

Sir

We received by Captain Chew your Letter of the 27th ulto advising your having purchased a Brigantine suitable for an Armed Cruizer in our Navy. On recurring to our letter to you of the 22nd August last, we find that our Orders were expressly that you should purchase and fit out the Schooner taken by Como. Hopkins in his return from the New Providence expedition and sent by his Fleet into your port. Our principal inducement in giving those Orders was, that a Vessel of that kind was then wanted for an expedition we had planned and Commodore Hopkins recommended that Schooner as suitable for our purpose.

If on examination you found that Vessel defective, you certainly did your duty to decline the purchase of her, but we cannot consider that you were authorized by the Orders we gave you to buy a Brigantine Eight Months after without having first consulted us on that head. Commodore Hopkins never has been invested with any authority from us to order the purchase of Vessels for our Navy and we beg leave to recommend in future an observance of our orders only, advising us when you think any alteration of them will be of service to the Public. From what we have thought proper to say on this subject you will perceive we do not consider ourselves bound to take this Vessel, but as we think the Public service will be benefited thereby we have concluded to take her, and have appointed Captain Samuel Chew to command her. We now request that you will assist him in getting her ready for the Sea with all possible expedition. You will please to put on board provisions &c for a four Months Cruize and make the necessary advances of Money which will be wanted for manning and fitting her out, and recommend your doing every thing in the most frugal manner. Should you have any Money belonging to the States in your hands for which you are to account with this Committee, you may apply it to this purpose, if not, you may draw on us and your bills shall be paid. You will please to furnish us in due time with accounts of the Cost and outfit of this Vessel with proper vouchers and a List of the Men on board at the time of sailing. Recommending this business to your attention we remain Sir

Your very hble servants

P: S: This Brig is to be called the *Resistance*.

[To Nathaniel Shaw, Jr.]

February 28th 1778

Sir

We have received your Letter of the 2d. instant & in consequence of your demand for money you have advanced by the Marine Service we have paid

[1] Of New London, Connecticut.

Mr. John Hertell whom you sent for that purpose Five thousand Dollars and have delivered to him a Warrant on the Loan Office of your State for thirty five thousand Dollars making 40,000 Dollars to your debit. Since the appointment of the Navy Board at Boston it has been our determination that all applications for money and other matters relative to Marine affairs should be made to them, for which reason we have charged that Board with the above sum and you must Credit them for the same. As it is high Time your Accounts with the Marine Department were settled, we request that you will with all expedition produce them to the Navy Board who will settle and pay the balance that may be due to you and in future you are to be governed intirely by their directions in Marine Affairs.

We are Sir

Your hble servants

[To Nathaniel Shaw, Jr.[1]]

April 13th 1779

Sir

We request you will immediately after the receipt of this furnish us with all accounts relative to the Prizes put under your care and sold by you, which were taken by the Continental Brig *Andrea Doria* Nicholas Biddle esquire Commander.

We are Sir

Your very hble servants

Eleven Out-Letters of the Board of Admiralty

(From copies in the Library of Congress)

[To John Bradford]

Admiralty Board Decem. 10th 1779

Sir

Congress having dissolved their Marine Committee did by a Resolve bearing date the 28th of October last, constitute a Board of Admiralty and appointed three Commissioners not members of Congress, two Members of Congress, and a Secretary to whose management all Affairs relative to the Continental Navy is committed subject nevertheless to the controul of Congress—Pursuant thereto it is the request of this Board that in future

---

[1] Continental agent at New London, Connecticut.

all letters and applications relative to the Navy be addressed to the Commissioners of the Admiralty of the United States.

Among other Instructions this Board is directed immediately to write to the several Continental Agents urging them to transmit Accurate Accounts up to the 31st. of this Month of all transactions relative to the Navy within their respective districts to which a due regard is expected. You will in particular immediately inform us as nearly as possible what balances are in your hands in Order that drafts may be made on you therefor, the Treasury being nearly exhausted and it being out of the power of Congress to preserve their resolution not to emit any more money unless they collect monies from every quarter where they are due & may be had.

\# From the Sales you have made of large quantitys of Sugar & Rum &c. Congress rationally suppose you have a very considerable sum in your hands belonging to the United States.

We are Sir
Your Hble Servants
By Order
John Brown Secy

\# N: B: The Above letter was circular (excepting the last paragraph) to the following Agents

John Langdon Esqr.............New Hampshire
Nathl. Shaw Esqr..............Connecticut
Danl Tillinghast ....Rhode Island

[To Nathaniel Shaw, Jr.]

May 9th 1780

Sir

The Board have this day received your letter of the 26th ultimo announcing the arrival of a *Polacca* laden with Wine & fruits, Prize to the *Deane* frigate Captain Nicholson.

You are directed to cause the Cargo to be divided and the Continental Moiety reserved until the farther Orders of this Board, but should the fruit from its present state be liable to perish soon, we would in that case have the fruit sold, unless you could procure a small fast sailing Vessel to bring it round to this port on freight. As Anchors, Cables and other Cordage are much wanted for the Navy, if any such can be spared from the *Polacca* we would advise the selling them seperate from the vessel, and purchased for the Navy. If it be practicable, we wish you to send to General Washington about a dozen Boxes Lemons which we shall inform him of by Post. You will also inform the Board by the first Opportunity with an exact Invoice of the *Polacca's* Cargo & condition of the Vessel. We are sir

Your Hble serts.

[To Nathaniel Shaw, Jr.]

May 22d. 1780

Sir

By letter from the Board dated the 9th. instant you were directed to reserve the Continental moiety of the prize Wines until farther Orders and to send the fruit by water to this place.—but from the present scarcity of money here, and the urgent necessity for the same in Order to fit out and Man two Ships of war now in this port we are compelled to direct that the Wines be immediately sold for ready money together with the *Polacre* &c as also the Fruit, if not already Shipped pursuant to the former Order (excepting 12 Boxes to be reserved for the General) and that the whole Money Arising from said sale be immediately sent to this Board and under a Safe gaurd if necessary. Mr. Ephraim Bill 2d Lieutenant of Marines to the Confederacy will deliver you this, who is directed at his return to call upon you, by whom we hope you will send us as much Money as you can possibly collect, for without an immediate Assistance from you the Confederacy &c cannot be fitted for Sea.

We are Sir
Your Hble servts
by Order.
JOHN BROWN Secy

[To Nathaniel Shaw, Jr.]

June 16th 1780

Sir

The Board are favoured with yours of the 25th Ultimo, and I am directed by them to Order that you immediately sell to the best advantage in your power one half of the Wines in your possession belonging to the public, Sales of which transmit to the Board and hold the proceeds ready for their Orders. It is not the meaning of the Board that you should delay the Sale of Prizes for their Orders. I am Sir

Your Hble servant
by Order
JOHN BROWN Secy

[To Nathaniel Shaw, Jr.]

June 24th 1780

Sir

The Board are favoured with your letter of the 9th inst. It is their Orders that you dispose of all the Continental Prize goods in your hands & immediately pay the proceeds to the Honble the Commissioners of the

Navy Board at Boston with whom you are to settle your Accounts. The Board expect you will execute this Business as speedily as may be consistant with the Interest of the public.

                               I am Sir

                                    Your hble Servt

                                       JOHN BROWN Secy

[TO THE COMMISSIONERS OF THE NAVY BOARD OF THE EASTERN DEPARTMENT]

                                       June 24th 1780

[Gentlemen]

    The Board have Ordered me to inform you of their Orders of this date to Nathl Shaw jr. Esq. Continental Agent at New London, immediately to dispose of the Continental share of all prize goods in his hands and pay you the proceeds, and render you his Accts which you will please to examine and adjust. The Money Arising in this way the Board desire you will apply towards building the frigate *Bourbon,* which they are extreamly Anxious to have compleated, or at least put in such a state as that the work already done may not receive damage until funds can be had to finish her.

                               I am Gentn

                               Your hble Servant

                               JOHN BROWN Secy

P: S: the Board expect you will urge Mr. Shaw to be speedy in the above business and that his Accounts will be immediately settled, as well his general Accounts, as those relative to his late Prizes.

[TO NATHANIEL SHAW, JR.]

                                       July 5th 1780

Sir

    I am ordered by the Board to advise you that I have this day drawn upon you at ten days Sight in favour of Mr. Thomas Mumford of New-London for one hundred thousand Continental Dollars being for the like Sum paid the Board at this place by his son Mr. Giles Mumford which you will duly honor and charge the Board with the same.

                               I am sir &c

                               by Order

                                   J BROWN Secy

[TO NATHANIEL SHAW, JR.]

July 7th 1780

Sir

Congress having resolved that this Board should take the most effectual means in their power for obtaining from time to time certain intelligence of the arrival of the enemys ships of war into any port or ports of North America, the number of their Guns and the condition they may be in together with such movements as they make from One port to another; and particularly to obtain the earliest intelligence of the arrival of any ships of war in or near the port of New York, You are therefore directed to obtain the best information in your power on this subject, particularly with regard to that part which respects the enemys ships at or near the port of New York, and transmit the same from time to time by the Post, unless you should have an earlier opportunity by some good private hand. You will also collect information from Captains of Vessels from the West Indies or any part of North America relative to the proposed subjects of intelligence, and transmit the same likewise to this Board. As it is of the utmost importance more especially at this juncture that speedy & Accurate intelligence should be had of the movements of the enemy by Sea as well as by Land. We desire your attention to this matter.—We refer you to our letter of the 24th. June with regard to the sale of the Wines &c and desire that you would use all possible dispatch in this business, but instead of remitting the whole Amount of the Sales thereof to the Navy Board in the Eastern Department as you was therein directed you are now required to send us immediately by a safe hand two hundred Thousand Dollars, our expected supplies having failed us it will be impossible to fit out the *Confederacy* an object of the greatest importance unless we are immediately furnished with that sum.—

I am Sir
Your hble servant
by Order
J BROWN Secy

[TO NATHANIEL SHAW, JR.]

July 18th 1780

Sir

In our last of the 7th. of July we referred you to our letter of the 24th June, and desired that you would use all possible despatch in selling the Wine, &c, and instead of remitting the whole amount of the Sales thereof to the Navy Board in the Eastern Department as you was in our letter of the 24th June directed to send us immediately by a safe hand two hundred thousand Dollars as it would be impossible to fit out the *Confederacy* unless we were immediately furnished with Money. The Arrival of the French Fleet hath made it absolutely necessary that we should complete the *Confederacy* with all possible dispatch in order to her Co-Operating with them; and without we receive that sum instead of proceeding in the slow manner we are now obliged to do for want of Cash, we shall soon be at a dead stand, therefore you will excuse our repeating our directions and urging you to the swiftest dispatch in this most important business.

I am Sir

Your hble servant

FRANCIS LEWIS by Order

[To NATHANIEL SHAW, JR.]

August 11th 1780

Sir

Yours of the 26th ultimo is received in which you mention your payment of our bill in favour of Thomas Mumford Esqr. for One hundred Thousand dollars. The remittance of two hundred thousand Dollars requested in ours of the 7th. July is absolutely necessary for the [use] of this Board and must be made in preference to any demand of the Navy Board in the Eastern Department as the business of fitting out the Ships on hand is of more pressing necessity than that of building new. You will therefore use your best efforts to remit the sums required with the greatest dispatch using your Prudence in disposing of the Unions Cargo to the best advantage you can, attending to the Public Interest in referring or disposing of the Wine after raising the sum above mentioned. We shall rely on your care to obtain & communicate such intelligence as you shall judge to be of importance to this Board. We are sir

Your very Hble Servant

JOHN BROWN Secy

[To NATHANIEL SHAW, JR.]

August 22d 1780

Sir

We have your letter of the 10th. instant by which we learn that the Sales of the Wines are yet at a Stand.

The want of money for fitting and manning three frigates now in this port is so pressing that we are necessitated to direct you to sell the Wines for the best price you can procure without limitation, and transmit 200,000 Dollars immediately by a careful purpose messenger, for without a Speedy supply of the above sum, in continental money a fair opportunity of rendering Singular Services to the United States will be lost.

We rely on your exertions in effecting this business and are sir

Your very Hble servants

by Order

JOHN BROWN Sec:

NEW LONDON PRISON SHIPS

Thomas Shaw of New London (brother of Nathaniel Shaw, Jr., and his assistant in business) was appointed deputy commissioner of naval prisoners. Previous to his appointment he had been in conversation with Governor Trumbull in regard to the welfare of the prisoners who had been brought into the port by our armed vessels, and furthermore had corresponded with the governor concerning the "wretches on our prison ship."

The first prison ship, an old prize ship, was in use only a short time, having been rented from her owner, Samuel Aborn of Warwick, Rhode Island. The second prison ship was named the *Retaliation* and moored two miles north of New London. It was from this ship that some eighty of the prisoners escaped but most of them were recaptured. The prison ships were under the supervision of the Navy Board, Eastern Department, in behalf of the Continental Congress.

IV

THE FIRST NAVAL EXPEDITION, UNDER THE AUTHORITY OF CONGRESS

THE importance of New London as a port, with her superb harbor and ample facilities for fitting out ships and opportunities for manning them, caused her to be selected as the place where the initial expedition of the first American Navy should be chiefly recruited.

In those early days of the Navy there was not time to train officers and men for the service, and instinctively the Continental Congress turned to the able seamen in the merchant service engaged in sailing to the Mediterranean and European ports, to the West Indies, Bahamas, Greater and Lesser Antilles, and the Windward and Leeward Islands.

The appointments of officers were made by the Marine Committee and then reported to the Congress. The first appointments were as follows:

"Friday, December 22, 1775"

"The Committee appointed to fit out armed vessels, laid before Congress a list of the officers by them appointed, agreeable to the resolutions of Congress, viz.:

Esek Hopkins, Esq[r] commander in chief of the fleet.

Captains

Dudley Saltonstall, Esq[r] of the *Alfred*.
Abraham Whipple, Esq[r] of the *Columbus*.
Nicholas Biddle, Esq[r] of the *Andrew*[1] *Doria*.
John Burrows Hopkins, Esq[r] of the *Cabot*.

1st Lieutenants

John Paul Jones, Hersted (Hoysted) Hacker,
Rhodes Arnold,   Jonathan Pitcher.
——— Stansbury,

---

[1] The correct name is *Andrea Doria*.

2ᵈ lieutenants

Benjamin Seabury, Thomas Weaver,
Joseph Olney, ——— M'Dougall.
Elisha Warner,

3 lieutenants

John Fanning, Daniel Vaughan
Ezekiel Burroughs,

Resolved, That the pay of the commander in chief of the Fleet be 125 dollars per calendar month.

Resolved, That commissions be granted to the above officers agreeable to their rank in the above appointment.

Resolved, That the Committee for fitting out armed vessels, issue warrants to all officers employed in the fleet under the rank of 3ᵈ lieutenants.

Resolved, That the Committee for fitting out armed vessels be directed (as a secret committee) to give such instructions to the commander of the fleet, touching the operations of the ships under his command, as shall appear to the said committee most conducive to the defence of the United Colonies, and (to) the distress of the enemy's naval forces and vessels bringing supplies to their fleets and armies, and lay such instructions before the Congress when called for.

Resolved, That the said Committee be directed to consider how the share of the prizes allotted to the captors ought to be divided between the officers and men, and report to Congress."[1]

At the beginning of the War there was not time to build ships, so merchant vessels were converted into armed cruisers. They were the *Alfred*, twenty-four guns; the *Columbus*, twenty guns; the *Andrea Doria* (named for a celebrated Genoese admiral and statesman), fourteen guns; and the *Cabot*, fourteen guns.

New London and its vicinity had the honor of furnishing eighty members of the crews. Among the officers were Dudley Saltonstall, senior captain, lieut. Elisha Hinman, midshipmen Peter Richards, and Charles Bulkeley,[2] all of New London.

The fleet sailed from Philadelphia on January 4, 1776,[3] but on account of the ice did not put out to sea until February 17. Then with a rendezvous at Abaco Island it descended on Nassau on New Providence, an island of the Bahamas, and

---

[1] *Journals of the Continental Congress,* Vol. III, pp. 443, 444.
[2] Caulkins, *History of New London,* p. 509.
[3] Beck, *Esek Hopkins' Letter Book,* p. 18.

New London, April 25th, 1776

Sir,

Inclos'd is an Invoice of the W't and Sizes of Thirty Four Cannon Rec'd from Admiral Hopkins, ten of which is landed at Groton—

Viz: 3 Twenty Four pounders
    2 Eighteen D˚
    5 Twelve D˚—

The Remainder are all at N. London, and are mostly fitted on Carriages, he has landed a Great Quantity of Cannon Ball, and shall pick out those that are suitable — Mr. Ledyard I suppose has Carriages already made for the Guns at Groton, so that we shall have the Carriages Rammers &c Ready, to pay a Compliment to any of the British Ships, let them come as Soon as they Please &c—

The Mortars and Shells General Washington desired might be sent to N. York, and the Admiral has sent them — The Remainder of the Cannon are Thirty Sent to N. Port and part on Board the Sloop, which he wants to Carry to N. Port. I shew him the Resolve of the Cong. rep Relative to their being Delivered here, but he says they cannot be taken out—

I am Sir Your humble Servant
Nath'l Shaw Jun'r

The Nine Pounders are but ordinary Guns, the Others are all very Good Ones — Col˚ Knox a Gentleman who Gen. Washington Desired to take a Particular View of the Harbour, thinks that it would be best to have four of the Twelve pounders mounted as Field Pieces, two on East Side the River which you will Consider of—

I am Sir
Yours &c
N. Shaw Jun'r

P.S. when all the Shot and Iron which is are landed will send you an Acc't of the Number of Each & Sizes—

LETTER FROM NATHANIEL SHAW, JR., TO
GOVERNOR JONATHAN TRUMBULL.

without much resistance captured at Fort Nassau eighty-six cannon and mortars and much ordnance, also at Fort Montagu seventeen cannon and some ordnance.[1] Commodore Hopkins reached New London April 8, and landed seventy prisoners,[2] one hundred and twenty sick seamen,[3] also the wounded and the stores. The sick seamen and the stores were left under the supervision of Nathaniel Shaw, Jr.[4]

The following is Commodore Hopkins' report to John Hancock of the expedition.

Ship *Alfred* at New London April 8th 1776[5]

Gentlemen

When I put to Sea the 17th Febry. from Cape Henlopen we had many Sick, and four of the Vessels had a large number onboard with the Small Pox. The *Hornet* and *Wasp* join'd me two days before, the Wind came at N. E which made it unsafe to lye there. The Wind after we got out came on to blow hard. I did not think we were in a Condition to keep on a cold Coast, and appointed our Rendezvous at Abacco one of the Bahama Islands. The second night we lost the *Hornet* & *Fly*. I arrived at the Rendezvous in order to wait for the Fleet fourteen days agreeable to Orders. I then formed an Expedition against New Providence which I put in Execution the 3rd March by landing two hundred Marines under the Command of Captn. Nicholas,[6] and fifty Sailors under the Command of Lieutt. Weaver of the *Cabot* who was well acquainted there.

The same day they took Possession of a small Fort of Seventeen pieces of Cannon without any opposition save five Guns which were fired at them without doing any damage. I received that evening an Account that they had two hundred and odd Men in the Main Fort (all Inhabitants). I then caused a Manifesto to be published the Purport of which was ("That the Inhabitants and their Property should be Safe if they did not oppose me in taking possession of the Fort and Kings Stores) which had the desired effect for the Inhabitants left the Fort and Governor almost alone.

Captn. Nicholas sent by my Orders to the Governor for the Keys of the Fort which was delivered and the Troops march'd directly in where we

---

[1] Middlebrook, *Maritime Connecticut*, Vol. I, pp. 11, 12.
[2] Caulkins, *History of New London*, p. 509.
[3] Middlebrook, *Maritime Connecticut*, Vol. I, p. 12.
[4] Caulkins, *History of New London*, p. 510.
[5] Beck, *Esek Hopkins' Letter Book*, p. 46.
[6] "Samuel Nicholas received a commission as Captain of Marines signed by John Hancock on November 28, 1775. It is the oldest Federal Naval Commission in existence today. Others may have been issued but the original commissions are not known to exist today." McClellan, *Hist., U. S. M. C.*, 1st ed., 1st rev., I, ch. III, p. 82.

found the several Warlike Stores agreeable to the Inventory inclosed, but the Governor sent 150 barrs. Powder off in a Small Sloop the night before.

I have taken all the Stores onboard the Fleet, and a large Sloop that I found there which I have promis'd the owner to Send back and pay him hire for.

The *Fly* join'd us at Providence and gave an account that she got foul of the *Hornet* and carried away her Boom and head of her Mast and I hear since she has got into some port of South Carolina.

I have taken the Governor Montfort Brown, the Lieutt. Governor who is a half pay Officer, and Mr. Thomas Arwin who is a Counsellor and Collector of his Majestys Quit-Rents in South Carolina, and it appears by the Court Callendar that he is also Inspector General of his Majestys Customs for North America.

Since we came out we have lost Company with the *Wasp*.

The 4th instt. we fell in with the East End of Long Island, and took the Schooner *Hawke* Commanded by young Wallace of Six Carriage Guns & eight Swivels—and the 5th took the Bomb Brig of 8 Guns, 2 Howitzers & 48 hands, well found with all sorts of Stores, Arms, Powder &c—the 6th in the Morning we fell in with the *Glascow* and her Tender and engaged her near three hours. We lost six men killed and as many Wounded— the *Cabot* lost four Men killed and Seven Wounded the Captain is among the latter—the *Columbus* had one Man lost his arm. We receiv'd considerable damage in our Ship but the greatest was in having our Wheel Rope and blocks shot away which gave the *Glascow* time to make Sail. I did not think proper to follow as it would have brought on an action with the whole of their Fleet and as I had upwards of thirty of our best Seamen onboard the Prizes and some that were onboard had got too much liquor out of the Prizes to be fit for duty thought it most prudent to give over Chace and secure our Prizes—and got nothing but the *Glascows* Tender— and arrived here this day with all the Fleet.

Among the dead are Mr. Sinclair Seymour Master of the *Cabot* a good Officer Lieutt. Wilson of the *Cabot* and Lieut. Fitzpatrick of the *Alfred*.

The Officers all behaved well onboard the *Alfred*, but too much Praise cannot be given to the Officers of the *Cabot* who gave and Sustain'd the whole Fire for some considerable time within pistol Shot.

I am with great Respect

Your most Obedt. humb Servt.

E. H.

To the honble. John Hancock Esqr.
Presidt. of the Congress at Philada.

The accompanying illustration is from a photostatic copy in the Library of Congress of Shaw's letter to Governor Trumbull, with statement showing the amount of ordnance and ammunition consigned to Shaw.

Invoice of 34 Cannon Received of Admiral Hopkins
Viz

```
                    35.2.18          51.2.3
                    35.1.4           49.3.0
                    34.0.2           50.0.0
                    38.3.25          51.2.10
    Sent to         34.0.11          52.2.4
    Groton          42.3.12          52.0.5
                    50.1.4           54.0.0
                    50.1.4           50.0.12
                    52.1.16          51.1.19
                    18.3.5           40.0.5
                   392.2.17          33.3.27
                                     39.2.20
                                     34.1.0
                                     34.3.25
                                     35.2.14
                                    601.2.20
       9 D°. 18.3.5 each — is  169.0.17
                                    850.3.19
                                    392.2.17
                                   1243.2.10
```

3 Twenty four Pounders
2 Eighteen — D°. — } Sent to Groton
5 Twelve — D°. —

8 Twenty fours
2 Eighteen —
4 Twelves —   } left in N. London the Nines are all for
10 Nines —   Guns D°

INVOICE OF 34 CANNON, FROM NATHANIEL SHAW, JR., TO
GOVERNOR JONATHAN TRUMBULL.

The colony of Rhode Island[1] was the first to provide armed ships during the War, and her delegates in the Continental Congress advocated a colonial navy. Connecticut[2] and Massachusetts[3] followed with their own armed vessels. The Continental Congress appointed Esek Hopkins as Commander-in-Chief of the Fleet. He was the first and only man to hold that office and was usually addressed as Commodore, occasionally as Admiral. In the *Journals of the Continental Congress* he is alluded to as Commander-in-Chief at the time of his appointment, and as Commodore in all subsequent entries.

The title of Commodore as adopted by the author is verified by the following letter.

OFFICE OF
NAVAL RECORDS AND LIBRARY
NAVY DEPARTMENT

Washington, D. C.,
June 5, 1933.

Dear Sir:

Your letter of the 29th ultimo, asking whether Esek Hopkins should be referred to as Commodore or Admiral, has been referred to this office for reply.

The only official title given to Esek Hopkins by the Continental Congress was "Commander-in-Chief of the Fleet." (*Journals of Congress*, Vol. III, 1775, page 443.) For possible explanations of the title see Paullin's *Navy of the American Revolution*, pages 52-53.

Throughout the *Journals of Congress*, as you mention in your letter, Hopkins is alluded to as Commodore. Photostat copies of the Hopkins Papers (from originals in the possession of the Rhode Island Historical Society) show that he was addressed as Commander-in-Chief by the Naval Committee of Congress, and as both Commander-in-Chief and Commodore by the Marine Committee, which superseded the Naval Committee. Other correspondents addressed him in both ways and also as Admiral.

In the Continental Navy, with the exception of Esek Hopkins, and in the United States Navy up to 1862, no officer was given a higher rank than Captain, but in both navies Commodore was a courtesy title given to a Captain in command of more than one vessel, and in the latter, to a Captain in command of a Navy Yard or Station. On November 15, 1776, however,

---

[1] Middlebrook, *Maritime Connecticut*, Vol. I, p. 9.
[2] *Ibid.*, pp. 9, 10.
[3] *Ibid.*, pp. 9, 10.

Congress fixed the relative rank of army and naval officers as follows: Admiral with General; Vice-Admiral with Lieutenant-General; Rear-Admiral with Major-General, Commodore with Brigadier-General, etc., but without designating any officer of the Navy as Admiral, Vice-Admiral or Commodore.

Taking all the facts into consideration, it cannot be said that either Admiral or Commodore is incorrect as applied to Hopkins. Either one was a title of courtesy used to designate the Commander-in-Chief. The one used by Congress would seem preferable however.

Very sincerely,

Mr. Ernest E. Rogers
New London County
Historical Society
Shaw Mansion,
New London, Conn.

(Signed) D. W. KNOX,
Captain, U. S. N. (Ret.),
Officer in Charge.

In the course of the war the Connecticut Navy comprised thirteen sea-going vessels, as follows: *Minerva*, brigantine; *Oliver Cromwell*, ship; *Spy*, ship; *Defence*, ship; *Guilford*, sloop; *Schuyler*, sloop; *Mifflin*, schooner; *Old Defence*, brigantine; *America*, brig; *Whiting*, galley; *Crane*, galley; *Shark*, galley; and *New Defence*, galley. In addition to these nearly three hundred privateers were commissioned.[1]

Nassau, New Providence, is now a popular winter resort. After one hundred and fifty-seven years some of the old landmarks still exist, as is shown by a letter from the Director of Publicity. This letter, together with an extract from *The Bahamas Handbook*, are both printed as they furnish interesting and pertinent facts.

From the Office of the Director of Publicity at Nassau

April 29, 1933.

Ernest E. Rogers, Esq.,
The New London County
Historical Society,
New London, Conn.

Dear Mr. Rogers,

Enclosed are two extracts which we have copied one from *The Handbook of the Bahamas*, the other from Stark's *Guide to the Bahama Islands*.

---

[1] Middlebrook, *Maritime Connecticut*, Vol. I, p. 10.

Old Fort Montagu, Nassau, New Providence, Bahama Islands.

Under separate cover we are sending a picture of Fort Montagu but regret that we are unable to send one of Fort Nassau—the New Colonial Hotel now occupies the former site of Fort Nassau.

If we can be of any further assistance please communicate with us.

Yours faithfully,

(Signed) HUGH BELL,
*Director of Publicity,
Development Board.*

Excerpts from the Bahamas Handbook

"The Bahamas must still have been regarded as of some account in 1760, when General William Shirley, formerly Governor of Massachusetts, was appointed Governor, and the islands increased in importance in consequence of the course of events in the neighbouring American colonies. During the revolutionary war, New Providence was the objective of the young American navy, the first fleet sent out by the rebel colonists having descended upon Nassau for the purpose of securing ammunition which they believed to be stored in the forts.[1] Although the expedition under Admiral Ezekiel[2] Hopkins was originally intended to be directed against Lord Dunmore, who with a naval force was ravaging the coast of Virginia, owing to the vessels having been held up by ice at Reedy Island for several weeks, they did not set sail from the Bay of Delaware until the 17th February and in the meantime they had been ordered to rendezvous at Abaco to make a descent upon Nassau. The squadron, consisting of the *Alfred* (24 guns), the *Columbus* (20 guns), the *Andrea Doria* (14 guns), the *Cabot* (14 guns), the *Providence* (12 guns), the *Hornet* (10 guns), the *Wasp* (8 guns), and the *Fly* (a despatch vessel), arrived off New Providence on the 3rd March, 1776, having stopped at Abaco on the way, approaching the island around Salt Cay and Porgy Rocks. A party of 200 marines, under Captain Nicholas, and 50 sailors under Lieut. Weaver, landed near East End point and marched to the town, both Forts Montagu and Nassau surrendering without resistance when the object of their visit was explained in a pamphlet which was issued and an undertaking given that the town would not be plundered. The Grand Union Flag (bearing the Union Jack in the corner and thirteen red and white stripes in the field representing the thirteen colonies) which had been adopted as a standard for their army and navy by the rebellious colonists,[3] was hoisted over Fort Nassau for one day, but the

---

[1] *American Naval Heroes, 1775-1898*, by John Howard Brown (Boston, Brown and Co.), and *History of the U. S. Navy, 1775 to 1894*, by Edgar Stanton Maclear. New York: D. Appleton and Co.

[2] His correct name was Esek.

[3] The Stars and Stripes were not adopted by Congress as the National Emblem until 1777.

invaders, having taken away the guns and a small quantity of powder from the forts, made no attempt to hold it or disturb the peace of the town. Most of the powder had been shipped to St. Augustine, Florida, the day before they arrived, but they took over 100 guns besides a large quantity of shells and fifteen barrels of gunpowder. The Governor, Montfort Browne, and Thomas Arwin, Inspector-General of Customs in North America, were taken away to be held as hostages. The Governor was subsequently exchanged for Lord Sterling, who was held as a prisoner by the British forces."

Later a letter was received from the American Consul at Nassau which gives such illuminating facts it is also printed.

AMERICAN CONSULAR SERVICE
Nassau, Bahamas, May 12, 1933

Mr. Ernest E. Rogers,
The New London County Historical Society,
Shaw Mansion,
New London, Connecticut.

Sir:

Receipt is hereby acknowledged of your letter of April 28, 1933, in which you request the Consulate to send you postals or illustrations of Old Fort Nassau and Old Fort Montagu, captured by the men under Commodore Esek Hopkins in March 1776, sailing from New London. You state also that any information regarding these forts would be appreciated.

The Development Board at Nassau has informed the Consulate that descriptive literature has been sent you regarding the forts in question. For your further information there is quoted below an excerpt from *The Bahamas Handbook* published by the *Nassau Guardian*, Nassau:

> "FORT NASSAU Of all the sites reminiscent of old Nassau, the one of greatest historic interest is that now occupied by the New Colonial Hotel. As early as 1672, two years after the islands were granted to the Lords Proprietors, a "King's flagg for the forte," presumably on this site, was applied for to the Governor of Jamaica, and two other small forts were erected before Fort Nassau was completed in 1697. This fort was partly destroyed by the French and Spaniards in 1703, and when Captain Woodes Rogers, the first royal Governor, arrived in 1718, he found it in very bad repair, with only one gun mounted. It was there that he was sworn in after he had been received by a guard of honour of pirates who were ready to surrender and take the oath of allegiance. It was also in this Fort that a court martial was held on a number of captured pirates in the following month, when nine of them were condemned to death and hanged in the

Fort on the 17th December. The Fort was almost entirely rebuilt by Peter Henry Bruce, who was appointed "Chief Engineer to fortify the Bahama Islands" in 1740, and it was again repaired in 1770 by order of the Commander-in-Chief of His Majesty's Forces in North America. In 1776 it surrendered to the naval expedition of the American rebels under Admiral Hopkins, who took the guns and what powder and ammunition they could find and then hauled down their flag which had floated over it for one day.

During Lord Dunmore's administration in 1789, application was made for the site and buildings of the Fort for public buildings, but this was not granted, and part of the garrison was quartered there in 1790. The Fort was neglected and finally pulled down in 1837 to make room for military barracks, which were in turn demolished in 1899, when the site was given to Mr. H. M. Flagler for the purpose of erecting the Hotel Colonial. After the destruction of this hotel by fire in 1922, the site was purchased by the Government, and the New Colonial Hotel was erected by arrangement with the Bahamas Hotel Company. On this site, under the Hotel, is a large well known as Blackbeard's well, from which the arch-pirate was supposed to water his ships.

FORT MONTAGU—A fort on this site to guard the eastern entrance of the harbour and close the back door through which the Spaniards might enter and surprise the town was apparently commenced as early as 1728, but it was not until 1741 that the present fort, a small redoubt named after the Duke of Montagu, was built by Peter Henry Bruce. The foundation stone was laid by Governor Tinker on the 10th June, 1741, the Assembly having ordered all vessels and boats to carry stones and mastic trees for pallisades. The fort and sea battery called Bladens Battery were completed in 1742, and mounted eight 18, three 9, and six 6 pounders. Inside were barracks for officers and soldiers, a guard room, powder magazine and a terraced cistern.

In 1776 the American rebels, whose fleet arrive at Salt Cay anchorage, landed at the east end of the island and marched on Fort Montagu, which surrendered without resistance when the object of their visit was explained. In 1782 the Spaniards under Don Juan de Carigal, Governor General of Cuba and the Havannah, attacked New Providence with a force of 5,000, and Fort Montagu surrendered, being held by the Spaniards until it was recaptured in 1783 by a body of loyalists under Colonel Andrew Deveaux, of South Carolina, who landed with about one hundred and sixty men, recruited in St. Augustine and Harbour Island, about a mile from the fort, which was abandoned by the Spanish garrison, whose plans to blow it up were frustrated by Colonel Deveaux when he took possession of it. On the removal of the Imperial troops in 1891 the guns were dismounted."

Trusting that the above information will be of interest to you, I am

    Respectfully yours,

        (Signed) JOHN P. HURLEY,
                American Consul.

V

THE SHIP GENERAL PUTNAM
NEW LONDON PRIVATEER

THE shipyards of New London were busy during the sixties building merchant vessels for the coasting and foreign trade. In the seventies armed vessels were being launched to cruise against the enemy. Many privateer ships sailed from New London during that period. Nathaniel Shaw, Jr., owned and operated not less than ten armed vessels during the war, in addition to his merchant vessels.

When he built the ship *General Putnam* at Winthrop Neck, New London, and commissioned her April 23, 1778, no effort had been spared to make her an honor to her owner. Her armament of 20 cannon, nine pounders, were purchased in Norwich and her timbers cut in adjacent towns. In the Shaw Collection at Yale, packet No. 79 contains 94 bills, receipts and papers pertaining to the building of this privateer ship. Thousands of hand-made copper and wrought-iron nails were used. Iron came from the furnaces in Salisbury, lead and sulphur from the Middletown mines, copper from Simsbury, powder from the West Indies and Elderkin & Wales' mills and Colonel Pitkin's mills.

Several records have been found referring to the fast sailing vessels of Nathaniel Shaw, Jr., but the *General Putnam* was said to be the fastest sailer from New England. Her first commander was Thomas Allon[1] of New London, who had a crew of 150 men. The ship cost £50,000, was owned by Nathaniel Shaw, Jr., and Company of New London, and was bonded for $10,000 by Thomas Allon, Nathaniel Shaw, Jr., and Michael Melally, all of New London.

When the ship was "advertised as lying at anchor in the harbor of New London, fitted in the best manner and ready for sailing under Captain Allon, May 13, 1778, when all

---

[1] Spelled Allon, Allen, and Allan.

TYPE OF PRIVATEER SHIP OF 20 GUNS.
By permission of the Essex Institute, Salem, Mass. Illustration in Maritime Connecticut, by Louis F. Middlebrook.

gentlemen volunteers who were inclined for a cruise were desired to apply on board or at Nathan Douglass's tavern at the sign of the Golden Ball,"[1] her owner wrote to Colonel Josiah Waters at Boston on April 26, 1778, "Pray forward the surgical instruments as the ship is ready to sail." There was more behind the scenes than the adventurous youth enlisting realized.

Altogether the ship took fourteen prizes. She was burned in the Penobscot expedition to prevent her from falling into the hands of the enemy.

Captain Nathaniel Saltonstall was not only an experienced sailor from youth but an expert artilleryman and patriotic soldier, and at the beginning of the Revolutionary War was placed in command of the garrison of the old fort that stood at the foot of the "Parade."

He had previously been employed by Nathaniel Shaw, Jr., in the merchant service and had sailed on some of his armed ships. He went out as First Lieutenant on the ship *General Putnam's* first voyage under Captain Allon. On the second cruise he was in command and secured several prizes for the owners.

In this chapter are printed the instructions of Congress to all masters of privateers; Saltonstall's commission when in command of Shaw's *Le Despencer;* the list of the crew of the *Putnam* when he was First Lieutenant; and Shaw's instructions to him when starting on the cruise as Captain. He was considered an able commander and a daring seaman.

A very interesting sketch of Captain Saltonstall was written by Jonathan Brooks in 1840, fifty-nine years after the burning of New London in 1781 when Brooks was only thirteen years of age. When writing his narrative of the attack on New London, Brooks quotes the exact words of Captain Saltonstall which demonstrated the Captain's good advice at a critical moment.[2]

---

[1] Middlebrook, *Maritime Connecticut*, Vol. II, p. 99.
[2] Rogers, *Sesquicentennial Battle of Groton Heights and Burning of New London*, p. 141.

". . . . At the head of the road we fell in with about one hundred citizens, volunteer soldiers armed and equipped. My father dismounted and joined them.

"The party then fell into conversation about how they should manage, having no commanding officer. Some who had no experience in war matters were for fighting at any odds, saying, 'let us form where we are and contest the ground inch by inch;' but Captain Nathaniel Saltonstall, who once commanded the ship *Putnam*,[1] said, 'gentlemen, whether I have as much courage as many who have given their opinion, I shall not undertake to say; but this I will say, for one I will not be such a fool as to stand here open breasted and be shot down by the very first volley of the enemy's fire.' The enemy were at this time in sight marching in solid columns . . . . . .

"The party now left to themselves, on the sober second thought happened to hit upon Captain Saltonstall, to whom they now looked to command them, and asked him what they should do—there was no time for parley now. He said, 'My advice is to divide ourselves into two parties, each taking the stone wall which is on each side of the road for our shelter; each man take care of himself, and get a shot at the enemy as best he can.' This course was taken, and Benedict Arnold and his army of traitors (for they were almost all of them refugees) were much annoyed by them."

On that memorable occasion Captain Nathaniel Saltonstall[2] did as many other brave men who had risen to the command of ships and of troops, and had been in various encounters, yet, happening to be home at that particular time, shouldered their muskets and went down to meet the approaching enemy as volunteers.

THE DUNMORE SILVER

The publication of the complete manuscript letter book of Nathaniel Shaw, Jr., will no doubt throw light upon many questions. It has done so already for the author.

The New London County Historical Society is the possessor of several pieces of Dunmore Silver consisting of

---

[1] While the official name of the privateer ship was *General Putnam*, she usually was called the ship *Putnam*.

[2] Captain Nathaniel Saltonstall was not a member of the New London family of which Governor Gurdon Saltonstall was the head. Evidently he came to New London when a young man, and made a remarkable record both in the army and the navy. Later he removed with most of his family to Marietta, Ohio, where he died August 1, 1807, aged 80 years.

The Dunmore Silver.

1 Tankard, W. R. D., Armorial bearings,
2 Goblets, W. R. D., Armorial bearings,
12 Tablespoons, W. R. D.,
11 Small teaspoons, W. R. D.,
1 Odd Teaspoon,
1 Cheese spoon,

bequeathed by the late Jane R. Perkins, and known as the "Dunmore Silver" which was the only statement accompanying the gift.

A note was found in the unpublished Caulkins manuscripts:

"Some valuable articles of plate were in possession of this family (Shaw) that were taken in one of the prizes of the revolutionary war. They are marked with armorial bearings and the initials W. R. D."
"Now in the family of Dr. N. S. Perkins."

The markings indicate solid silver, made in the period 1736-1739.

Upon scanning the mercantile letter book for unusual items after it had been photostated and typed, the letter of Nathaniel Shaw, Jr., to Colonel Isaac Sears, merchant in Boston, December 23, 1778, was significant:

" .... As to ordering the prize to Boston that was at Falmouth, in case she had been lost, I imagine I should have been blamed by the concerned. There were no dessert knives, I will furnish you with an acco^t of all the Plate and in case you had rather have your part in anything else you may have it. Am determined to have no dispute with you about anything. Yours, &c."

Another letter was found in the mercantile letter book under date of September 6, 1778, to Amaziah Jocelin, one of the Prize Masters of the *General Putnam*, then in Falmouth, Casco Bay, Maine, with a prize, one of the six taken by Captain Allon. There are two other letters in the mercantile letter book under date of September 19, 1778, mentioning the *Putnam* as arriving in New London, September 18, but no record appears of the silver. In all probability it was brought to Nathaniel Shaw, Jr., by Captain Allon on September 18, but from which one of the six prize brigs it was taken is not known at present.

Letter from Nathaniel Shaw, Jr., to Captain Deshon

(From the copy in the Shaw Collection at Yale)

New London February 27th 1779

Dear Sir

  The Ship *Putnam* is now Ready for Sailing has all her Stores on Board. Yesterday I sent to his Excellency Goven^r Trumbull for a Commission for Capt Nathl Saltonstall as Command^r and he wrote one in answer that he had not any att Pref. Neither did he Expect any sooner than two or three Weeks this being the Case have only Chance to apply to you for one, which I beg you will be so kind as to get me and Send by Harris, or I shall be Ruined. The Ship mounts Twenty Guns has one hundred and Fifty Men on Board and Two hundred Cask of Provisions and About Four hundred Tons own'd by my Self & Co. I Suppose this is all thats Nefsary to know, I have Inclos'd the Bond which you Can fill up to your liking or you Can Send me one to Sign if this is not Agreeable, and I will Comply with your Directions. In Short I will do anything. The Commifsion must Come, and I beg you to send it as soon as Pofsible, for the Ship waits for Nothing Else, and the Consequence of its not Comeing will be the breaking up of the Cruise. Capt. Pinkham in the *Nancy* arived here last Wednesday from Martineco the 27th ulto, says that Count De Estaing was att Fort Royal with his Squadron and had Received no Reinforcement from Europe. The Brigg *Fair Play* was Sunk by the Fort att Guadalupe for not Shewing Proper Signals and some of the People lost, but that the Goven^t has made the Capt Reftitution by that Capt Manly in the *Cumberland* was taken by a Friggate, he Engaged her by a Mistake and Could not get off. The Small Pox I Really believe will go through the Town do all we Can, three Persons are to be Remov'd today, where am I to be Repaid the Expense attending the Sick Prifoners that came here from N York belonging to the Continental Navy—the Expense has been very Great.

Letter from Nathaniel Shaw and Company to Captain Nathaniel Saltonstall

(From the copy in the Shaw Collection)

New London Mar 14, 1779

Sir,

  You are to go on board our Ship *Putnam* Arm'd and fitted in a Warlike manner for a Cruise against the Enimies of the Independant States of America as p^r your Commifsion and Instructions from the Presedent of Congrefs and whose Instructions you are strictly to obey.

We would recommend your sending into this Port in preference to any other all the Prizes you take giving the Prize Masters orders to fall in with the Shoals of Nantuckett, and get intelligance of the Situation of the Enemies Ships, and if they the Block-Island channal to be so guarded that they Cannot proceed here, in that case would recomend their geting into Boston. And where you should Cruise must leave intirely to you and your Officers descretion, and would have you Continue your Cruise as Long as your Stores will allow of it. We wish you a Succefs and Safe Return to your Friends and Owners

               Nathl Shaw & Co.

To Capt Nathl Saltonstall
 Present
  a true Copy of the Original
   Pr Nathl Saltonstall

A List of the Officers and Men on Board the Ship Putnam

(From the original in the Shaw Collection at Yale)

Thomas Allon Capt
Nathl Saltonstall 1st L^t
Nathl Coit 2nd L^t
Seth Warner 3^d L^t
Richard Potter master
Jedediah Hyde Capt of marines
Timothy Rofsiter Surgeon
Robert Smith 1st mate
Christ. Deshields 2nd D^o
John Spencer Prize master
Danl Eldridge D^o
Phineas Stanton D^o
Elnathan Hatch D^o
Amaziah Jocelin D^o
Obadiah Spencer D^o
John Chatfield D^o
  Gunner
David Pool Boatswain
Thomas Edgar Carpenter
Noah Scranton Capt of Hold
Joel Webb Lieut of marines
Thomas Slattery Clerk
Jefse Dowe Steward
William Denison Cooper
Ebenezer Goddard Junr Capt Stew^d

Joshua Lathrop
Luther Burney
Jeptha Benell
Reuben Davis
Roger Robins
John Danielson
Ebenezer Corkins
John Glison
Saml Haskins
John Ripley left Sick
Danl Unkas
Ebenezer Tanner
Thomas Pagy
Joseph Squibb
Gourdin Warricks
John Stephens
Saml Williby
Timothy Butler
William Babbit
Joseph Tibbals
Elnathan Norton
Jefse Gilbert
David Clinton
Agrippa Smith
Thomas Catlin

John Bolles armourer
Milatiah Norton Sailmaker
James Young Gunners mate
William Boulton Boatswains Do
Jonathan Setchel   Do
John Sheffield Carpenters
Julius Willard   Do
Frederick Ridfield Surgeons mate
Moses Palmer Master of Arms
Thomas Bowtriy Quarter master
Jefse Murray   Do
Nathan Baldwin   Do
Sylvanus Smith   Do
William Champlin
John Waterman
David Ensign
William McBride Stewards mate
Thomas Goddard Capenters Yeoman
    Cuffs   Cook

Stephen Davis
Patrick Simot
Reuben Clarke
Thomas Rogers
Isach Hammond
Jonathan Whaley
Joseph Wheeler
Joseph Colly Negroe
Saml Frisby
Joshua Squire
William Young
Paschal Deangelis
William Cooper
Justin Miller
Constant Webb
Hezekiah Canfield
Theodore Harrison
Peter Nugans
Enoch Brookway
Ephraim Tiffidy
John Gwinn
Thomas Bancroft
John White
Stephen Heffern
Henry Card
Drake Mills
Ezra Allen
John Baxter
Timothy Stocken

Burrel Smith
Joseph Smith
Jefse Smith
John Tantiquigin
Edward Staplin
Darius Brewster
Benjamin Williams
Michael Torrey
Solomon Hyde
John Peck
Uriah Roundy
Asa Woodward
William Nasin
Saml Smith
John Harvey
Joseph Manly
Amos Morrison
Lemuel Smith
Danl Twigg
William Tyack
John Caulkins
Benjamin Bowel
Henry Ranson
James Wall
John Wall
Saml Fargo
George Wiatherlike
Joseph Peck
Cato Jones
Isaac Oliver
Timothy Church
James Everts
Amos Mansfield
Elihu Copely
Charles Elliot
John Mansfield
Paris Bernard
John Hubbard
Mathew McClure
John Needham
Thomas Averil
Saml Smith Junr
John Needham Junr
Thomas Berry
James N Griffin
Danl Conkling
William Charley
Michael O'Brien
John Edmunds

Elias Neadham
Eurastus Allen
Elias Sage
Charles Wright
James Parsons
John Vandervoort
Thomas Parsons
Miles Dudley
Peter Darra
Joel Johnson
William Stone
John Brewster
Reuben Shelly
Lewis Fairchild
Cesar Landon
John Salmon
Amasa Hyde
John Mathers
Stephen Tubbs

James McMullins
John Barr
Dan¹ Newcome
Joseph L Saltonstall
Christopher Deane
Thomas Eldridge
Cesar Sabens
Amos Pendleton
John Pendleton
Sam¹ Champlin Junr
John Mason
William Babcock
Thomas Stanton
Henry Elliott
Nath¹ Dyer
Joseph Cook Hubbs
John Elliott

Petition Presented in Boston by Josiah Waters

(From the copy in the Shaw Collection)

To the Honorable the Senate and the Honorable the House of Representatives of the Commonwealth of Mafsachusetts in General Court Afsembled in Boston

Humbly Shews the Petition of Josiah Waters Junr in Behalf of the Owners of the Private Ship of War the *General Putnam*

The Ship of War *General Putnam* was built in 1777 at New London by Nathaniel Shaw Esq for the Sole purpose of a Cruising Ship; and no cost or pains was wanting to compleat her for the businefs, and by means of unfavorable Winds the said Ship put into the Harbour of Boston on the 26th June 1779 at which time an expedition was forming against Penebscot and your Petitioner who was Agent for the owners (Seven Eights of whom were Inhabitants of the state of Connecticutt) was applied to for the said Ship to proceed with them on the said Expedition, and as he did not conceive it to be his duty to consent, without first obtaining leave from the owners; The said Ship was seized by the Sheriff of the County of Suffolk who was fully authorized for the purpose to proceed on the said Expedition: and although your Petitioner was requested to join with the then Board of War in naming the Persons for the appraising the Said Ship, on his refusal for the reason, before mentioned they the said Board of War did appoint, Captains Prince—Fleet and Waldo to appraise the said Ship who accepted the appointment, and did appraise the said Ship at *Ten thousand pounds Sterling*, but in as much as their was no Specie circulating *at that time* they named the sum of *One hundred and ten thousand pounds* in the then *paper Money,* supposing it, to be equal to the aforementioned sum of *Ten thousand pounds Sterling.* But sometime after a Scale of depreciation being fixed; the afore mentioned sum of *One hundred and ten thousand Pounds* in paper Money at which the said Ship *was appraised,* amounted to no more by the said Scale than about *Seven thousand Pounds Lawfull Money*—In consequence of which several petitions from your Petitioner and the owners of the said Ship, have been before the former Hon[ble] General Court, and through the multiplicity of buisneis nothing has yet been finally determined upon—Your Petitioner therefore now prays this Honorable Court, to take the matter into their wise consideration, and appoint a Committe to enquire into the truth of the above representation in order to the owners receiving the sum that the said Ship was intended to be appraised at, with Intrest from the time it became due Confiding in the Justice and Integrity of the Honorable Legislature, and not doubting of a speedy completion of this buifnefs will as in duty bound ever pray

Josiah Waters Jun[r]

Boston Sept[r] 24. 1783

Instructions from Congress to the Commanders of Ships of War, Authorizing Them to Capture British Vessels

(From the original in the Shaw Collection)

IN CONGRESS

Wednesday, April 3, 1776

INSTRUCTIONS to the Commanders of Private Ships or Veffels of War, which fhall have Commiffions or Letters of Marque and Reprifal, authorifing them to make Captures of Britifh Veffels and Cargoes.

I.

You may by force of Arms, attach, fubdue, and take all Ships and other Veffels belonging to the Subjects of the King of Great-Britain, on the High Seas, or between High water and Low-water Marks, except Ships and Veffels bringing perfons who intend to fettle and refide in the United Colonies, or bringing Arms, Ammunition or warlike Stores to the faid Colonies, for the Ufe of fuch Inhabitants thereof as are Friends to the American Caufe, which you fhall fuffer to pafs unmolefted, the Commanders thereof permitting a peaceable Search, and giving fatisfactory Information of the Contents of the Ladings, and Deftinations of the Voyages.

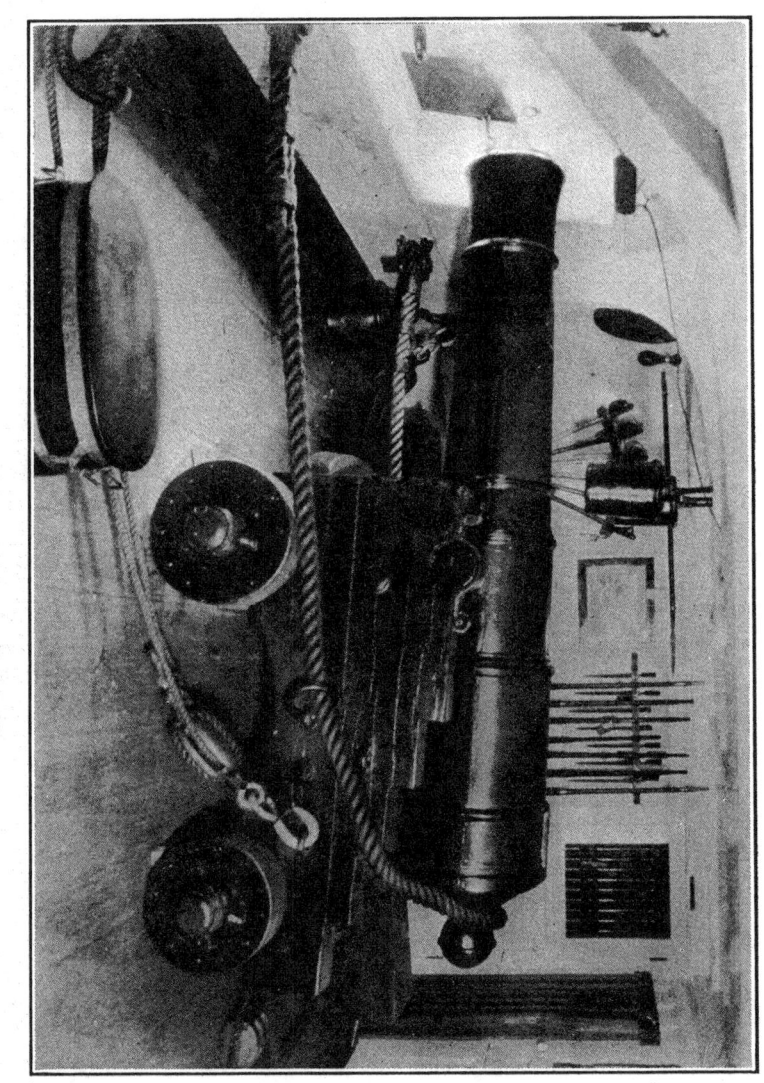

CANNON, 24-POUNDER ON U. S. S. CONSTITUTION.
By permission of the Navy Department, Bureau of Construction and Repair.

II.

You may, by Force of Arms, attack, subdue, and take all Ships and other Vessels whatsoever, carrying Soldiers, Arms, Gun-powder, Ammunition, Provisions, or any other contraband Goods, to any of the British Armies or Ships of war, employed against these Colonies.

III.

You shall bring such Ships and Vessels as you shall take, with their Guns, Rigging, Tackle, Apparel, Furniture and Ladings, to some convenient Port or Ports of the United Colonies, that Proceedings may thereupon be had in due form, before the courts which are or shall be there appointed to hear and determine causes civil and maritime.

IV.

You or one of your Chief Officers shall bring or send the Master and Pilot, and one or more principal Person or Persons of the Company of every Ship or Vessel by you taken, as soon after the Capture as may be, to the Judge or Judges of such Court as aforesaid, to be examined upon Oath, and make Answer to the Interrogatories which may be propounded, touching the Interest or Property of the Ship or Vessel and her Lading; and at the same Time you shall deliver or cause to be delivered to the Judge or Judges, all Passes, Sea Briefs, Charter Parties, Bills of Lading, Cockets, Letters and other Documents and Writings found on Board, proving the said Papers, by the Affidavit of yourself or of some other Person present at the Capture, to be produced as they were received, without Fraud, Addition, Subduction or Embezzlement.

V.

You shall keep and preserve every Ship or Vessel and Cargo by you taken until they shall, by Sentence of a Court properly authorised, be adjudged lawful Prize or acquitted—not selling, spoiling, wasting, or diminishing the same, or breaking the bulk thereof, nor suffering any such Thing to be done.

VI.

If you, or any of your Officers or Crew, shall, in cold Blood, kill or maim, or, by torture or otherwise, cruelly inhumanly, and contrary to common Usage and the Practice of civilized Nations in War, treat any Person or Persons surprized in the Ship or Vessel you shall take, the Offender shall be severely punished.

VII.

You shall, by all convenient Opportunities, send to Congress written Accounts of the Captures you shall make, with the Number and Names of the Captives, Copies of your Journal from Time to Time and Intelligence of what may occur or be discovered concerning the designs of the Enemy, and the Destinations, Motions and Operations of their Fleets and Armies.

VI

THE SHAW MANSION

By Elizabeth Gorton

(In September, 1901, upon urgent solicitation, Miss Elizabeth Gorton became Secretary of the New London County Historical Society.

The Society is grateful for the thirty-two years of faithful, devoted and conscientious service continuously rendered as Executive Secretary and also for this article which by reason of her association with the Shaw Mansion and long experience as a writer is so ably produced. E. E. R.)

THE Nathaniel Shaw House, in New London, Connecticut, commonly known as the Shaw Mansion, is an old historic homestead, owned by a public organization, interested in its past, its present and its future. As one enters New London on the post road from New York and drives through the business section, the house is plainly visible across Perkins' Green, a small parklet separating it from Bank Street. Before the highway was laid out over Long Bridge, the gardens of the Shaw and Perkins families were directly in the street path. Formerly, there was a sandy beach opposite the house and an unobstructed view of Shaw's Cove and the upper harbor. Now, the building faces a busy street lined with stores and the constant hum of modern traffic resounds through the once quiet neighborhood.

Miss Jane Richards Perkins, who passed away March 26, 1930, at the age of eighty-six years, distinctly remembered the open water front, within a stone's throw of her front door, where she kept her rowboat, and spent many happy childhood hours. She was the last lineal descendant of the original owner to occupy the ancestral home, and also the last surviving member of a family of fourteen children.

The changes made to the interior of the house, by her father, Dr. Nathaniel Shaw Perkins, which he considered improvements, are deeply deplored by people of a later generation. The wainscoting in the long parlor, and the chimney piece of wood, were taken out; the room was plastered, and a

ELIZABETH GORTON.
When assuming the office of Secretary in 1901.

marble mantelpiece was put in place of the original one. The original stairs were narrow, and the mantelpieces were undoubtedly high, to allow for the large openings in the chimneys.

Dr. Perkins and his family lived in a house standing a short distance back from Bank Street a little farther up on the same side as the stone house, until he inherited the latter from his father, Judge Elias Perkins. When he moved down to his inheritance, Miss Jane R. Perkins, the youngest member of the family, was carried as a child in her father's arms. The passing years brought inevitable changes. The one who came to the old homestead as a little child lived to witness the passing away of all other members of the immediate family, leaving her and her niece as the sole inheritors of the property and a wealth of valuable material. After the change of ownership, her love for the old home never waned, for it was full of sacred associations, and she never ceased to think of it as her own property. Until the time of her passing, a portion of the house was reserved for her personal use, and she came and went with the freedom of one perfectly at home.

Many times, in a reminiscent mood, she has lingered in her former dining room, now used as a library and office, and revealed intimate touches of family life to the writer of this article as she lived over again, in imagination, many well remembered events of the past connected with life at the Shaw Mansion. Among these was a vivid word picture of one evening in May, 1861, when two of her brothers returned from a mass meeting in the old Court House, held in response to President Lincoln's call for troops to preserve the Union, to tell their parents they had volunteered. The details were made so very real that the listener momentarily seemed to become an eyewitness in the large parlor on that eventful occasion. As a sequel, it is interesting to know that the following year, Lieutenant William W. Perkins, only twenty-one years of age, was killed in action at Kinston, North Carolina. The other brother, Major Benjamin R. Perkins, died at Fort Whipple, Arizona. Their crossed swords and one sash are hanging with their portraits in their boyhood home.

The room known to visitors as the Washington room, was always Mother's room to her. Her graphic descriptions of family events, both of joy and of sorrow, which had occurred there and in other parts of the house, were very realistic. Until failing health prevented her from doing so, she always claimed the happy privilege of arranging flowers in that room, and helping to make other preparations, when there were special social events at the Shaw Mansion. At her own request, made many years ago, her funeral services were held in the old home she loved so well. After her death, it was learned that she had made a very generous financial bequest to the Society, in addition to the family portraits, and some furniture—including that in the Washington room, which, as a loan, had long been among the chief attractions in the house.

Nathaniel Shaw, Sr., ship master and ship owner, during whose life the house was built, and whose name it bears, was a native of Fairfield, Connecticut. He came to New London as a young man and for many years was a sea captain in the Irish trade. The first known local reference to him is that made by a contemporary resident in his diary under date of November 7, 1732:* "Natt Shaw Master of the Norwich Scooner came in from Ireland & have had the Small Pox in their passage, Absolom King Jonathan Douglas (who was Shaw's mate) & Shaws Brother & two Indians died 5 out of 15." On August 23, 1741, the following entry was made concerning his wife: "Temperance Shaw took into the Chh."

In 1734, Shaw purchased from George Denison of Westerly, the land on which the Shaw Mansion stands. It was originally a portion of the Picket house lot. Brewer Street, opened through this lot in 1745, was known as Picket Street. He resided in a frame dwelling, in the rear of the present house until the winter of 1756. On January 21 of that year, a ship arrived from Nova Scotia bringing three hundred French Acadians, including both men and women. In retrospect, this bit of Acadian life within its borders forms a golden link binding together the early history of the Shaw Mansion and

---

* *Diary of Joshua Hempstead*, p. 253.

that of the primitive town, with the life history of these "simple Acadian farmers" so vividly depicted in Longfellow's story of *Evangeline*. At the time, their presence in the town brought the civil authorities face to face with a real problem of unemployment, a fact well authenticated by the following quotation from Joshua Hempstead: "In the evening I was at G. R. with the Rest of the Civil Authority & Selectmen to Consider how to Dispose of the French Neutrals."

It was an inauspicious time for this large band of exiles to earn a livelihood. Captain Shaw graciously came to the rescue by allowing them to remove a large portion of the granite ledge from his property, and build him a substantial stone residence. A visit to the cellar reveals the interesting fact that the house, literally, is built upon a rock-hewn foundation. For a century and three quarters, it has withstood the countless storms which have beaten upon it. Mere antiquity, however, does not constitute the only charm of the Shaw Mansion. To enable one to visualize it, some technical details are necessary, but they are of secondary importance and will be given simply as a background for the people who have dwelt there and the history which centers in it.

Originally there was a wooden wing on the house. The outside door leading into it was always left unfastened, for, according to Captain Shaw's orders, when the house was built, the original owners of the soil were not to be debarred from entering. A fire was kept burning in the huge fireplace, and the wood was piled high at night. In the morning, it was not unusual to find that several Indians had spread their blankets in front of the open fire and spent the night in comfort.

During Dr. Perkins' life, the porch was added and the old wooden wing was taken down and one was built of stone, similar to that in the main house. His office, now used as a work room, was on the ground floor, adjoining a small, square entry having an outside door, from which a short pathway leads directly to the street. The wing is quite complete in itself as a place of residence. It contains two stairways, upper and lower halls and three outside entrances, the one in the kitchen, and one in the rear of the hall opening directly into the garden. There are two rooms on the main floor, four in the second story, and a modern bathroom. It is now occupied by resident caretakers, while the main house is open to the public.

The house stands a short distance back from the street, with a broad flight of brown stone steps leading to the main entrance, which is slightly to the left of the center. It is surrounded by a lawn, with spacious grounds in the rear, and is enclosed, in front, by an artistically designed fence of wrought iron. Extending across the entire front of the main structure is a porch one story high, supported by seven square posts of wood, with ornamental iron work between them. The roof, including that of the wing, is surmounted by a balustrade of wood. The front doorway is recessed with long side lights of glass in three panes, and three wide panes above the door. It opens into a central hallway, extending through the house. This is widened in the rear to accommodate the stairs, which ascend on the left side. From the door at the end of the hall a winding path through the garden leads up a gentle slope to an octagonal shaped summer house which, like an ever watchful sentinel, is perched on the highest part of a granite ledge. From this vantage point, in olden times, the incoming and outgoing ships were easily discernible.

Built into a grassy bank near it is an ancient root cellar, called the *muggs*, formerly used for the preservation of roots and vegetables. This is so tomb-like in appearance that it was used, during a pageant, in August, 1924, to represent the tomb of Washington. Lafayette advancing reverently, laid a wreath upon it as one feature of a century party, celebrating the one hundredth anniversary of his visit to the Shaw Mansion. A group of people, impersonating old time residents of the house, who apparently had stepped from their frames in the portrait gallery, welcomed him once again to their home as he arrived in an old-fashioned coach, accompanied by his Secretary.

THE SUMMER HOUSE AND ROOT CELLAR.

On the first floor, in the main house, there are four rooms, opening into the central hallway. The main stairway, having a newel post, banisters (two on a tread) and a rail of mahogany, has one quarter turn, with a small landing, and leads into a large square hall, or *salon*, which was used as a family sitting room. From the large double windows in the rear, there is an extended view of the grounds.

On its walls are ancient portraits of people identified with the early history of the house. Among them is the stately portrait of Lucretia Shaw, heroine of Revolutionary times, and a full length portrait of Judge Elias Perkins, who entertained General Lafayette in 1824. The portrait of Madame Temperance Shaw hangs near the entrance to the room occupied by General Washington when he was a guest in her home. Arrayed in her old time costume, with white neckerchief and cap, she sits with placid expression in a large winged chair, with spectacles in one hand, and the other hand resting upon the open Bible in her lap, the personification of genial hospitality.

Hanging beside that of his mother is a life-size portrait of Thomas Shaw. He is represented as rather stern of visage, sitting by an open window in his home, through which one catches a glimpse of Shaw's Cove, and the harbor beyond Tongue's Rocks, standing like a gateway in the cove. His youthful and attractive sister, Mary Shaw Woodbridge, in her colonial dress of white satin, is pictured standing out-of-doors against a background of sky and foliage. People of a later generation, who also belong in the family group, are represented in portraiture on the same walls. Permanent picture plates of brass, appropriately lettered, have been placed on the frames enabling one to ascertain "who's who" in this unique and valuable collection of portraits.

Opening into this square hallway, there are five bedrooms, now used for exhibition purposes. The bathroom opens out of a short passage-way connecting the main house with the annex.

On the third floor, in the main house, there are six rooms, including two under the eaves, also a square hall, with a stairway leading to a dark, low attic under the roof, having two skylights of wood. The walls throughout the house are plastered, and most of them are covered with wall paper. Five of the mantels are of black marble and two are of wood. The window sills are deep and the inside shutters fold into the window casings.

At the outbreak of the War of the American Revolution, Nathaniel Shaw, Jr., a man of great wealth and influence, had succeeded his father as head of the Shaw Mansion. He was commissioned by John Hancock, President of Continental Congress, to serve as Naval Agent at New London, and had charge of fitting out all war vessels making port there, and of caring for disabled ships and sick and wounded sailors. He was a member of the committee of five appointed to draft resolutions condemning Parliament for closing the port of Boston in 1774. As a member of the Committee of Correspondence he was in constant demand for consultation with the Governor and Council of Safety in frequent sessions at Hartford, for he was an authority on naval affairs.

His home,—the Shaw Mansion,—was used as a naval office for Connecticut. Locally, it was the center of authority. Most of the distinguished strangers and official guests visiting the town were entertained there. Governor Trumbull, who was an intimate personal friend of the family, was always the guest of the Shaws when he came to New London from the war office in Lebanon. Much valuable manuscript material relating to the Revolutionary War period, including correspondence with General Washington and others regarding naval affairs, was carefully preserved in the family archives. A portion of it has been presented to Yale University, and some of it, including five letters from George Washington to Nathaniel Shaw, Jr., has been given to the New London County Historical Society.

Because of its strategic situation near the entrance of Long Island Sound, New London was able to be of great service

JANE RICHARDS PERKINS IN THE SUMMER HOUSE.

to the country. It was on the direct road from Boston to New York and Philadelphia, and people, passing through, would stop at the naval office—the Shaw Mansion—for the latest news and rumors.

In the midst of the busy and turbulent days of the Revolutionary War period, Lucretia Shaw was the constant companion and helpmate of her husband, Nathaniel, sharing with him the experiences of service and sacrifice. The Shaw Mansion, over which she presided, always famous for its hospitality had become an important center of action, and a place where many deep laid plans were made. Large things were required of her. Both Mr. and Mrs. Shaw were in the very prime of life. He was forty years old and she was about two years younger. She was a woman of large wealth and social position, living in the midst of conditions affording unusual opportunities for patriotic service.

When New London was burned one hundred and fifty-two years ago, the Shaw Mansion caught fire, but was saved by a neighbor who poured some vinegar from the scuttle down the roof and extinguished the fire. An article in a local newspaper, late in 1781, paints a graphic word picture of conditions at that time which clearly portrays the devotion of New London people to the victims of war and those sick with gaol fever. It says in part: "The little portion of this town that was preserved from fire on the 6th of September, is so crowded with those that have been burned out of house and home, that it is dreadful indeed to take these poor, infectious, dying people in. In short, if there is no redress of this intolerable evil, this town and Groton must be depopulated. It is enough to melt the most obdurate heart to see these miserable objects continually landing here from every flag (of truce) that comes; to see them poured out upon our desolated wharves, sick and dying, and the few rags they have on covered with vermin, their friends, if they have any, at a distance, and no public hospital or provision made to receive them. Thus it is that the compassionate among us are compelled by their dying groans to take them into their families at the expense of their lives, without the least recompense in this world, notwithstanding, whole families have been ruined by this means."

Despite the danger to herself, Lucretia Shaw took into her hospitable home some of the sick and friendless prisoners landed under her husband's supervision. She was most impartial in her ministrations to the suffering. "With an open hand for want, a pitying eye for suffering, a loving kindness to solace and a Christian love to comfort,"* she found abundant opportunity for helpfulness. On December 11, 1781, she paid the price of her kind deeds, with her life. It is a most fitting tribute that Lucretia Shaw Chapter, Daughters of the American Revolution, has chosen her name for their organization.

Her husband's death occurred the following April, some time before the welcome news of peace. In the "Towne's Antientest Buriall Place" they were laid side by side, and the place is marked by a double tomb-stone. They lived in stirring and crucial times, and well deserve the local fame they have acquired.

One of the interesting incidents connected with the Shaw Mansion is Washington's visit to it. He came to New London as a young man 24 years of age, and again, twenty years later. Although holding the office of Commander-in-Chief, he arrived on horseback without ostentation, attended by two officers and his faithful colored servant. He spent the night of April 9, 1776, at the Shaw Mansion as the guest of Captain Nathaniel and Madame Temperance Shaw, also Nathaniel Shaw, Jr., and his wife Lucretia. The room in which he slept is a never ending source of delight to visitors. The chimney end and one entire side of the room are panelled and the floor boards are wide. Antique furnishings of the colonial period, including a mirror which reflected the face of Washington at the time of his memorable visit, add to its attractiveness. Unfortunately, the original mantel was among those replaced by marble.

---

* Jane R. Perkins.

Nathan Hale was a friend of the family, and a frequent visitor at the home of Mr. Shaw, who was a trustee of the Union School and instrumental in securing Hale as a teacher. There is said to be still in existence a letter written by him to a young woman, who was a guest of the Shaws. In it he invited her to accompany him and watch the sunset from the rocks behind the Shaw house. The letter was found among the possessions of one of her descendants, and was sold to a collector for $975.00.

On Sunday, August 22, 1824, General Lafayette was a guest, for a few hours, in the same home. In the morning, on his way from Saybrook, he was met in Waterford by a committee of citizens from New London, and escorted to the mansion of Judge Elias Perkins, who had offered to entertain him.

Upon his arrival at the house, Lafayette was received with a national salute of twenty-four guns from Fort Trumbull. While there, he was taken to the Washington room. It is said that he knelt at the bed-side in silent prayer, and then withdrew. He attended service at the Congregational Church, where Rev. Mr. McEwen officiated, and at St. James Church, where Rev. Mr. Judd was the rector. He returned to the home of his host, and received a few callers, after which dinner was served at three o'clock. Seated with him at the table was a small circle of friends, including General William North, General Ebenezer Huntington, General Burbeck and Dr. John R. Watrous. After dinner, he departed with his suite for Norwich, on his way to Boston. It was a day never to be forgotten in the history of New London and the old stone house. The plain, substantial dining room table of mahogany, around which Washington, Lafayette and many other persons of distinction have feasted in that home of bounteous hospitality, is treasured as a priceless heritage by the present owners of the property.

It is with a feeling of unusual interest that one acquainted with the history of the Shaw Mansion ascends the brown stone steps and enters the house visited by George Washington, General Lafayette, Nathan Hale, Commodore Hopkins, "Brother Jonathan" Trumbull and many others distinguished in the revolutionary service, and in various walks of life.

It is a significant fact that the house remained in the same family for a period of one hundred and fifty-one years, being occupied continuously by successive generations of the Shaws and Perkins. In 1907, the crucial time arrived when it must change ownership. Its fate was in the balance. Could it possibly be saved, or must it be sold for business purposes? One by one most of the old colonial houses in New London which had escaped the traitor's torch had been destroyed, until those worthy of preservation were few and far between.

Among the most valuable of the buildings extant was the Shaw Mansion. Certain members of the New London County Historical Society determined to take the initiative in the matter, and attempt to preserve for future generations this place so closely associated with colonial and revolutionary history, and, at the same time, secure a much needed home for the Society. Under the leadership of Hon. Ernest E. Rogers, President of the Society, and largely through his initiative and personal solicitations, the entire purchase price of thirty-three thousand dollars was secured by individual gifts and public subscriptions in less than three months. The prompt and generous response to the appeal for funds was ample proof that the task was undertaken at the psychological moment. Events of the years intervening since the fulfillment of that vision comprise a separate and interesting story.

Rescued from commercialism, the Shaw Mansion, bearing over its entrance the name of the New London County Historical Society, now bids a silent welcome to all visitors. If endowed with the faculty of speech, it could relate many interesting tales of bygone days and reveal many visions for the future. In historical significance and possibilities for future usefulness, this ancient homestead is second to none in the State of Connecticut.

THE SHAW MANSION.
(Rear view.)

VII

THE SHAW AND THE PERKINS FAMILIES

NO New London family, over so long a period, has been more prominent, public spirited and patriotic than members of the Shaw family and their descendants, the Perkins. The records show that all generations promoted good citizenship and community service, were loyal to their native City of New London, and furnished prominent leaders in its social, business and religious life.

It would be interesting to step aside from the direct line of these immediate families and mention some allied to them by marriage, as the Woodbridge, Mumford, Mitchell, Bingham, Williams, Nevins, Griswold, Haven and other families, but it is the plan to confine the record chiefly to those who owned the Shaw Mansion, or were born, lived, or died in it.

CAPTAIN NATHANIEL SHAW, the head of the New London family, is said to have been the son of "Nathaniel Shaw of Boston—married Margaret Jackson of Virginia—removed from Boston to Fairfield, Connecticut where they died—left son Nathaniel who settled in New London."[1] "Nathaniel Shaw a mariner from Fairfield appears at New London as early as 1722, being then about 17 years of age and serving in vessels sailing from this port. Advancing to manhood he became owner and commander of a vessel and was soon afterwards known as a thriving merchant. He married in 1730, Temperance, daughter of Colonel Joseph Harris. The eight children of this marriage all lived to maturity, but only one of them, viz.: Mary, who married Rev. Ephraim Woodbridge, has any descendants remaining."[2] Only in the Caulkins manuscripts was it found that Shaw was born September 23, 1703. Consequently in 1722 he was 19 years of age, instead of 17 as stated above.

NATHANIEL SHAW, JR., around whom center the contents of this volume, was, as stated in a previous chapter, New London's most valuable contribution to the success of the

---
[1] Caulkins MSS.
[2] *Ibid.*

American Revolution. His wife, Lucretia Harris Rogers Shaw, as elsewhere mentioned, was the New London *heroine* of the American Revolution. The local Lucretia Shaw Chapter, Daughters of the American Revolution, was named for her.

THOMAS SHAW, brother of Nathaniel was an ardent patriot, a Deputy Commissioner of Naval prisoners, selectman of the town, and aid to Nathaniel.

HON. ELIAS PERKINS, born in Lisbon, Connecticut, a young lawyer and graduate of Yale, at 23 married Lucretia Woodbridge, the niece of Thomas Shaw, then living with her uncle in the Shaw Mansion, and moved to his wife's home. He became a judge of the superior court and the outstanding citizen of the town.

DR. NATHANIEL SHAW PERKINS, their son, became the leading physician of the town. His son, Major Benjamin Richards Perkins, was the first volunteer in New London at the opening of the Civil War. Another son, Lieut. W. W. Perkins, was the second volunteer; he was killed in action. The W. W. Perkins Post G. A. R. is named for him.

JANE RICHARDS PERKINS, the youngest child of Dr. Perkins and the last to reside in the Shaw Mansion, left a large portion of her estate to the New London County Historical Society.

ELLINOR SHAW GRISWOLD, the daughter of Mary Perkins Griswold, was the last child born in the Shaw Mansion. Of the fourteen children of Dr. Nathaniel Shaw Perkins, Mary was the only one to leave a descendant; with the passing of her daughter Ellinor on February 24, 1932, the line became extinct.

As some discrepancies appeared in such genealogical records as were found in the Shaw Collection and elsewhere, the plan has been followed of visiting the cemeteries for the gravestone inscriptions, and printing in italics those found. The cemeteries visited were the First Burial Ground, New London (Antientest Buriall Place), the oldest in New London County; the Woodbridge Cemetery in Salem, Connecticut; the Griswold Cemetery in Old Lyme, Connecticut, and Cedar Grove Cemetery in New London.

The first two generations were buried in the First Burial

LUCRETIA HARRIS ROGERS SHAW, MARY SHAW WOODBRIDGE.

Ground, New London, except Daniel Shaw, who with his wife was buried in the Second Burial Ground, New London, and afterwards removed to Cedar Grove Cemetery. The third, fourth and fifth generations are buried in Cedar Grove Cemetery, except Nathaniel Shaw Woodbridge, who with his first wife, was buried in the Woodbridge Cemetery; and Mary Perkins Griswold, who with her two daughters of the sixth generation lies in the Griswold Cemetery.

GENEALOGICAL RECORD OF THE SHAW AND THE PERKINS FAMILIES

*CAPTAIN NATHANIEL SHAW, SR., b. Fairfield, Conn., Sept. 23, 1703;[1] *d. Aug. 26, 1778*;† m. Nov. 5, 1730,[2] Temperance Harris, b. May 24, 1709;[2] *d. June 27, 1796*.

EIGHT CHILDREN BORN IN NEW LONDON

Sarah, b. March 29, 1734;[1] *d. Sept. 11, 1759*; m. Nov. 20, 1757,[3] David Allen. Son David *d. Nov. 17, 1762 aged 3 years, 7 months*.

*NATHANIEL SHAW, JR., b. Dec. 5, 1735;[2] *d. Apr. 15, 1782*, no children; m. July 20, 1758,[2] Lucretia Harris Rogers, widow, b. ———; *d. Dec. 11, 1781 aged 44 years*. She had one child by first marriage to Captain Josiah Rogers. The Captain d. Sept. 11, 1757,[4] son Josiah *d. March 20, 1764 aged 7 years, 8 months*.

*THOMAS SHAW, b. March 16, 1739;[2] *d. Sept. 26, 1795*; not married.

Daniel Shaw, b. ———; *d. June 16, 1798 aged 56 years*; m. June 12, 1769,[2] Grace Coit, b. ———; *d. June 14, 1800 aged 55 years*; no children.

---

* Resident Owners of the Shaw Mansion.
† Gravestone records are in italics.
[1] Caulkins' MSS.
[2] Perkins, *Chronicles of a Connecticut Farm*.
[3] Rev. Mather Byles.
[4] *Diary of Joshua Hempstead*.
[5] Caulkins, *History of New London*.
[6] Shaw Collection.
[7] Caulkins' *Necrology*.
[8] *New London Town Records*.

Joseph, aged 20, died at sea.[1]
John, aged 21, died at sea.[1]
William, aged 22, died at sea.[1]
Mary (Polly), b. Sept. 6, 1751;[2] *d. June 10, 1775*; m. Oct. 26, 1769,[5] Rev. Ephraim Woodbridge, b. June 20, 1746;[2] *d. Sept. 6, 1776*, three children born in New London.

THREE CHILDREN OF MARY (POLLY) SHAW AND REV. EPHRAIM WOODBRIDGE BORN IN NEW LONDON

Nathaniel Shaw Woodbridge, b. Nov. 4, 1771;[2] *d. June 16, 1797 aged 26 years*; m. (1st) June 24, 1790,[2] Elizabeth Mumford, b. ———; *d. Feb. 21, 1795, 25th year of her age*; three children born in Salem. M. (2nd) May 5, 1796,[2] Lois Mather, b. ———; d. Feb. 15, 1823;[2] one child born in Salem.

*LUCRETIA SHAW WOODBRIDGE, *b. Aug. 7, 1773*; *d. March 6, 1802*; m. March 11, 1790,[6] *HON. ELIAS PERKINS, *b. Apr. 5, 1767*; *d. Sept. 27, 1845*; seven children born in New London. Elias Perkins m. (2nd) Mary Mumford of Salem, Feb. 11, 1805;[2] *b. Apr. 17, 1774*; *d. March 22, 1830*; two children born in New London.

Sarah Woodbridge, b. Jan. 7, 1775;[6] *d. Sept. 5, 1775*.[6]

SEVEN CHILDREN OF LUCRETIA SHAW WOODBRIDGE AND ELIAS PERKINS BORN IN NEW LONDON

*DR. NATHANIEL SHAW PERKINS, b. Feb. 11, 1792;[6] *d. May 25, 1870 in 79th year*; m. May 10, 1818,[6] Ellen Richards, daughter of Captain Benjamin Richards; b. Jan. 28, 1801;[6] *d. March 3, 1885 aged 84*; fourteen children born in New London.

---
* Resident Owners of the Shaw Mansion.
† Gravestone records are in italics.
[1] Caulkins' MSS.
[2] Perkins, *Chronicles of a Connecticut Farm.*
[3] Rev. Mather Byles.
[4] *Diary of Joshua Hempstead.*
[5] Caulkins, *History of New London.*
[6] Shaw Collection.
[7] Caulkins' *Necrology.*
[8] *New London Town Records.*

Ellen Richards Perkins, Dr. Nathaniel Shaw Perkins, Joanna Burnham Perkins Caulkins, Nathaniel Shaw Perkins, Jr., Dr. Nathaniel Shaw Perkins.

SHAW AND PERKINS FAMILIES

Thomas Shaw Perkins, b. Aug. 10, 1793;[2] d. Oct. 14, 1844 aged 51, at sea; m. (1st) Jan. 4, 1818,[2] Cornelia Leonard, b. ———; d. May 8, 1818,[2] on passage from New York to Bordeaux; m. (2nd) Feb. 23, 1820,[2] Mary Ann Griswold, b. ———; *d. Sept. 22, 1869 aged 67.*
Joseph Perkins, b. Sept. 21, 1794;[6] d. an infant.
Daughter, b. Oct. 2, 1795,[6] lived 12 hours.
Lucretia Woodbridge Perkins, *b. Feb. 22, 1797; d. April 12, 1829*; m. Hon. Thomas Williams, May 15, 1817.[2]
Ellen Elizabeth Perkins, b. May 23, 1799;[2] d. Feb. 26, 1877;[2] m. Nov. 14, 1820,[2] Charles Griswold.
Oliver Ellsworth, b. Aug. 16, 1801;[6] d. Nov. 25, 1801.[7]

TWO CHILDREN OF MARY MUMFORD AND ELIAS PERKINS BORN IN NEW LONDON

Oliver Ellsworth, b. Jan. 26, 1806;[6] d. Aug. 9, 1847.[7]
Elias, Jr., b. July 28, 1808;[6] d. April 13, 1816,[6] *aged 7 years, killed by being thrown from a carriage upset by a frightened horse.*[7]

FOURTEEN CHILDREN OF DR. NATHANIEL SHAW PERKINS AND ELLEN RICHARDS BORN IN NEW LONDON

Elias Perkins, b. Feb. 6, 1819;[6] *d. Oct. 22, 1883 aged 63* at Merced, Calif.[6]
Benjamin Richards, b. Nov. 1, 1820;[6] *d. July 21, 1821 aged 6 months.*
*NATHANIEL SHAW PERKINS, *b. April 19, 1822; d. Feb. 8, 1905, last surviving son of N. S. and E. R. Perkins.*
Henry Coit, b. Feb. 12, 1824;[6] *d. May 19, 1824 aged 3 months.*

---

* Resident Owners of the Shaw Mansion.
† Gravestone records are in italics.
[1] Caulkins' MSS.
[2] Perkins, *Chronicles of a Connecticut Farm.*
[3] Rev. Mather Byles.
[4] *Diary of Joshua Hempstead.*
[5] Caulkins, *History of New London.*
[6] Shaw Collection.
[7] Caulkins' *Necrology.*
[8] *New London Town Records.*

Jonathan Coit, b. April 15, 1825;[6] d. Dec. 26, 1826 aged 20 months.
Ellen, b. April 15, 1827;[6] d. Sept. 9, 1827 aged 4 months.
Mary Richards Perkins, b. July 6, 1828;[6] d. Oct. 1, 1863 aged 35; m. June 24, 1861,[6] James Griswold, b. Feb. 8, 1828; d. May 7, 1892. Two children, Theodora, b. April 28, 1862; d. Sept. 17, 1862. *ELLINOR SHAW GRISWOLD, b. Sept. 6, 1863;[8] d. Feb. 24, 1932.
Thomas W. Perkins, b. Aug. 15, 1830;[6] d. Sept. 7, 1881 aged 51 years.
Major Benjamin Richards Perkins, b. Aug. 2, 1832;[6] d. Feb. 7, 1871 at Fort Whipple, Arizona Ty, aged 38 years, 6 months.
W. Lewis Perkins, M.D., b. Dec. 8, 1834;[6] d. Dec. 12, 1864.
Ellen, b. Feb. 24,[6] 1837; d. Dec. 11, 1839, aged 2 years, 9 months.
Francis A. Perkins, b. March 18, 1839; d. Feb. 11, 1875; m. Dec. 11, 1872,[6] Anna W. Haven, daughter of Henry P. and Elizabeth L. Haven, b. May 22, 1841; d. Jan. 28, 1890.
Lieut. Wm. W. Perkins, b. April 7, 1841; d. Dec. 14, 1862, killed in action at Kinston, N. C.
*JANE RICHARDS PERKINS, b. Jan 23, 1844; d. March 26, 1930. "A quiet life of fortitude and courage."

Tombstone Inscriptions of The Shaw Group in "Ye Towne's Antientest Buriall Place," New London

The Dust of Nathaniel Shaw Esq[r] Who died 26th August A.D. 1778 Aged 75 years	In Memory of M[rs] Temperance Shaw Relict of Nath[l]. Shaw Esq[r] who died June 27th 1796 Aged 87 years

---

* Resident Owners of the Shaw Mansion.
[6] Shaw Collection.
[8] *New London Town Records.*

WILLIAM W. PERKINS, BENJAMIN R. PERKINS (above).

The
Dust of
Nathaniel Shaw Esqr
who died 15th April
A.D. 1782
Aged 47 years
and
of his Wife
Lucretia
that died 11th Decm^r
A.D. 1781
Aged 44 years

In Memory
of
Thomas Shaw Esqr
who died Sep 26th
1795
Aged 56 Years

Sacred to the Memory
of
Ephraim Woodbridge A.M.
Sixth Pastor of the 1st Church
New London
Ordained Oct. 11, 1769
deceased Sept. 6, 1776
AE xxx
Zion may in his fall bemoan
A Beauty & a Pillar gone.

Here lies the Remains
of
Mrs Mary Woodbridge
Wife of the
Rev. Ephraim Woodbridge
and Daughter of Capt
Nathaniel & Mrs Temperance Shaw
Who died at Bolton
June 10, 1775
In the 24th Year
of her age
When as a signal of her leave to go
Home to her Saviour free from Sin & Woe
Death from his Quiver show'd a fatal Dart
A sudden Pulse of Joy leap'd from her Heart
Enough of Life & all its Charms, she cried
Welcome my Father's Messenger, & died.

In Memory
of Sarah ye wife of
Mr David Allen &
Daught'r of Mr Nathaniel
& Temperance Shaw
who died Septr 11th
A.D. 1759   Aged 25
Years, & 5 months.

In Memory
of David y^e
son of David
& Sarah Allen
who died Nov^r
ye 17th 1762
Aged 3 years
& 7 M^o.

In Memory
of Josiah Son
of Josiah and
Lucretia Rogers
who died March
20th A.D. 1764
Aged 7 years
& 8 M^o.

VIII

THE SHAW COLLECTION

THE New London County Historical Society justly values with pride its Shaw Collection, not only on account of its intrinsic worth, but also for its educational value to students of history, and its interest to the public.

The Shaw Collection came to the Society through the agreement of February 15, 1907, as excerpt:—"The undersigned, Jane R. Perkins and Ellinor S. Griswold also hereby agree that in case said land and house shall be conveyed to said society, pursuant to the option hereby given, they will also donate to said society such papers, books, furniture and other articles as they may select, having historical value and interest and now in said house, to be known as 'The Shaw Collection,' and to be preserved by said society in memory of their ancestors and kindred who have occupied said house."

It consists of portraits, furniture, Dunmore silver, books and approximately 1,000 pieces of manuscript material including letters and documents.

The portraits are those of Temperance Harris Shaw, Thomas Shaw, Mary (Polly) Shaw Woodbridge, Lucretia Harris Rogers Shaw, Joanna Burnham Perkins Caulkins, Judge Elias Perkins, Lucretia Shaw Woodbridge Perkins and infant son Nathaniel Shaw Perkins, Dr. Nathaniel Shaw Perkins (two portraits), Ellen Richards Perkins, Nathaniel Shaw Perkins, Jr., William W. Perkins, Benjamin R. Perkins, Captain Benjamin Richards, Jonathan Coit and James Coit. There are also miniatures and daguerreotypes.

Persons competent to judge claim that some of the early portraits were the work of Ralph Earle who painted portraits in Connecticut.[1]

---

[1] "Ralph Earle was born at Leicester, Massachusetts, in 1751, and painted portraits in Connecticut, in 1775, after the manner of Copley. After the war he went to England, studied under Benjamin West, became a member of the Royal Academy, and returned to America in 1786." Perkins, *Chronicles of a Connecticut Farm.*

To the present time the author has not located either in the New London or Yale Collection the letters from the Marine Committee of the Continental Congress which he saw in 1896, or any letters from Governor Trumbull. However, copies of the letters from the Marine Committee have been procured from the Library of Congress and printed in "The Naval Office" chapter. It was the custom for all the committee members present to sign the letters. Through changes in the membership from time to time the letters contained the signatures of thirty-two signers of the Declaration of Independence.

THE SHAW PAPERS AT YALE

Yale College is the *Alma Mater* of Miss Jane R. Perkins' grandfather, Judge Elias Perkins; her father, Dr. Nathaniel Shaw Perkins; and her brother, Nathaniel Shaw Perkins, Jr. To this institution was presented on September 6, 1926, a sea chest containing 8,882 pieces, now in the Yale University Library.

The entry at the time of their accession reads as follows:

"The Nathaniel and Thomas Shaw Letters and Papers given to Yale College as a memorial of Nathaniel Shaw Perkins, M.D., by his daughter, Jane R. Perkins and her brothers, September 6, 1926.

"The manuscripts, consisting of 35 account books and ledgers, and 150 packets of letters, bills, receipts, etc., numbering 8,882 pieces are packed in a large wooden chest, which belonged formerly to Elias Perkins one of the donors.[1] A manuscript inventory in two 'Order Books' accompanied the gift.

"Account Books—Accounts for prize ships, sales of cargo, crews, care of prisoners, supplies for the Continental Army, etc."

An important item was found by the author in the Shaw Collection at Yale in the handwriting of Nathaniel Shaw, Jr., showing delivery of powder and ball to Lieutenant Hale. Nathan Hale resigned July 7, 1775,[2] as teacher in New Lon-

---

[1] Miss Jane R. Perkins gave the collection to Yale in the name of herself and brothers, but attention should be called to the fact that all of her brothers were deceased before the collection was given.
The sea chest containing the papers was the property of her brother, Elias, named after his grandfather, the Judge.

[2] Johnston, *Nathan Hale 1776*, p. 61.

don to accept his commission as lieutenant in the Continental army, and began recruiting in New London. Nathaniel Shaw, Jr., delivered the powder and ball to him on August 30, and about September 20[1] a part of Colonel Webb's regiment including Lieutenant Hale's company left New London for Cambridge, the headquarters of the American army.

Levingworth	30^{lb} Ball	———	——	del^d.	Nath Wheeler
Tyler . .	40	———	10^{lb} powder	—	Ens^n Hale
Rowlee. .	40	———	10	d^o	Jo^s. Carver
Shipman .	40	———	10	d^o	Simeon Fuller
Latimer .	——	———	10	d^o	Serg^t Chapman
Bostwick .	40	———	10	d^o	Ens^n. Brinsmaid
Tuttle . .	40	———	10	d^o	Lemuel Gibs
Hubbard .	12	———	6	d^o	Wm Tallmage
	242		66		

} Aug^s 30th del^d Lieut. Hale 1775

Of the many account books it seems advisable, in one case at least, to enumerate the headings of the separate accounts, often comprising many pages each, which will give an example of the voluminous accounts kept in those days.

Account Book No. 4 of Nathaniel Shaw, Jr., Merchant, in the Shaw Collection at Yale

ACCOUNTS WITH INDIVIDUALS

Joseph and William Packwood	1764
Capt. Josiah Rogers	1757
Peter Vandevoort & Co.	1765
William Miller	1765
John Chapman—Master of *Pompey*	
Thomas & Isaac Wharton	
N. Saltonstall—Master *Lucretia* 13th voyage	
Azariah Jones—Master *Pompey*	1770
Michael Melally—Master Sloop *Thames*	
John Chapman—Master Sloop *Dove*	1771

ACCOUNTS WITH SHIPS

Brigantine *Lucretia*	
Sloop *Nancy*	17 voyages
Prize Ship *La Isan Teresa*	
Sloop *Speedwell*	1763
Schooner *Lucy*	1765

---

[1] Johnston, *Nathan Hale 1776*, p. 61.

THE SHAW COLLECTION

Sloop *Lively* — 1766
Sloop *Elizabeth Freeman* — 1767
Brigantine *Nancy* — 14 voyages
Sloop *Dove* — 8 voyages
Schooner *Pompey* — 1767
Brigantine *Thames* — 1767
Sloop *Lively*
Schooner *Three Sisters* — 1768
Schooner *Hawk* — 1770
Brigantine *Little John* — 1770
Schooner *Delight* — 1770
Schooner *True Blue* — 1771
Sloop *Thames*, Michael Melally, Master, 1771
Schooner *Neptune* — 1771
Schooner *Lark*
New *Pompey*
Brig *Mermaid*—M. Melally
Sloop *Polly* — 1772
Ship *America*
Sloop *Sally* — 1773
Brigantine *Disco* — 1773
Sloop *Black Joke* — 1773
Brig *Marianne* — 1773 Wm. Powers Master
Schooner *Defiance* — 1774
Brig *Polly & Getty* — 1774
Sloop *Macaroni*
Sloop *Commerce* — 1775
Sloop *Groton Packett* — 1775
Sloop *Betsey* — 1775 Edward Chappell Master
Schooner *Industry* — 1775
Sloop *William* — 1775
Schooner *Happy Return* Nath Howard 1775
Schooner *Endeavor* Stephen Stimson
Sloop *Thomas* — 1776 Jo Packwood
Schooner *Ceaser* — 1776
The Colony Brig *Defence* — Seth Harding Master
The Continental Brig *Cabot* — Elisha Hinman Commander
Sloop *Lucretia* — 1777 Stephen Tinker Master
Sloop *American* — 1778
Brig *Favourite* — 1778
Sloop *Providence* — 1778
Schooner *Mefflen* — 1777
Schooner *Hannah & Molly* — 1778
Sloop *Guilford* — 1779
Brig *Eliot* — 1779 afterwards called *Polly*..

IX

GEORGE WASHINGTON'S CORRESPONDENCE WITH NATHANIEL SHAW, JR.

LAST year, as the contribution of the New London County Historical Society to a proposed celebration of the bicentennial of the birth of George Washington, it was planned to issue a brochure containing the letters of Washington to Nathaniel Shaw, Jr. When it was ascertained that copies of the letters of Shaw to Washington were obtainable, it was decided to print all in the present book for greater permanence.

Washington was in New London when a young man and again when he was on his way to New York from Boston after the British had evacuated the latter city. It seems appropriate in connection with his visits to New London to reproduce here the article written for a periodical called the *Repository*, by Frances Manwaring Caulkins, New London's historian, November 20, 1858, titled *Washington's Visits to New London.*

"In the year 1756 Washington was twice in New London. He was then but twenty-four years of age yet had distinguished himself in the frontier wars with the French and Indians, and was chief commander of the Virginia forces. He was on a journey to Boston for the purpose of conferring with Gov. Shirley, and tarried a night at New London both in going and returning. It is probable that he lodged at the sign of the *Red Lion* in Main St., which was then the principal house of entertainment for travellers, and was kept by Capt. Nathaniel Coit.

"Irving, in the Life of Washington, says that this journey of 500 miles was performed on horseback. Col. Washington was accompanied by his aid, Capt. George Mercer, and Capt. Stewart of the Virginia Light Horse, and the three men each had an African servant in livery. The whole party were splendidly equipped and made a brilliant appearance.

"We can imagine that the populace of New London, which at that period was very gay and excitable, was considerably moved when this dashing party came galloping into town. Washington was a skillful rider, and a noble figure upon horseback, eminent also for his martial bearing and stately courtesy. Undoubtedly our gallant fort at the foot of the parade, displayed old England's cross, and fired its six pounders in a salute to the

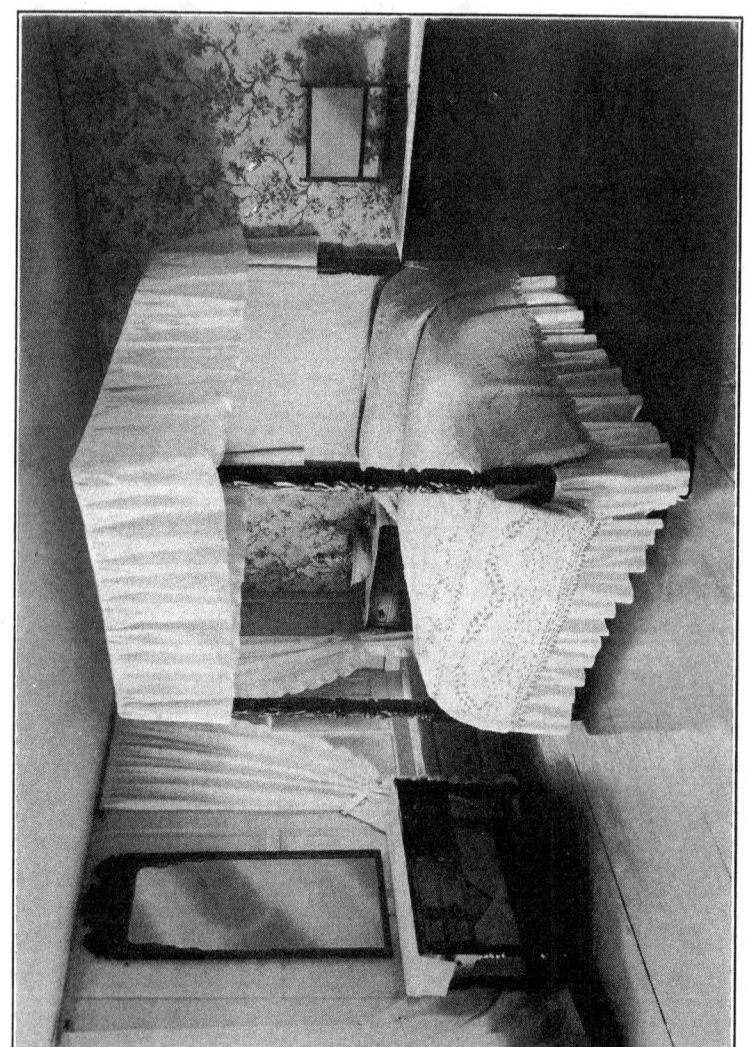

THE WASHINGTON ROOM.

brave young Virginians. In the evening probably, bonfires blazed and the strangers were saluted with a martial serenade.

"Unfortunately, this was before any newspaper had been established in the place, and no one chronicled the event. But the return of the party after ten days stay at Boston, is noted in a private diary, kept by a citizen of the place.

"March 8, 1756.—'Col. Washington is returned from Boston and gone to Long Island, in Power's sloop; he had also two boats to carry six horses and his retinue; all bound to Virginia. He hath been to advise with Governor Shirley, or to be directed by him, as he is chief general of the American forces.'

"Washington was again in New London twenty years later, just after the British had evacuated Boston, and while the American army was on the march from that place to New York. He came this time also on horseback, not with the army but almost alone, in a quiet, unpretending way. Though holding the office of Commander-in-chief, he made no display whatever.

"The writer of this article was told by the late Col. John Raymond of Montville, that he was at work upon the road between Norwich and New London with a team and several assistants, when Gen. Washington came riding with a rapid pace over the Mohegan hills, attended by only two officers and his faithful colored servant.—Raymond had performed duty at Boston as Lieutenant of a company, and recognized the General at the first glance.

"'I knew him,' he said, 'at a distance, by the stately way he sat upon his horse, and his grand, magnificent air.'

"The workmen threw down their implements, and standing aside with deference and respect, waved their hats and gave a loud huzza. Washington bowed his head and without slacking his pace, gave them in passing, a silent but courteous salute. Raymond and his men leaped upon fences and rocks to gaze after him, and keep him in sight as long as possible.

"This was on the 9th of April, 1776.—New London wore a lively aspect that day and night. Commodore Hopkins had just returned from an expedition against New Providence, one of the Bahama Islands. A part of his fleet lay in the harbor, and he was landing his prisoners and the military stores he had captured. General Greene, with a part of his brigade, on their march to New York, arrived the same night and encamped in and around town.

"Washington was the guest of Capt. Nathaniel Shaw, at his stone house in Bank St., and some of the members of the Council of Safety of Connecticut, and conferred with them respecting their future operations against the enemy. The chamber which Washington occupied that night at Mr. Shaw's, has acquired from the circumstances an enduring interest. The owners of the mansion have endeavored to keep it unchanged in appearance. . . . .

"When the Marquis LaFayette made his celebrated tour through the United States, 40 years after the revolutionary struggle in which he had borne a part, was over—he visited New London and was a guest for a few hours in the Shaw house, then owned by the Hon. Elias Perkins; while there, he was conducted to the Washington chamber. After surveying it with tearful eyes, he knelt for a few minutes by the bedside, communing no doubt, in reverential silence with God and the spirit of his departed friend, and then withdrew.

"There is certainly a superadded value attached to whatever has been connected with the person and life of Washington. Certain localities that he is known to have visited, acquire new interest. The articles he wore and implements that he used, the books he read, the words he wrote, the things that he merely touched and beheld with complacency become thereby worthy of preservation and admiring regard.

"It is this principle which will make the generations that come after us remark, (with even a stronger interest than we now experience) as they walk the streets—'Here stood the Red Lion Inn, where Washington and his brilliant companions were entertained when they came here in the time of the old French war! This was the Ferry wharf from which he took his departure to Long Island, waving his adieus to the curious throng that lined the river bank! And there, too, is the house where he was received with magnificent hospitality, and the very chamber, where he found repose as he was hastening forward to commence the arduous campaign of 1776.'

"It is this hallowed principle of affectionate interest in all that concerns the noble and pure-minded Washington, that has roused the Ladies of the Union at this time, to unite their efforts to redeem the Home and the Tomb of the Hero from decay, and to take measures for preserving them evermore as sacred memorials of the gratitude of his country. The blessing of Providence will surely crown an enterprize which springs from a grateful reverence for our greatest earthly Benefactor and Defender—the man who, as warrior and statesman, all will acknowledge, stands unrivalled in the annals of history."

Five Original Letters from George Washington to Nathaniel Shaw, Jr.

One Copy of a Letter from George Washington to Major General Greene

The New London County Historical Society is fortunate to have among the many valuable letters in its possession five original letters from George Washington, and takes pleasure in publishing them. It has also a copy of one of Washington's letters to Major General Greene.

Letter from George Washington to Nathaniel Shaw, Jr.

(From the original in the Shaw Collection)

Head Quarters N. York 7th. Aug. 1776

Sir

I duely received your fav^r. of the 1st. Inst. by Doct^r. Wolcott with an ^extreme fine Turtle, which was very acceptable, & for which I return you my best thanks—Am exceedingly sorry to hear the Prize ship was lost when so near the Harbour, but conclude it was an unavoidable accident, & as such we must be reconciled thereto—I wrote you the other day by some french Gent^n. to wch. I refer, and am with due Regards

Sir

Your very humble Servt.

G^o. Washington

Nathl. Shaw Junr. Esqr.

Letter from George Washington to Nathaniel Shaw, Jr.

(From the original in the Shaw Collection)

Head Quarters Bergen County 10th: July 1780

Sir

It is more than probable that we shall, in the course of our expected cooperation with our Allies, have occasion to make use of the Navigation of the Sound, for which reason we should have some of the most expert and trusty pilots engaged.

I am recommended to apply to you Sir to undertake this business, which I am convinced you will cheerfully execute. You will have only need for the present, to fix upon certain Characters, and engage their promise to repair, at a moments either on board the Fleet, or to any place to which they may be directed. They shall be amply paid for their time, should they go upon service. I am convinced I need make no apology for giving you this trouble. The occasion will be sufficient.

      I am with great Respect
        Sir
       Your most ob.^{t} Servt
       G° Washington

Nathan^l. Shaw Esq:

Letter from George Washington to Nathaniel Shaw, Jr.

(From the original in the Shaw Collection)

    Head Quarters Robinsons House 31st. July 1780

Sir

  In the present situation of affairs, it is indispensably necessary that we should have the most instantaneous advices of the movements of the Enemy at Rhode Island. For this purpose I have posted relays of Dragoons at every 15 Miles distance between New London and the Head Quarters of the Army. This taking as many as we can conveniently spare. I shall be exceedingly obliged to you to hire as many trusty Men with their Horses as will continue the Chain from New London to Tower Hill, posting three at every 15 Miles, with orders to ride by night or by day whenever dispatches arrive at their quarters. I will be answerable for their pay while in service, which will be as long as the British Fleet and Army continue at or off Rhode Island. Should you not be able to accom: plish this Business, you will inform the Officer, the Bearer of this, who must in that case carry the Dragoons the whole way through, however inconvenient it may be. I shall also be obliged to you to have a constant look out kept upon the sound, and if the Fleet appear standing from the Eastward towards New York, to give me instant intelligence of it by the Chain of Expreses—

I am with great Respect
Sir
Y^r. most ob^t. Servt.
G^o. Washington

Nathl. Shaw Esq:

Letter from George Washington to Nathaniel Shaw, Jr.

(From the original in the Shaw Collection)

Head Quarters near Orange Town.
Augst. 8th. 1780

Sir

I have been duly favoured with your two Letters of the 5th. and 6th. Instant; and thank you for the intelligence contained in them —

I am also much obliged by your offer
of assistance to Captain Hurlbut of expediting
the communication—And entreat you will continue to give me the earliest notice ∧ which
of any movements
may be made by the Enemys shipping in
the Sound, or of any thing else of consequence
which may come to your knowledge.

    I am Sir
      Your most Obedient
       Hble Servant
      G°. Washington

Nath Shaw Esquire.

Letter from George Washington to Nathaniel Shaw, Jr.

(From the original in the Shaw Collection)

  Head Quarters Orange town 16th: Augt 1780

Sir

  I have rec^d. your favors of the 11^h: and 13^h: instant. I perceive that you have transmitted the intelligence contained in the last to Rhode Island, and I would always wish you to do the same whenever you gain any information which may be interesting to the French General and Ad: miral.

    I am Sir
      Your most ob^t. & hble Servt.
      G°. Washington

Nathaniel Shaw Esq:

WASHINGTON—SHAW CORRESPONDENCE 95

Letter from George Washington to Major General Greene

(From a copy in the Shaw Collection)

Head Quar near Passaick
July 19. 1780.

Dear Sir,
In answere to yours of this evening the whole of the Cloathing & Arms are to be sent to Fish Kill Town in the first instance unless orders should be given to the contrary—and tho' it is a matter of great importance & infinitely desiraiable to save expense, by bringing them by water transportation part of the way; yet the present State of navigation will not permit or justify me in giving an order for their coming otherwise than by land

The Arms will be adressed to General Knox—the Clothing to Mr Wilkinson or John Moylan Esq. The powder & lead on board the Fleet for the States—if they cannot be sent with safety to New London must be sent to providence

I am Dr Sir
Your most obed^t S^t
G^o. Washington

Major Genl Greene
Q M G^l.

Fifteen Letters from Nathaniel Shaw, Jr., to George Washington

Letter from F. Greene to General Washington

Invoice for Arms from Clark & Nightingale to Nathaniel Shaw, Jr., for account of General Washington

Invoice for Arms from Daniel Tillinghast to Nathaniel Shaw, Jr., for account of General Washington

Letter from Thomas Shaw and Others to Governor Trumbull

The late Nathaniel Shaw Perkins obtained from the Secretary of State at Washington copies of all letters from Nathaniel Shaw, Jr., to George Washington; copies of two invoices for arms sent to Shaw for the account of Washington and copy of one letter from Thomas Shaw and Others to Governor Trumbull.

These copies are now in the Shaw Collection at Yale. They are all printed here.

New London July 18th 1776

Sir

Inclos'd you have Capt Jehiel Tinkers Receit for three Chests of Arms and One Barrell & One Kegg of Flints, as pr Invoice Inclos'd, the Arms were Sent to me by Daniel Tillinghast Esqr the Flints by Messrs Clark & Nightingale Merchts In Providence desiring I would forward them to you by the first Oppertunity, hope they will come Safe to hand & am Sir

Your very hume Servt˙
Nathl Shaw Junr

(Addressed)
on the Service of the
United States of America   To
His Excellency
George Washington Esqr
General & Commander in Chief of the
Forces of the United States of
America
Pr ye *Crane* Galley   In
Capt Tinker   New York

New London Augst 1st 1776

Sir

The bearer Doctor Wolcott will deliver you a Turtle wich was taken in a Ship bound from Jamaica to London by

Capt Biddle in the Brigg *Andrew*[1] *Doria*, & was Sent into this Port but Unfortunately was Lost on the Rocks of Fishes Island, being Chas'd by a Man of War, we Sav'd About Ninety Puncheons of Rum, the Sugar 250 hh^{ds} all Lost & ye Ship—and as the Turtle was Intended for the Support of our Enemys, we thought best to Send him to head Quarters, to be Dealt with.

I am Sir
Your very hum Servt
Nathl Shaw Junr

(Addressed)
To
His Excellency General Washington
Command^r of all the Forces of the
United States
In
New York

Pr Doc^t Wolcott
wth a Turtle

New London October 1st 1776

Sir

The 29th Ult^o I shipt by Capt Webster Seventy Two Tents which was sent me by Daniel Tillinghast Esqr of Providence and hope they will get Safe to hand—I now by Capt Thos King Send you Nine Marque and Ninety Seven Common Tents which I hope will also Come Safe.

In Case any of the Brittish Ships Should come down this way, I think we Should have the Earliest Notice of it, as we are Daly Shiping Goods up the Sound for the Army, I am Sir

Your very hum Servt
Nathl Shaw Junr.

---

[1] The correct name is *Andrea Doria*.

New London August 5, 1780.

Sir

I Received yours by Capt Hurlbutt who sett out for New Port this day in order to Post the Dragoons for the Purpose you Mention and Every Assistance in my Power you may Depend, I shall give him—their is now a fleet of Ships Just come to an Anchor of this Harbour, Consisting of about Fifteen or Sixteen, I believe moastly large Ships of the Line and Imagine they are the same that were of Block Island, they have French Colours Flying, what their Intentions is I Cannot Conceive, the Headmoast Ship came to an Anchor att 3 O'Clock P M and the Stern moast att 8 O'Clock, as the wind is they might have Continued their Coarse up the Sound, but their not makeing up of the Oppertunity, I Suspect they have sum Design Against this Port, we have about one Thousand men hear, & Suppose Goven^r Trumbull will Imediately order more, if any movement to morrow will Advise you. I am Sir

Your very hum^e Servt.
Nathl Shaw

New London Augt 6th 1780

Sir

I wrote you last Evening that their was a large fleet of Sixteen Sail of Ships lying of this Harbour att Anchor, they Continue in the Same Position this Morning 9 oClock one Ship came down from the Westward and Join'd the Fleet.

I am Sir
Your Hum^e Servt
Nathl Shaw

P S its now Eleven O'Clock and the fleet are under Sail with ye Flood tide Consequently bound to the Westward. N S.

New London Augst 9th 1780

Sir

The Brittish Fleet Come to Sail last Sunday from of this Harbour and mov'd up as farr as Gardners Island where they have been att Anchor Ever Since, only Three or four frigates Cruse between Block Island & the Fleet.

We have Sent a Boat over to the Island to get Intelligence, and when she Returns Shall Inform you. I am Sir

Your hum Servt
Nathl Shaw

New London Augst 11th 1780

Sir

This Serves Just to Inform you that the Brittish Fleet Continue att Gardners Island, our Boat is Return'd from the Island, and ye Inhabitants say the Brittans are Procuring Small Stock wood & Water.

I am Sir
Your hum Servt
Nathl Shaw

Thursday 12 O'Clock

New London August 13th 1780.

Sir

This day Six Persons deserted from the Brittish Fleet and Came into this Harbour in a Small boat, the Information they give, is that the Fleet were to Return to their Station of Block Island this day, and that General Clinton was Imbarking his troops att White Stone, and were to Come down the Sound to Procede Against New Port, and that two Ships was dispatch'd from the Fleet to Convoy the Transport to New Port.

The Brittish Fleet are now Under Sail Steering to the Eastward, Inclos'd is a List of their Force, I am Sir Your moast Obed.

Hum^e Servt
Nathl Shaw

Sunday 8 O'Clock P.M.
P S   The Above is Sent to New Port.

New London Augst 18th 1780

Sir

Since I wrote you 13th Ins^t the Brittish Fleet are Return'd, and are now att Anchor in Sight of this Port, and Yesterday Six Ships Came from up the Sound, I Suppose from New York and Join'd them, I look't att them with a Good Spy Glass, and Imagine their was one Frigate and Five Store Ships.

Shall Inform our Friends at New Port Agreable to your Request, of Every movement of ye Brittish Fleet as long as they Continue hear.

This Evening we Send a Small Boat Over to the Island for Intelligence when she Returns Shall Inform you. I am Sir

Your moast Obed^t hum^e Servt.
Nathl Shaw

Fryday
7 O'Clock P M.

New London Augt 20 1780

Sir

The British Fleet consisting of Sixteen Sail, came to Sail from Gardiners Island Yesterday & stood for Rhode Island with a fair Wind & must have got their by the next

Morning—at the Same time Six Ships got under way & stood up Sound, and have returned & anchored again of Plumb Island.

We have sent a boat over to the Island to gain Intelligence & shall expect her return to morrow morning.

> I am with the greatest respect
> Sir Your Hum^{le} Servt
> Nathl Shaw

P S those Ships that are now att Plumb Island I Suppose were Those that Came from N. York.   N S

Sunday 9 O'Clock P.M.

New London Augt 24th 1780.

Sir

In my last I wrote you that the Brittish Fleet last Satturday, and a Sloop belonging to this Port arrived last Evening from the West Indias, and Informs me that he fell in with Twelve large Ships and three friggates, Seventy Mile Southward of Montaug, and Imagines they were bound to N. York, I make no doubt but that they were the Brittish Fleet, I am Sir

> Your most Obed^t
> hum Servt
> Nathl Shaw

Thursday 9 O'Clock A M.

New London Octo. 30. 1780

Sir

Last Thursday Thirteen Sail of Brittish Ships (by their Appearence) are of the line, were discover'd Standing in for Block Island, on Satturday, it look't like for a Storm and they all Came in to Gardners Bay, where they now are att Anchor, when any further movement is made I will Inform you of it.

      I am Sir
       Your moast Obed^t
        Hum^e Servt
         Nathl Shaw

       New London Novr 23^d 1780.

Sir

 Agreeable to your Excellencys Letter of the 31st July last to establish a Chain of Expresses from N London to Tower Hill, and that you would be answerable for their pay while in Service, I found it necessary only to employ three trusty men & their Horses for this & the Post at Tower Hill for five days, before the French General releav'd those at Tower Hill, & Capt Hurlbut of Col. Sheldons Reg^t Dragoons extended his Light Horsemen to this Post. The expence of which am^o £453.18^s/ as pr Bill Inclosed. After Capt Hurlbut had established his men at this post, I was obliged to find their Horses with Hay & Oats &^{c} untill I could apply to His Excellency our Govenor to get an assistant D Q M appointed at this Post (which was much wanted before) the am^o of which is £1462.10/, as pr Inclosed Bill. The Post is now supply'd by this D Q M who is furnished with money from our Govr & Council. I was in hopes of not troubling your Excellency with this triffling affair, as I made no doubt but it would be settled by this D Q M & according wrote by him to N. Hubbard Q M G for his orders, & rec^d the following reply.

 ". . . . neither can I pay the expence of the Express Riders provided by you, as I am entirely destitute of money, and have not the most distant prospect of a Supply—I should imagine you might get your money soonest by applying at Head Quarters." I am obliged therefore to take this liberty of Inclosing those Bills to your Excellency, and hope it will not be long before they are settled. The different Bills & Receipts if necessary can be forwarded. I have taken the most prudent care and attention in the expences.

The Brittish Fleet still lie at Gardiners Bay, as I wrote you in my last, making no movements excepting one or two Ships that are frequently running off Block Island & returning to them again.

I am with the greatest respect and esteem

Your Excellency
Most Ob^t & very Hum^{le} Servt.
Nathl Shaw

N.B. The above Fleet lies 3 miles W N W Gardiners Point, (consisting 9 Sail of ye Line) 3 or four Miles South Plumb Island. It is said that Admiral Arbouthnot is to go to New York to take the Command their, when Admiral Rodney leaves it, & Admiral Graves to command in the Bay this Winter.

Y^{rs} &c
N. S.

New London January 31st 1781

Sir

I Imagine it would be Agreable to you to be Inform'd of the movements made by the Brittish Fleet, have now to Inform you that on the 22^d Ins^t three French Ships Sail'd from New Port as I am Inform'd to Secure the Comeing in of Two French Friggates and a Store Ship that was Expected from Boston, and Imediately Four Brittish Ships of ye Line Sail'd from Gardners Bay to meet them, but a Gale of Wind arising, the French Ships Return'd to New Port, the Brittish Ships came to Anchor in the Evening without Fishes Island, and in the Night there were many Cannon heard—Suppose to be fir'd for being in distress, & the Next Morning One Ship was discover'd to be Standing to the Southward of Montaug, Under Jury masts, one Ship was of our port with all her masts Gone by the Board, and one Ship run on Shagwomanack Reaf near Gardners Island and is Intirely lost many of her hands drown'd, and by Report the Ship of our Harbour threw over her upper Teir of Guns, I am Just now Returnd, from the Lt House, and Can Observe with a Spy Glass that they are now takeing out the Masts from the Ship on Shore, I suppose for the one that is Dismasted and att Anchor with the Fleet.

There is Eight Ships in Gardners Bay now Riding att Anchor and by the best Information we Can get they Consist of the Dismasted Ship, Five other Ships of ye Line and Two Friggates, in order to get an Acco^t more Particular we have Sent over a Boat to Long Island, and all the Intelligence we Can Obtain Shall Continue to Send our French Friends att New Port, who we Wrote to directly Upon hearing of ye Disaster, and Shall write you Again as Soon as we hear from the Island. I am Sir

Your moast Obed^t
hum^e Servt
Nathl Shaw

P S The French Ships that were Expected from Boston Received no damage in the Gale and Arived Safe att N P.

New London Feby 6th 1781

Sir

I wrote you pr post last Week Informing of ye Disaster ye Brittish Fleet mett with, by ye Storm on ye 22 Ult^o. Since that I Observe they have Rigg'd ye Dismasted Ship with Jury Masts, the Ship that drove on Shore is Intirely lost, and y^e

Ship that is Missing has not Return'd Since. This day a Friggate Sail'd from ye Brittish Fleet and their Remains now att Anchor Three Large Ships, & y^e *Bedford* Dismasted, Two Ships of Sixty Four Guns & One of Fifty. Y^e *Culloden* is ye Ship that is on Shore y^e *America* is ye Ship that is Missing.

I am Sir
Your very hum^e Servt
Nathl Shaw

Copy of a Letter from Mr. F. Greene to General Washington

Provid^{ce} July 15, 1776

Sir
    Agreable to the request of his Honor Govr Cooke I have sent Forward to the care of Nathl Shaw J^r the small Arms flints & cutlasses imported by Saml Chace for the Continent, wish them A safe arrivall at New York & your Excellency health and the Arms of the United States success ag^t our common Enemies.

Y^{rs} With Respect
F. Greene.

P S there is
  14,500
    30 Cutlasses
    20 Small Arms

Copy of Invoice for Arms from Clark & Nightingale to Nathaniel Shaw

Providence 15 July 1776

Inv^o of Seventeen Thousand Gun Flints Sent by Willm Brown from Clark & Nightingale of Providence to Nathl Shaw Esqr at New London & by him to be forwarded to his Excellency General Washington at New York Viz^t:

N° 6 a Barrell⎫
    7 a Cag ⎬ Q^t 17 m Gun Flints
Providence 15 July 1776
Errors Excepted
Pr Clark & Nightingale

Copy of Invoice for Arms from Daniel Tillinghast to Nathaniel Shaw

Providence July 15th 1776

Invoice of One hundred & Seventeen Small Arms, Eighty Nine Bayonets, Twenty Broad Swords & Three Fuzees, sent by William Browns Team from Daniel Tillinghast of Providence, to Nath¹ Shaw Esqr at New London who is Immediatly to forward them to his Excellency General Washington at New York. Viz^t:

S A 3 Cases q^t Scotch Arms taken by the *Andrew Doria* at Sea } Viz^t:

   N° 1a Case q^t 36 Small Arms
               36 Bayonets
                2 broad Swords
     2 a Case q^t 42 Small Arms
               42 Bayonets
     3 a Case q^t 39 Small Arms
                3 Fuzees in Cases
               11 Bayonets
               18 Broad Swords

Providence 15th July 1776

{ Copy Orig¹ sent }   Errors
{ Nath¹ Shaw Esqr }   Dan¹ Tillinghast Agent

N B N° 6 & 7 a barrell & Cag q^t 17 m Gun Flints sent in the above Team to Mr Shaws Care by Clark & Nightingale & are to be forwarded his Excellency Gen¹ Washington wth the above arms the first Oppertunity.

To Governor Trumbull from Thomas Shaw and Others

Stonington, August 10th 1780.

May it Please Your Excellency.—

We your Excellency's Complainants, and Petitioners, beg leave at this time, to lay a Matter, before your Excell^y (which to us appears of the most alarming kind; and as we Conceive of great Importance; both in its present Operations, as well as future Consequences;—

About the 25th of July Past We rec^d undoubted Information, that an Armed Vessel, from Long Island, richly laden with British Manufacturers, had run down Fishers Island Sound, and Entered the mouth of Paucatuck River, which Divides the State of Connecticut, from that of Rhode Island, said Information Obtain'd from Two Arm'd Boats, Commission'd from your Office, who enter'd Stonington Harbour, and reported, they had pursued said Vessel down the Sound, and had made a Demand (Consonant to their Duty) of the Persons on Board, relative to their Intentions, and Designs, together with what Authority they were permitted to Cruise in said Arm'd Vessel as above. They were Answer'd that s^d Vessel, was legally Commission'd and that they were possess'd of a Permission from Congress, to Transport Goods & Effects from Long Island, to any of the United States of America; the People of said Arm'd Boats strongly suspicious of Iniquity in the matter, made a second Attempt to Board said Arm'd Vessel, but were strictly prohibited by the People on Board, and threatened even with Destruction, should they prosecute their Attempt, by Cannon Loaded, Matches light^d &c. A strong Argument of the perniciousness of the Undertaking. We therefore Your Petitioners, upon the strongest ground of Conjecture, that said Goods were illicitly convey'd from Long Island to the Main; did apply to proper Authority, State of Connecticut, (Agreeable to the Laws of said State, as Well as Congress) and procured a proper Warrant, for the Seizure of said Goods, thereby Endeavouring that a full Discovery of the affair (by strict Inquiry) might be made; And, if any Iniquitous Transactions (relative to said Goods,) were Committed, the Conductors thereof might be Detected; and the Peace and Safety of the Community Secured. In the prosecution of said Business, We found that said Arm'd Vessel, was at a Wharf at East side of s^d Paucatuck River, within the State of Rhode Island: We therefore Advanced into Said State, and made Application to Authority within said State to have said Warrant render'd, which was granted, & committed to a proper Officer to Execute &c. (By the way) we were Seconded, and Encouraged by many of the good & Respectable People of s^d State, in the prosecution of said Matter, who then appear'd, and still continue, to Express the highest Indignation, against that Trade, which in its Consequences, must prove ruinous to the People of these States: *A Justifiable Resentm^t* indeed. When we were possess'd of positive Assurance, that every necessary Expedient was obtain'd for Legal Procedure, we repair'd to a Storehouse Belonging to Doctor Joshua Babcock of Westerly, in which Store, said Goods were deposited; But to our great Surprize & Astonishm^t we found s^d Store under Protection of the Guns of said Arm'd Vessel, and a Gentleman of Rank & Distinction, Col^o Henry Babcock, by Name, did so far proceed in the protection of said Goods, as to take the Tomkin's from the Guns, prime them, light the Matches, and in the most determin'd manner (to appearance) did declare he would Defend said Store & Goods, to the Destruction of the Prosecutors, but as a State of Determinedness on their part, had taken place, they did proceed to Enter said Store, and made a Tendry of said Goods, to the Officer, for Seizure &c upon which he refus'd to serve said Warrant and did proceed to cover said Goods, under a Protection, as we imagin'd fraudulently obtain'd from the Governor of said State of Rhode Island; in consequence of which Our Procedure, was quash'd and every Exertion on our part, for making full discovery of the Affair, at that time Defeated. We would Observe, that at the time of our Endeavouring, to enter said Store, some of the Persons belonging to s^d Vessel, and as we suppose interested in said Goods, did publicly Assure the Officer, that if he would desist from Serving Our Warrant, they would indemnify him, at all Adventures. There were Belonging to said Vessel fourteen Persons in Number, Who tho' in character of Marines &c appear'd to be Gentlemen of Distinction, Elegance &c. An Argument with us of the Extensive connection in said Goods Tho' Transported under the Sanction of a Permit granted to an Individual:—A Copy of said Permit, if obtainable shall transmit enclosed. The Grant of said Permit is made to George Howel, by Name, belonging to the State of New York, who has resided, within the Enemies lines steadily since the Subjection of Long Island to the British Arms: And as we are inform'd, and are confident, can fully prove, has carr^d on an Extensive & Profitable Trade, within said lines; having been a Purchaser of Vessels, Cargoes, &c, from us, Captured by the Enemy. The Names of the Persons belonging to s^d Vessel shall transmit if they can be Obtain'd, the principal part of the number, we are inform^d are Inhabitants of the State of Connecticut. We beg leave to Observe that a Permit granted by the Honble Continental Congress, to any Individual (more especially to one holding long Residence within the Enemies Lines) of so Extensive a Nature, being unlimited, as to Quantity or Value, is to us Unaccountable and really irreconcileable to those favourable Sentiments, which we have, and hope to have, of that August and Respectable Body; it really is a matter of general Speculation, and what at this time generally commands the Attention of the People of this Quarter, who express strong Desires that a full Explanation of the matter may be Obtain'd. Further the Persons on Board said Arm'd Vessel, did publicly declare that the amount of Value of s^d Goods in s^d Store was £50,000 Sterling and that the One half of those granted by s^d Permit, or were intended to be transported, under s^d Permission had not arriv'd, which fills us with strong Apprehensions, that said Permit, was fraudulently Obtain'd or Iniquitously Applied. We would Inform, that said Goods were remov^d from s^d Store in Westerly for Conveyance to Providence within s^d State; and when on their way, complaint was made to the Goven^r of s^d State by the People of the Eastern part of s^d State setting forth their Suspicions, of Iniquity, in the matter, The Quantity being so large and Valuable; upon which the Govr was pleas'd to Order the Sheriff in s^d State, to seize said Goods, which was complied with, and the Goods Stored in the Town of Greenwich, and as we were inform^d The Govr did personally appear, and upon Examination made, did release said Goods from any further prosecution. And now may it Please Your Excellency. The intent & Design of the foregoing Complaint and Representation, must appear Obvious. In that The Honble Continental Congress have been pleas'd to Enact Laws for the Regulation of Trade & Commerce evidently design'd & wisely adapted for the Interest, and Security of the People of the United States. And which, have been, Laudably strengthened, Supported & encouraged by Your Excellency's Exertions in Council manifested in an Act entitled an Addition to an Act, to prevent illicit Trade &c pass^d 2^d Thursday of May 1780, together with other Acts, to prevent a Trade with the Enemies of the United States. A Trade which in its consequences must prove Destructive to the Interest of the People; Strongly tend to weaken the Continental Army, by depriving the People of solid Coin, the Sinews of our present War, and the principal Dependance & Expectation of our Soldiery in the present Campain; And as the most zealous Exertions, in Supporting the good & Salutary Laws of these States, are necessary for the Salvation of the whole; We do Therefore implore Your Excellency's Interposition in the matter herein related; Assuring Ourselves, (from your known Character of strict Justice in Every Department, and zealous Attachment to the Interest of your Country) that Your Influence will be improv^d in Laying the Affair before Congress That thereby a full Discovery may be made, and if anything Iniquitous, has been committed, the perpetrators thereof may be brought to proper Punishm^t. Otherwise, by a full Explanation the Country may be Satisfied, and relieved, from their present Disturbances, Uneasinesses, & Jealousies, respecting, so large liberal and Extensive Permissions, in a Trade so strictly Prohibited.

With the utmost Respect & Esteem We Subscribe Your Excellencys most Devoted Humble Servants.

Robert Stanton
Andrew Palmer
Peter States   Complainants
Cabeb Brown
John Cotton Rosseter

His Excell^y Jon^a Trumbull Esqr.

We the Underwriters, haveing well Acquainted Ourselves, with the above and foregoing Representation, Beg Leave to Unite and Join with the above named Complainants, Ernestly Requesting Your Excellency's Influence and Assistance in said matter, which to us appears of the most alarming Consequence; & Importance.

In the meantime Subscribe
Your Excellency's most Obedient Humble Servants.

His Excell^y Jonathan Trumbull Esqr.

Nathan Palmer	Jabez Dean	John Herltell
Nathan Palmer Jun	Jonath^n Gray	Joseph Packwood
Peter Crary	John Hillard	Ephraim Miner
Asa Palmer	Latham Hall	Eliph^t Carew
Nath^{el} Chesebrou	Lebulon Stanton	Azariah Lathrop
Andrew Stanton	Nathl Cheesebrough	Oliver Hillard Dennis
Oliver Hillard	Enoch Stanton	Eliphalet Hobart
Steors Sheffield	Eliphalet Hobart 2^d	Joseph Vincent
Ebenezer Cobb	Joseph Page	Daniel Cowlins
Wait Rathbun	Theo^p Mumford	Thomas Palmer
Jonathan Crary	David Mumford	Gilbert Fanning
Jo^s Fellows	Wm Ledyard	Jno Dean
Daniel Hobart	Thos Shaw	James Dean
Gilbert Wright	Giles Mumford	Joshua Williams
David Randal	Marvin Wait	Christopher Dean
John Dean Jn^r	Step^n Babcock	Joseph Dennison
Abram Wescott	Adam Shapley	John Breed Jun

X

JOHN HANCOCK'S LETTERS TO NATHANIEL SHAW, JR.

NATHANIEL SHAW, JR., received two letters from John Hancock, president of the Continental Congress and the first signer of the Declaration of Independence. Hancock's name is probably better known to posterity, from his famous signature than from the facts that he was a leading merchant of Boston, a governor of Massachusetts, and a delegate to the Continental Congress, and twice the president of the Congress during the most momentous days of its existence.

Hancock's first letter of April 23, 1776, is printed in Chapter III, and is also reproduced in facsimile. Only his second letter is printed here.

Letter from John Hancock to Nathaniel Shaw, Jr.
(From the original in the Shaw Collection)

In Marine Committee Philadelphia 15th July 1776

Sir

It is necessary that the Cannon, stores &c made prize of and delivered to you should be appraised, for which purpose you are hereby directed to appoint three or more judicious persons to perform this service under Oath—and that you immediately make a return of such appraisement to this Committee— A proper return will be made to you of the officers and men who have a right to share in such prizes as have been, or may be committed by .... [1] care.

I am in behalf of the Marine Committee,

Your very hum^l. Servt.
John Hancock P^t.

Nathaniel Shaw Junr Esqr.
Agent for prizes in Connecticut

---

[1] No word appears in the original letter.

XI

ESEK HOPKINS' LETTERS TO NATHANIEL SHAW, JR.

ESEK HOPKINS of Rhode Island was the first and only *Commander-in-Chief* of the American fleet by act of Congress. He was appointed by the Naval Committee on November 5, 1775, which action was confirmed by the Continental Congress on December 22, 1775.

It was said by Spears in *The History of Our Navy*, "Commodore Hopkins received his appointment chiefly through the influence of John Adams." Adams was a far-seeing statesman. It was he who in the Continental Congress had previously nominated George Washington from the South as *Commander-in-Chief* of the army of the United Colonies. Now he sponsored a man from the North for the navy.

Commodore Hopkins made Providence his home; the house in which he lived is still standing and is used for a museum.

The Rhode Island Historical Society in 1932 issued *Esek Hopkins Letter Book*, edited by Mrs. Alverda S. Beck. Therein appear copies of four letters to Nathaniel Shaw, Jr., May 21, June 5, and September 9, 1776; and February 14, 1777. The originals of these letters are among the six originals owned by the New London County Historical Society:

> Six Letters from Esek Hopkins to Nathaniel Shaw, Jr.
> Receipt from Esek Hopkins to Henry Billings
> Receipt from Esek Hopkins to Nathaniel Shaw, Jr.
> Receipt from Samuel Lyon (Esek Hopkins' Secretary) to Thomas Shaw
> Two Letters from Thomas Shaw to Esek Hopkins
> Letter from Esek Hopkins to Thomas Shaw
> Receipt from Thomas Shaw to Samuel Eddy for Esek Hopkins

Esek Hopkins to Nathaniel Shaw, Jr.

(From the original in the Shaw Collection)

Know all Men by these Pressents that I Esek Hopkins (Command^r. in Chief of the Arm'd Vessells belonging to the United Colonies) do Constitute and Appoint Nathl Shaw Junr. Merch^t. to be my Agent and in my Name and behalf to Appear in all Causes Whatso Ever and to have full Power to transact any Business for me as though I were Pressent in this Port or Colony —

New London April 17th 1776

        Esek Hopkins

Letter from Esek Hopkins to Nathaniel Shaw, Jr.

(From the original in the Shaw Collection)

      Providence May 21st 1776

Sir

  You know when I left the Guns at New London I told you that if the Congress sent for them they must have them which you then said must be Comply'd with, and as there is now an Express Order without Reserve for twenty of the heaviest Cannon to be sent to Philadelphia I expect if Governor Trumbull is not at New London you will Immediately deliver them to Messrs. Hollingsworth and Richardson who are sent to Receive them as the failure may be attended with fatal Consequences —

    I am Sir

      Your most humb^l Servt.

       Esek Hopkins

To
 M^r. Nathl Shaw
  Merchant at
   New London

Letter from Esek Hopkins to Nathaniel Shaw, Jr.

(From the original in the Shaw Collection)

Providence June 5th. 1776

Sir

Please to send me by Captn. Saltonstall as good an Account of the Guns and Stores left in your hands as you can get, and likewise should be glad you will send me an Account of your Schooners Cargo, which Captn Biddle Retook as the Officers blame me for delivering her till she was Tryed—should be glad to Satisfy them that they will receive no Injury by that Step—

I congratulate you on being appointed by the Congress Agent of the Fleet, and all Prizes sent in to your Government, which I have Receiv'd on Account of—Expect you will Act as such whether you have Receiv'd the Order or not, and get the three Prizes Libelled and Condemn'd as soon as possible; and as to your Schooner I make no doubt but you will Satisfy the Officers and People without a Tryal—

I now have the Gentlemen here from the Committee of Saftey of Philadelphia, but I expect they will not be able to get more Cannon here than they did, or I expected they would at New London—What will be the Event of their not Succeeding I can't at present tell! I am well Convinced the Sending them away, will be of very ill Consequences to the Continent—And their not going will have no other bad Effect but on me, who had better Suffer than the Community—

I am with great Respect
Your Friend & humb^l Servt.
Ezek Hopkins

Mr Nathl Shaw

Letter from Esek Hopkins to Nathaniel Shaw, Jr.

(From the original in the Shaw Collection)

Providence Septemb^r. 9th. 1776

Sir

I receiv'd yours, and desire you will supply Captn. Hacker with every thing that may be necessary to enable him to get with dispatch his Vessel ready to Cruise—

As to purchasing the Schooner you best can tell, as you had directions in procuring the Vessel—My instruction is to mann her and Order her where to Cruise—I have no Orders to buy, or to direct any other Person to buy—perhaps you would do well to write to the Marine Committee for Orders in that matter, as I believe they had no apprehension of any Warlike Vessel, Guns or Stores of any kind being sold without their especial Orders, so to do—

I expect to come to New London soon, and am

          Sir

               Your humb^l Servt.

M^r. Nathl. Shaw   Esek Hopkins

Letter from Esek Hopkins to Nathaniel Shaw, Jr.

(From the original in the Shaw Collection)

Warren, in Providence River
Jany. 20th 1777

Sir

Please to pay the bearer M^r. Samuel Lyon my Secretary; all my part of Prize Money in your hands, (which is One twentieth of the Captors Part)—and his Receipt shall be your discharge for the same, from

          Sir

               Your humble Servt.

                  Esek Hopkins

Nathaniel Shaw Esqr
    Agent for the Continental Fleet
        at New London

Letter from Esek Hopkins to Nathaniel Shaw, Jr.

(From the original in the Shaw Collection)

Providence Feby. 4th 1777

Sir

Captn. Whipple late of the Columbus Sent for his Money from New Hampshire and Boston and has divided it out to his people—and as M^r. Thomas Mumford has a Power from Captn. Hinman his Officers and people I think it will be best for the Service that you pay him the Captors part of what Captn. Hinmans last Prize came to, all except my part which is one twentieth and his Receipt will be your discharge for the same—

I am

Sir

Your humble Servt.

Esek Hopkins

Nathl. Shaw jun^r. Esqr
Cont^l. Agent

(From the original in the Shaw Collection)

Rec^d of M^r. Henry Billings M^r. Joseph Russels Receipt for one Thousand and Ninty Three Pounds Powd^r Which he Rec^d. for M^r. Williams of M^r. N Shaw

Providence Aprill 29. 1776

Esek Hopkins

(From the original in the Shaw Collection)

Providence Feby. 11 1777

Rec^d of Nathl Shaw Junr. Continent^l Agent his order on Daniel Tillinghast Esqr. for Two hundred pounds L Money, which I Promise when paid to Ano. with S^d. N Shaw

Esek Hopkins

(From the original in the Shaw Collection)

New London Jan 27 1777

Received of Nathl Shaw Junr. One thousand Dollars, which I promise to deliver Com modore Esek Hopkins being in part pay of his prise Money—

Saml. Lyon

Letter from Thomas Shaw to Esek Hopkins

(From a copy in the Shaw Collection)

New London Nov 24 1784

My Dear Friend

    I have been waiting for a final Issue to this litigious as it is cruel prosecution in which you have been unhappily involved in order that I might make you some veritable acknowledgement for your friendship to my late brother & myself. I am sensible that you have been at expence & trouble I am in hopes it is now drawing to a close & as soon as I hear of this happy event I will make manifest the Generosity you always found in my brother

Your friend

Esek Hopkins Esq
    Provid

Note: No signature, but possibly initials (illegible). From contents of letter, Miss Jane R. Perkins said, undoubtedly, it was written by Thomas Shaw.

ELIZABETH GORTON,
Secretary,
New London County Historical Society.

Letter from Esek Hopkins to Thomas Shaw

(From the original in the Shaw Collection)

Providence Goal Ap^l. 28th. 1788

M^r. Thomas Shaw

Sir

I have Rec^d. Y^r. two several letters by Doct^r. Clarke & P^r. Post; The sorrow which you express for my imprisonment & the assurances which M^r. Helme has given you of my being speedily Relieved, afford but very ineffectual support, To one confined in Prison suffering already too much for having trusted to the like assurances & Depress^d. with Age and Dissease your late worthy Brother assured me I should suffer no damage or Injury for having become his Bondsman and he kept his word most faithfully while he liv^d. I am Inform^d. that on his Death Bed he enjoined his Executor to see that his promise to me was never broken But I have been Commited to Goal on this very Account, am put to great expence to Support myself in Prison, my Disorder requiring constant Watchers & I Solicitted by Doct^r. Clarke a little cash, to defray this expence. certainly, Sir, when you declined to comply with this request, your Brothers Dying Injunction must have escaped your memory. you will pardon the warmth of these expressions, my situation will furnish an apoligy to any candid mind. having already experienced so severely the Inconvenience & disadvantage of confiding my defence against the suit of Stanton & Noyes, to the management of others. I am resolved to have the future direction of it more in my own hands—To defray the expence of my subsistence in Goal to be liberated from Imprisonment, To get rid of the present Judgment of Court and to bring the Cause to a speedy and final Issue to us both requires the advance of a Considerable sum of money. Doct^r. Clarke the

Bearer hereof waits on you for this purpose, and flatter myself that when you reflect on my situation and on the Justice of my Claim for assistance you will not decline to comply with it; Indeed I think your Interest and duty will equally prompt you to afford me some pecuniary assistance. If this application shall fail I shall be Oblidged to endeavour to effectuate my own Releif & liberation by such means as shall appear to be practicable safe & proper—

From Y^r. Hb^l. Servt.
Esek Hopkins

Letter from Thomas Shaw to Esek Hopkins

(From a copy in the Shaw Collection)

New London May 3^d 1788.

Sir

I received your Letter of the 28th Ult^o. and am much concerned at your situation, but am assured by Mess^r Helme & Channing, that they will prefer a petition to your General assembly which setts in Newport the first Wednesday of this Month, & they have the greatest reason to believe you will be relieved thereby—I do not see what I can do more—I have been at every expence—& am sorry that you should think me deficient herein, or that I have been negligent. I am however conscious to myself of doing every thing in my power to bring this litigious suit to a close & have no doubt but it will now be terminated, but if your Assembly should refuse to pay any kind of defference to their own Acts admitting of Appeals to Congress & not govern themselves by said Court of appeals, I can do no more—I shall think myself fully justified, but I cannot think they will be so unreasonably cruel & oppressive

In full expectation of your happy release

I am Sir with the greatest respect
Your Most Hum^{bl} Servt.

Note: Signature to letter is missing; undoubtedly that of Thomas Shaw. (Information received from Miss Jane R. Perkins.)

ELIZABETH GORTON,
Secretary,
New London County Historical Society.

Receipt from Samuel Eddy to Thomas Shaw Written on the Back of Power of Attorney from Esek Hopkins to Samuel Eddy

(From the original in the Shaw Collection)

Received Jany. 3^d 1792 of Thomas Shaw Esqr. three hundred pounds Lawfull Money for Esek Hopkins Esqr. of North Providence in the State of Rhode Island in Consideration whereof, I, Samuel Eddy of Providence in s^d. State; do in Virtue of the within Letter of Att^y. hereby in behalf of the s^d. Esek, Release exonerate and discharge the s^d. Thomas Shaw Executor to the last Will & Testament of Nathaniel Shaw Esqr. deceased from the within mentioned Action and from all claim and Demand of every name & nature whatsoever which, the s^d. Esek hath or might have against the s^d. Thomas either as Executor as afores^d. or in any other way or manner. . . . .

           S^l. Eddy

Witness— B. Griswold
     Joseph Perkins

XII

BENEDICT ARNOLD'S LETTERS TO NATHANIEL SHAW, JR.

BENEDICT ARNOLD was a New London County man, born in Norwich Town. He was a successful merchant in New Haven; an able and courageous military leader who rose to the position of major-general in the continental army.

A month before the final battle of the war, as Brigadier-General in the British army he led an expedition against his former neighbors and friends and left behind him in a single day, for all time, a sad picture of destruction, desolation and death. On many gravestones of the heroes of that day may be found this inscription, "Slain by traitor Arnold's murdering Corps."

He knew full well when he gave the order for destruction, that the ships, wharves and warehouses of his former friend, Nathaniel Shaw, Jr., would be destroyed. "Arnold himself took some refreshment that day at the house of an old acquaintance in Bank Street, but even before they rose from the table the building was in flames over them."[1] This was probably a block north of the Shaw Mansion.

Four Original Letters from Benedict Arnold to Nathaniel Shaw, Jr.

Bill of Sale from Captain Truxton to Benedict Arnold.

Letter from Benedict Arnold to Nathaniel Shaw, Jr.

(From the original in the Shaw Collection)

Philad^a. June 8th 1777

Dear Sir

This will be handed you by Colonel Samuel Griffin, a Gentleman of Character, and property who, wishes to be

---

[1] Caulkins, *History of New London*, p. 534.

Concernd in a privateer, any Services, or
civilities, rendered him, will be esteem'd
and acknowledged a favour done

>Dear Sir
>>Your Obed^t Hbl Servt
>>B Arnold

Nathl. Shaw Esqr

Letter from Benedict Arnold to Nathaniel Shaw, Jr.

(From the original in the Shaw Collection)

>Ramapaugh 10th. July 1777

Dear Sir
>Some time since I received a Line from
M^r. John Broome, acquainting me had Authority from you
to assure me I might have one Eighth or one Sixteenth
of your Ship, I have defered answering his Letter, supposing
Colonel Griffin would have settled that Matter with you,
as he has not done it, I take this Opportunity, to
advise you I have given my Sister, who is at Middletown
Orders to pay your Draft for one Sixteenth of the Ship—
I set out immediately for Albany, where I shall
be glad to hear from you

>>I am D^r. Sir
>>>Your ob^t. humble Servt.
>>>B Arnold

M^r. Nathl. Shaw
> Merch^t
>> New London

Letter from Benedict Arnold to Nathaniel Shaw, Jr.

(From the original in the Shaw Collection)

Sir
                    Middletown 2d. March 1778

When I proposed taking one
Sixteenth of the Ship *Putnam*, Mr Broome inform'd
me she would cost only Twenty Thousand Pound
M^r. J. Broome informs she will cost at least
Forty Eight Thousand Pound, a Sum far beyond
my Expectations, He also informs me it will be
no disappointment or dammage to you if
I am not concern'd, I must therefore decline it
and am Sir
                    Your most Hble Servant
                        B Arnold

Letter from Benedict Arnold to Nathaniel Shaw, Jr.

(From the original in the Shaw Collection)

                    Head Quarters Robinsons House
Dear Sir   August 10th 1780

I have taken the liberty of Inclosing
Sundry Letters, Bills Sale &c; by which it appears that
Capt. Joseph Packwood in Aug^st. 1778, sold to Capt. Thos. Truxton
One fourth part of the Sloop *John* with Her Cargo, Amount^g.
to £1070, Lawfull Money, for which amo^t. Capt. Truxton drew
on me (then in Philad^a.) which draught I stood ready to
honor when presented; It also appears by Capt. Packwoods Letter
that He had no doubt of the draughts being honored. It also
appears by the Papers that the Sloop made one Voyage, and
returned safe from the W^st. Indies in March 1779 with a Cargo
of Rum, Sugar, & Molasses;—How many Voyages She has
made since, or what has become of Her, I have never heard.
Capt. Truxton informs me that Capt. Packwood wrote to him
some time since, requesting him to draw for Two thousand
pounds Lawful Money, part of the Profits on the Voyage, and

at the same time objected to his sharing his full Proportion
alledging for reason, that the Sloop was not paid for when
bought and that the money had greatly depreciated;
This is an objection that Capt. Packwood has no right to make
as it was his own neglect (not the owners) that He did not
present the draught and receive the money, which lay
Ready for him, and Capt. Packwood has had the Neat Proffits
of the Voyage in his hands, as well as the Vessell seventeen
Months.—It appears to me but Just that after deducting
The prime Cost of the Vessell and Cargo, The Ballance of
the proceeds should be accounted for by Capt. Packwood,
and as He has had the Vessell and Ballance in his hands
and to his use since Her arrival in March 1779 or since
the Sales of Her Cargo, without advising us that we
might Draw for the same it is but reasonable He should
make good the Depreciation.

        Neither Capt.Truxton or myself
know if the Vessell Has been sold or is still runing
on our Acco^t. I am requested by him and the other Owners
to beg the favor of you to inquire into the Matter, and
make a settlement with Capt. Packwood which you
think Just & reasonable. If you should differ in
sentiment with him I beg you will submit the
Affair to Arbitration, which I conceive He can have
no reasonable objection to.—It is the wish of the
Owners if the Vessell is in being, and not sold, to have
their Quarter part sold, the Acco^t. Closed and the Ballance
Remitted to me at this place, by the Post or any
Safe private Conveyance

        Your Compliance will be
Esteemed a very particular favor done

            D^r. Sir

                    Your most Obed^t.

                          Humble Servt.

Nathl. Shaw Esqr.   B Arnold
    New London

(From the copy in the Shaw Collection)

N. London Augt. 26th. 1778

Major General Arnold

Bought of Thomas Truxton one Sixteenth part of the sloop *Success* now called the *John* at the rate of Eight hundred pounds lawful money with all her Appur^s. as Bo^t. at Auction

Thos. Truxtun

XIII

CAPTAIN CHARLES BULKELEY

NO seafaring man was better known or more respected by his fellow citizens of New London in the century in which he lived than Captain Charles Bulkeley, a naval officer of the American Revolution. His home was on the west side of Bank Street not far from the home of Nathaniel Shaw, Jr. He lived to the great age of ninety-five years, dying in 1848.

His name appeared in 1826 at the head of the petition to the General Assembly asking for aid to erect a monument on Groton Heights in memory of the brave men who fell at Fort Griswold. He was chosen President of the Groton Monument Association, and his son, Leonard H. Bulkeley, Secretary. It is doubtful if his record of sixty years of active service on the ocean has been surpassed by any New London sailor.

At the time of the attack on the town his vessel, the privateer *Active*, which had arrived a few days before, was burned at the wharf. Like Captain Nathaniel Saltonstall on that fateful day, he shouldered his musket and fought with the minute men, capturing a prisoner.

He was successful in privateering and the merchant service. During 1812 he was active in fighting the enemy, having command of the Letter of Marque ship *Mars*. His property was inherited by his only surviving son, Leonard H. Bulkeley, who upon his death, a year later, bequeathed it to found the Bulkeley School for boys.[1]

---

[1] Captain Charles Bulkeley had seven children all of whom died single. With the death of Leonard the family became extinct.

Captain Charles Bulkeley's Narrative of Personal Experiences in the War of the American Revolution from His Original Manuscript

PRESENTED TO THE NEW LONDON COUNTY HISTORICAL SOCIETY BY HELEN R. FITCH IN 1913

"In September 1775 I was from the West India bound to New London in the Sloop—Capt. Daniel Starr. We were captured by a tender belonging to the *Rose* Man of War off Block Island, and soon after it became calm, and remained so all that day and night. Just at night a Block Island boat with two men and a boy came off and within hail and they were ordered to keep off. I then ran out on the squaresail boom and jumped overboard and swam to the boat and then went ashore on Block Island and arrived there in the night and manned that boat and got another boat to assist us to recapture the Sloop. We went off and lay until daylight and after day broke we discovered the Sloop and retook her and brot her in to New London.

"The following winter I went into the Old Fort as a Volunteer near the Market.

"In the Winter of 1775 and 1776 Capt. Dudley Saltonstall was appointed to the command of the Ship *Alfred*, lying at Philadelphia. I then was appointed a midshipman under him. Lt. E. Hinman, Lt. Malby, Sailing Master Phips, Midshipman Peter Richards, Alexander P. Adams, Capt. Clark, myself, and about 74 others, sailed from N. London to join the fleet then lying in the Delaware and were distributed on board of said fleet and I was ordered on board of the *Alfred*.

"The fleet consisted of the Ship *Alfred*, Commodore E. Hopkins, Capt. Dudley Saltonstall, John Paul Jones, 1st Lt., *Columbus*, Capt. Whipple of Providence, Brig *Cabot*, Capt. John Hopkins of Providence, Brig *Andrerin*, Capt. Biddle of Philadelphia, Sloop *Providence*, Capt. Harzen and one small Sloop, Capt. Hacker. Sailed from the Capes of Delaware Feby 17th 1776 and arrived at New Providence, March 3d and took the place and brot Govr Brown and his Secry on board of the *Alfred*. We took all the cannon from the Fort and elsewhere and loaded a Sloop and from thence we sailed for New London.

"April 7 off Block Island took a tender belonging to the Ship *Rose* and a Bomb Brig and towards morning fell in with the *Glasco* Man of War and engaged her and recd a shott through the Main Mast and one of our tiller blocks being shott away we came into the wind and the enemy then stood to the eastward and we arrived at New London Apl 8 1776. Left N. London and arrived at Providence Apl 28.

"Oct. 1776 Capt. J. P. Jones took the command of the *Alfred*. The *Alfred*, Capt. Jones, and the Sloop *Providence*, Capt. Hackers, sailed on a cruise of about six weeks from Newport to the eastward and took a number of prizes and the *Alfred* and *Providence* returned to Boston.

"Capt. Jones was ordered and took charge of the Ship *Ranger* at Portsmouth and Capt. Hinman was ordered to take charge of the *Alfred*. After repairing the Ship, she was ordered to Portsmouth, New Hampshire to join Capt. Thomson of the Ship *Raleigh* and sailed in company on a criuse and for France and on our passage took several prizes and among them two Ships from Jamaica, and anchored them under an Island, on the coast of France, and then went into L'Orient in sham distress. Whilst lying in L'Orient, Capt. Niles in a Packet arrived with dispatches of the Capture of Genl Burgoine. Next day after his arrival you would be saluted by every Frenchman you met. Bon Bostonian, Bon Bostonian. Whilst we lay in Port, the English Minister making representations and such a noise that we were shipping men, a French Officer was then sent on board to examine and he passed by about forty-five and could not see one.

"There were two English Frigates off cruising for us, and a French Sloop of War was sent from Brest to see us off the coast and we sailed just at night and she proved to us a good Pilot. We sailed from thence to the coast of Africa and took a Sloop and went in to the Island of Gorer and then to the Cape de Verde Island and then to the windward of Barbadoes and then we fell in with two English ships, the *Ariadne* of 20 Guns, Capt. Pringle, and the Sloop of War *Ceres* of 18 Guns, Capt. Dacres, we commenced action and the *Raleigh*, Capt. Thompson (he being an Englishman) ran away and left us without firing a gun. After his return home he was tried by a Court Marshall and broke.

"After a running fight of two hours we were captured and were carried into Barbadoes and here I lost my trunk. All the officers and men were landed, except Capt. Hinman, Lt. P. Richards, Capt. Welch and Lt. Hamilton of the Marines and myself. After remaining on board some time, we went to St. Christopher and there were put on board of the *Yarmouth*, 64 Gun Ship, Capt. Vincent, this being the same ship that engaged the *Randolph*, Capt. Biddle, that was blown up and afterwards picked up four or five of her men after being on the wreck several days. I conversed with one of the men and he could give no account how the accident took place.

"We sailed for England and arrived at Portsmouth, were landed at Gosport and examined and confined in Fortune Prison about one mile from Gosport. We were confined in the upper part of the Prison, with the Liberty of the Yard in the daytime and at night Lamps were placed all around the prison to prevent escapes. In consequence of complaints of the bad treatment the prisoners recd, a Presbyterian Priest by the name of Wren was permitted to come into the prison Weekly and to supply many of the wants that the prisoners stood in need of.

"We now made arrangements to make our escape. We cut through the floor into the black hole and then through another floor for the purpose of digging out, the Black Hole being the place that the prisoners were confined in on account of any offences they may have committed. Before breaking out we agreed in case we got separated to meet at a certain place in London. We dug in a slanting direction so that there might be dirt overhead sufficient that it might not cave in. The tools we had to work with were an old chisel and a broken fencing foil. We made small bags to put the dirt in. We found great difficulty in secreting the dirt at first. We put some in our chest, the fireplace below being stopped up we took some bricks out of the chimney in the upper loft and took the bags and lowered them down to the bottom and with a tripping line emptied them so that they might not be any noice heard from the falling of the dirt. We were over three weeks in digging out. We made a lottery for the purpose of having regular turns in going out, for the prevention of confusion and noise, the guard being very near to the hole dug for our escape. Before going out we put a pair of trousers, shirt and stockings over our other clothes and covered our heads and hats and after getting out we took them off and threw them away. The hole was so small that Capt. Harrison of a States Brig of Virginia, after trying to get out was wedged in. We were obliged to pull him back by the legs.

"After our escape we went to Gosport for the purpose of crossing to Portsmouth. Three of us got a Post chaise (Mr. Richards having separated from us by accident). We had to go by the prison just at daylight and before any alarm was given and arrived at London in the afternoon, being 75 miles and here we all again met and staid a few days and visited St. Paul's Church and the Tower and were well worth seeing.

"Capt. Welch and Lt. Hamilton went to Holland and Lt. Richards and myself went to Deal, 75 miles from London, and got a passage in an open Smuggler's Boat and crossed the channel for France in the night and landed at Calais and then went to Paris and then waited upon the American Ministers Doct. Franklin and Mr. Adams and after remaining some time in Paris we went to Bordoux. We traveled about 700 miles in France. We staid about seven weeks in Bordoux waiting for an opportunity to get home and we took passage in a Schr. Capt. Alexander Cane, for Baltimore and off the Capes of the Chesapeake we were captured by a privateer from New York and remained on board some days and they having so many prisoners on board they set us ashore south of Cape Henry and we travelled to Philadelphia via Portsmouth, Va. and Baltimore and then I received a large sum of money from Col. Pickering, he being, I believe, Quarter Master Genl, to carry to New Hampshire.

"I went to Boston and then returned to N London and went a privateering and commanded a privateer at the time N London was burned and she was partly destroyed, her mast being out. When the enemy retreated after burning N London, by that Traitor Arnold, they were pursued by a small party of men and I being in advance on Manwaring Hill I took a prisoner. I took the command of the Brig *Marshall* of 14 Guns and all the officers and men we could get to man her was forty-nine. The cause was if captured they would be sent to the Jersey Prison Ship and they were almost sure to die. This cruise we captured a Schooner from the W. I. and a Ship and brig from Jamaica—the Ship and Brig we took in tow about a week and never cast them off until we arrived opposite Fisher's Island Point."

Inscription on Marble Shaft in Cedar Grove Cemetery

(FRONT)

Capt.
Charles Bulkeley.
A Naval Officer of the
American Revolution
was on board the *Alfred*
in the Delaware River
and witnessed the first
unfurling of the Stars
and Stripes* to the wind
on board that vessel.
An ardent Patriot
he served his Country
faithfully and loved her
with the devotion
of a Son.
born Dec. 19th 1752.
died Feb. 16th 1848.

(REVERSE)

Peter Bulkeley B. D.
a nonconformist to the
English Church
emigrated to this
Country for Religious
Liberty. He arrived
in Cambridge 1634 and
was a leader of those
resolute and self denying
Christians who soon
after went further into
the Woods and settled
on the Plantation in
Musketaquid.
He died in Concord, Mass
March 9th 1659
in his 77th year.
The family motto
"neither rashly nor timidly"
was eminently
characteristic of the
American family.

Second Marble Shaft Same Size as the Captain's

Leonard H. Bulkeley
born
Dec 22, 1791
died
Dec 19, 1849.
The
Founder
of
Bulkeley School

THE FIRST AMERICAN ENSIGN

The inscription on Captain Charles Bulkeley's monument* regarding the Stars and Stripes should not be accepted in the light of present research. The reader should bear in mind it may not have been Captain Bulkeley's own statement, for the inscription no doubt was placed after his death by those responsible. Evidently he did witness the unfurling of the first American Ensign, of whatever design it may have been.

The flag with the stars and stripes was not officially adopted by the Congress until June 14, 1777, and was used at first principally in the Navy. Much controversy has arisen concerning the design of the flag unfurled on the *Alfred* on December 3, 1775. In *Esek Hopkins Letter Book*, Mrs. Beck states proof that the Great Union flag was used at the sailing of the fleet from Philadelphia on January 4, 1776. However, her statement does not specifically say this was used on the *Alfred*. A letter from Captain McCandless of the U. S. Navy, Boston, Massachusetts, May 23, 1933, indicates that he is still looking for final proof of his contention that the Great Union flag was flown from the *Alfred* on December 3, 1775.

Letters from the nautical historian, Louis F. Middlebrook of Hartford, May 29 and May 31, 1933, giving a copy of the original entry of the charge of bunting for the first American Ensign on December 2, 1775, would indicate that only red and white stripes were used. Mr. Middlebrook's proof is the most convincing thus far.

May 29, 1933 ". . . . As I was over at the State Library I thought I would call for the photostats of the Day Book of James Wharton of Philadelphia which I deposited there in May 1931 and I quote there-from as follows for your information, data and needs:

'December 2, 1775, Ship *ALFRED* DR.

49 Yds. Broad Bunting @ 2/	4: 18-0
52 ½ Yds. Narrow Bunting @ 1/	2: 12-6
To making Ensign, canvas and thread	1: 2-8
	£ 8: 12-2
Cr. Margaret Manny for making Ensign	£ 1: 2-8'

"This therefore is the first American Ensign to be flown by an American Warship and for which Congress paid the price later on when they got the bill for the refitting of the *Alfred* amounting to over £1000 . . . ."

The second letter of May 31 states, "I have received carbon copy of your letter of May 29th addressed to Captain McCandless, U. S. N., Boston, for which accept my thanks. In addition to the letter I wrote you a day or two ago relating to the First American Flag, the more I think of it the more I am convinced that the flag made by Margaret Manny was the First Continental American Flag, but I have been trying to find out why there were 49 yards of broad bunting and 52½ yards of narrow bunting, and I think I have at least satisfied myself . . . . From the data I submitted to you from the ship chandlery of James Wharton of Philadelphia, I am more inclined to believe that the first all American Flag which was made December 2, 1775 by Margaret Manny was a flag consisting of 13 red and white stripes. By reference to *Stars and Stripes* by Peleg D. Harrison (Little, Brown & Co., Boston, 1917) Page 42, Par. 3, he says 'A flag worn by American vessels during the early part of the Revolution, composed of 13 horizontal alternate red and white stripes alone, was an exact copy of a signal used in the British fleet,'—which would indicate that Harrison conceded the *stripes alone* as the Continental Ensign of the time; and I have also encountered 'the stripes' (Brit. Pub. Rec. Office, American Naval papers) . . . ."

XIV

THE NEW LONDON LIGHTHOUSE

THE question is often asked not only by visitors but also by citizens, "When was the lighthouse built?" The present lighthouse was erected by the United States in 1801.

New London from her earliest days has been the chief port of the Commonwealth of Connecticut. For a long time all the shipping of the colony was cleared from this port.[1] No merchant had so many ships passing in and out of the harbor as Nathaniel Shaw, Jr. A lighthouse at the harbor's mouth has always been a necessity.

"A lighthouse of some sort had previously been erected at the mouth of the harbor. Allusions to it are found after 1750, but nothing that shows when it was built or how maintained."[2]

The lighthouse is of especial significance in connection with this volume of Collections because the land on which it was built was sold to the governor and company by Nathaniel Shaw, Jr.

"In 1760, a lottery was granted to build a light-house at the entrance of New London Harbor. This was the first light-house upon the Connecticut coast. Near the rocky ledge chosen for its site, members of the Harris family have dwelt since the first generation from the settlement. The particular spot on which the house was erected, was sold to the governor and company by Nathaniel Shaw, Jr. It was part of the inheritance of his wife, Lucretia, only child of Daniel Harris. In 1801, this structure was superseded by another, built by the general government, which had assumed the charge of the light-houses of the country."[3]

The Harris family is one of the oldest in New London and furnished a *heroine* of the American Revolution in the person of Lucretia Harris Rogers Shaw, as is mentioned earlier in this volume.

---

[1] Caulkins, *History of New London*, p. 477.
[2] *Ibid.*, p. 474.
[3] *Ibid.*, p. 474.

THE NEW LONDON LIGHTHOUSE.

Lucretia Harris Rogers, young widow of Captain Josiah Rogers and daughter of Daniel and Lucy Tinker Harris, was baptized April 22, 1739 (Blake 503), married Nathaniel Shaw, Jr., July 20, 1758, and died December 11, 1781.

Daniel Harris, the son of Joseph, was married by justice Hempstead on April 18, 1738, to Lucy Tinker, daughter of John. Daniel Harris died, not quite twenty-one years of age, in 1739 soon after his marriage, and left one child, an infant daughter Lucretia, who married first, Captain Josiah Rogers; second, Nathaniel Shaw, Jr.

Captain Josiah Rogers died September 10, 1757, as recorded in the *Diary of Joshua Hempstead*, p. 691:

"Capt. Josiah Rogers died with the smallpox. He was in a small sloop privateer fitted out in the West Indies this summer and took a French ship and brought her in to Rhode Island where she was condemned &c. He went up to New York and took the smallpox, was sick one week, aged 20 odd."

In the Caulkins MSS. it is further recorded:

"He was buried in a plot of graves near the Light House at Harbor's mouth where a stone was erected in memory of Capt. Josiah Rogers, who died of smallpox Sept, 10, 1757, Aged 26 years."

Their little son Josiah died in the Shaw Mansion, March 20, 1764, aged seven years eight months.

In order to ascertain how the lighthouse was supported before it was transferred to the federal government, the *Colonial Records of Connecticut* were consulted, and, fortunately, several illuminating facts concerning its maintenance were discovered in Volume XIV. They are as follows:

October, 1773—p. 191

"Upon the memorial of Nathaniel Shaw, of New London in the county of New London, shewing to this Assembly that in the year 1771 the memorialist was the sole director, provider for the light-house in New London, and that he was obliged to expend of his own money in that business about twenty pounds, lawful money, more than he received, and that the fund for the support of the said light-house is not sufficient to repay your Hon[rs] memorialist; praying that the same may be ordered to be paid out of the treasury &c., as per memorial, dated October 18th, 1773."

January, 1774—p. 236

"Resolved by this Assembly, that the said Jeremiah Miller, Esqr, be and he is hereby directed and impowered to pay and satisfy said sum of £ 19 12 5 to Nathaniel Shaw out of said duties, and also to charge the balance of duties in his hands with said balance of £ 85 7 6, due to him for supplies to said light-house."

January, 1774—p. 216

"An Act in Addition to and Alteration of an Act entituled An Act for raising a certain Sum to be appropriated to the Erecting and Maintaining a Light-House near the Port of New London, and for laying a Tax on Shipping for the Support thereof.

"Whereas by said act it is enacted, that all vessels entering and clearing out for any port or place more remote than Philadelphia in Pensylvania, and Portsmouth in New Hampshire, above twenty tons and not more than fifty tons the sum of four shillings and six pence, lawful money, and for each vessel above fifty tons and not more than one hundred tons the sum of six shillings, and so in proportion as they shall be larger: And as the tax aforesaid is found insufficient for the support and maintenance of the light-house,

"*Be it further enacted*, That from the first day of March next, each vessel in burthen twenty tons and not more than fifty tons shall pay the sum of six shillings, lawful money, and each vessel above fifty tons and not more than seventy tons the sum of seven shillings and six pence, and each vessel above seventy tons and not more than ninety tons the sum of nine shillings, and each vessel more than ninety tons and not more than one hundred tons ten shillings and six pence; and so in proportion as they shall be larger.

"*And be it further enacted*, That all vessels not belonging to this Colony which shall enter and clear at the said port shall be subjected to a tax double what is hereby laid on the navigation of this Colony; and all vessels that shall harbour and anchor in the port of New London shall be subjected to pay, towards the support of the light house, at the same rate as the vessels belonging to this Colony pay when they clear out; which tax becoming due as aforesaid shall from time to time be paid to and collected by the naval officers of the ports where any such vessel shall be cleared out, deducting for their fees as they are allowed for collecting other duties. And the naval officer of the port of New Haven is hereby directed to forward the tax he shall collect, quarterly, to the naval officer of the port of New London, for the convenience and speedy accommodation of the light house; which is to be by him appropriated to the use aforesaid; any law, usage or custom to the contrary notwithstanding."

The United States still owns and maintains the lighthouse, although the keeper's residence and the larger portion of the grounds and beach were sold to Mrs. Alice Bunner in 1929.

JUDGE ELIAS PERKINS.

XV

MARQUIS de LAFAYETTE'S VISIT TO NEW LONDON

LAFAYETTE'S visit to New London on August 22, 1824, was ably described by Nathaniel Shaw Perkins, grandson of Judge Elias Perkins, in the *American Historical Register* for August, 1895.

The article in full is as follows:

"The General left Saybrook early Sunday morning, taking his breakfast at the house of Richard McCurdy, Esq., an eminent citizen of Lyme, and proceeded to New London. It was uncertain for some days whether Lafayette would go on to Hartford from New Haven, or would take in Providence in his route to Boston, visiting New London and Norwich. It was learned in New London on the evening of the 18th, positively, that he was to be expected there. The citizens convened without formal summons, spontaneously, and passed the following vote:

Learning with pleasure that General Lafayette may probably pass through this city on his tour to or return from the eastward, and being anxious to show that respectful attention due to so illustrious a citizen, to manifest to him the high sense of gratitude which we entertain for his patriotic exertions and generous aid during the Revolutionary War; and that his virtues and benevolence are still cherished by those who are now enjoying the fruits of his noble and disinterested deeds;

Voted, That the Hon. Elias Perkins, Richard Law, Chas. Bulkeley, John P. Trott, Oliver Champlin and John Hallam, Esquires, be a committee to make such arrangements for his reception and accommodation during his stay with us as will evince our respect and attachment to the benefactor of our country and the ardent friend of the rights of man.

Attest: Elias Perkins, Chairman
Robert Coit, Secretary.

The committee, with energy and promptitude, made all arrangements to welcome his arrival, which was expected that evening. Judge Perkins offered his house, famed for hospitality, for his reception. The military, in full uniform, under command of Captain Allyn, with a band of music, marched to meet the expected visitor, and preparations for the illumination of that part of the town, which he was expected to pass through, was made, the citizens arranged to fall into line and cheer him on his progress.

Some members of the committee took carriages to meet the General on the west side of the river, to accompany him from Saybrook. Others of the committee, with a number of citizens went out to Waterford to meet him and escort him to his lodgings. But, retarded by the respectful attentions which every town and village through which he passed was anxious to manifest, the General advanced no farther than Saybrook that night.

He was then met at Waterford by the delegates from New London, who were introduced to him by the committee that had accompanied him from New York. These gentlemen, on their introduction, presented him an address and, ardently expressing their admiration and esteem, solicited his acceptance of the hospitality of the citizens of New London. He happily responded, accepting the invitation. His duties during the war had never taken him to New London, but its name was associated with the brilliant assault of the redoubts before Yorktown, the first measuring of steel in the final conquest of the Revolutionary War. The story of the conflagration and massacre there by Arnold, the traitor, was but a few days old in the beleaguering camp when the assaults on the batteries were made by Hamilton and Lafayette, and his memory recalled the stern whisper to the silent stormers, "Remember New London," and vividly recalled the brilliant action. There were also resident there officers of his own legion whom he recollected in the field in the dark days of doubtful struggle. One of his earliest recognitions was of Captain Ranson, a gallant veteran who had served under him.

He was escorted to the mansion of Judge Perkins, where, with the spontaneous acclamations of a great body of citizens, and with sincere and heartfelt gratulations, he was received under a national salute of twenty-four guns from Fort Trumbull. He was introduced to the crowding citizens, greeted with an affection respectful and earnest and the scene remains among the purest and most sacred memories. His manner of receiving the enthusiastic guests was with a friendly informality that charmed, every word and gesture manifesting his affection for each and all Americans. There was in his demeanor an affectionate simplicity, an unaffected gentleness, which softened all whom he welcomed.

The church bells proclaiming the hour of divine service, he accompanied his host, Judge Perkins, to his pew in the Congregational church, the Rev. Dr. McEwen and the whole congregation rising as he passed reverently up the aisle. On reaching the pew he turned, fronting the congregation, and silently saluted. Later he passed to the Episcopal church the Rev. Mr. Judd officiating, and participated in the service. On leaving the churches he paid his respects to Madam Huntington, widow of the late General Jedediah Huntington, and Madam Perry, mother of the late commodore.

On his return he spent an hour in further social courtesies with gentlemen and ladies who called upon him. His recognitions of old companions, distinct and invariable were very felicitious and gratifying. There had been the intimacy of young companions, as well as that of young soldiers, between himself and General William North, a former aid to Baron Steuben, then a resident of New London. The meeting of this occasion was very interesting. The writer recalls the incidents as narrated to him some years since by the gentleman who introduced them. He simply announced General North as an "old companion in arms." As Lafayette looked on the face and the recognition grew upon him, the exclamation

Lucretia Shaw Woodbridge Perkins and son, Nathaniel Shaw Perkins.

broke forth, "Is it my dear North?" followed by a tearful embrace and most affectionate greeting.

He met many old friends whom he had not seen since they were in the camp and field together—General North, General Eb. Huntington, General Burbeck, Dr. John Watrous, a surgeon in the Revolutionary War, Captain Ransom, Captain Adam A. Larrabee and a number of others, all associated with scenes of conflict or campaigning.

At 3 o'clock dinner was announced and, surrounded by distinguished veterans, his old comrades, and the family of the mansion, he passed an hour at the table in delightful converse. Before he said farewell, knowing that Washington had been a guest of an older member of the family, he asked to be shown the room and permission to retire there. Previously committees from Norwich and Stonington had been introduced to the General, who waited upon him with invitations to visit their towns. The route as decided upon was through Norwich, and the Stonington delegation could receive but kindly regrets and thanks for their courtesy.

He was escorted by a numerous cavalcade of New London gentlemen as far as the half-way house on the turnpike, between Norwich and New London, where the final adieux were said and the Norwich committee received him as their guest. The General and suite reached Norwich at 6 o'clock where he stopped several hours and then went to Plainfield to lodge Sunday night."

When searching to find items pertaining to Lafayette's visit to New London the following were located among Judge Elias Perkins' papers in the Shaw Collection:

> Receipt for Payment of Use of Horses by Lafayette from his Aide-de-Camp
> Letter from William Jones to Ebenezer Way
> Letter from Frederick Lee to Ebenezer Way
> Address by Judge Elias Perkins, in his own handwriting

Receipt for Payment of Use of Horses by Lafayette

(From the original in the Shaw Collection)

New London Sepr. 3, 1778 Received of Nathl. Shaw Junr. Two horses to perform a Journey to General Washington, with Dispatches Said Horses were Rode from N Lond^n. to New Haven & back again to N Lond^n—by order of ye Marquis La Fyatt on Acco^{tt}. of the King of France.

Major (surname illegible) a. d. c.

By order of Major general Marquis de la fayette

Letter from William H. Jones to Ebenezer Way

(From the original in the Shaw Collection)

New Haven August 19— 1824

Eben Way Esq
   Dr Sir

     Genl. La Fayette will breakfast at New Haven on Saturday & leave here about 11—o clock for New London where he will probably arrive about Sunset or soon after. I give you this information that your citizens may be prepared to give him such attentions as they may wish.

                             Respectfully Y^r friend
                                   W^m H Jones

P S.
  The General intends to be in Boston on tuesday Morning—Cambridge Commencement is on Wednesday.

Letter from Frederick Lee to Ebenezer Way

(From the original in the Shaw Collection)

New Haven 1/2 Past 8 P M   All is bustle here waiting for Layfaette he is expected every Moment
    Three guns are to anounce his arrival and the city will be Immediately Illuminated they have got a large box of transparancy suspended in the Middle of the street between Bishop, and Morses on one side Welcome Layfaette & Right, of man on one and Liberty on the other there is to be a Public Breakfast tomorrow Morning and at 12 he leaves this for N London on his way to Boston

                                     in haste yours &c
                                         Fred^k Lee

P S
   The Gen^{rl} will Stay Pratts tomorrow night and arrive in N London on Sunday.

Address by Judge Elias Perkins[1] to General Lafayette

(From the original in the Shaw Collection)

To Gen¹ Lafayette

The Citizens of New London filled with gratitude for the great & eminent services rendered their Country, in the highly distinguished part you took in achieving their independence & deeply impressed with the lofty & Elevated stand you have taken in the defense of the liberties of the civilized world thereby walking in the footsteps of your great prototype & friend of your early life beg leave to address you.

We congratulate ourselves upon the arrival in our Country of so distinguished a Visitor & one whom we can hail as a fellow citizen. While retrospection reminds us of the solemn fact that few of the mighty chiefs, with whom you were associated remain as the pillar & the cloud to the succeeding generation our hearts are elevated & cheered at the prospect of seeing among us from a distant country one of the most distinguished of their number—Here may you enjoy that tranquility & secure those honours which ought ever to await him who hazards all, in Defence of the right of humanity.

The Citizens of New London under standing that you contemplate a tour through this state most earnestly request that their city may have the honour of entertaining you—that their hearts may be rejoiced at the presence of the early friend & companion of their beloved Washington

we have the honour to be in behalf of the City your

most obed¹ Serv¹

---

[1] Surnames are acquired through heredity and marriage, and Christian names by choice of the parents. People sometimes wonder why certain Christian names have been chosen. The choice may have been made because of the desire to continue the Christian names from generation to generation, in other instances the children have been named for relatives and friends, or merely because of the appeal of certain names, and again, according to a custom prevailing in the past, they have been named for prominent personages local or national.

My father was one of a numerous family. After the continuous name had been bestowed and names of relatives given, he was named for the most prominent man of the community, Judge Elias Perkins. After my call on Nathaniel Shaw Perkins in 1896, my father informed me of this fact and said Judge Perkins gave him, in person, a silver dollar for his name. My middle name, Elias, was acquired from my father.

E. E. R.

XVI

THE NEW LONDON CUSTOM HOUSES

THE colonial Custom House was situated on the east side of Main Street above Hallam Street on Winthrop Cove. This building together with the collector's dwelling, was burned on the sixth of September, 1781.[1] In 1761 a list of the shipping of the district of New London which included the whole colony returned 45 vessels, 1668 tons, 40 guns, 387 men.[2] If to these are added the coasting vessels, the total would amount to 80 vessels. Duncan Stewart was appointed collector in 1764 and was the last to hold office under the King's customs in this port, his duties ceasing with the Declaration of Independence.[3]

The Declaration of Independence was the line of demarcation between the colonial and state governments. The first meeting of the Connecticut General Assembly after the Declaration of Independence was held on October 10, 1776, and Connecticut changed over from a colony to a state by a legislative act.[4]

---

[1] Caulkins, *History of New London*, p. 553.
[2] *Trumbull Papers*.
[3] Caulkins, *History of New London*, p. 478.
[4] "Whereas George the third, King of Great Britain, hath unjustly levied war against this and the other united States of America, declared them out of his protection, and abdicated the government of this State, whereby the good people of this State are absolved from their allegiance and subjection to the crown of Great Britain: And whereas the Representatives of the said United States in General Congress assembled have published and declared that these United States are and of right ought to be free and independent States, and that they are absolved from all allegiance to the British Crown:

"*Resolved by this Assembly*, That they approve of the Declaration of Independence published by said Congress, and that this Colony is and of right ought to be a free and independent State, and the inhabitants thereof are absolved from all allegiance to the British Crown, and all political connections between them and the King of Great Britain is, and ought to be, totally dissolved.

"*And be it enacted by the Governor, Council and Representatives, in General Court assembled, and by the authority of the same,* That the form

The New London Custom House.

The necessity for State supervision of customs on account of a state of war caused the General Assembly in May, 1776, to authorize the governor to act as the naval officer and directed "that there shall be kept at the port of New London one naval office, at the port of New Haven one other naval office, at the port of Middletown one other naval office, and the port of Norwalk one other naval office; and that the governor for the time being depute some proper person at each of said ports as naval officers."[1] Later Norwich and Stonington were added to the list of offices. Jeremiah Miller was appointed naval officer at New London. He was succeeded by Gurdon Saltonstall.

Brigadier General Jedediah Huntington of Norwich was appointed the first collector of this port by President Washington in 1789, and held the office until 1815. It was at General Huntington's home in Norwich that Washington was entertained on his way from Cambridge to the home of Nathaniel Shaw, Jr., on April 9, 1776. Later in the war, he was officially attached to Washington's military family. He removed to New London and built his home at the corner of Huntington and Broad Streets, and, to a certain degree, modeled it after Mount Vernon. The office of the collector was in the second story of a building on the corner of State and Bank Streets.

In 1833 the United States purchased land on Bank Street and commenced to build the present custom house, so the building this year completes its centennial. Most of the stone came from the Millstone quarries; the front of the building was built of stone from Waterford near the city. The present doors (they are the original) were made from planks taken

---

of civil government in this State shall continue to be as established by Charter received from Charles the second, King of England, so far as an adherence to the same will be consistent with an absolute independence of this State on the Crown of Great Britain; and that all officers, civil and military, heretofore appointed by this State continue in the execution of their several offices, and the laws of this State shall continue in force untill otherwise ordered. . . ." *Records of the State of Connecticut*, Vol. I, p. 3.

[1] *Colonial Records of Connecticut*, Vol. XV, p. 280.

from the old frigate *Constitution* at the time repairs were made to that famous ship.

As the books previous to September 6, 1781, were burned with the first custom house, the records of the local customs begin with the first collector under the federal government.

Washington was elected President in 1789, and soon afterwards he appointed Alexander Hamilton Secretary of the Treasury. There follows a copy of a letter written by Hamilton, the first Secretary of the Treasury, to Jedidiah Huntington, the first Collector of the Customs, New London. It was written on a plain sheet of paper (showing the primitive governmental stationery at that time) and is entirely in Hamilton's elegant penmanship.

(From the original in the collection of the New London County Historical Society)

Treasury Department Novr 6th 1789

Sir

I have this day drawn on you in favor of Mr James Watson the fum of One Thousand Dollars in a fole Bill of Exchange.

You will be pleased to pay the said fum, and transmit the Bill in Lieu of Specie to the Treafurer of the united ftates, addrefsing your Letter to him under cover to me, and a regular warrant Shall be transmitted to you for the amount.

I am
Sir your Ob^t ferv^t
A Hamilton
Sec^y of the Treafury

Jedediah Huntington Esqr
Collector of the Customs
New London

At the present time there are, for the District of Connecticut, a collector, with office at Bridgeport, and deputy collectors in the sub-ports of New London, New Haven and Hartford.

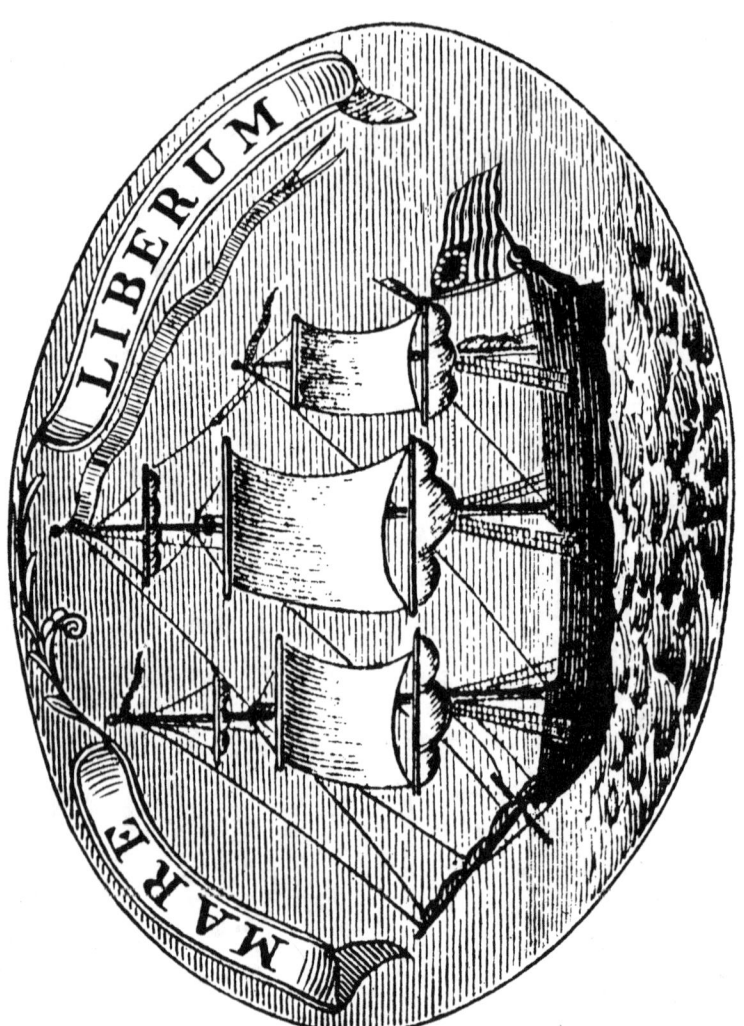

The Seal of the City of New London, adopted in 1784.

The City of New London was incorporated in January 1784, and stands second on the list of incorporated cities of the state.

XVII

THE LATER PORT OF NEW LONDON, 1783-1933[1]

AFTER the Treaty of Peace of September 3, 1783, concluding the war of the American Revolution, the commerce of the United States and consequently that of New London experienced great prosperity. Thomas Shaw, inheriting his brother Nathaniel's business, succeeded finally in settling the estate successfully as a whole, complicated as it was by many accounts with foreign customers. With thirteen years of prosperity from the passing of his brother until his own death in 1795, Thomas Shaw's estate consequently was much larger than Nathaniel's.

The decline of the West India trade followed by the embargo, nonintercourse and war of 1812 broke down the commerce of New London which was followed by the rise of the whaling industry.

New London was surveyed by Warren in 1807 and Meyer in 1846. Warren's survey did not indicate any wharves whatever. Theodore Barrell (a wharf owner) produced a map, evidently by taking the central portion of the city from Warren's map, mounting it on cardboard, designating the wharves, some changes in the suburbs, and hung it in his office. It is inscribed "Plan of a Part of the City of New London taken July 1820 from the City's survey (1807) by Theodore Barrell." The map is now in the collection of the New London County Historical Society.

Theodore Barrell Map, 1820

Wharves near Federal Street, W. Williams, John Hallam, Saltonstall; Douglass Street, Perkins,[2] Ezra Chappell, (illeg-

---

[1] Population of New London, 1782, 5,688; 1800, 5,150; 1850, 8,991; 1900, 17,548; 1930, 29,640.

[2] Judge Elias Perkins inherited the Shaw wharves.

ible, possibly Forsyth); John Street, C. Kimball; Prison Street, (illegible); Market Square, Market Wharf, Elias Perkins,[1] David Frink, Steamboat; Golden Street, Theodore Barrell, Ephraim Frink; Tilley Street, Brown. Theodore Barrell published later a large map.

Colfax and Holt Map, 1847
(From Survey of 1846)

Island of Rocks; Hallam Street, Billings; Federal Street, Williams, Williams and Barnes; Douglass Street, Williams, R. Coit; John Street, Prentis and Learned, Gorton; Prison Street, Hobron, Holt; Market Square, Ferry, Perkins,[1] Frink, French; Golden Street, Steamboat, Lawrence, Frink; Pearl Street, Custom House, Bassett; Tilley Street, Brown, Brown; Brewer Street, Smith (Perkins[1] & Smith).

City Map Without Date Gives Names of City Officers— F. L. Allen, Mayor. He was Mayor from 1865 to 1871

Hallam Street, Moses Darrow, Woolen Wharf, Williams & Barnes, Badet & Cornell; Douglass Street, Williams & Havens, F. & H. Coit; John Street, J. M. Huntington & Co., New London Ferry, Hamilton Powers & Co., R. R. Ferry, Stonington R. R. Wharves Nos. 1 and 2, C. Smith, Steamboat Wharf; Golden Street, Lawrence Wharf, A. F. Prentice, Custom House Wharf; Pearl Street, Starr Dock, Bassett's Wharf; Tilley Street, Brown's Wharf, wharf (no name); Brewer Street, H. B. Smith. At the present time all these names are changed except Custom House and New York Steamboat, the latter changed its location.

The whaling industry reached its height in January, 1846, with 78 vessels sailing from New London in pursuit of whales. In 1820 there were 4 vessels. New Bedford ranked first in the whaling industry in the world, New London second and Nantucket a close third.[2] A large and important

---

[1] Judge Elias Perkins inherited the Shaw wharves.
[2] Caulkins, *History of New London*.

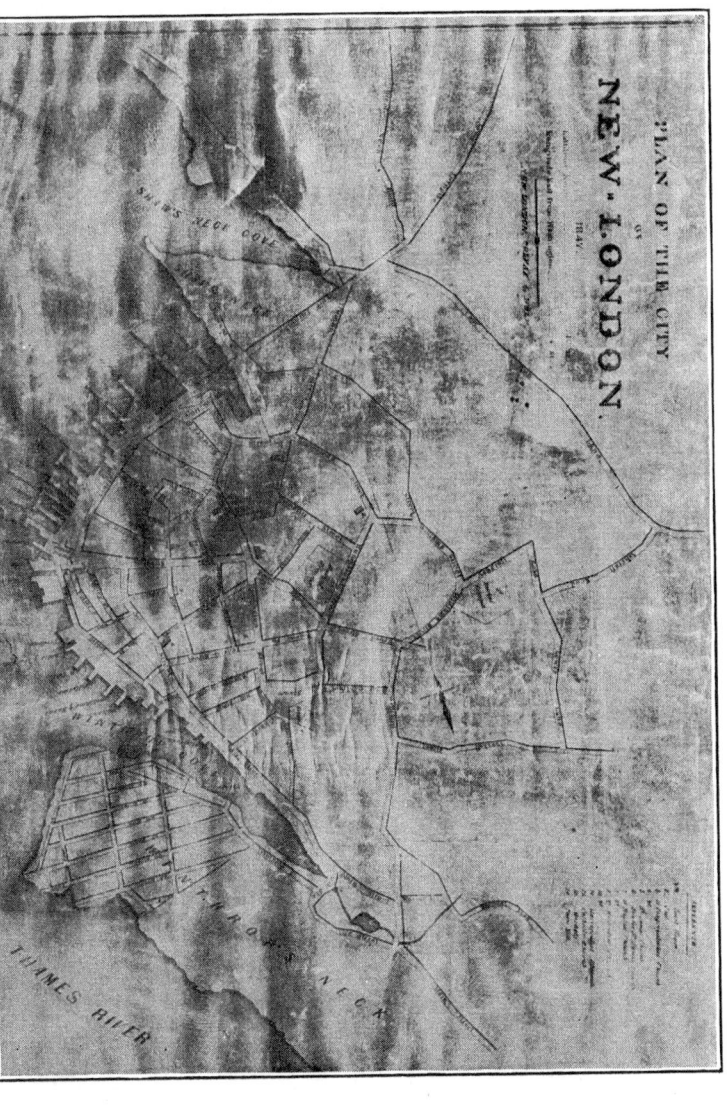

Map of the Later Port of New London, 1847.

Courtesy of the Public Library of New London.

museum containing implements and relics of the whaling industry in Connecticut is that of the Mariners Savings Bank of this city, collected by its Vice-President, P. LeRoy Harwood. The Jibboom Club No. 1 and the New London County Historical Society, both of this city, have important collections. An interesting incident is connected with the figurehead from the whaling ship *Flora* which sailed from this port.

A whaling ship built in Groton, Connecticut, during the years 1810-11 and named *Flora* was later sailed by Captain John L. Ward of New London. In the gold rush of '49 to California, he took his wife on this ship around Cape Horn. A child born on the voyage was named Flora. Many years later the child, grown to womanhood, owned the figurehead of that ship and at her death a few years ago left it as a bequest to the New London County Historical Society when her husband should care to part with it. It is now in the possession of the Society, the gift of her husband, Joseph Smith, 2nd, of New London, now deceased.

United States Submarine Base

John R. Bolles of New London was the father of the New London Navy Yard. The plan was his and the pamphlet and newspaper articles published by him in the early sixties met a ready response on the part of our citizens. The following excerpt from the speech of former congressman from this district, Hon. Edwin W. Higgins of Norwich, May 27, 1912, shows the importance of New London's harbor and port:

"The history of the location of this station goes back to before 1862. At the direction of Congress in the early sixties the Secretary of the Navy appointed a naval board, composed of the most intelligent naval officers then in the service, to examine Narragansett Bay, the harbor of New London, and League Island, and to report back to Congress which would best serve the public interest. Commanders Stringham, Gardner, and Van Brundt and Chief Engineer Sanger composed this board, and to the report which they made was appended the following resolution:

Resolved, That the harbor of New London possesses greater advantages for a navy yard and naval depot than any other location examined by this board.

In 1864 Congress directed the Naval Committee of the House to visit the proposed site at New London to make a thorough investigation and report back to the House. They made a personal examination, and their report concluded in the following language:

The site near New London, presenting such great natural and economical advantages, has been tendered as a free gift to the Government. The committee recommend its acceptance, and for the purpose of locating thereat a navy yard and depot such as is contemplated by the naval authorities they recommend the passage of the accompanying bill for a public act.

Congress in 1867, convinced of the wisdom of locating a station at this point, passed the following resolution:

Resolved, That the Secretary of the Navy be, and he is hereby, authorized to receive and accept a deed of gift when offered by the State of Connecticut of a tract of land with not less than 1 mile of shore front on the Thames River, near New London, Conn., to be held by the United States for naval purposes.

The State of Connecticut appropriated $15,000 for the purchase of this tract of land, and in addition the city of New London was authorized to appropriate any sum of money not to exceed $75,000 for the purchase of land to be deeded to the Federal Government for naval purposes, and the city of New London joined with the State in the gift. I will print as an appendix to my remarks a certified copy of the deed, which conveyed this land to the National Government upon a distinct condition and for a definite purpose, and it was accepted by the Government upon that condition.

This conveyance was made on the 11th day of April, 1868, and this Government entered into possession and has been in possession ever since, holding it, as agreed, for naval purposes."[1]

A wharf was built at the Navy Yard, but few improvements were made until it became a coaling station for government boats. The coal shed was removed upon the establishment of the submarine flotilla. In 1915, the author, then Mayor of New London, was en route to Savannah and when calling upon the Hon. Josephus Daniels, the Secretary of the Navy, at Raleigh, North Carolina, was authorized by him to telegraph the people of New London as follows:

"Upon expressing to the Honorable Secretary of the Navy, Josephus Daniels, the appreciation of the citizens of New London for establishing the naval base of the submarine flotilla at New London, he personally authorized me to forward his greetings, accompanied with hopes that the ample

---

[1] *Congressional Record*, Vol. XLVIII., Part VII., p. 7234, May 27, 1912.

facilities for submarines at New London may be more fully utilized in the near future."

Secretary Daniels also said he expected to make New London the chief Submarine Base of the United States, which plan was soon realized.

United States Coast Guard

The Coast Guard, a part of the naval forces of the United States, is composed of the Revenue Cutter Service, founded August 4, 1790, and the Life Saving Service established in 1878. The rank of cadet was created in 1876. New Bedford was the seat of the first Academy which was stationed on shipboard until 1894.

In 1900 a shore establishment was made at Arundel Cove, Maryland, near Baltimore. The Treasury Department, which has jurisdiction of the Coast Guard, removed the Academy to Fort Trumbull, New London, in 1910, as this fort had been vacated by the removal of the Headquarters Harbor Defenses of Long Island Sound to Fort H. G. Wright, Fishers Island, New York.

In 1933 the Coast Guard Academy removed to its new buildings in the northern section of the city. The cost of the buildings and grounds was nearly $2,500,000.

The Coast Guard Destroyer Force removed from the State Pier and now occupies Fort Trumbull. This branch of the Treasury Department has four destroyers and twenty patrol boats in its service with rendezvous at Fort Trumbull.

Connecticut's State Pier

The late Bryan F. Mahan was the father of the State Pier. He conceived the idea, possessed the vision, and his bill for $1,000,000 introduced in the General Assembly in the session of 1911 when he was state senator, with the aid of his fellow citizens here and throughout the state was successful and it was signed by the Governor, June 25, 1911.

The pier is 1,020 feet long and 200 feet wide. So far this calendar year thirty-one cargoes of lumber from the West Coast have been received and twelve of wood pulp from Europe.

A noteworthy incident which caused a real sensation, was the arrival of the undersea freighter *Deutchland* on November 1, 1916, from Bremen. She docked at the state pier which was not quite completed.

Although America had not at that time entered the war, the author, then Mayor, before accepting the invitation to call on Captain Paul Koenig, placed himself in communication with representatives of the U. S. Treasury Department and ascertained the *Deutchland* was rated as a neutral merchantman.

The Mayor called at the Nathan Hale schoolhouse for his son E. Gorton Rogers, next at the Post Office for Postmaster B. F. Mahan and the three made the official call. The Mayor insisted that Postmaster Mahan should be the first to officially step aboard the boat, the first craft carrying a foreign flag to dock at the pier which Mr. Mahan had secured for New London. Mr. Mahan had served as Mayor of New London for three terms of three years each, state senator, congressman for this district, and had recently accepted the office of postmaster.

After the decline of the whaling industry the coasting trade employed many schooners carrying freight. The *Day* of October 1, 1882, mentioned the fact that the weather bound fleet of over one hundred vessels, some of which had been in port for over a week, left the harbor with favoring breezes.

At the present time only an occasional schooner carrying freight comes into this port. Tugs with barges of coal, gasoline and fuel oil, ocean going power ships, submarines and boats of the Navy, boats of the Coast Guard together with passenger and freight boats to New York and nearby stations form the usual routine of water craft. However, the Yale-

Harvard regatta held here with few exceptions since 1878 brings enthusiastic devotees from the entire country who become acquainted with the many natural advantages of New London. The New York Yacht Club has a yearly rendezvous of its fleet in New London which makes a picturesque appearance.

Much could be written concerning the later history of this ancient seaport. While the study of the history of New London is interesting, yet to have seen "history in the making" during recent years has been far more fascinating to the author.

XVIII

A JOURNEY OF THIRTY-ONE YEARS IN RETROSPECT

By ERNEST E. ROGERS[1]

Address delivered at the annual meeting of the New London County
Historical Society, September 22, 1931

DRIVING over a New England highway is always interesting because of the diversity of the landscape, including city and village, mountain and lake, hill and valley, forest and stream, and often a glimpse of the sea. All of these we have in New London County. Furthermore, there is no county in the state more replete in historical interest than our own, with its romantic or aboriginal, heroic or revolutionary, and commercial or whaling eras.

There has been a marked change in transportation since the opening year of this century from horse drawn vehicles and bicycles to high-powered automobiles and aircraft. Then one could observe each rock, tree, and object with additional time for contemplation, while now one may grasp only the outline of the terrain with hardly a possibility for details. Likewise, methods and systems of business and organizations have changed, and as Epictetus, the Roman philosopher, said, "The times change and we change with them."

Little was it imagined by any-one, much less by the speaker, that his journey commenced in 1900 would be so long, for it was his aspiration to make it intensive rather than extensive. The journey of 31 years commenced September 7, 1900, was continuous to March 8, 1916, and from September 20, 1921, to September 22, 1931, a period of 25½ years as President of the society and Vice President for the 5½ years intervening. There has been no strife for office; indeed, it has been difficult to escape office. I speak from experience, having made the

---

[1] Mr. Rogers served six years as Vice President and twenty-five years as President, retiring as President on September 22, 1931.

ERNEST E. ROGERS.
When assuming the office of President in 1900.

attempt several times and succeeded only once when burdened, during the war period, with the heavy responsibilities of Mayor of the city. Thus it has been my privilege to be in the service in an official capacity for nearly one third of a century, and almost one half of my life, with a continuous membership of 39 years.

While this journey covers the latter half of the society's existence, allusion should be made to the first half of the society's life, especially to its founding. The act of incorporation states the names of the incorporators: Henry P. Haven, Charles J. McCurdy, John W. Stedman, Richard A. Wheeler, Learned Hibbard, John T. Wait, John P. C. Mather, Ashbel Woodward, Nathan Belcher, William H. Potter, S. G. Willard, Thomas A. Clark, and Isaac Johnson. The act was approved by the General Assembly July 6, 1870, but the organization meeting did not take place until October 17, 1871, being held in the common council chamber of the city hall, New London. At this meeting, LaFayette S. Foster of Norwich was chosen President and continued in office until his death in 1880. The name of Mr. Foster, who was the moving spirit in the organization of the society, does not appear in the list of incorporators, no doubt modestly omitted by him, as he was speaker of the General Assembly while the act was under consideration.[1] Mr. Foster resigned the speakership on June 16, 1870, having been elected a justice of the Supreme Court of the state. Mr. Foster, previous to this period, was United States Senator from Connecticut, President *pro tempore* of the Senate, Acting Vice President of the United States after the assassination of President Lincoln when Vice President Johnson became President.

---

[1] In October, 1931, Miss Emma Douglas (then living at the Mohican Hotel aged 85, but now deceased) informed me she became a member of the family of Henry P. Haven when fourteen years of age as her father was a brother of Mrs. Haven. She recalled the organization of the New London County Historical Society and the interest displayed by Mr. Haven who was the first named in the articles of incorporation specifying he should call the first meeting. He prevailed upon LaFayette S. Foster of Norwich to accept the presidency and entertained him in his home on the day of the meeting.

Mr. Foster was succeeded in office by David A. Wells of Norwich, 1880-1882; by Charles Augustus Williams of New London, 1882-1900; by Ernest E. Rogers, 1900-1916; by George S. Palmer, 1916-1921; by Ernest E. Rogers, 1921-1931;—five presidents in 60 years.

When the Society of Antiquity of Worcester made a patriotic pilgrimage to New London in 1903, Ledyard Bill of Paxton, Mass., was among the number. He formerly lived in Norwich and informed me he was a charter member, and being in the publishing business was appointed chairman of a committee to provide a seal, which he personally designed.

While not explicitly stated, it is inferred from the early records that the first home of the society was in the city hall building. In 1875 rooms were leased in the Union Bank building, the rent being paid by a generous member of the society. The society moved back to the city hall in 1888 because of increase in rent. The next removal was in 1891 to the upper floor of the public library building, which had recently been built. From July, 1902, to August, 1907, rented rooms in the Harris building known as Apartment E were occupied. Finally in August, 1907, removal was made to its own home, the Shaw Mansion on Bank and Blinman streets.

The courage of the early members was undaunted. Like pilgrims of a night with no permanent abiding place, they wandered from pillar to post, without an income or a home. For more than half of its 60 years of existence, the abode of the society was as uncertain and shifting as the sands of the seashore. However, with the help of more recent friends it reached its present substantial home in an old renowned colonial stone house, built on a ledge of solid rock.

In 1886, the able, active and versatile Thomas S. Collier was elected Secretary. The project for the placing of a statue of Captain John Mason on the site of the Pequot fort in Mystic was completed, and in 1890 Mr. Collier published Volume I. Part I., *Records and Papers*, and started an exchange list with the historical societies of the country which has been continued to the present. Time forbids the mention of many loyal officers and friends of the society in those early days. The celebration of the 250th anniversary of the founding of New London, inaugurated by this society, was observed on May 6, 1896, by the laying of a cornerstone of the foundation for a statue to the memory of John Winthrop the Younger, founder of the town; the dedication of the Soldiers and Sailors monument, the gift of the late Sebastian D. Lawrence; and the mammoth military, naval and civic parade which was the largest during my memory.

On September 7, 1900, the late former Mayor, George F. Tinker, called on me at the office of the Brainerd and Armstrong Company, where I was employed as head bookkeeper and said the New London County Historical Society was in annual session at the public library building, and as chairman of the nominating committee, he had come to inquire whether or not the presidency of the society would be accepted by me. I declined, remarking that I was employed, and only my evenings and an occasional day could be devoted to the society. He said that would be satisfactory. Then I accepted provided he would give his financial and moral support. Mr. Tinker was most helpful until his decease.

The years have brought many changes to the officers and advisory committee elected with me. All have passed away except Charles B. Ware, former Treasurer, now of Bridgeport, with a summer home in New London, and myself. Officers then: President—Ernest E. Rogers, New London; First Vice President—Frederic Bill, Groton; Second Vice President—William A. Slater, Norwich; Third Vice President—George C. Strong, New London; Secretary—Mary Eddye Benjamin, New London; Treasurer—Charles B. Ware, New London. Advisory Committee: Ernest E. Rogers, New London; Hon. George F. Tinker, New London; Charles B. Ware, New London; George W. Goddard, Salem, Mass.; Hon. Robert Coit, New London; William A. Slater, Norwich; Walter Learned, New London; Frederic Bill, Groton; Frederic S. Newcomb, New London; Richard A. Wheeler, Stonington; John McGinley, New London; Lewis D. Mason, M.D., Brooklyn, N. Y.; H. Wales Lines, Meriden; Amos Lawrence Mason,

M.D., Boston, Mass.; Jonathan Trumbull, Norwich; Major Bela Peck Learned, Norwich; J. Lawrence Chew, New London; Sebastian D. Lawrence, New London. The Treasurer's report showed cash on hand $117.58, and in savings bank $78.72. The Secretary reported 5 honorary, 25 life, and 60 annual members.

The publishing of the *Hempstead Diary* had been delayed for lack of funds, but on October 3, a meeting of the advisory committee was called, and, as the subscriptions were not more than half of the cost, the committee underwrote the balance and proceeded with the work. Our very helpful member of the advisory committee, Jonathan Trumbull of Norwich, volunteered to take charge of the proof reading and indexing if provided with a competent assistant. A copious index of 39 pages of both names and subjects was prepared under his supervision. Five hundred copies of the *Diary*, containing 750 pages, were issued the next year and have been sent to all sections of the United States. An official of the Connecticut Historical Society recently told me this book is consulted more than any other reference book in its library.

The Winthrop family tomb is in the "Antientest Buriall Ground" in New London, and it was a revelation to me to ascertain in 1895 that John Winthrop the Younger was not buried there. There was no memorial to him in Connecticut, not even a headstone. He was taken ill and died when on a visit to Boston, and was buried in the tomb of his father, Governor John Winthrop of the Massachusetts Bay Colony, in Kings Chapel cemetery.

The General Assembly of the state convened in January, 1901, and the first month was allowed for the introduction of bills. As my resolution adopted by the Society in 1895 had been fulfilled, with the exception of the procurement of the Winthrop statue, the time seemed opportune for the movement. The resolution was:

"Whereas, the 6th day of May, 1896, will be the 250th anniversary of the founding of New London by John Winthrop the Younger, subsequently Governor of the colony, and

"Whereas, it is eminently fitting and proper that the New

London County Historical Society should originate plans for the erection of a public memorial to Governor John Winthrop,

"Moved, that this society take the initial and active steps toward placing on the elevation in the new park a statue of Governor Winthrop of commanding size, the cornerstone to be laid not later than the above mentioned date.

"Moved, that a committee of three, of which the president of the society shall be an ex-officio member, be appointed by the society to develop plans and methods for securing the necessary funds, and to report to a special meeting of the society to be held during the third week of September."

Accordingly, early in January a call was made upon Augustus Brandegee, and he was asked to take the chairmanship of a committee to represent the New London County Historical Society. Mr. Brandegee considered the matter carefully, and although very much interested, decided his health would not permit him to undertake the task, but requested me to ask his friend Robert Coit. Mr. Coit when asked made no reply, but, lawyer that he was, after some moments said: "Who sent you to me?" My reply was: "Augustus Brandegee." Without a moment's hesitation, he said: "If Mr. Brandegee sent you, I will take the office," which he did and worked indefatigably, assisted by his son W. B. Coit, who represented New London in the legislature in the sessions of 1901 and 1903.

Shortly after this the president of the society was authorized to appoint a committee, which consisted of Robert Coit, M. Wilson Dart, Alfred H. Chappell, Walter Learned, and John McGinley. The hearing was held in Hartford, and assistance given by a delegation from this city and also one each from Norwich and Hartford, to show that it was a state-wide project. However, it was not until the next session of the legislature that the $10,000 grant was made and commissioners appointed, consisting of Robert Coit, ex-Governor McLean, Colonel N. G. Osborn. Bela L. Pratt of Boston, a native of New London County, was chosen sculptor, with the result that the statue was unveiled with imposing ceremonies on New London's natal day, May 6, 1905, after ten years of persistent effort.

In the meantime, it was necessary to locate a boulder pedestal that would meet the requirements of the sculptor. Mr. Brandegee, who was fond of driving, volunteered to take Mr. Coit to hunt for a boulder, but Mr. Coit was taken ill and passed away in June, 1904. Mr. Brandegee died in November of the same year. After Mr. Coit's death, Governor Chamberlain appointed the president of the society chairman of the commission. It was incumbent upon him to locate a pedestal at once as the request of the sculptor became urgent. The boulder was found just north of the Glenwood Avenue bridge in Waterford. It was shaped exactly for its location in the triangle with base and top flat, not requiring even a cut of the chisel, also a flat space on one side for the tablet. The funds for the pedestal were raised by public subscription, and the bronze tablet presented by Mr. Pratt was the work, it will be interesting to know, of his assistant, George Guest of New London.

While the journey at times was in high altitude, it must be borne in mind that at other periods it led through deep valleys, for it became necessary when renting the apartment in the Harris building for the president personally to solicit subscriptions to pay the rent. These were never refused, for such members as F. L. Palmer, B. A. Armstrong, Sebastian Lawrence, Frederic Bill and others came to the rescue. Of course this condition could not last indefinitely and emphasized the need of a permanent and more spacious home.

In January, 1907, learning that the owners of the Nathaniel Shaw property, Miss Jane R. Perkins and Miss Ellinor Shaw Griswold, wished to sell the property, including Perkins' Green, the board of directors authorized the president to secure an option, and a price of $33,000 was named. The president was completely surprised the following month to have Miss Cornelia W. Chapell hand him a subscription paper which she had drawn and headed with her pledge of $10,000. From his experience as president of Nathan Hale Branch, Sons of the American Revolution, in raising funds by public subscription (both in New London and throughout the state), your president realized the result would not be accomplished by small gifts. Knowing that Alfred Mitchell had been interested in the Shaw Mansion from boyhood, a letter was written to him at his winter home on the island of Jamaica. This brought the second subscription of $10,000.

Mrs. Richard H. Chapell sent for me and added $2,500 to the list. Since taking the presidency of the society, Sebastian Lawrence had been very helpful both with moral and financial support, and at one time went so far as to authorize me to make a bid of $10,000 for a house without grounds as a home for the society, but the offer was not accepted. Upon calling on him he asked me if I had seen the Palmer brothers, and when he was informed in the negative, said he would give $2,500 if they would give the same amount. Within a few minutes the subscription of $2,500 from the three Palmer brothers, Elisha, Frank and George, was made, bringing the total amount to $27,500. Then the subscription list was opened to the general public, with the result that at the expiration of the three months' option, the entire amount of $33,000 was raised. The subscription list in full is recorded in the *Records and Papers*, Vol. III. Part II., pages 330 to 333. It should be noted that the subscription of Walter Learned is $100.69, which is accounted for by the fact that a few days before the expiration of the option, when the sum of approximately $500 was needed, Mr. Learned volunteered to give the amount needed at the completion of the option, which proved to be $100.69.

After the acquirement of a home replete in historical associations and occupied by generations of the family who built it, our journey again descended from the hilltops and led through more valleys. The society met a great loss with the passing of a large coterie of influential members. It has been only with the strictest economy and thrift that the property has been kept up, the society has functioned, no indebtedness has been incurred, all bills have been paid, no obligations have been made without first knowing whence the money to meet them would come, yet the progress has been gradually forward and upward.

The early announcement that an endowment of $50,000

was needed was not lost sight of, and may I call your attention at this time to the fact that we own without encumbrance this property, including Perkins' Green, purchased in 1907 at a cost of $33,000. Furthermore, we expended $2,000 to make the house suitable for the occupancy of an institution before moving into it. In addition you will notice from the detailed report of the treasurer that our endowments together with certain allocated but unexpended funds amount to a total of $44,294.92.

This is the most historic homestead still extant which survived the burning of New London, and was ably described by our secretary, Miss Gorton, in her radio talk last April in behalf of the Connecticut Daughters of the American Revolution, which paper the society should print.

There were entertained here such notable men as General Washington, General Lafayette, Nathan Hale, Generals Greene, Huntington, North and Burbeck, Commodore Hopkins, Jonathan Trumbull and many others.

Nathaniel Shaw, Jr., commissioned by the Continental Congress as agent for continental prizes in the colony of Connecticut, used his home as a naval office for the colony, just as Governor Trumbull in Lebanon used his store for the war office. Miss Jane R. Perkins, whose family had occupied the house since 1756 when it was built to the time our society took possession in 1907, asked me some ten years before her decease to arrange for her funeral services to be held in her former home. She passed away in 1930 and her wishes were fulfilled. Later on it was made known by her attorney that she had bequeathed to the society the portraits by Ralph Earle and the other family portraits, the furniture including those pieces in the house when Washington spent the night there and certain valuable historical documents and letters, and made us the residuary legatee of a portion of her estate after the expiration of certain trusts. However, it will be necessary for the present to adhere to our plan of rigid economy if we wish to accomplish our objective.

In the past this county has sent out many sons and daughters, to all parts of our country. Soon after assuming office it was my observation that much interest was shown by them or their descendants in their ancestral New London County. This was noticed by numerous letters concerning genealogical matters, inquiries for the *Hempstead Diary* and other publications. It was realized that this demand for information should be supplied, and accordingly a publishing fund was endowed, the income only to be used. When the interest had sufficiently accumulated, $2,000 of the income was used for the publishing of *Life on a Whaler,* of which 250 copies were given gratis to our membership, 66 were sent to historical societies in exchange for other publications, and the balance placed on sale. The income from the sale of these books is added to the publishing fund, therefore making it to a small extent a revolving fund, so that at the present time there is $1,055.81, sufficient money to start immediately the next volume of *Collections.*

Considerable amounts have been expended recently upon the property, new plumbing and heating systems installed, the caretakers' apartment renovated, thus requiring little further expenditure in the near future. On account of the recent release of the entire income to us of the Fanny S. Wetmore bequest, we will be in a position to publish from our regular income, Volume III. Part III., *Records and Papers*, for there will be sufficient funds at our disposal by the time the book is completed. We are many years behind in the publishing of *Records and Papers,* and calls for these records are being made by our contemporary historical societies. Furthermore, there is sufficient money on hand in the binding fund to bring the binding of the newspapers and pamphlets up to date.

Our valuable reference library has been acquired through gifts and exchanges of our own publications. The time has now come, in my opinion, when we should expend yearly $100 for genealogical, historical, and important publications. Unless such action is taken and carried out, our library in the future will not so favorably compare with the libraries of other historical societies as it has in the past.

The Lewis D. Mason Library fund of $1,000 less the

inheritance tax, has now accumulated to the $1,000 mark, and the income from this fund should be supplemented yearly by approximately $50 making $100 available for purchasing books.

At the present time we are storing valuable manuscripts, papers and autograph letters in a bank vault, as a long hoped for fireproof vault has not been constructed in our home for lack of funds. There seems to be no way to obtain this necessary acquisition otherwise than by gift.

I am storing in the vault of the state library in Hartford a valuable film taken during the World War period in New London; also a film of the historical pageant produced on these grounds in August, 1924, upon the occasion of the centennial of General Lafayette's visit here; and a film of the Connecticut Society Sons of the American Revolution, taken at my home the same year; all of which I now give to the New London County Historical Society and will have them transferred as soon as the vault is built.

No attempt is made to give a complete history of the society for the past 31 years, but merely to touch upon some of its accomplishments. For example, in 1922 the society voted to offer its services to the city manager for the care of the Old Town Mill, under the direction of the city, provided an appropriation be made to finance the work. Only last Friday the press reported that 1,800 visitors registered in the mill during the past summer for the three days a week it was opened, and no doubt vast numbers of others viewed the historic spot without registering. The city authorities should be complimented, for, when the matter was called to their attention they took charge of the situation without assistance.

New England has recently discovered that its greatest assets during the recreational season for tourists are its historic landmarks. I should be pardoned for taking especial interest in the Old Town Mill because my ancestor, the first James Rogers, came from Milford in 1655 upon the request of Governor Winthrop to operate the mill, and his descendants have lived in New London and vicinity for 276 years.

It does not seem to be generally known that under the laws of Connecticut, the Governor is obliged to appoint the president of the New London County Historical Society a member of the Fort Griswold and Groton Monument Commission. Your president during all those years of membership has faithfully attended to the obligations imposed, both as secretary and as president of the commission. Naturally he took much interest in the preservation of Connecticut's chief battle-field, for he was born in sight of Fort Griswold and Groton Monument, and has always lived where he could view them daily.

The sesquicentennial of the Battle of Groton Heights and Burning of New London, occurring September 6 and 7, with the historical exercises Sunday afternoon, the reproduction of the battle Monday morning, and the large military, naval and float parade Monday afternoon, is fresh in your memory. The occasion culminated in the transfer of the deed of the fort from the United States of America to the State of Connecticut. Your president, who is also president of the Fort Griswold and Groton Monument Commission, and was general chairman of the Sesquicentennial Celebration, takes this occasion to thank all who in any way contributed to the success of the celebration.

It would be a delight to recall scores of names of those who have long since passed away, as well as those who remain and who have been helpful in many ways. The name of Frederic Bill should not be omitted, for he helped with his means in emergencies and always with his counsel. One day he walked into my office and laid down $3,000 in bonds as his contribution to the endowment. Permit me to say that most of the endowments were obtained upon my personal solicitation.

The second year after I assumed office Daniel L. Phillips of Jewett City read a paper on the Town of Griswold at the winter meeting in Norwich. Upon the completion of the reading the president expressed the hope that Mr. Phillips would prepare a history of Griswold. Recently Mr. Phillips completed his history and generously presented the entire edition to the society so that the society could receive the proceeds from the sale. Already the fund amounts to $821.29.

While material success is very necessary and important, yet there is a subtle and indefinable influence for success found in the personal equation. It is this human element and fine spirit of co-operation in altruistic endeavor on the part of officers and members that have brought slow but sure success.

Too much credit cannot be given to our secretary, Miss Elizabeth Gorton, who for 30 years has cheerfully, patiently and efficiently acted as secretary and custodian and performed the many detailed duties pertaining to the organization.

Furthermore, it would not be fair if I did not mention the assistance of Mrs. Rogers, who has unselfishly released me from many home duties so that I could perform public service.

The journey that to me apparently began as a prosy trip proved within a short time to have expanded into new fields of romance, accompanied with extraordinary and unexpected events along the pathway of new adventures. The opportunity to use one's imagination in promoting new projects has been most interesting. The pleasure and the experience gained have more than repaid the effort, and the contacts made with people of the county and the state interested in educational and historical affairs have been delightful.

May I right here allude to the remark of an aged official of a university who was present at one of the early meetings soon after I was elected to office. After being introduced, he looked surprised and said: "Mr. Rogers, I always assumed that the presidency of an historical society presupposed gray hair, and you haven't one."

The audience will now observe that his supposition has finally come true, whether occasioned by burdens of office or by the length of the journey, you may decide.

At last we have reached the highest hill in this particular journey and are looking over into the promised land, confident that those who succeed us with the foundations laid and the superstructure reared, with all the facilities placed at their disposal, will see that our fondest hopes are fulfilled.

Commemorative Tablet.

XIX

UNVEILING OF COMMEMORATIVE TABLET ON THE SHAW MANSION

THIS chapter was added after the entire volume was in type, on account of the important event of the unveiling of a bronze tablet on the Shaw Mansion, August 19, 1933, designating the building as the Naval Office. It was planned to have the unveiling on September 3, 1933, just one hundred and fifty years after the Treaty of Peace, September 3, 1783, the closing event of the Revolutionary War, and the last Sesquicentennial of that period to be observed. As the proposed date would fall on Sunday it was decided to celebrate the event on August 19 which was the most convenient date for all concerned.

The tablet was unveiled in the presence of a large assemblage of spectators including officers and members of the New London County Historical Society, officers of patriotic societies, officers and men from the United States Navy at the Submarine Base, and from the United States Coast Guard Training Station at Fort Trumbull. The United States Coast Guard Academy Band and a delegation of about 150 of the Connecticut Society Sons of the American Revolution from various towns in the state were also present.

The Shaw Mansion and grounds were open to the public and many people responded to the invitation to be present. The presence of many officers and men of the United States Navy and Coast Guard gave it a distinct naval flavor.

The program and addresses of Mrs. Minor and Mr. Rogers follow. Necessarily Mr. Rogers' historical address is composed chiefly of excerpts from the previous chapters.

PROGRAM

2:30 P. M. (Daylight Saving Time)

Presiding—Mrs. George Maynard Minor, *President New London County Historical Society, (Honorary President General National Society Daughters of the American Revolution.)*
America—United States Coast Guard Academy Band
Invocation—Rev. J. Romeyn Danforth (*Past Chaplain General National Society Sons of the American Revolution.*)
Greeting—Mayor Malcolm M. Scott
Presentation of Tablet—Ernest E. Rogers, *Chairman of Tablet Committee.* (*Past President General National Society Sons of the American Revolution.*)
Unveiling—Master Graham L. Platt, *Direct descendant of Captain Nathaniel Shaw, Sr.*
Music—United States Coast Guard Academy Band
Acceptance of Tablet—Mrs. Minor
Star Spangled Banner—United States Coast Guard Academy Band

Naval Platoon (36 men) from U. S. Submarine Base
  Lieutentant L. D. Follmer, U. S. N., *commanding*
United States Coast Guard Academy Band
  Bandmaster H. O. Jenks, *conducting*
Detail of Sailors (36 men) of the U. S. Coast Guard from Fort Trumbull
  Lieutenant R. M. Ross, U. S. C. G., *commanding*

Tablet Committee

Ernest E. Rogers, *Chairman*
George T. Brown
Mrs. Leander K. Shipman

The exercises will be held in front of the building.
The public is cordially invited to be present.

Presentation by Ernest E. Rogers

Madam President, Mayor Scott and Friends:

We are convened for an unusual occasion at this historic homestead in this ancient seaport, for, we are not assembled to commemorate a brave soldier, a daring sailor or a great statesman, but we are here to pay tribute to a merchant. Of all her native sons during that war period, it should be said that Nathaniel Shaw, Jr., was New London's most valuable contribution to the success of the American Revolution.

Shaw inherited and lived in this house known throughout all the years as the Shaw Mansion, which was built by his father, a sea captain and merchant. Paullin has written of him, "Shaw was the Continental Agent at New London, Connecticut. He was a wealthy and public spirited citizen, and was on intimate terms with Washington and other Revolutionary leaders."

May we now review briefly his career as citizen, merchant, patriot and Naval Agent.

As a CITIZEN, Shaw was friendly and neighborly. He was elected several times First Selectman of the Town, the highest political office; sent often as a representative to the General Assembly and helped unstintedly in advancing the social, business and religious life of the community.

In 1767 he purchased a fire engine in Philadelphia, had it brought to New London on one of his vessels, and presented it to the citizens. During the Revolutionary War the house in which the engine was stored was burned by Arnold's expedition but the engine previously hidden in the suburbs was returned unharmed. The volunteer fire company formed to operate it, is still in existence now known as the Niagara Engine Company.

Shaw was one of the proprietors of the Union school taught by Nathan Hale who was a frequent visitor here. Hale wrote to a young lady, inviting her to sit on the rocks at the Shaw residence to watch the sunset. Years afterwards, Hale's letter to the young lady sold for $975.00. The summer house built on the rocks soon after the Revolution, is open for inspection to-day.

As a MERCHANT, Shaw in his twenties upon the retirement of his father succeeded him and conducted his mercantile and shipping business under the name of Nathaniel Shaw, Jr., Merchant. Among the many merchants of New London he did more than any to develop the commerce in those early days. Under his able management the business rapidly grew and his ships sailed to the Mediterranean, European, and West Indian ports.

He belonged to the mercantilistic group of New England merchants who often did not conform to the Acts of the British Parliament and which nonconformity was an important factor in fostering the revolt of the colonies in the critical period of pre-Revolutionary days.

As a PATRIOT, Shaw was a member of the first Committee of Correspondence in 1774, being the only member to serve continuously during the war. He was an active member of the Sons of Freedom. Before the shot "heard round the world" was fired, his ship brought an extra supply of powder from the French islands in the West Indies, and tradition in the family says it was used at Bunker Hill. Washington, when on his way from Boston to New York, was his guest here on April 9 and 10, 1776; visited Forts Trumbull and Griswold then in the process of construction; and went on board the flagship *Alfred* of the Continental fleet then in the harbor. Commodore Hopkins had just returned from his expedition to Nassau, New Providence, Bahama Islands and was landing the captured prisoners and ordnance. Shaw corresponded with Washington throughout the war.

His wife, Lucretia, was the New London *heroine* of the war. She took into their home sick prisoners, nursed them and died of the malignant fever. Her name has been perpetuated by the Lucretia Shaw Chapter, Daughters of the American Revolution.

As NAVAL AGENT, Shaw was advised by Samuel Huntington, President of the Continental Congress, on May 4, 1776, as follows: "I had the pleasure of procuring you to be appointed Agent, being the most suitable person I could think of." He was appointed continental Naval Agent on April 23, 1776, by the Continental Congress.

The Colony of Connecticut appointed him Naval Agent on July 10, 1776, to represent the Colony.

The State of Connecticut on October 21, 1778, realizing there was no one in the state so capable in marine matters, appointed him "Marine Agent for this State to take the oversight and to give direction for the management and equipment of all armed ships or vessels, which are the property of and fitted out by this State when in port, to direct and order what cruises they shall go upon, to receive and dispose of the prizes that shall be taken by them."

In addition to his merchant vessels, Shaw owned and operated during the period of the war not less than ten privateers.

When Arnold burned the town, all the residences and mercantile establishments on Bank Street were burned except this Shaw Mansion, twice set on fire, and the house next south.

The Shaw Collection, composed of some 10,000 valuable letters, papers and account books, was given partly to Yale College and the balance to the New London County Historical Society by the late Jane R. Perkins.

The New London County Historical Society has published and will have ready for distribution in a few weeks a book titled "Connecticut's Naval Office at New London During the War of the American Revolution."

Now, in behalf of the Tablet Committee, I have the honor to report our work completed and the tablet, designating this Shaw Mansion as the Naval Office, will be unveiled by a direct descendant of Captain Nathaniel Shaw, Sr.

Acceptance by Mrs. Minor

Mr. Chairman:

In the name of the New London County Historical Society I accept this tablet, with great appreciation for the work of this committee and especially to you, Mr. Rogers, for your tireless efforts and co-operation in behalf of our organization.

To record in enduring bronze the names of those illustrious patriots, members of the Shaw family, who were reared and lived in this fine old historic mansion and also the names of Washington, Lafayette and other distinguished guests who are closely associated with its history, is a proud achievement for the New London County Historical Society.

It means much to our city and in fact to all Connecticut, to have a house like this preserved for all time.

Here are gathered many valuable records and papers, so arranged as to be available to the historian and genealogist; there are many pieces of rare old furniture, china, glass, portraits, implements of the old whaling industry of New London and many other interesting things.

In these times of unrest and change, when much that is fine and valuable is being ruthlessly set aside or forgotten, we are fortunate to have people who are interested and willing to support our Historical Society; whose appreciation of our history prompts them to collect and save for future generations these records and traditions of the past.

We welcome you to join with us on this day to honor the memory of those illustrious patriots and to rededicate ourselves in our efforts to preserve not only the tangible mementoes but to perpetuate the ideals which inspired their heroic service to God and Country.

XX

THE MERCANTILE LETTER BOOK

December 27, 1765 to July 23, 1783

THE Mercantile Letter Book of Nathaniel Shaw, Jr., after remaining in one family for one hundred and sixty-one years since the first letter was copied into it, was given, with other books and papers, to Yale College on September 6, 1926, as stated in the chapter "The Shaw Collection."

The book contains 233 pages of copies of important mercantile letters, nearly all in the handwriting of Nathaniel Shaw, Jr., but a few were written by Thomas Shaw. Nathaniel's last letter was written April 10, 1782, two days before his fatal accident. Copies of other letters were filed in "packets."

The New London County Historical Society has had the book reproduced by the photostatic process. The sheets will be bound and placed in its library for reference.

To Doct^r Moore New London Decem^r 27: 1765
on Long Island

    Sir Capt John Rogers of this Town called on me a few days Ago to let me know that he had Received a Line from you desiring him to let me know that you had in mind to Purchase Negro Prince, I have by this Opportunity Sent him the Price is Eighty pound York Currency if you Intend to have him I Should be glad you would Send me word by the first Opportunity. I am Sir your hum^l Servt. In behalf of the Concernd.

                                                    Nathl Shaw Junr.

To Mr Elias Desbroses New London Decem^r 27: 1765
Merch^t In New York

    Sir by the bearer Capt Peter Lattemore I should be glad you would Send me two p^s of blew half Thicks 1 p^s bearskin 1 C^t Goose Shott 1 C^t Duck Shott two Cask of powder 6 doz buck handle knives & Forks 1 bundle of Frying pans which Charge in Acc^{tt} to Sir Your hum^l Servt.

                                                    Nathl Shaw Junr.

To Mr Peter Vandevoort & Co.   New London December 27: 1765
Merch{ts} In New York

  Gentlemen I have shipt by the bearer Capt Peter Lattemore as pr the Inclosed bill of Lading Twelve hogsheads and Nine Terses of Molaſses which I would have you dispose of as Soon as they Come to hand as I Imagine that Article will not be much higher. I want a very Fine p{s} of Frise for Severall Gentlemen to make Coats of if you Can Find a p{s} of that kind please to Send it of a Cloth Col{d} also 40 wt of three thread wine and the Ballance in Bills of our Colony—I am Gentlemen Yours &c.

              Nathl Shaw Junr.

To Capt Nathan Moore   New London Decr 27th: 1765
Att Guadalupa

  Sir Since you left New London this is the third letter I have wrote you Just to let you know that Molaſses still keeps up very high att least 2/4 York Currencey and I Really beleive that it will not fall before May next and I think you had best purchase as soon as Poſsible so as to be able to be att home one of the first Veſsells in the Spring—their never was so Great a Demand for Sugars att this time. Comon Brown Suargrs Sell for £4 & £5 York Currency pr. Mrs Moore and all Friends are well and hope this may Find you so I am Yours &c.

              Nathl Shaw Junr

To Mr Wm Millir   New London Decemr 30th: 1765
att Boston

  Sir I have hear Inclosed you our Acco{tt} Current Ballance due in my Favour thirty two Pound Seventeen Shillings Lawfull Money which Please to pay Meſs{rs} Green & Boylstone and take their Rec{t}. I have also Inclosed your Note you Gave to Meſs{rs} Perry & Hayes which I have paid. Mr Stewart Desires you would Ship him pr the first Coaster for New London a Box which Came in the Last Ship from London Consign'd to Mr Werden to be forward{d} to him. I am Dr Wm—yours Affectiontly

              Nathl Shaw Junr.

To Meſs{rs} Jo{s} & Wm Packwood   New London January 20th 1766
att Martineco

  Gentlemen the Severity of the Season has been so extreeme Cold that it has been almost Impoſsible to do any kind of Labour which has been the Occaſsion of the Briggant{ns} being so long detaind, but I flatter my Self that we Shall Come to a better markitt then if we had Saild before.

I was Confined within doors for near a fortnight, after you left us Since that, I have been to New York where I disposed of my Molaſses so as to Neate two Shillings Currency and I Really beleive that it will not fall from that Price this next Sumer. Brown Sugars was never known to be in so great Demand as att Preſsent—Capt Seabury is arived from the Mount with a Cargoe of Molaſses which he purchased att Sixteen peaces of Eight p^r hogshead of 150 Gallons and very plenty, this I advise you of that you might Govern yourself in Regard to purchasing att Martineco Sugars where att 4½ and 5 p^r. I think if you Can make a Small Sloop a french Bottom so as to Send her down to the Bite of Logan if it is not attended with too much Expence it would turn to a very good Acco^{tt}. all these things I must leave to your discretion and hope that you will manage matters so as to make money by the Voyage—when I was att New York I caled on Mr Beache to know if he had any acco^{tt} of our Friend I. C. order being paid but he Aſsured me he had not Received a line from St Eustatia Since he wrote but promised to let me hear from him as Soon as the Order was paid or Returnd—Matters in Regard to our Friend seem to be much in the same way as when you left us their being no Courts to take any Notice of Affairs on Acco^{tt} of the Stamp Act which has put a Stop to all Buſsineſs—their being no Stamp papers in this Colony I have Run the Risque of Clearing out the Brigg *Lucretia* and Getting a Collecter to Insert att the Bottom of the Clearence that no Stamp paper is to be had so that In Case any of the men of warr Should Carry the Brigg into Port Capt Saltonstall must Imediately Apply to the ſtamp Maſter to have his papers Stampt which I think will be of Service to him. I have hear Inclosed you an Invoice of Cargoe also a Coppy of Captain Saltonstall's Orders and hope they will arive Safe and to a good Markett. I think I have putt on Board as Good a Cargoe of Cattle as was ever Shipt they being much Larger then Comon. I make no Doubt but they will turn out att least £25 p^r head and if you Can purchase Goods so as to Clear anything by them I am Sure we Shall do Something this Voyage.

Mrs Shaw Sends a Small Venture of a few Dolphin Cheases you must git her a N^t Umbraella. Mrs Packwood and all Friends are well and hope these may find you so. I beg you will write me by all Oppertunitys—the *Cygnett* man of Warr is Returnd to this Port I hope you will take a Special Care that nothing is put on Board the Brigg that will any ways danger the Veſsell by Seizure—you will I make no Doubt Dispatch the Brigg as Soon as Poſsible as I Imagine that the Sooner we git home the higher price Molaſses will fetch. I should be glad you would bring a hh^d or two of Coffee and Sugar as I want a trifle of Such things for Retailin. Now Gentlemen on the whole I leave all to your Prudent Management in Regard to the transacting this Voyage as you are on the Spot you must Certainly know better how to Manage Affairs then I Can Direct you so that I would have you do Every thing and take Every Step that you think for the Benefit of the Voyage as I would not have you Imagine that I would Confine you to any sett of Orders but do as you think best for my Intrest. Capt Waterman is Just now Come in from the Mount he tells me that Molaſses was very plenty their and was Certain that if you was to go down their with Cash you Could Load as fast as you Could take it in their being a great Number of Spanish Craft Imployed Continually in bringing up Molaſses from the Cape and I Really beleive if Molaſses is Scarse to Windward you had better go Down their—Capt Watterman tells me that he mett with a ſloop att ſea the Capt of which Inform'd him that all English Veſsells where Orderd away from Martineco and Guadalupe, if this Should be the Case I am Afraid we Shall make a poor hand of it and I think it would be best if so to Sell the Oxen att Dominique or St Christopher and then go to Leeward I Can add nothing further but hope you will be Able to gitt the Brigg in Either att Martineco or Guadalupe. I am Gentlemen yours Affection^{t}ly.

To Meſs^{rs} Joseph & Wm Packwood   Nathl Shaw Junr.
att Martineco

To Mr Peter Remsen   New London February 3: 1766
Merch^t In New York

    Sir I Received yours of ye 29th Ult^o. and have now to Inform you that Capt Rogers is Indebted to more People then I Imagind and he will not deliver up his Effects unleſs it be for the benefit of all his Creditors and him Self sett att Liberty which will be the Case as soon as he Can take the Benefit of an Act pas'd in this Colony for Insolvent Debtors, but if you will Send up the whole of your Demand against him I will have the whole of his Effects disposed of and see that you have your Proportional part without much Charge if you Agree to this, we Can have the matter Settled without much Expence. Other ways Rogers will take the steps of the Law, wich will be to have his Estate Sold att Vendue by Aſsigneas and ye N^t Procedes p^d to the Creditors who lay in their Claim. I should be glad you'l Send me an Answer p^r the Return of the Bearer—I am Sir Your hum^l Servt.

         Nathl Shaw Junr.

To Capt Hugh Ledlie   New London Febuary 5th: 1766
Merch^t att Windham

    Sir I have hear Inclosed you an Order on William Malcom for £50 York Currency drawn by George Kidd Payable att Ten days Sight wich I am Certain will meet with due honour, this being all I Can pay you att Preſent on Acco^{tt} of the Bond due to you from Mr Chew, Deſhon & ſelf for wich you Can give me a Receit when in Cash, this being the whole I have Received of Mr Mumford for that Purpose—Mr Chew is to ſett out for Windham tomorrow who will hand you this and Expect he will att least pay you on the Same Acco^{tt} £250—however you'l be so good as to Inform me by a Line the Sum he pays you on Acco^{tt} of our Bond—Capt Kidd will ſail in a day or two for New York and I think you had much better take a Paſsage with him then go by land. Y^{rs}

         N Shaw Junr.

To Mefs^rs Gregg Cunningham & Co. New London 12th Feb^ry 1766
Merchants in New York

  Gentlemen as Soon as Mr Peirce the drawer of the within bill arived att New London I desird him to pay the money with 20 p C^t. Damages wich he Refused to do and Produced a letter from his wife wherein he was much Supprized that the bill had not Come to hand, he has now given further directions which I have hear Inclosed, and as Mr Peirce is very sure the bill will meet with due honour I begg you'l send it Once more and In Case it is not paid have it Properly Protes^d that I might have my Remedy against the drawer or the Indorser untill that time he will not pay it.—Mr Peirse has drawn Severall bills with the same directs wich have always been paid and thinks it very hard that to pay 20 p C^t. damages when he is sure the person who you fent the bill to was att no pains to find out the person on whom it was drawn and thinks if he allows the Intrest from the time of drawing the bill to this day with Charge of Post^s if any you have no Occafsion to Complain.

                Nathl Shaw Junr.

P S the Lads who you Desir'd me
to Apprehend were Eloped before yours Came to hand

To Mr Peter Kettletafs   New London Febuary 19th 1766
Merch^t In New York

  Sir I Received yours by the Post & would have you Send me Ten Reals of yern by Capt Tinker who I Imagine is now in New York, if Capt Tinker is Saild for N L their is a Small Sloop hear wich is Just on Sailing for New York & shall send an order for them by that Conveyance. I am Sir Your hum^l Servt.

                Nathl Shaw Junr.

To Mr Peter Kettletafs   New London March 5th 1766
Merch^t In New York

  Sir—I should be glad you would get Nine hundred pounds York Currency Insurance on the Sloop *Roadney*, half on the Vefsell and half on the Cargoe From Martineco to Hispaniola and New London Joseph Packwood Mafter, the last advise I rec^d was ye 9th January last att Martineco where in he wrote me that he Expected to Sail the Next day for Hispaniola and should there dispose of his Cargoe and purchase Produce and Return to New London. I would have only Just a Comon Policy Against the danger of the Seas—I mention this as I do not Expect the Underwriters to Run any Risque of Seizures for want of any Nefsary papers and do not Expect to pay more then a Comon Premium the Insurance you'l have on Acco^{tt} of N Shaw Junr & Co. and I will send you the Premium Imediately. I am Sir Your hum^l Servt.

N Shaw Junr.

P S I wrote you for ye Yerns by Capt Bebee—N S

To Mefs^{rs} Joseph & Wm Packwood   New London March 6th 1766
Merch^{ts} In Martineco

    Gentlemen I Received your Favour p^r Capt Robeson Mumford and Agreable to your Request I have wrote to New York for Nine hundred pounds Insurance on the Sloop *Rodney* for your Acco^{tt}. I am Determined to Risque my Intrest on Board—I wrote you p^r Capt Dav^d Mumford that In Case you Could not purchase Molafses in Plenty to go to the Mount Since that, as by the Inclosed News Paper you will see that all the English Vefsells are Orderd away from the Mount so that you must Endavour to Load the Brigg with Molafses att Martineco—Capt Saltonstall's Wief is Recoverd of her Ilnefs very Suprizingly being now able to take the Air Abroad. I am Gentlemen Y^{rs} Affection^{tly}.

N Shaw Junr

To Mr William Millir   New London March 9th 1766
Merch^t In Boston

    D^r W^m I hear Inclose you pr Mr Leffingwell an Order on Andrew Oliver Esqr for Six pounds Lawfull Money drawn by David Latham which when Rec^d the Contents for C^r my Acco^{tt} & Charge 48/ which I Received from Duncan Stewart Esqr. I am D^r W^m yours &c

Nathl Shaw Junr.

To Mr Theopulas Morgan   New London March 12th 1766
Merch^t In Killingsworth

    Sir I Received a letter from Capt Joseph Packwood dated ye 9th January last wherin he wrote that he wast Just on Sailing in the Sloop *Rodney* for Hispaniola with a Cargoe of Fish and desird me to git fome Insurance made for his Acco^{tt} from Martineco to Hispaniola and New London which I wrote for last Post and if you Intend to make any you must write by this Post as I hourly Expect his Arival—I expect some Molafses in a short time if you then want Can Supply you I am Sir

Your hum^l Servt.

Nathl Shaw Junr.

To Mr John Spooner   New London March 13th 1766
Merch^t In Boston

     Sir we Received both your fav^{rs} by the Post and when the Reasons arive shall do the Best we Can in Disposing of them if you ship any for this Post to be forwarded to New York I can ship them att Nine pence pr Cash. We are Sir Your hum^l Serv^{ts}.

                                               Nathl & Thos Shaw

---

To Mr Peter Kettletaſs   New London March 19th 1766
Merch^t In New York

     Sir Yours 7th Ins^t Came to hand by Capt Havens with Fifteen Reals of Yern and the Iron this day which gave he great Joy for Really Imagine Bebee must have met with some Accident as I have not heard from him Since he left this—your Sending Five Reals more than desir'd will make no Difference and Shall Endavour to make Paym^t att the time—the Iron I will take to my own Accot^t have no Occasion for any Steel att Preſs^t—I wrote you ye 5th Ins^t for £900 Insurance on the Sloop *Rodney* Joseph Packwood Maſt^r from Martineco to Hispaniola and New London since that have not Rec^d any of your Fav^{rs} but Expect an Answer this Evening by the Western Poſt. I am Sir Your hum^l Servt.

                                               Nathl Shaw Junr.

To Mr Richard Alsop   New London March 26th 1766
Merch^t In Middletown

     Sir if you have not already shipt the pipe wine I wrote you for you'l send it by the Bearer—I have taken up the Bill on you in favour of Mr Stewart. I have hear Inclosed Tim^o Millir's N^t on Demand for £10 with Intrest dated 29th June 1765 which he Aſsur'd me Mrs Millir would pay on Sight which Please to Preſsent for paym^t and if you Receive the Contents C^r my Accot^t.—the Bearer has a few Casks of good Reasins to Dispose of if you want any you have them att 48/ pr Cask. I am Sir &c

                                               Nathl Shaw Junr.

To Meſs^{rs} Gregg Cuningham & Co.   New London 16th April 1766
Merch^{ts} In New York

     I Received yours of the 31st Ult^o. and shall ship your Salt for New York by the first Oppertunity if you think it best—however if you'l let me know ye lowest termes you will sell it att time of paym^t &c I will take the whole or part if Agreable.
     I have made Inquiry for Some Carpenders and find that I Can procure Four who are Active young Fellows that will go to Pensecola for a Dollar

pr day from ye time of their leaving N L to their Return unleſs they Choose to tarry there. Yesterday our Courts Sett and was Adjournd without doing any Buſineſs to June Next when I Expect they will go on as Usual. I find that our Friend Intends to Stand tryall and Mr Law Refuses to appear Against him, if you will have the Action go on you must Apply to some other Person I am Gent^lm Your Hum^l Servt

Nathl Shaw Junr

To Mr William Packwood   New London May 6th 1766
att St Pieres Martineco

    Sir I Received yours of the 2 of March last which gave me great Joy to hear of the Arivall of the *Lucretia* since that I have not Rec^d any of your Favours—your Brother Joseph is not Arived which gives me much Concern as I have not Rec^d any Acco^tt of him Since he left Martineco—I have Procured the Insurance you wrote for in New York att three & half p C^t.—Sugars are now much fal^n in Price by the great Quantity Ariving from St Croix and if you have more Casks than will Purchase a Load of Molaſses you had best Purchase Cotten as that Article is in great Dem^d. I begg you'l write by every Oppertunity. In Case your Brother Arives I will fitt him out with a Cargoe Imedit^ly. All Friends are well, I am Sir Y^rs

Nathl Shaw Junr.

To Mr Peter Vandevoort   New London May 13th 1766
Merch^t In New York

    Sir I have shipt by the bearer Capt Edward Tinker Eighty Casks of Molaſses which Please to dispose of for Cash. I shall want about £200 pr Cash Tinkers Return which must be in our Bills Silver or Gold and the Ballance shall give Orders for when you advise me of being Cash—if west India Rum is to be bo^t for 3/ or Under send me Four hh^ds that is Good and 12 C^t of ship bread in Bulk I have sent a Canister which fill with good Bohea Tea if Tinker should have Occasion for Ten or Twelve Pound you'l let him have it, if any Virginia or Connec. Corn att markitt and you Can have itt for ab^t 3/ or Under pr bushell Send a hundred bushells. I am Sir Your hum^l Servt.

Nathl Shaw Junr.

Mr Kettletaſs   New London May 13: 1766

    Sir I have Sent some Molaſses to Mr Peter Vandevoort and as Soon as he is in Cash for it I Shall Order you the Premium on Packwood. I Just now Rec^d a letter from Wm Packwood who is in a Briggant^n of mine att Martineco dated ye 12th day of April and he Expects to Sail in about Four days for the bite of Logan and take in a load for N L under French Colours—he writes me that he is Qulified the Vefsell in Such a Maner that he Imagines it will be attended with little or no Risque of any Seizure he has only ye Capt Mate boatswain two Coopers and a Boy of ye English People the Rest being French men and Expects to be att home the latter End of June next. I should be glad you would let me know by ye Return of Capt Tinker what Premium I must pay against all Risque, Seizures &c & what for a Comon Policy.

N. S.

To Meſs^rs Gregg Cuningham & Co.   New London June 4th 1766
Merchants In New York

    Gentlemen I Received yours of the 22 and 26th Ult^o. yours of the 21st April did not Come to hand, I will keep the Salt either att the Cash price or the C^r and as Soon as I Can have itt Measured will then Determine. I very well Remember the Promise Mr Chew made R W in Regard to Settling the Bond before it Came to Court—but in my Oppinion I Sincearly do beleive that if the bond had been only £50 that it would have been Impofsible for him to have paid it and In Case you Recover a Judgement of Court Against him I am so well Aquainted with his Affairs that I Afsure you I would not give you £5 for it. What Plan he Intends to Pursue I know not he Really seems to be in a very Distresed Situation. I am Gentlemen your hum^l Servt

N Shaw Junr.

To Mr Theophalict Beach   New London June 4th 1766
Merchant In New York

    I Received yours 26th Ult^o which is the only line I have Rec^d from you this Six M^o Past. I am Suppriz'd that I should Mis of your favour ye 12th March last as I have been att the Post Office every week and haveing no line from you Expected that Mr Chews Order was paid. I have Mentioned the Affair to Mr Chew and he Complains of some Mistake in your Acco^tt Current with him and proposes to have that Settled and will then give you Security for the Ballance he tells me that he will write you on the Subject by this Post, it being too late to bring an Action to this Court now sot that I beleive it will be best to let the Matter rest Untill the next Court which will be in November next when I will bring an Action Against the Person who has Indemnified Packwood which should have done this Court had I know Mr Chews Order was not paid I dare say you'l Settle any Mistake thats made in the Acco^tt.
P S deliver ye Inclosed.   N. Shaw Junr.

To Mr Peter Vandevoort   New London June 9th 1766
Merch^t In New York

    Sir I wrote you by Mr Sherebrook that I had drawn an Order on you in favour of John Hertell for Sixty pound. I have now by the bearer Abijah Bebee Shipt as pr the Inclosed bill of Lading Nineteen hogsheads and Four Terses of Molaſses which you will find to be very good and Six Chests of Ayl which you'l dispose of for Cash and Send me Ten Terses of Ship bread and as much Corn as the Sloop will Carry Either Virginia or this Cuntry (and two barrells of milk bread and a Box of Candles and the Ball. in our Bills or hard money, I want Bebee to Land his Cargoe without Entring and Return to New Lond^n and take another Cargoe of molaſses on Board & Return to New York with the Same Clearance if you think it may be done, wich I must leave to you) for I Cannot Clear out any more Molaſses att the Custom House haveing all Ready Cleard as much as have p^d the Dutys for, I think the Plan may do well Enough for theirs no Occasion for him to Clear out att N York or Enter hear as he will not take any thing on board but Cuntry Produce and being a Small Veſsell you'l take out the Ayl as Soon as he Arives. I am Sir

                                  Your hum^l Servt
                                  N Shaw Junr.

To Mr Peter Vandevoort   New London July 14th 1766
Merch^t In New York

    Mr Vandevoort Sir I have shipt you by the bearer Abijah Bebee Ten hogsheads and Five Terses of Molaſses wich is not Cleared in the Custom House and would have you do the best in Landing and Disposing of it and for this and the former Ballance Please to Send me the Cash. I am Sir yours

                                  Nathl Shaw Junr.

To Mr Peter Vandevoort   New London July 16th 1766
Merch^t In New York

    Sir I have by the bearer William Potter shipt you Fourteen Kases of Ayl wich Dispose of for Acco^tt of Your hum^l Servt.

                                  Nathl Shaw Junr.

To Mr Peter Vandevoort   New London July 18th 1766
Merch^t In New York

    Sir I have by the Bearer Capt Hancok shipped you as pr the Inclosed bill of Lading thirty Four Casks of Molaſses wich I have Clear'd att the Custom house att about sixty Gall^on they being very large Casks I would have you dispose of them before Hancok hauls into the Dock and then have them Carried off Imediately, as I Imagine if any of the Cust[o] House Officers should see them they would take notice of their being very large and Pofsible have them Gauged Again, wich I should not Choose to have done. Send me Six peices of paper that is Genteel to paper a Room & bordering for Ditto One box of Candles and the Cash for the Remainder I have some very Good Brandy in Keggs let me know what they will Sell for. I am Sir Your Hum[l] Serv[t].

                Nath[l] Shaw Jun[r].

Send a Kegg w[t] Lead Ground
in Ayl. N S

To M[rs] Ann Devisone   New London July 18th 1766
In New York

  I Received yours 16th Ult[o] Covering Amasa Jones two Bonds in your favour wich I will settle with him in the best manner I Can for your Intrest he lives about Twenty miles from this and as I wrote him of your Sending me the Bonds I Expect to see him very Soon and shall then Inform you what steps I Shall take. I have been looking out for Some Effects of y[e] Forseys to take hold of for your Acco[tt] but cant find anything. I am Informd by a Mafter of a Vefsell who arived hear a few days Agoe that their affairs were in a very bad Situation att S[t] Croix and that Tho[s] keeps all the Effects that y[e] sent him by his Brother and that he really beleived that their would not be anything shipt home that any Person Could take hold of for their Acco[tt] so that I Really know not how to advise you to Act. If they owed me that sum I would attach Ben. Imediately for I see no better Profpect. I am yours Refpectfully

                   N Shaw Jun[r].

if you would pursue this method you
will let me know it. N S

To M[r] Theophalict Beach   New London July 23–1766
Merch[t] In New York

  Sir I Received yours 8th Instant by M[r] Morgan Concerning M[r] Packwoods Protested bill wich you must Send me with a Power that I may git a writ Served on him before he goes to the west Indias wich will be in ab[o] Ten days. The Indemnifying Bond he has is payable in Sixty days after a Suit is Commenc'd against him wich he leaves in my hands to Sue to the next Court, In Case it is not paid before. I mentioned to him your Request that he would pay part of the money, but he Afsures me that but a very little part of it is the Intrest in his hands is his and that he Expects to have the whole settled Next Fall & that if you should Insist on Imediate paym[t] it must Infalibly Ruin him. Yrs

                      N S

To Mr Peter Vandevoort　　　　　　New London July 22: 1766
Mercht In New York

 Sir I wrote you ye 18th Inst by Capt Hancok by whom I shipt you thirty four Casks of Molaſses wich I hope will Arive Safe. I Received yours by Bebee with the Inclosed Accott and Cash for the Ballance wich was all Right. Please to Send me Four thousand feet of Jersey boards Suitable for Sheathing by the first Oppertunity.

 Please to Inquire of Mr Jno Alsop what Premium he would take to underwrite on a Small Sloop from St Croix with Rum Against all Risques, if he does not Choose to underwrite ask him what he Imagines it to be worth when the *Cygnet* lies in Port. Please to Deliver the Inclosed to Mr Beach. I am Sir yrs

              Nathl Shaw Junr.

Mr Theophalict Bache　　　　　　New London Augst 10:1766
Mercht In New York

 Sir, I Received yours by Mr Perritt of ye 29th Ulto Inclosing a power and Since that I have Received Packwoods Protested Bill by your Apprentice and should have had a writ Against Packwood but the Attorneys tell me that a writ must be in favour of Meſsrs Pennington & Son as they are the Persons that the bill is now in favour of, being the last who it is made payable too and on that Accott must know Pennington and Sons Christn Names wich you'l let me know by the first Oppertunity. I find by Mr Law that he Obtained a Judgement of Court Against Allyn Wilson & Shackmaple for the Amo of your Bond Against them and that Execution was Levyed on Shackmaples House for the Amount of the whole Debt wich Sattisfyed the Execution Bond &c. You have now sett of to you a part of Shackmaples House for the Sum of £704.3.6 debt & £4.1.4 Costs as Apprized by people Chosen by Each Party and I Really do beleive if it was now ſold it would not ſell for above £300 Lawfull Money. Mr Law has never taken Poſsesion of it and as Shackmaple is now in the West Indies their Can nothing be done in the Affair untill November Court next when I Imagine they will Quietly Reſign it up to you. I am very Certain that you will never be in Cash for Near the Amo of your Debt, your Execution should have been first Levyed on Willson's Estate and the Remainder on Shackmaple who would have been Oblig'd to pay the money, as his Estate was more then Sufficient to pay his Debts but now is too late. I am Sir, your huml Servt.

              N Shaw Junr.

To Meſsrs Lane & Booth　　　　　　New London August 12th 1766
Merchts In London

 I Received the Goods you shipt wich Came safe to hand and in Good Order. Since that I have not received any of your favours. I have now as pr the Inclosed bill of Lading, Shipt you by Capt Wm Billings in the Brigg *Betsey*, Four Casks and three bails of Cotten wool wich is the Growth of Martineco and is Esteem'd as good as any in the west Indias, and One Cask of Cocoa wich Dispose of for my Acco^{tt} and as Soon as you let me know the ballance I will Remitt it you. I am, Gentlemen, Your hum^l Servt.

Nathl Shaw Junr.

To Meis^{rs} Gregg Cuningham & Co.   New London August 13th 1766
Merchants In New York

Gentlemen, I Received yours 28th Ult^o Respecting the Salt, wich I will take att the Cash price and make the paym^t for it very Soon. Untill that you are in Cash shall Expect to allow the Intrest, I should have sent you the Quanity of bushels but the store being so full it is Inposible to measure it unleis it be removed to some other store, wich will Create an additional Expence of Cartage. I Expect to sell a Great part of it very Soon and will then measure the whole and send you the Acco^{tt}. I am, Gentlemen, Your Obed^t Hum^l Servt.

Nathl Shaw Junr.

To Mr John R. Myers   New London August 27th 1766
Merch^t In New York

Sir, I Received yours by the past 18th Ins^t and will take the yern att Sixty Five Shillings pr C^t. payable in three Months and the Intrest after that time. If you will send them att that price let me know it by the Return of the Post, as I intend to purchase some hemp wich I Can have made into Cordage so as to turn out Equal to yerns att that Price, but had rather give the Preference to an Old Friend. I am, Sir, Your very hum^l Servt.

N Shaw Junr.

To Mrs Ann Devisone
In New York

I Received yours 23 and 24th Ult^o and Agreable to your Directions have taken out a writ Against Forsey, wich has been Served on him and he has procured a Bondsman for his Appearance (with much Difficulty) to November Court next. Forsey exprest much Concern on your Acco^{tt} as that you must now Come in only for your proportion of his Estate, as he should be Oblig'd to give up the whole of his Intrest att Novem^r Next for the Benefit of his Creditors, and that if you had not served this writ he should if Poisible paid you ye whole as you had shewn him so much lenity. The writ was served on him Just att the time of Capt Packer's Ariving from ye West Indias, who saild from this in a New Brigg^{tn} of his wich is Sold with the Cargoe and the whole Effects is in his Br⁰ Thos hands and I beleive on the whole that you have the best Chance of Obtaining your money then any other of his Creditors, as their is a report hear of Ben. going to the west Indias to his Bro. if that should be the Case the Bondsman is then lyable. Since I wrote you 18th Ult⁰ Mr Jones has been in Town and tells me that it is not in his power to make you any paymt and beggs that you will not take any harsh steps with him for he intends in a very short time to be in New York and if Pofsible make you a paymt of part as their is no Court untill November. Can let it Rest untill then wich I think will be the best Plan. I am Yours &c.

N Shaw Junr.

To Mr Peter Vandevoort   New London Sepr 3: 1766
Mercht In New York

    Sir, I Received yours by the Post and find you have not disposed of the Molafses wich I beleive will be att two shillings in a short time & Untill you Can git it I beleive it best to let it lye on hand—however I leave it to your discretion Either to sell or keep it as you think best. I should be glad you will Send me by Capt Lattemore Ten Terses of Bread & Sixty wt of three thrid twine. I wrote John R. Myers for some Reals of holland yern by the last post, I should be glad you would Inquire of him if he Intends to send them. If not you must git me a Cable, 65 fathom Eleven Inches, as I shall want it for a Vefsell wich is Just on Sailing. When you are in Cash for ye Molafses, pay Peter Kettletas thirty pounds on my Accott. I am, Sir, Your huml Servt.

Nathl Shaw Junr.

To Mr Peter Kettletafs   New London Sepr 3: 1766
Mercht In New York

    Sir, please to Send me Four Ton of Iron by the Bearer Capt Lattemore. I have desird Mr Peter Vandevoort to pay you for the Ton you sent me last as Soon as he is in Cash for some Molafses I sent him. Yrs

N Shaw Junr.

To Mr John R. Myers   New London Sepr 3; 1766
Mercht In New York

    Sir, I wrote you by the last post.

To Mr John Spooner   New London Sepr 11th 1766
Merch^t In Boston

    Sir, We Received yours 1st Ins^t & should have wrote you by the Return of the Post but Mr Smith was out of Town. We have now Inclosed you ye Acco^{tt} Current that Mr Coffin rendered Mr Smith which he has Indors'd, and if you have Occasion for a Power of attorney will procure it for you, it will be Attended with some trouble as their must be the Colony Seal to itt. We Imagine if you have a power wrote on the Acco^{tt} it will be Equal'y as well—all you Can git from Smith will be this as he has given up his whole Effects for ye Benefitt of his Creditors.
  Yesterday We was looking on some sugars which were Imported in the same Vefsell as those shipt to you and find them much better then we Expected. We are Sir Your hum^l Serv^{ts}.

                                                                 N & T Shaw

---

                                       New London Sepr 20th 1766
Gentlemen

    I Received yours by the post and have now Inclosed you a Sett bills of exchange for thirty pounds Sterling drawn by John Connor on Mefs^{rs} Om Manney & Marsh, London for which C^r my Acco^{tt} for the exchange they sell for and advise me by the Return of the bearer that I may settle with ye drawer.
To Mefs^{rs} Gregg Cunningham & Co.   N Shaw Junr
  N York

To Mr Peter Kettletafs   New London Sepr 20th 1766
Merch^t In New York

    Sir, I Received the Iron you shipt by Lattemore and as I wanted it for ship use it is not so Suitable their being but very little Sq^r Iron. Please to Send me by the Bearer One Ton of Sq^r Iron and Charge in Acco^{tt} to Your hum^l Servt.

                                                                 N Shaw Junr.

To Mr Peter Vandevoort   New London Sepr 20th 1766
Merch^t In New York

    Sir, I Received yours by Capt Lattemore with the Goods you shipt, please to Send me by this Oppertunity two barrels of milk bread, two hundred weight of Loaf Sugar and Eight pound of Congo Tea. After paying Peter Kettletafs send the Ballance if Rec^d by Mr Way. If any Vefsell from Martineco be so Good as to Inquire for Capt Moore in a large Shoon^r from this. Y^{rs}

                                                                 N Shaw Junr.

To Mr John R. Myers　　　　　　New London 20th Sepr 1766
Mercht In New York

　　　I Received yours by Lattemore with the yerns which I Orderd to the Rope yard to make a Cable of 12 Inch and the Rope maker was Oblig'd to take the yerns part of Five Reals for onReeling of the yerns to about Middway. He found them Milldew'd sum more then the Others and so Rotten that they would not bare a 28c weight. It was Occasioned by the Spinners putting on so much size wich Contracted a Dampnefs, have not had much time to Examine them but will let you know how I find the Rest. If they had not Recd any Damage they are much Inferior to any I Ever Bot from you. I am Sr Yrs

　　　　　　　　　　　　　　　　　　　　　　　N Shaw Junr.

To Mr John R. Myers　　　　　　New London Octobr 15th 1766
Mercht In New York

　　　Sir, Inclosed is a Sett Bills of Exchange drawn by Thomas Slaid for £20 Sterg on Wm Slaid, also Joseph Irvings Bill on Henry Corts for £10 Sterg which Cr me in Accott for. I Just now by a Vefsell from Martineco am Inform'd that Capt Nathan Moore who was Cast away in a Veisell of mine has Since Purchased a Schooner for my Accott and Saild from their abo the 12th Ulto to go to Leeward to Load, I Suppose Either with Salt, att Turks Island, or Anguilla or to St Croix or Mount a Christi and from thence to N L. I have had no letter from him Since he purchased nor do I know the Name of the Vefsell, or Mafter, but Suppose that he is the Master. I should be glad you would git £400 Insurance made on the Vefsell from Martineco to N L wth Liberty to go to any Port or Ports and Load.

　　　I have a Briggtn which Sail'd from this Port the 4th Inst. for Martineco Were I Expect they will dispose of their Cargoe and Procede to Hispaniola and purchase a Cargoe and to Return to New London. I should be glad you would let me know what Premium I must give on this Vefsell. The Insurance on Moore must be made for Accott Nathl Shaw Junr & Co. I am Sr Your huml Servt.

　　　　　　　　　　　　　　　　　　　　　　　N Shaw Jr.

To Mefsrs Gregg Cuningham & Co.　　New London Octo. 15th 1766
Merchts In New York

　　　Gentlemen, I Received yours by Mr Way 23 Ulto. The price of Flaxseed will be I Imagine att about Five Shillings York Currency. If you want a Quantity I beleive Can purchase att that. Next Month our Court Setts when I Expect you will have a Judgemt Against Mr Chew, and I should be glad you would let me know if you Intend an Execution shall be Levied on him and he Comitted to Goal for I well know he has not any Estate whereon you Can Levy the Execution. I shall Expect an Answer by Hancoks Return. I am Gentlemn Your huml Servt.

　　　　　　　　　　　　　　　　　　　　　　　N. Shaw Junr.

To Mrs Ann Devisone　　　　　　　　New London Octo. 21st 1766
In New York

　　I shall this day withdraw the writ Against Forseys on your Acco^tt and have Given him a Bond that you shall not Arrest him Again in twelve months, for which have only a Bill of Sale of a house and Land about twenty Mile from this in the Town of Lebanon which Cost him Four hundred pound York Currency (and have Given him a Receit for that Sum on your Acco^tt.) I Sent a Man to Lebanon to See that the Land &c was Clear of any Incumbrance and find the Deed good and have put it on Record. It was given Forsey as Security for that Sum by a Person who is Expected from the West Indias very Soon when Forsey Aſsures me that the Money will be paid and the Land Redeem'd. As you left the whole Affair with me I Really Imagine that their was nothing better that Could be done for you. The Person who was Security for his Appearance was to Deliver him to the Sherriff ye Next day and he must been Comitted to Goal, and then he is to Deliver up the whole of the Estate that is in his hands, and my Real Opinion is that it is not in his power to pay more then One Shilling in the pound. He has now two Executions Against him which if Levied must Oblige him to go to Goal and deliver up his Effects for the Benefitt of all his Creditors and then you must Come in for the Remainder. Forsey begs you would keep it as a Secret his makeing you any paym^t as it would vex the Other Creditors.

　　Amasa Jones has been in Town since he Sent a Man to New York, and tells me that he is Determined to pay no Person One Shilling this twelve month, as he Suspects his Affairs are in a bad Situation and that this was the Advise of his Creditors in Generall—so that if you Comence a Suit Against him he must Deliver the whole up for to be Equaly Divided. He tells me that his Credit is Good (att home) and he Expects that In Case no one puts him to trouble that he shall pay the whole in a twelve month and that he is well Aſsured Unleſs you Arrest him no Person will. I beleive it will be as well to Lett the Matter Rest for the Charge in Distributing Aſsigneas &c is attended with so much Charge Coniving &c that very Seldom the Creditors git any thing. Mr Belding Aſsures me in a few days he will Settle his note. If he does not I shall not let it paſs this Court. I am

　　　　　　　　　　　　　　　　Your very hum^l Servt
　　　　　　　　　　　　　　　　Nathl Shaw Junr.

To Mr John R. Myers　　　　　　　New London Novr 8th 1766
Merch^t In New York

　　Inclosed is an Order for Sixty pound York Currency drawn by Geo. Kidd on Wm Malcom att Fifteen days Sight, also a Bill of Exch^a for twenty One pound Sterling drawn by Jno Sullivan ye 20^thOct^o att 30 days Sight on Richd Kee Esqr, London which Creditt me in Acco^tt for. Please to Send me by the Bearer Six Terses of Bread and Desire Mr Peter Kettletaſs to Send me two Ton of Iron and 2 C^t of Jarmin Steel. Please to git me One Thousand pound Insurance on the Brig *Lucretia*, Jo^s

Packwood Master from New London to Martineco & Hispaniola and back to N L with Liberty to go in to any Port during her Voyage, Untill she Returns to New London. Y^e Brigg Saild ye 4th Octo. and has not been heard of Since. My Orders were to try ye Marketts att Martineco and if they were low, to Procede to any Island that he Imagind he should better himself—and my Intention is to have that Sum Insured att Six p C^t. during the whole Voyage to her Return to N L and if they will not Underwrite for that I Choose not to have Insurance made. I Expect a Comon Policy without the Risque of Seizures. The Vefsell is as Good a One and as well fitted as any that Ever Saild from this Port.

N. S.

To Mr John Foster   New London Novr 21st 1766
Merch^t att South Hampton

Sir, I Received yours 18th Ins^t and the Plan you proposed in Regard to fitting out our Schooner does not sute me—if you will Charter her att One Dollar pr Ton pr Month I am Content and ye Owners to Risque her Against the Danger of the Seas for a Voyage to the west Indias and back Again, or if an Oppertunity presents to Sell her for the money she Costs us, if you send to Guadalupe Capt Hicks can advise with Capt Moore in Regard to Selling her their. If it does not sute you to Charter the Schooner on these termes, I will take her and Allow you att the Same Rate the Charty party to begin as Soon as I Can have her Ready to take on board and Should be glad you would Send her over directly, and In Case I have not an Oppertunity to Sell in the West Indias so as not to loofe money by her you may have her the next Summer on the same termes. Your Answer by the first Oppertunity will much Oblige

Your hum^l Servt
Nathl Shaw Junr.

To Mr Peter Vandevoort   New London Novr 26 1766
Merch^t In New York

Sir, I have Shipt by the Bearer Capt Peter Lattemore three hogsheads of Commune Sugars which dispose of for my Acco^tt and Send me One Ton of Iron half Sq^r and half Flatt barrs. Mr Ludlow I am Inform'd is Owner of the Warf and Store that Mefs^rs Forseys hired in this Town. They are now both of them left us and gone to the West Indias. I Should like to hire or Purchase, if the price is not too high, it is very Nefsary that some person should take Care of it as it is very much in want of Repairs on the Warf wich will Suffer very much this Winter Unlefs taken care of. If the Rent be not more then twenty or twenty Five pound Currency I would Rent it Untill I Come to New York. Your Inquiry will much Oblige

Your Hum^l Servt
N Shaw Junr.

To Mr Gabriel Ludlow   New London Decemr 10 1766
Merch{t} In New York

Sir, I Received yours under Cover from Mr Vandevoort and Agreable to your Request Apply'd to Mr Wm Coit (a Person Forsey left as his Attorney) for the Keys of your Store, but he would not deliver them. His answer was that when Forsey left him the Care of his Affairs, it was his Particular Order not to let any Person have the Store untill Mr James Depeister had Settled with you in Regard to the Store, as he says there was a bond given for it and some Hampshire money left in your hands, the Particulars of which he has wrote to Mr Depeister, and as Soon as you Settle with him Mr Coit will have no Objection to delivering up the Store to your Orders. I think the best method will be for you to Settle with Mr Depeister and let him by a line advise Mr Coit of itt and their will be no further Difficulty—for they are Determin'd to keep it (unlefs Mr Depeister advises them to Deliver it up) untill you Can Disposes them of it by a Course of Law which will be very tedious. I think if by Gentle means we Can git in Pofsesion it will be much the best—they seem to be Intirely Ignorant of the Contract between you and Mefs{rs} Forseys—shall be glad of a line by ye Return of ye Post and am Sir

Your hum{l} Servt
Nathl Shaw Junr.

To Capt Mackdugale   New London Decemr 20th 1766
In New York

Sir, I have made a little Estamation of the Charge attending ye Plan you proposed to me when in N L and In Case you pursue it I will give you all the Afsistance in my power, that is for the Charge of Landing, Storage and ReShipping Five p Cent on the N{t} Sales in New York and if you should find any part of it answer in this Markett I will Dispose of it for two and half pr C{t}. I have Converst with severall Gentlemen who are Importers of Rum from ye English Islands and I find it will be very Difficult to Obtain Certificates from them—but you may depend on my Shipping as much under that head as Pofsible, and for the Remainder I do not apprehend much Risque in Shipping it in Small Quantitys. I am Sir

Your very hum{l} Servt.
Nathl Shaw Junr.

To Mefs{rs} Gregg Cuningham & Co.   New London Decemr 20th 1766
Merch{ts} In New York

Gentlemen, I Received your Favours by the Post, but att Prefsent it is not Convenient for me to Comply with your Request, when I Purchased ye Salt I expected by allowing you the Intrest you would be Content to wait twelve Months or I should Certainly shipt it for I have not Sold One Quarter part of it. I will Endavour to send you the Ball. in the Spring. Your Law suit with Mr Chew came on this Court and his attorney's Plea was that the bond being given in this Colony for Seven pr Cent Intrest (which is Directly against the Law) Judgem^t should not go Against him— and it is the Opinion of every Attorney that In Case you stand a tryall it will Intirely kill the bond. On thatt Acco^{tt} the Attorney I Imploy'd has got the tryall put over to the next Court, and his Advise to you is to have the Action withdrawn before the Setting of the Court (as he is very Certain their is not the least Chance of Getting Judgement on the Bond) and then you Can find him or his Effects. I am Gent^l Your Hum^l Servt

Nathl Shaw Junr.

To Mr John R. Myers   New London Decem^r 20th 1766
Merch^t In New York

    Sir, I Received your Favour by Capt Kelly with the Bread, and Observe that it was a matter of Doubt, if Malcom would pay the Bill. Since that I have Rec^d no line from you and Imagine it is paid.

    The *Lucretia* is safe Arived att Martineco and has Saild on her Voyage to Leeward. I want about Ten Real Yerns and twenty bolts Rouſsia Duck, should be glad you would let me know what they may be bought for, and you'l Oblige Your hum^l Servt

Nathl Shaw Junr.

To Mr Peter Vandevoort   New London Decem^r 22 1766
Merch^t In New York

    Sir, I have shipt you by the Bearer Capt Edwd Tinker, Sixty three Casks of Molaſses and Twelve Casks of Sugar, which Dispose of for Cash. I have this day drawn on you in favour of Henry Van Vleck for £99.4 and would have you Send by Return of Capt Edwd Tinker £500 in Cash, two bar^{ls} Milk Bread, One bar^l Flour and 6 C^t w^t Flatt barr Iron 3½ Inch w^d. I am Sir

N Shaw Junr.

P S   let Capt Tinker have w^t Cash he has Occasion for.   N S

Capt Alexand^r McDougale   New London January 21st 1767
  In New York

    Sir, I Received yours 6th Instant and am Content to Aſsist you as far as in my power in your Plans Agreable to what you Propose for my trouble &c, but I aſsure you it will be Impoſsible to git any Certificates for Sugar, and In Case you have any Come this way it must be Reshipt for New York without any Clearence att all in Small Quantitys. I have Sloop wich will Sail for St Croix in about ten or Fourteen days, if you have any Comands. I am Sir Your hum^l Servt

Nathl Shaw Junr.

To Mr Gabriel Ludlow   New London January 21st 1767
Mercht In New York

Sir, I Received yours of ye 27th Ulto with a line Inclosed for Mr Wm Coit, wich I Deliverd him, on Receipt of wich he gave me the Pofsesion of your Store and wharf wich I have this day taken into my hands. The Store has been very much Abused by their putting a great weight in the upper loft wich is Sprung all the Summer. The warf very much in want of Repair. I Expected (when I wrote you first) to be in New York by this time, but I find it is now very Uncertain when I shall be their, should be glad if you'l let me know the Lowest Price, time of pay &c you will take for the Store and wharf as I shall want to make some Additions and Repairs to it if I Purchase. I am Sir Your huml Servt

N Shaw Junr.

To Mr John R. Myers   New London January 21st 1767
Mercht In New York

Sir, I Received yours by Capt Lattemore with the Cordage wich is Middg in regard to Goodnefs but not Equal to what we make in this Town and does not sute me so well as to have Yerns as I am Concern'd in a Rope work Cordage will turn out to me much Cheaper. I this day Received a Letter from Capt Joseph Packwood who is Safe arived att Monti Christi in ye Brigg *Lucretia*, and Informs me that he Saild from Martineco the 10th of November in Co with John Shackmaple in the Sloop *Nancy* and Wm Packwood in the Sloop *Dove*. I should be Glad you would git £1000 pound Insurance on the Sloop *Nancy* (½ on Vefsell & ½ on Cargoe) John Shackmaple Master from Martineco to Port Auprince & New London for Accott of Nathl Shaw Junr & Co—and £500 York Currency on the Sloop *Dove* & Cargoe, Wm Packwood Master from Martineco to Port A Prince and New London (½ on Vefsell & ½ on Cargoe) on Accott of Joseph & Wm Packwood. Capt Jos Packwood writes me that he had Fifteen days Pafsage to the Mount, and parted with the two Sloops in a hard Gale of wind, wich you'l let the Underwriters know of (but att ye Same time I would not give more then One Pr Ct. Extra for that for I do not Imagine that any Gale of wind att that time Could do them any Damage.) I would have both these Insurances made with Liberty to Unload att the mount and Return to ye Cape Francois or Port A Prince and Load again & then Return to New London, as I little Expect that the Sloop will bring there Cargoes up to the Mount, and Load the *Lucretia* and Return and take in a Load for New London, so that I would have the Insurance made from Martineco to Port Au Prince & New London att so much pr Ct. as you Shall Agree and In Case they Unload att the Mount & Return and take in Load and then Sail for New London then So much pr Ct. The Premium I will Desire Mr Peter Vandervoort to pay you as Soon as I know how much you pay. Your huml Servant

Nathl Shaw Junr.

To Mr John Barrett　　　　　　　　New London Febuary 4th 1767
Mercht In Boston

　　　Sir, we have Shipt you by the bearer Capt Wm Hancok, Ten hogsheads of Good Muscovado Sugars wich Please to Dispose of to the best Advantage for our Intrest and when in Cash Cr our Accott. We want by the Return of Capt Hancok Sixteen Bolts of Roufsia Duck, Five Bolts of English Do No 4 and Five bolts of Raven's Ditto & 50 wt of English sewing Twine for our own use wich must be good. We have some more Sugars on hand wich shall ship if we find the Price will do, we have paid Hancok ye Freight already. We have Inclosed the Tare of ye Casks wich were weigh'd before the Sugars were put in them. We are Sir Your huml Servts

　　　　　　　　　　　　　　　　　　　　　　N & T Shaw

To Mr Peter Vandevoort　　　　　　New London Febuary 5: 1767
Mercht In New York

　　　Sir, I Received yours by Capt Edward Tinker & Harris with ye Accott Sales and Cash all Right. The Ballance Send me by the Bearer Capt Peter Lattemore by whom I have shipt twenty hogsheads of Good Muscovado Sugars wich I would have you dispose of to the best Advantage Either for Cash or One, two or three months Creditt as you think best but for my Intrest (but take Care that you put them in good hands). I Could only Clear out Twelve Casks and have shipt the Other Eight as Flax Seed & would have you take Care to have them Carried off as Soon as they are landed. Send me three Ton of Iron & lett their be two Dozn of Shear moulds with itt. I have about twenty Casks more of Sugars which I Cannot Clear att ye Custo House. If you think they Can Come down with Safety I will fhip them; att foot you have ye No & Tare of ye Casks. I am Sir Your very huml Servt.

　　　　　　　　　　　　　　　　　　　　　　Nathl Shaw Junr.

To Mrs Ann Devisone　　　　　　　New London Febuary 10th 1767
In New York

　　　Inclosed is a letter I Received from Mr Jones by wich you'l see the Proposals he makes. I Advise you to Accept them. The land I am Certain will not sell for the money soon, but I beleive his Affairs are very bad—shall wait your Orders. I am Your Huml Servt

　　　　　　　　　　　　　　　　　　　　　　N Shaw Junr.

to Amo £673—Currency

To Mr Peter Vandevoort　　　　　　New London Febuary 13th 1767
Mercht In New York

　　　Sir, I have by the bearer Joseph Latham, shipt you Six hogsheads of good Muscovado Sugars wich dispose of to the best Advantage. I begg you'l take Care to have them landed in the most Secret manner for we have not Clear'd them att the Custom house.

Send me Six pounds Good Bohea Tea, three Keggs of white and One Kegg of Red lead ground in Oyl.

I want a Cushion made of blew Plush for a Cuntry Church, wich send by the first Oppertunity. I have hired Latham by the Voyage and if you have not Shipt the Iron I wrote for by Lattemore send it by Latham. Please to deliver the Inclosed to Mr Robinson. I am Sir Your hum^l Servt.

Nathl Shaw Junr.

To Mr Peter Vandevoort   New London March 7th 1767
Merch^t In New York

Sir, I wrote you ye 13th Ult^o by Jo^s Latham with Six Casks of Sugar. Since that I am not Rec^d any of your favours. I have now by Capt Bebee shipt you Ten Casks more of Sugars for wich I must have ye Cash by y^e in One month att farthest as they do not belong to me. The Cask markt R S must be sold Seperately. I have sent a Canister wich fill with good Bohea Tea, and if you are in Cash for any Sugars send it by Bebee. I am S^r Y^{rs} &c

Nathl Shaw Junr.

To Mr Thomas Wharton   New London April 8th 1767
Merch^t In Philadelphia

Sir, In Mr Goddard's paper N° 9 I see that their is a Fire Engine Advertiz'd for Sale by Daniel Ellis Esqr and I want one of that kind very much. Should be very much Oblig'd to you to Ingage it for me on the lowest Termes you Can (if it be a good One). In two or three days Capt Wm Harris will sail for your Place in a Small Sloop with Fifty or Sixty hogsheads of Molaſses wich shall ship to you for to Dispose of for my Acco^{tt} & would have you ship me ye Engine by his Return. Should be glad you'l write by the Return of the Post if I may depend on ye Engine on acco^{tt} that I must git one made in Boston if this should be Disposed of before ye letter comes to hand. Please to favour me with the Price Curr^t of West India Goods & you'l oblige Sr Your hum^l Servt.

Nathl Shaw Junr.

To Mr Thomas Wharton   New London April 12th 1767
Merch^t In Philadelphia

Sir, Inclosed is a Bill of Lading for Fifty One Casks of Molaſses by Capt Wm Harris for which have already paid him the Freight, and would have you dispose of it to the best Advantage for my Intrest. I shall want by the Return of Capt Harris the Engine, Fifty barrels of Flower, One Ton of hemp and Twenty barrels of Ship Bread and the Ballance in Cash. If I find that the Molaſses Answers your markett better then in N York I shall Frequently ship it to your Addreſs. The Comiſsⁿ they Charge me in N York is two & half pr Cᵗ. on Sales and 2½ pr Cᵗ. on Returns when they purchase Goods & no Comis. on Cash. I Expect you'l Charge yᵉ Same. Let me know yᵉ Price of Refind Iron. Yʳˢ

N Shaw Junʳ.

To Mʳ Peter Vandevoort   New London April 16ᵗʰ 1767
Merchᵗ In New York

    By the Bearer, Mʳ Power I have Shipt you two hogsheads and One Terse of Molaſses and Six hogsheads and three Terses of Molaſses Sugar wich I hope will sell for much more then Molaſses, as I think it must be vastly better for Either a Distiller or a Sugar house. I should be glad you'l Send me as much Cash as Convenient by the bearer for I Aſsure you am in great want. Mʳ Packwood is Arived from the Mount and is very uneasy on Accoᵗᵗ of the Insurance I mentioned to you not being made on Capᵗ Shackmaple as he was Concernd with me & is much Supriz'd that Capᵗ Jones who came in from Port A Prince should Report that the Sloop was Safe Arived, when Capᵗ Packwood Inform'd Jones every Particular of yᵉ Misfortune that had hapened to Shackmaple before he Saild. Packwood is Suspicious that the Insurance was made before Jones Arived & that on hearing the bad News, the Policy was Alterd, now as I am well Aquainted with Mʳ Myers & yᵉ Underwriters I am very sure that it is Impoſsible they should do a thing of yᵉ kind and should be glad you would Enquire of Jones what Report he had given of Shackmaple and when Jones Arived, for by the Accoᵗᵗ of yᵉ Insurance it was made yᵉ 2 of Febuary. I Imagine Jones must have arived yᵉ Latter End of January. Please to Send me Fifteen barrels of Lamp Oyl, one beaver hatt, two Large black barcelona handkercheifs & 8½ yᵈ bla. Callimenco. I am Sʳ Your humˡ Servᵗ

N Shaw Junʳ

To Mʳ John Foster   New London April 28ᵗʰ 1767
Merchᵗ att South Hampton

    Sir, I Received yours 27ᵗʰ Insᵗ and am Sorry to find that our Schooner is in so bad Order, but find that what you propose in Regard to the Schooner does not Sute me—when I Consented to Charter you my half last November for a Voyage I Expected to have the Same Priviledge of Chartering your half the next Voyage and att the Same Rate, which you have Agreed to by your letter of yᵉ 16ᵗʰ December. On that Expectation I have Pland a Voyage to Carolina and have a Load of Lumber lying their Ready as Soon as a Veſsell Arives to take it in. Your Son has Shewn me the Accoᵗᵗ of yᵉ Diſbursments in fitting out the Schooner which I have no Objection to. The Disbursements in the West Indias can say Nothing About as I can see no Accoᵗᵗ of them, but if you'l send me the Veſsell over hear I will have the whole Accoᵗᵗ Adjusted & pay you what Ever I am Deficent in—this I think no Reasonable person Can object Against.

You'l let me know by a line by the first Oppertunity what you are Determined to do for I want to have the Schooner on her Voyage as Soon as Pofsible. I am Sir Your very huml Servt

Nathl Shaw Junr.

To Mrs Ann Devisone   New London May 20th 1767
In New York

     I Received yours of ye 30th March and Since that I have made two Journeys to Colchester to Settle your Affair with Mr Jones, but to no Purpose, he Refuses to let the Land go att the Price he gave for it, and Insists that you give him what it was Appriz'd att two years Ago. I find that his title to the land is Disputable, and he Insists on a full Discharge from you, when he gives a Deed and will not on any termes give Security to pay the money any time—and as you left the whole matter to me I came home without doing anything, and I Expect he will take ye benefitt of the Insolvent Act. I made as much Inquiry about Mr Jones Affairs as I Pofsible could and their is many People who Imagine that his Plan of Shutting himself up is only to pay his Debts with his Real Estate att a great Price. I Afsure you their is such Villanous Procedings in all our Bankrupts that the Creditors Scarsely git anything. I am Your very huml Servt

Nathl Shaw Junr.

To Mr John R. Myers   New London May 20th 1767
Mercht In New York

     Sir, I Received yours of ye 2 of Febuary with an Accott of the Insurance being made on the Sloop *Nancy* and *Dove*, and was much Rejoiced that they had Safe Arived att Port A Prince and that you had Saved me two pr Ct. but you may Judge how much Suppriz'd I was in About three Weeks after when One of Shackmaples hands came home and Inform'd me that both Sloop and Cargoe was lost in going down to Port A Prince from Martineco, and what should Induce Capt Jones to Report such an Accott I Cannot Imagine, however I must Impute it to bad luck. The Sloop *Dove*, Wm Packwood Loaded att Port A Prince and Came up to the mount and put her Cargoe on Board of the Brigg *Lucretia* as I Expected and Returnd to Port A Prince and is Since come up to the Mount with the Second Load and Finding a good Markett Capt Wm Packwood is Disposed of his Cargoe and wrote me from the mount of the 17th of April that he Expected to fail from the Mount in About three days for Cape Francois, and should their load his Vefsell and fail for New London—and as he is now Departed from the Policy, I would have you make Five hundred and Fifty pounds Insurance, One half on ye Vefsell and One half on the Cargoe from the Mount to the Cape and to New London. I think for this Insurance it would be Reasonable for to give up the first Policy and to pay as much more as the Risque is from the mount to the Cape and back Again to the mount, as that is all that the Risque will be Increased. I Expected to have paid you the Premium before now but Mr Vandevoort sold some Sugars of mine on C^r to the first of Next Month when I shall Order him to pay itt. The Insurance must be made on Acco^{tt} of Jo^s & Wm Packwood.

I am Sir Your hum^l Servt
Nathl Shaw Junr.

To Mr John R. Myers   New London June 17th 1767
Merch^t In New York

    Sir, the foregoing is a letter I wrote you by the Post wich I saw put in the Mail my Self and am very much Suppriz'd that I have had no Answer from you. Capt Packwood Arived Safe in this Port Yesterday. Should be glad you'l let me know by the Return of the Post if the Insurance was made. I am Sir your hum^l Servt.

Nathl Shaw Junr.

To Mr Peter Vandevoort   New London June 26th 1767
Merch^t In New York

    Sir, I have by the Bearer Capt Nathl Coit shipt you thirty hogsheads of Rum markt S P wich I would have you dispose of. If you Cant have the Cash, give One Months Credit but let it be to a Punctual Person and then Should Rather have the Cash unlefs you Can get a Larger Price for it; the Rum seems to be very good and is high Proof. Pay when you are in Cash for the Sugars One hundred pound to John R. Myers and Ninety pound Six Shillings and three pence to Peter Kettletafs for my Acco^{tt}. Send 12 Loaves of Sugar, 10^c Tea and One bar^l Milk bread.

Please to Deliver the Inclosed to Mr Robinson as I have wrote him for some Goods wich must come by this Oppertunity. I Rec^d yours by Capt Lattemore with ye Cash.

Nathl Shaw Junr.

To Meifs^{rs} Thos & Isaac Wharton   New London July 1st 1767
Merch^{ts} In Philadelphia

    Gentlemen, I Received yours with ye Goods & Cash by Harris, Acco^{tt} Sales of ye Molafses &c, all wich I find to be right, and should have wrote you before but have been Endavoring to find what Pretentions your Collector had for obliging you to pay 1^d Ster^g pr Gallon on the Molafses after it had paid the duty in this Port, and am Inform'd by Persons who know as much about Acts of Parliment as Mr Swieft that it is not the Intention of the Act that Molaſses should pay the Duty more then Once, and I Should Imagine that when Mr Swieft finds (wich is Certainly Facts) that no Other Collect^r on the Continent takes the duty but himSelf he will Repay you the money back Again on that Acco^tt. I shall let the matter Rest a little longer, and if I Find that he Continues to keep the Duty, I shall Imploy an Attorney to git it from him att Common Law and make no Doubt but I shall be Able to Recover it. If Molaſses should take a Rise let me know it and if I should have any Arive will order it to you without Entring of it hear. Am much oblig'd to you for the Two Cheeses wich I find to be Excellent. The Ball. shall let Rest in your hands till I know Mr Collect^rs Determination. I am Gentlemen, Your hum^l Servt.

Nathl Shaw Junr.

To Mr Samuel Cornell   New London July 1st 1767
Merch^t In Newbern N^o Carolina

    Sir, this will be handed you by Capt Samuel Hern in the Sloop *Dove*, who we have sent to your Addreſs to git the Effects of the Molaſses left in your hands in June 1765 and beg you'l put on board of the Said Sloop the Staves our J. P. left Directions for if they are not Disposed of and One hundred barrels of Tarr and One hundred and Twenty barrels of Turpentine with such other kind of Lumber as Capt Hern thinks best and Dispatch him as Soon as poſsible, as he is to Meet Capt Packwood in the West Indias. The Voyage wholly depends on Dispatch. Capt Hern has the Bill Lading and Acco^tt of the Molaſses wich he will furnish you with, and if we find the Voyage turn out to any Advantage shall send the ſloop back Again. Should be glad you'l forward the Acco^tt Curr^t and if a Ballance due to us a Bill pay. in New York would be very Acceptable. We are Sr Your hum^l Serv^ts

Jo^s Packwood & Co.

To Mr Peter Vandevoort   New London September 24th 1767
Merch^t New York

    Dear Sir, I have by the bearer Capt Tinker Shipt you ninety four hogsheads and six terses of Molaſses, which is as good as any imported, and hope you'l dispose of it for a good price. I shall want Cash soon and shall draw on you for it. Take up the Bill of Sulivans which John Myers has, and send it me by the first opportunity. Please to send me five bolts of Ruſsia and two bolts of Raven Duck, and one bolt of Ticklingburge and one Cask of 20^d Nails, and sixteen yards of black Padusoy, and 4 gro. Corks. Send me the Acco^t of Sales as soon as convenient. I Received yours with the Acco^t Cur^t and find a mistake of £10 in P^r of your former Ballance. am S^r   Your hum^l Servt

N Shaw Junr.

196   CONNECTICUT'S NAVAL OFFICE AT NEW LONDON

To Mr Joshua Elderkin   New London Septem^r 25th 1767
Merch^t In Windham

    Sir, I shall want in about three weeks From you, Twelve Neat good shipping Cattle & two horſes that are young and Fatt and three hundred bushels of Corn in Ears and Four Thouſand good hoops and Fifty or Sixty Shotes from 40 to 1 C^t w^t and if you Can let me have Ten barrels of beaf att 36/ pr bar^l I will take it. The Oxen I Expect to have att 16/8 pr C^t which is the price I am to have 30 head att Apprized by Capt Champion. The hoops I would have you send as soon as Poſsible as I want to ship them directly, I beg you'l see that they are good, and let me know the time when it will sute you to Cart the Corn and I will have a Small Sloop Ready att the Landing to take it in. The Stock I will let you know the time when to bring them in. I have now a Cargoe Just Arived of Good Muscovado Sugar & Molaſses and a few Casks of Clarrett wine if you should want can Supply you. I am Sir Yours &c

                                                                            Nathl Shaw Junr.

To Mr John R. Myers   New London Octo 21st. 1767
Merch^t In New York

    Sir, I should be glad you would git me One Thousand pound York money Insurance on ye Brigg^{tn} *Lucretias* Cargoe, Samuel Hern Master from Mount a Christ. to New London. My last Acco^{tt} from them was ye 17th Ulto wherein Jo^s Packwood ye Person who ye Brigg was Consign'd to writes me that she was to Sail in Fifteen days from that date. I will not give more then three p Cent, and Nine hundred pounds on the Sloop *Dove* and Cargoe, John Degine Master from ye Mount to Port A Prince and New London with Liberty to touch in att ye Mount. When you let me know what Premium you pay will Remitt it you. I am Sir Yours &c

                                                                            N Shaw Junr.

To Meſs^{rs} John Barrett & Son   New London Nov: 27. 1767
Merchents in Boston

    Gentlemen, I have by the bearer Capt Jeſse Harlow Shipt you as by the Inclosed Bill of Lading three hogsheads of Melaſses and Seven hogsheads of Sugar which are different in their quality, and would have you dispose of them and Credett our Acco^t with the neat proceeds. Should be glad when you render us an Acco^t of sails, you will take notice of the markes of the ſugar (as they are Owned by Several Perſons). We wrote you some time agoe and Inclosed you a Bill of Exchange for £50 Ster^g and an order of Char^s Chadwick on you. But have Rec^d no answere Since, should be glad you would let us know what the bill Sold for, that we might Charge it in Acco^t. We intend to pay you the ballance as soon as we can, and are Gentlemen Your very hum^l Serv^{ts}.

Nathl & T Shaw

1 hhd of the best Brown Sugar				IP
2 d^o	.	d^o . d^o	.	WP
2 d^o Comon	d^o . d^o	.		BL
1 d^o d^o .	.	. d^o	.	INPL
1 d^o Infearer	.	. d^o	.	SD
3 d^o Melaſses	.	. .	.	BL

To Meſs^{rs} Green & Boylston   New London Nov: 27, 1767
Merchests in Boston

  Gentlemen, We have by the bearer Capt Jeſse Harlow shipt you as by the Inclosed bill of Lading Twenty hhd^s of Melaſses which is very good, and would have you dispose of it to the best Advantage and Credet our Acco^t with the Neat Proceeds, and the ballance we Intend to pay you as Soon as we Can, and are Gentlemen Your very hum^l Serv^{ts}

Nathl & Thos Shaw

To Mr James Richardson   New London Decem^r 7th 1767

  Sir, the bearer Mr Thompson I have sent on purpose for Twelve Young horſes which I want to ſhip Imediately, I beg you'l let him have them and Expect you'l Charge them as we Agreed when you was att New London. They must be from Six to Eight pound price and shall depend on your Honour In Regard to their Price, and as I find them turn out will depend on my haveing further Dealings with you in this way. The other Eighteen I shall want in About a Month and would have you purchase Ten Mill horſes that are large and well ſett about Ten pounds Vallue and Six Saddle horſes about Fourteen Pounds or Fifteen pounds price and Two very Neat horſes not Exceding Twenty pounds Each and when I want them will Send you word. I am Sir Yours &c

N S

To Mr James Richardson   New London December 29th, 1767
att Leomenister

  Sir, I Received yours 11th Ins^t by Mr Thompson with the horſes which Came safe to hand, Excepting two of Them which had the Distemper which Effects the horſes by Swellings in the throat and Runing att the

Nostrills. I shall want the Other horses Viz: Eighteen, they must be hear without fail the 20th day of next Month. I beg you'l not fail of bringing them by the time and take Care that they have not the distemper. Their is no Person in this Town that I Can Recomend, that wants horses att Present. I am Sir Your very huml Servt

                  N Shaw Junr.

To Mr Peter Vandevoort   New London January 16th 1768

  Sir, I Received yours by Capt Peirse and Harris, and would have you pay John R. Myers One hundred pounds and take his Receit for it on my Accott. I shall want One hundred pounds more left in your hands, the Remainder should be glad you will send by the bearer Capt Wm Billings and want it Cheifly in hard money. I am Sir Your huml Servt

                  Nathl Shaw Junr.

To the Revd Marther Byles Junr   New London, May the 11, 1768
In Boston.

  Dear Sir, I Just now received advice of our friend Sullivan's going to London; and on that Account have Inclosed you his Note-hand for One hundred pounds, Seven Shillings, Sterling, with Interest from ye tenth October last. Which I should be glad you would take with you to London; and if you see him oblige him to pay it. His agent was Richard Kee Esqr at Savage Garden Tower Hill, where I imagine you may know if he be in London, or not. If he is not arrived, I would have you leave the Note with Mefsrs Lane, Son, & Frasier, Merchants in London, and desire them to keep a good look-out for him, when he returns, and arrest him, if he does not immediately pay the money; and advise me when in Cash. In case you git ye money from him, I would have you leave it with those gentlemen, and take their receipt for it: after deducting for your trouble.

  I am sorry to give you this trouble, but as you are so well acquainted with the affair between Sullivan and me, I imagine if you see him he cant have the afsurance to deny paying me.

  I realy wish you prosperity in your voyage; and shall rejoice to see you once more settled with your family, to your sattisfaction; and am, dear Sir, Your Affectionate Friend, & very humble Servent.

                  Nathl Shaw Junr.

Copy of the Note.
            New London October 10th 1767.

  I promise for Vallue Received to pay Nathaniel Shaw Junr of New London the sum of One hundred pounds Seven shillings Sterling in Six Months from this Date, with the Lawfull Interest untill paid, as witnefs my hand.

                  John Sullivan.

To Messrs John Barrett & sons   New London, June 2, 1768
Merchts In Boston

Gentlemen, Yesterday Capt Clay Arived hear from the Granades and Tells me that on his Passage he Spoke with Capt Jed Waterman who was bound to Boston and he Informd him that he Saild in Co with Capt Nathl Saltonstall in the Brigg *Nancy* from Cape Nuhola Mould for Boston, which Brigg I orderd into Boston and as Soon as she Arives I Intend to settle that Ballance with you—and that you Should not be Disapointed in Receiveing your Debt I would have you make One Thousand pound Insurance on the Brig *Nancys* Cargoe, Nathl Saltonstall Master from the Mould to Boston on my accott. I have hear Inclosed you a line for Capt Saltonstall and Desir'd him to Deliver you One hundred hogsheads of Molasses and I would have you Dispose of it to the best Advantage you Can. If the Markett should be low and any Prospect of doing better with it by Storing, I would have you do it if you think it best, all which I must leave to your Discretion & am Gentlemn Yours &c

N Shaw Junr.

To Messrs John Barrett & Sons   New London June 3, 1768
Merchts In Boston

Gentlemen, This Moment Brigg *Nancy*, Nathl Saltonstall Master, Arived hear from the Mould haveing had Contrary winds, & falling into the Westward, and I now send an Express to Overtake the Post to Prevent the Insurance being made and make no Doubt but he will be able to do it. Shall Endavour to pay your Ballance also One hundred pound on Accott of Silas Church in a few days, & am Yrs &c

N Shaw Junr.

To Messrs Thomas & Isaac Wharton   New London June 3, 1768
Merchts In Philadelphia

Gentlemen, This will be handed to you by Capt Stephen Clay in the Brigg *Thames* who has on Board Two hundred and Fifty Five Casks of Molasses which I would have you dispose of on as Good Termes as you Can, and let the Brigg Return as Soon as Possible. In Regard to the Dutys, I hope you'l settle with ye Custo House on as Good Termes as you Can. I shall want fifteen hundred bushels of Coarse Salt or more if the Capt Imagines it will not be Enough for Ballast if to be bought att or Near Eighteen Pence pr bushell—and shall want the Ballance in Cash, and should be glad you would Send what you Can Collect by ye Return of Capt Clay. If I find the price of Molasses Continues as it was when you wrote me last, shall Send Capt Harris with a Load. Capt Packwood who Came home in the Brigg is a very Sick Man, on that Accott have given Capt Clay the Comd of the Brigg and Suppose it Can make no Difference with the Cust⁰ House on Acc^ott of Entring ye Vefsell. Att foot you have the Marks and Numbers of ye Casks which you'l note in your Acc^ott Sales. I wish the *Thames* safe in Your River & am Your hum^l Servt.

Nathl Shaw Junr.

207 hh^ds N° 1 to 207. BT
28 Terses   1 to 28. BT
5 barrels - 1 to 5 B T   Terses Poor Molafses
14 hh^ds - - 1 to 14 W P

To Mefs^rs Thomas & Isaac Wharton   New London June 8, 1768
Merch^ts In Philadelphia

    Gentlemen, This by Capt Wm Harris in the floop *Bridgett* with feventy Six Casks of Molafses on Board Marks BI and IP, the Particular marks would have you take Notice of in the Gaugeing. I Expect to pay the Am⁰ of this Cargoe in N. York and when you are in Cash shall draw on you for itt. I would Rather have it ftored then fell it for lefs then One Shilling and Nine Pence pr Gallon. I little Expect Harris will in his way home git a Load of Shingles & if he is Determined to do it lett him have as much Cash as he Imagines will do for it or if he wants any more let him have itt & you'l Oblige Gentlemen, Your hum^l Servt

Nathl Shaw Junr.

To Capt William Harris   New Lond^n June 8, 1768
    Prefsent

    Sir, I have wrote Mefs^rs Thomas & Isaac Wharton that you have feventy Six Casks of Molafses on Board, so that you may dispose of the two Casks you have of Mrs Shaws and make Use of the Money on Acc^ott of the freight and I hope that will be all you'l have Occasion for their, & the Remainder will Settle with you for when you Return. If you Can git a Load of Shingles for Twelve Shillings or Under deliverd hear Clar of all Charge I would have you do it.

N Shaw Junr

Git 4 Sides Sole Leather & 4 Calf skins.   N. S.

To Capt Stephen Clay   New London June 8, 1768
on Board Brigg *Thames*

    Sir, if you Can find any bords of the Same Kind as you Carried in the Schooner last Voyage to the west Indias and git them att About 55/ pr in. desire Mefs^rs Wharton to Send Twenty Thousand. If they were a little wider then those you Carried I think it would be much better. All friends are well & am S^r Y^rs &c

Nathl Shaw Junr

To Meſs[rs] Thomas & Isaac Wharton   New London June 8, 1768
In Philadelphia

    Gentlemen, I wrote you last Post and Since that the Brigg *Thames* Saild for Phil[a] y[e] 3 Instant and as the wind has been Favourable I hope she is safe Arived, and this day the ſloop *Bridgett*, W[m] Harris Master with Seventy Six Casks of Molaſses Saild for Philadelphia to your Addreſs. For Particulars Refer you to my letter of y[e] date by Harris. I would have you to Send me three p[s] Irish Linin & three p[s] fine Cheque and three p[s] of Coarse Ditto more then what I wrote you for by Clay. Let the Irish Linin be from 4/ to 5/ pr yard. One Ton & a half of hemp and a Ton of Iron, send them in the Brigg, and I hope you'l Send her Away as soon as Poſsible. Inclosed is a Letter for Cap[t] Clay wherein I have Desir'd him to take in 20 in. bords In Case he finds any that will Answer. I begg you'l let me know the ſtate of your Marketts by Every Post. I am S[r] Y[rs] &c

                                                               N. S.

Send me 6 Glaſester Cheeses.

To M[r] Peter Vandevoort   New London June 10th 1768
Merch[t] In New York

    Sir, I have shipt by the bearer Cap[t] Edward Tinker Ab[o] Eighty Casks of Molaſses, the Particular Number am not Certain of and should be glad you will Dispose of the whole and take a Particular Acco[tt] of y[e] marks and Numbers. You may sell it for Cash or on a Short time of Paym[t] as you think best. I beleive you'l find it much better then what I Shipt you last and hope you'l be Able to get a better Price for it. I shall want the Greatest part of Y[e] Money hear, and our Bills will ſute me as well as any, and as they Cannot Change them att Hartford, I Imagine its Probable you might be Able to Dispose of y[e] Molaſses on Better Termes by takeing it in our Bills. Should be glad you'l send me by Tinker what you Can Conveniently Collect, let Tinker have what Cash he wants in N. Y. I am Sir

                                      Your hum[l] Serv[t]
                                      Nath[l] Shaw Jun[r].

To M[r] Peter Vandevoort   New London August 5th 1768
Merch[t] In New York

    Sir: I have shipt you by the barer Cap[t] Edward Tinker Ninety Two hogsheads of Molaſses, BL and One hogshead of Molaſses Sugar markt IP which dispose of for my Acco[tt]. I have drawn an Order on you this day in favour of Theopulas Morgan for five hundred pounds, which I Imagine will be Presented you for paym[t] in Ab[o] a Month from this and

I hope by that time you will be in Cash for the Molaſses. I have Inclosed you a Memo to pay Sundry Persons for Accott John Hertell & Patrick Robertson to the Amo of £232.14.1 when in Cash & Send me their Receits. Send me Ten Terses Ship Bread. Yrs

N Shaw Junr.

To Mr Peter Vandevoort   New London Septemr 6th 1768
Mercht In New York

    Sir, I have hear Inclosed you a Mortgage deed from Singleton Church to Wm Cobham & Indorsed over to Major John Mannsell who desir'd Mrs Devisone to dispose of it when she was in New London & I Agreed with Mrs Devisone to her One hundred pounds York Currency for a Quit Claim to the Estate which must be made on the back of the Mortgage Deed in the words following Viz: Know all men by these Preſsents that I John Mannsell Lieutt Coln being the Person to whom the within mentioned Mortgage is Aſsign'd over by the within Mentioned Cobham in Consideration of the Sum of One hundred pounds York money Received to my full Satisfaction of Nathaniel Shaw Junr of New London in the County of New Londn do therefore hereby for my self, my heirs & Aſsign set over Remise & forEver Quit Claim unto him the Said Nathl Shaw Junr his heirs & Aſsigns forEver all ye Right title Intrest & Estate whatsoever wich accreus to me by Virtue of the within Mortgage & Aſsignment as Wittneſs my hand & Seal. Sign'd Seald & Delivered in Preſsence of ——————— and must be Acknowledg'd. Should be glad you would git it Executed and pay the One hundred pound first Deducting Mr Laws Charges for this and some other matters of Coln Mannsells which he Charges 69/4 Currency for. If I Should not have any Molaſses Arive in a day or two I will git an Order from Capt Mumford for the Money. Send me by the barer one Cask of 10d and One Cask 20d Nails, also the Skreen if its finished. Yrs

N Shaw Junr.

To Mr John Dies   New London Sepr 8, 1768
Mercht In New York

    Sir, Inclosed is a letter I Recd from Norwich Concerning your debt with Mr Beckus, its beleived that his Estate will be Insolvt and if you would have me take the Navall Stores for your Accott att the Price Mentioned by Mr Perkins, let me know it by the Return of the Post. I Really beleive you had better take them, for he Certainly cannot Continue very long and then when he dies it will be a long time before its Settled.

MB Tarr 8/6 ⎫ pr barrell   Yrs
Pitch   13/ ⎭   N Shaw

To Mefs^rs Thomas & Isaac Wharton   New London Novem^r 23, 1768
Merchants In Philadelphia

 Gentlemen, I Received yours 28th Ult^o with Thos Barlow Junr Order on John Hertell for 160 doll^rs wich have given Credit for in your Acco^tt. Am Much Disapointed in the price of Molafses, I Really Expected it would have been higher. HowEver I think it best to finish the fale of it and dispose of it for the most it will fetch as their is Severall Concernd in it & we want to Close the Acco^tt and Remitt the Ballance when in Cash to Mr Peter Vandervoort, Merch^t In New York if you can git a Bill payable in New York. If you Cannot git a Bill, let Mr Vandervoort know the am^o of what is in your hand & desire him to draw on you for it.

To Mr Peter Vandervoort   New London Decem^r 28, 1768
Merch^t In New York

 Dear Sir, I Should be glad you would git Three Thousand pound Insurance on the Brigg *Thames*, Joseph Packwood Mafter (The Insurance must be made Two thousand pound on the Cargoe and One Thousand Pound on the Vefsell) from the Cape on my Acco^tt to New London. The last News I had from him was by his Letter of ye 11th Novr last from Cape Nuholafs mould, that he had come down their from the Cape in a Boat and was going to Port A Prince to Settle Acco^tt with a French Capt who was in a floop of mine and would not deliver her up Untill Packwood Came down their—that he was Unwell and should take Physick the Next Day and after that he Intended to Procede on his Bufinefs to Port A Prince—his Brigg att the Cape was Loaded already and waited only for his Return which he Imagind would be the last of November. In Case of any Accident to Packwood, John Daly will come home Master of the Brigg. You may let the Underwriters know that their is as Good a Crew and Vefsell as Ever Saild from this Port. I want only a Common Policy Against the Danger of the Seas.

 Sir, the Foregoing is for Insurance on the Brigg *Thames* and In Case the Underwriters will do it for three pr C^t or Under well, if not I would not have any made, the Premium shall pay when the Vefsell arives. I Rec^d yours by Hancock with my Acco^tt Current and find four pound over Charge in the Money by Thos Harris, also 6/8 in your favour in the Order gave Willson. The Money by Robinson I Received which was Right. After paying Judah for the House send me by Harris what Cash you may have of mine in your hand, not forgetting the Order in fav^r of Morgan, send by Wm Harris. A Friend of mine Defird I would ask you what Circumstances Mr John Weatherhead of N. Y. was in as he has a Vefsell hear which Requires something Advanct for him for which he has Defird them to Draw on him in N York. If you think it fafe let me know in your Next.

                 N Shaw Junr.

To Mr George Erwin   New London March 23 1769
Mercht In Boston

 Sr. The Barer Capt Nathanl Saltonstall in the Brigg *Nancy* with a Cargoe of Molaſses comes to your Addreſs which Please to Dispose of on as Good Termes as you Can for my Accott and send me Forty Thousand of Mercht pine boards, twelve Thousand of Brick and 150 hhds from the ſtill houſes that are Suitable to fill with Molaſses. Shall write you by post and am Sr
            Your huml Servt
             Nathl Shaw Junr.

To Mr George Erwin   New London March 23 1769
Mercht In Boston

 Sir, this day Capt Nathl Saltonstall in the Brigg *Nancy* with Two hundred and Thirteen Casks of Molaſses sails for Boston and I have given him Orders to Deliver them to you, which Please to Dispose of for my Accott. I Imagine that Molaſses will be very Plenty Soon and I beleive if you Can Ingage any Person to take it as Soon as it Arives at 10/ it will be better then to run the Risque of its falling. I shall want part of ye money paid in Boston which I shall draw on you for when in Cash. Should be glad you would send me two hundred Joanesis by Return of Capt Saltonstall.
 Our Mutual Friend Mr Stewart desird I would Consign this Cargoe to you and I make no doubt but you will do the best you Can for my Intrest. I Expect to Import a great deal of Molaſses and when Ever I find your Marketts higher then they are in N. Y. shall ship to you. The Commisn I pay in N York is 2½ pr Ct on the Sale of Goods and the same on the Goods I have shipt to me and no Commisn on Cash and I Expect you'l Charge me the same as Molaſses is a Cargoe that is Disposed of with as little trouble as any kind of Goods what Ever. I beg you'l write me by the Return of the Post and let me know the state of your Marketts in Regard to West India Goods as I have two Veſsells that I hourly look for with Molaſses and Sugar and if I find they keep up shall Order them down. I am Sir Your huml Servt
            Nathl Shaw Junr.

To Mr John Stoddard   New London May 15th 1769
Mercht In Boston

 Sir, I Received yours 10th Ulto and Shall Remitt you Agreable to your Request to ye Amount of what Indigo I have disposed of which I find to be to the Amo of Ninety pounds so that the ballance will be Abo Fifty pounds which I shall Order Meſsrs Ervings to pay as soon as they are in Cash for the Molaſses I Shipt by Capt Saltonstall. Att the same time I

Afsure you I have not Received the Cash for One half and was Oblig'd to putt it of att a great Lofs by Reason of its being of a very bad Quality. You mention my Sending the Remainder of the Indigo by a Coasting Vefsell but the Risque is too great as the floop *Liberty* is now Stationed hear and Searches Every Vefsell in ye most Stricktest manner so that no man of any Consideration will Venture to take it on board, I think you had best give some of the Coasters that belong up ye River Orders to Receive it and Endavour to Dispose of it their. I am Sir, Your hum^l Servt

N Shaw Junr.

P S Pofsible ye barer Capt Ledyard may buy it.

To Mefs^{rs} John & George Erving   New London May 15th 1769
Merchants In Boston

    Gentlemen, I have drawn two Orders on you in favour of Ebenezer Ledyard of One hundred pound Each also an Order in favour of Charles Eldrige for Seventy pounds all Payable when you are in Cash on my Acco^{tt}. Should be glad you'l Advise me when you pay them, also the Order in favour of Hubbard as I am to Receive the money hear when they are paid. Am Extreamly sorry for the Accident to Capt Erving and hope its not so bad as we have heard, as we are very Anxious to hear ye Particulars. If their should be any rise of Molafses you'l let me know it.

N Shaw Junr.

To Mefs^{rs} John Barrett & Sons   New London May 15th 1769
Merch^{ts} In Boston

    Gentlemen, we Expected to have been Able to have sent you an Order on Mefs^{rs} Ervings to the Am^o of the ballance of our Acco^{tt} but as yet have not Received any Advise of their being in Cash, as they sold great part of the Molafses on Credit. They mentioned to our N S that if he wanted any bills of Exchange they would let him have them Soon, and he wrote them that he wanted to make a Payment to you, and if it Suited, you might receive them and give an Order on us to the Am^o of ye Ballance.

    Inclosed is a bill of Exchange for Eighteen pounds Sixteen Shillings and ½ penny Ster^g drawn by James Athell on Mefs^{rs} Richard & Thos Oliver 24th Augst 1768 in favour Thos Oliver which Bill he Received a Long time Agoe and is been waiting for the others to come to hand, but Imagine they are Mifcarried. Should be Glad you'l take it and Creditt our Acco^{tt} and send it home by the first Oppertunity and if it Should Mifcarry will Repay you the money with ye Intrest. We are Gentlemen

N & T Shaw

To Peter Vandervoort   New London May 15, 1769
In New York

    Dear Sir, I received yours by Rogers Inclosing my Acco^t and I find it Right, and have drawn an Order on you in favour of Guy Richards for one hundred pounds, and in favour of Patrick Robertson Eighty pounds, and in favour of Nathan Douglaſs Twenty Six pounds 13/4, and hope you will be in Cash to pay them.

  I would have you take a Receipt from Capt Leak (for the Amo^t of the Melaſses you Sold him) on Acco^t of the Bond he has against my Father, John Church & Daniel Braynard, & have the Receipt dated at ye time of ye delivery of ye Melaſses, that it might prevent the Interest. I expect a Cargo of 250 hhd Melaſses in about ten days & hope the price will keep up with you, as I had much rather send it to New York then Boston. After paying ye above Orders, if David Manwering should want about £100, should be glad you would let him have it & take his Rece^t or pay it to his Order, when you are in Cash on my Acco^t. Should be glad you would engage 200 Melaſses hhd^s from the Distellirs, and have them put up as those you shipt by Bushnell against I send down a Veſsell. Our Cruseing Pyrate Saild yesterday for New Port and hope she will not return. I am Sir,

                                             Your Hum^l Servt
P. S. Pray send me a Rheam of good Paper.   N. Shaw Junr.
                       N. S.

To Peter Vandervoort   New London June 12, 1769
  Dear Sir,

    This comes by Wm Rogers who has on Board a Cargoe of Molaſses which dispose of as you think best for my Intrest and send me two hundred and Fifty barrels of flower, One Ton of Iron, One Cask Large deck, One Cask 20^d, one ditto 10^d, One ditto 6^d, One ditto Sheathing Nails, 3 in. Sheathing Boards and Six Ream of Brown Paper for Sheathing, two beaver hatts, Cask of Ship Bread.

  I have now on Board of Tinker 110 hh^{ds} of Molaſses which will Remain hear untill I hear from you Concerning the Marketts—have also a Quantity of Brandy, Ayl & Soap which I will send you if you think it will Answer. I would have you Send what Molaſses Casks you have on hand and Engage as many more as I shall want them that are Good as fast as they Empty them.

To Mr Theopulas Backe   New London June 12th 1769
Mercht In New York

    Sir, Inclosed is a letter from Capt Joseph Packwood which he desir'd might be forwarded to you. He is now in the West Indias, and when he will Return is Uncertain. You'l see in his letter the many Circumstances that is the Occasion of your being so Long out of your Money on Acco^{tt} of the Protested Bills which agreable to your Directions I putt in sute Against him and he att the same time Commenct an Action Against ye Persons who had given him Indemnifying Bonds, but in Court Mr Chew Produc'd an Acco^{tt} Current with you (which was settled in N York in a great hurry) and Pointed out to ye Court many Errors and severall Articles that he had sent you on Purpose for a Remmittance in Consequence of these bills being Protested, and that if you would come or send to N London and have the Acco^{tt} Adjusted, their would then be found a Suffeciency in your hands to Answer ye bills as you had Charg'd him Five pr C^t Commis^n instead of 2½ and with severall bad Debts which he was sure ye Court would never allow, and on the whole I Really would advise you to Accept Packwoods offer as he is mett with many sevear Lofses, has a Family to Support, hard times, &c and I have many Reasons that might be added which I shall omitt Mentioning. Only Remember that I advis'd you to take this offer. I am Sir

Your hum^l Servt
N Shaw Junr.

P. S. Packwoods offer £200 down & Security for £100 pay in 12 M^o

---

To Meſs^{rs} Wartons   New London June 20, 1769
Gentlemen,

    I wrote you ye 16 Ins^t by Capt Edwd Tinker in ye Sloop Sally who had on Board 121 Casks of Melaſses, who was to Proceed to N. York & in Case ye price of Melaſses was not Equal to what you wrote one by the Post, I gave him Orders to Proceed to Philadelphia & deliver his Cargoe to you. This is now by Capt Leeds in ye Schooner *Pompy* who has on board Eighty Five Casks of Melaſses which Please to dispose of & Send me two hundred & fifty barrels of Flower—and if you can collect ye Cash Should be glad you'l send the ballance by Leeds. Hope you'l do the best you can for my interest in regard to the dutys as y^e *Pompy* has not entered here. You'l let me know ye price of Melaſses by ye Post, I am Gentlemen Your Hum Servt.

N. Shaw Junr.

To Meſs^{rs} Thos & Isaac Whartons   New London June 21, 1769
Gentlemen,

    The above is a Coppy I wrote you by Capt Leeds in the Schooner *Pompy* who saild yesterday and hope he will be safe arrived by the time this comes to hand. Have nothing further to add only that I think if you can engage ye flower att 14/ you had better do it Imediately for I really imagine it will Rise. I make no doubt but you'l dispatch y^e *Pompy* as soon as poſsible. I am Your Hum. Servt.

Nathl Shaw Junr.

N. B. Send me by Leeds 10 Cask Ship bread & 2 Cask fine flower.

To Mr Peter Vandervoort   New London June 26th, 1769
Merch^t In N. York

    Sir, I received yours by Rogers & Tinker & am very Sorry you could not obtain 22^d pr Gal for ye Melaſses by Tinker, but I really expect it will Neat that price or more at Philadel^a. I observe what you mention in regard to the Rec^t I desired you to take from Capt John Leak, but as he refused to give one dated at the time of Receiving the Melaſses, I am now fully determined never to trouble myself about the matter it being an affair that is not of any consequence to me, and I find he is Resolved to be as troublesome as in his Power.

    I have sent you by the bearer Fifty boxes of Sope which dispose of to the best advantage. Send fifty weight of Good English sewing Twine. I am Sir Your Humble Servent.

                                                           Nathl Shaw Junr.

Mr John Myers   New London August 16th 1769
Merch^t In New York

    Sir, I Received yours of ye 1st Instant and I Really am very much Suppriz'd att the Contents, if the Underwriters are Determined never to pay any Loſses they meet with, I Suppose that I must Suffer with the Rest of my Neighbours, who have been so Unlucky as to have their Veſsells Insured in New York. If the *Lucretia* had come Directly into New London, I should not have been so much Supriz'd att their Disputing the Matter, but her coming in by Way of New York where the Underwriters had an Oppertunity of seeing the Veſsell themselves & must Certainly be Convinct that she must have Rec^d very great Damage, all her top timbers on one Side broke of, and her waist Lying flatt on ye Deck, her whole Cargoe shifted so as to bring one Streake of the Deck in ye Water, two hh^{ds} in her hatch way stove to peices which unstow'd almost all the fore hold, the pump well was broke & one hh^d in Either the first or Second Teir but was moved by the Violent Sea which Drove in her waist, and as the hh^{ds} moved some of them were turn'd with their bungs almoast down and some of them in part—and as Soon as we Opened the Hatches, I had two Maſters of Veſsells to Survey the hold, who gave it as their Opinion that ye Cask had been well stow'd and that the Damage was Received by the Sea.

    I also putt two Other Persons on Board to Examine Every Cask and to take the Wantage of those which appeared to be moved by the others being loose and to see Every Cask before they were Unstowed. Their was a Number of Other Casks which wanted very Considerable of being full which they took no Acco^{tt} of as they Appeard not to be moved. The two Masters who Survey'd the hole are now att Sea and as Soon as they Come home I will Send you their Affidavits.

    The Insurance you made att the same time on ye Sloop *Dove* & Cargoe, John Degine Master from Monto Christo to Port Au Prince at & from thence to N L with Liberty to touch att Monto Christo in her way from Port Au Prince to N L was att 4½ pr C^t. This Sloop saild from ye Mount to Port Au Prince & came up to Cape Nicholas Mold and their Sold her Cargoe and Returnd to Port Au Prince for another Load and has been Employ'd Ever Since in that trade so that ye Risque the Underwriters run was only from ye Mount to Port Au Prince and up to the Mole, Consequently I think they in Justice Should Return part of that Premium.

I want much to Come to New York but att Prefsent my bufsinefs is such that I Cannot Pofsible leave home, and I Flatter my Self that if ye Underwriters do (as they would others should do to them) they will pay ye Money. I can send you the Affidavits of the two Persons who Survey'd and Gaug'd Every Cask to prove that the Lofs of ye Molafses was Occasioned by the hole shifting if that will Sattisfy ye Underwriters. I am Sir Your hum^l Servt.

            Nathl Shaw Junr.

To Mr Gabriel Ludlow   New London August 16th 1769
Merchant In N York

  Sir, I Received yours 28th Ult^o Concerning the Rent due for your Warf and Store. I now Inclose you an Order on Peter Vandervoort for Eighty Four pounds York Currency for Two Years Rent and the Occasion of my not sending you ye Money before was, because, when I Agreed with Capt Tiley to pay that Rent I Really Did Intend to have purchas'd it before the Year was up and Imagind if that had been the Case You would not have made me pay any Rent, but now I find so great a Scarsety of Cash that its very Propable I shall never Purchase it—and for the future Cannot afford to give more then Thirty pounds pr Year Rent—and their must be att least Fifty pounds lay'd out on ye Warf before winter or Else it will take three times that Sum to Repair it next Summer. Capt Tiley was hear about three weeks Agoe and I made him Sensible it will go to Ruin very fast if I did not. The last Year I putt one teire of Logs all Round ye Warf which Cost me att least Forty Pound which I should never have done had not I Intended to Purchase. The warf was very badly Built att First which is the Occasion of its Sinking down Every Year & Unlefs you keep putting on more logs it will not be tenable. I am Sir

            Your hum^l Servt
            Nathl Shaw Junr.

To Mefs^{rs} John & George Erving   New London Septem^r 14th 1769
Merch^{ts} In Boston

  Gentlemen, I Received yours of the 28th Ult^o and am very much Oblig'd to you for your Advise in Regard to the Prosecution that is Intended Against me. Att Prefsent I Cant Conceive on what Acco^{tt} they Intend to trouble me, as I am as Innocent of Destroying the Sloop as Either of you, and can make it Appear so to the Sattisfaction of any Court or Jury in this Colony, and I am of the Opinion if I can do that, it will be Suffecient and In Case they are Determined to have the Matter try'd in Boston att a Court of Admiralty, should be glad you would Inform me in your next what method they are to take to Oblige Either Packwood or me to Appear their or if it goes Against us by Default what Plan they are to Persue to get the Money. Att Prefsent we have no Judge of ye Admiralty in this Colony and I beleive no Person hear would att this time Except of it. Mr Stewart has Seiz'd a Sloop which he Suspects is the Sloop that was Carried of att N Port the Night the *Liberty* was Destroy'd. It is now Seventeen days Since the Seizure was made and he has done nothing towards having her Libel'd. Neither can he git any advise from the Commifoners what steps to take with her, he has no Evidence hear to Prove this to be the Sloop, nor Cant have any, unlefs Capt Read or some of his People should come hear, & I beleive it will not be Convenient for them to make their appearance very Soon and haveing the Sloop detain'd so long must Consequently Create an Expense which must fall some where, I Proposed to Mr Stewart to have ye Sloop Appriz'd as she now is & give him Security for ye Vallue In Case she be Finally Condemn'd, that we might go on with her Repairs as she wants much before she is in a Condition for the Seas, I should be glad you would Consult some Person who can Advise me in this matter, what steps to take for I Suppose Mr Stewart will not do any thing untill he has Orders from y^e Commisoners.

You'l let me know if the Price of Molafses keeps up as I Expect a Vefsell or two in a few days which shall order your way if the Price suits— also if you have Settled with $Mefs^{rs}$ Barrett. I am Gentlemen, Your hum^l $Serv^t$.

$Nath^l$ Shaw Junr.

To Mr Theophylact Bache   New London $Septem^r$ 27th 1769
$Merch^t$ In New York

Sir, I Received yours of y^e 19th June and have Agreable to your Desire Comprimis'd y^e Affair of the Protested Bill of Exchange with Capt Joseph Packwood and he has paid me two hundred pounds N Y Currency and given me good Security for the Ballance Payable in Twelve Months, and I have now given him up the Bills—and as Soon as that was done Mr Chew came with an Officer and Lay'd an attachment on the Intrest I have of yours in my hands as being an Attorney to you as you'l see by the Inclosed writt. I find this has been a Long Plan of Mr Chews & the Persons who was Security to Packwood. Chew had Objected to so many Errors in y^e $Acco^{tt}$ Settled with you that he brings you a great deal in Debt and has give in this $Acco^{tt}$ with a Power of Attorney to those Persons to Secure them.

I have Consulted an Attorney and they tell me that you must Certainly be oblig'd to have y^e $Acco^{tt}$ Settled over Again by Referees Chosen by Each

Party In Case you Cannot Agree between your Selves—and in Short att Preſent their Seems to be no End to the Law for if an Accott is Settled with Ever so much Fairneſs and Receits Paſ'd Either of ye Partys can bring a writ to Court and have the whole Accott Disputed again, Instances of this kind we see Daily to the very great Prejudice of Every Honest Man. Mr Chew tells me that he has wrote you very fully this Post & makes no Doubt butt you'l Settle the Accott Again by leaving it to Different Persons before the Court comes on. I am Sir Your huml Servt.

N Shaw Junr.

To Mr Peter Vandervoort   New London October 5, 1769
Merchant In New York

    I have yours before me of ye 28th Sepr by Wm Rogers and Reſpecting the freight of the Rum Capt Wm Billings Aſsures me that he Poſsitively Agreed with Mr Law to be paid Five Dollars pr hhd deliverd in New York and Cannot Accott for the two Bills of Lading being fill'd up for Four only. How Ever must leave it with you to Settle the Affair on as good Termes as you Can and I think as Mr Law fill'd up the bills himself he should in Justice pay Five Dollars.

    I have Shiped you by Capt Tinker Fifty Five hogsheads of Molaſses which dispose of to the best Advantage. I have this day drawn an Order on you in favour of Wm Ledyard for Forty Nine pounds three Shillings and Four pence—I have also by Capt Tinker shipt Six hogsheads of Rum and Four Terses for Mr John Wattles which he would have you forward as pr the Inclos'd Directions and send Ten Keggs of Brandy as I did not Choose to send any by Tinker. I hope you'l have the Terses taken out Soon as they may appear Suspecious. I am Sr Your huml Servt.

Nathl Shaw Junr.

To Mr Isaac Hazlehurst   New London December 6th 1769
Mercht In Philadelphia

    Sir, I wrote you by the last Post that Mr Blakency was Expected in Town. Since that he has Returnd and Agreable to your directions I have taken out a Warrant to have him taken but he keeps him Self shutt up att a house hear in Town, and desird to see me and I went to him and he tells me that the Occasion of his Shutting himself up is that In Case the Warrant is Served on him he Consequently must be Committed to Goal as no One hear will be Surety for his Appearence att Court and that he has a Quantity of Goods att New Port and some Cash Suffecient to Sattisfy the Debt and that he Intends to have the Goods hear in this Town in Ten Days and will then Secure the Payment of the Debt. How much Dependance may be putt on this Promise you may Judge, but you may Depend on my doing Everything in my Power to git the Debt Secured.

N. Shaw Junr.

To Mr Peter Vandervoort   New London Febuary 14, 1770
Mercht In New York

    I Received your Several favrs 1st, 15th, 26th Ulto also of ye 5th Inst. I have an Order from Allin for you to Dispose of it and Accott with me for ye Neat Procedes. Saml Herns debt to Mr Lawrence is Seventeen Pound Nineteen Shillings York Currency which you may pay to him and Charge me with it. Observe what you mention in Regard to Mr Pomeroy, I must have £150 of ye Effects to my Creditt. Shall write you more fully on this head as Soon as he Comes to N L. I am to have some of his Rum att what it Should Neat in N Y att the time he Shipt it to you & Should be Glad you would let me know what Price I ought to give him. I am very much out in my Judgement if Sugars do not Rise as Soon as the River Opens. I drew an Order on you in favour P. Robinson ye 3 Ulto for £40 and in favour Rogir Gibson for Sixty pound ye 6th Ulto & as they are not come to Hand I Suppose they sent them by Peter Lattemore. I should be glad you would give me an Order on Jed. Huntington for Two hundred Pounds as I have Engag'd to pay you that sum for his Accott. I Just now have Advise of Capt Packwoods drawing a Bill on me for Four hundred Dollars to be paid in Boston and Should be Extremely Oblig'd to you if you Could Procure me a Bill Pay. their for that Sum. And you must Charge me Interest when you are in Advance for me. Yesterday Capt Latham arived in a Sloop of mine from Cape Francoise and I am now Loading Harris with molaſses and Sugars for N Y, the Sugars shall Clear as Seads. I find by Capt Latham that Jos Packwood in ye Brigg *Thames* and William in the Brigg *Nancy* had both Liberty to trade att the Cape and were Loading with Molaſses. The *Thames* was to Sail in Eight days After him and I am in hourly Expectation of her Arivall. I think I have a Good Chance of doing something this Voyage. I am very Sorry to hear that your Aſsembly has Granted Money to the Soldiers, am much of ye Opinion that it is Contrary to the minds of their Constituents. I think the Maſsachusetts house of Aſsembly & the Sons of Liberty in New York behave with the best Spirrit. I am Dr Sir Your huml Servt.

    I Just now have been settling Accott with my Rope Maker and find that the two Reals of Yern as per the Incloſed Invoice had not the tare of the Reals deductd which I Suppose you may Easily have Rectify'd.

                                                                            N. S.

To Mr Peter Vandervoort   New London Febr 17, 1770
Mercht In New York

    Sir, I have shipt you by the barer Capt Wm Harris thirty hogsheads of Molaſses and Twenty One Casks Sugar which Dispose of for my Accott. I want you should send me by Capt Harris Four or Five hundred Dollars if you Can Poſsible get them as I am In Debt to ye Custom house for Dutys which must be paid in Silver. I have drawn on you in favour of Saml

Beldin for Fifty pounds Paym^t Fifteen days Sight and in favour of Jno Hertell for £50 Payable att 15 days—and I have this day Given George Irish (a Gentleman at New Port) an Order on you for Two hundred & thirty Six pounds which Order he is to make use of In Case he makes a Purchase for me, but do not much Expect he will make use of it. If it Comes to hand Should be Glad you would Answer it, but Imagine before you see it Tinker will be down with a Load of Molaſses. I have a Quantity of Clarrit wine and Ayl on hand and would Send it down In Case you Could putt it of which be so Good as to Advise me of in Your Next. I am Sir, Your hum^l Servt.

Nathl Shaw Junr.

To Meſs^{rs} Thomas & Isaac Wharton   New London July 20, 1770
Merchants In Philadelphia

Gentlemen, Inclosed is A Bill of Lading for thirty Five hogsheads Molaſses which you'l dispose of for my Acco^{tt}. In Case that Article is Plenty and will not Command ye Cash I beleive it would be better to putt it some little time in ſtore which you must be the beſt Judge of.

My Friend Roſwell Saltonstall is to pay me a Sum of Money, in order to Raise it has Shipt you Twenty Four hogsheads and Twelve Terses N E Rum which you must Dispose of and Creditt my Acco^{tt} for the Neat Procedes only he is to have One hund^d and Twenty pounds, as per his Letter hear Inclos'd. Should be Glad you would keep me advis'd of the Price Current. I have a Quantity of Sugars on hand, but am att a Loſs how to git them to your Marketts. In Case I should Ship them with Molaſses do you think their would be much danger. Send me 4 Calf Skins & two Sides Sole Leather.

To Mr George Erving   New London Augst 14, 1770
Merch^t In Boston

Sir, I have shipt by the Bearer Capt Wm Harris Sixty Six hogsheads Melaſses Four Tierces and Eight barrels ditto as by Inclosed Bill of Lading, which I wish safe to hand, and a good markett. I believe you will find it to be very Good; in the sale of it should be glad you would keep the markes of the Casks they being part of two seperate Cargoes. You must send by the Return of Capt Harris, Fifty hogsheads of Jameca Codfish, fifty barrels of Mackrell & thirty Kegs of Sounds & tongues, and if any Veſsell should sail for New London before Harris send me Ten hogsheads of Fish & Twenty barrels of Mackerell more as I want them to go in a Veſsell that sails sooner then the one that is to carry the others, you must pay Capt Harris 7/ pr hhd, 3/6 pr Terse & 1/9 pr barrel freight for the Melaſses, if any Callico to be had Suitable for Curtains send 36 Yards, I am Sir Your Hum Servt

Nathl Shaw Junr.

To Mr George Erving   New London August 23, 1770
Merch^t In Boston

    Sir, I Received yours 20th Instant Advising the Arival of Capt Harris with ye Melaſses which you must take Care that he Delivers ye whole that I shipt and pay him ye Freight for as I wrote you and give him a Rec^t for what you Receive as I am not Certain he has the Quantity on Board that is mentioned in the Bill of Lading.

You must Send me all the Fish I wrote for only the Last Twenty Barrels of Mackrell.

I have a Cargoe of Melaſses Just Arived which I have not taken out. Its Probable I may send part of it your way. I am Sir, Your hum^l Servt.

                                          Nathl Shaw Junr.

To Mr George Erving   New London August 30th 1770
Merch^t In Boston

    Sir, I Received yours 27th Instant and hope by the time you Receive this, Harris has Saild for N L with the Fish, when the Western Post comes in I shall Determine Either to send you 70 hh^d Melaſses or send it to Phil^a.

Concerning the Voyage to Europe, I beleive it best for me not to be Concern'd, as my trade is in a Different branch and I think it will be best for me to persue the trade wich I have Experienc'd. How Ever I wish you Good Luck, and if I Can do anything for you hear you may Depend on it I will.

I dont Imagine any Green Tea would sell hear as their is not more then 3 or four Familys who use it. Let me know the Lowest Price for Ruſsia Duck. I am Sr Your hum^l Servt.

                                          N. Shaw Junr.

To Mr George Erving   New London Sepr 1st, 1770
Merch^t In Boston

    Sir, this by Capt Tinker in the Brigg *Little John* with 68 hh^{ds} & 3 Terses of Melaſses which you will Find to be very Good and I hope you'l be Able to git 17^d for it. I would have you Endavour to git the Brigg away as Soon as Poſsible; and git her what Freight you Can, and In Case you Cant git any Purchase me as many Merchantable pine Boards as will fill the Brigg^s hole.

I would have you sell for Cash and send me as much money as you Conveniently can by Tinker. I have Cleared out att the Custom House 30 hh^{ds}, 30 Terses and Six Barrels, and I Suppose as the Duty is already paid, their will be no Officers on Board to make any Difficulty. Send me one Chaldron of Coal and some Nails as by the Inclos'd Mem^o.

                                          N. Shaw Junr.

To Meſsrs Thomas & Isaac Wharton   New London September 3, 1770
Merchants In Philadelphia

Gentlemen, Inclos'd is a Bill of Lading for Forty Two hogsheads and Twelve Terses of Melaſses shipt in the Schooner *Hawk*, John Chapman Master, which I hope will Arive Safe and to Good Markitt. Send me three hundred bushels of Lisbon, Cadiz or English Salt, and would have you Dispatch the Schooner for N L as Soon as Poſsible. The Amo of this Cargoe shall draw on you when in Cash. I am Gentlemen, Your huml Servt.

Nathl Shaw Junr.

New London Novr 9th 1770
Gentlemen,

I received yours 23 Ulto. and observe you have past the ballance due to Roswell Saltonstall to my Creditt, but you did not Mention the Sum he tells me, that is £188.6.11 which I suppose is right and have charged you that Sum.

I have now sent you by the bearer William Harris Junr Fourteen Teirces, twenty two hogsheads and Sixteen Barrels of Sugar, and Four Barrels Indigo, which would have you to dispose of and send me the Accot of Sales soon as poſsible as their is several Persons concerned in it and am to Accot with them and should be glad you would observe the numrs & Marks on the Casks & put them down at the foot in the Accot of Sales. I have sum good Sugars in N. York and have desired Mr Vandervoort to ship them to you in case he cannot dispose of them. I have Received the Money from Chappell for your Note, the order on W. Saltonstall I expect will pay in a few days.

I have several Cargos of Melaſses arrived since Chapman was at Philadelphia but the price is at 23d in N. Y. and the Commisn is only 2½ pr Ct. which makes it turn out better. I Really believe between friends if you were to Charge only 2½ that in the Cource of a Year you would be no Looſers by it. The Chamber of Commerce in New York have putt it at 2½ and think it ought not to be more in Philadela.

Send me by Harris Ten Barrels of Ship Bread, and as much flower as he stow in his hold.

I am Gentlemen, Your very Huml Servt.

Nathl Shaw Junr.

10 Teirces Sugar EF
 4 ditto   ditto EW
22 hhds   ditto P
 3 barl   ditto P
13 ditto   ditto N.S.
 4 do Indigo   N.S.
—
56
—

P. S. Let Harris have what little Cash He may have occasion for expences.

To Meſsrs Tho. & Isaac Whartons   N. S.
Merchts Philadelphia

To Mr Peter Vandervoort New London Nov. 9, 1770
Mercht In New York

The bearer William Harris Junr. has on board Fourteen teirces, Twenty two hogsheads and sixteen Barrels of Sugar, and Four barrels of Indigo, which you must git Cleared for Philadelphia in the Method we proposed, and you'l let Harris have some Duck and what other Necefsarys he may have Occasion for in New York and take his order on me for it.

In case Eleazer Pomeroy draws on you for One hundred and Fifty Pounds York Currency should be glad you would pay it.

Send me Two bolts Rousia Duck by the first opportunity. I hope the Schooner *Lark* is on her way to New London. I this moment Received yours of ye 7th Inst and if you cannot dispose of the Sugars that Came in the Schooner, I think you had better ship as much by Harris as he can take in to Mefsrs Whartons for my Accot.

To Mefsrs Griffiths & Thomas New London Janry 30th 1771
Merchts In Bristol

Gentlemen, I have hear Inclosed you a Bill of Exchange drawn by James Athill on Mefsrs Thos & Richd Oliver Esqrs for thirty Nine pounds 5/9 Sterg and should be Glad you would send me by the first Oppertunity One Cask deck, 1 Cask 24d, 1 do 20d, 2 Do 10d, 2 Do 8d, 2 Do Sheathing 2 Do 6d, 2 Do 4d, Do, 1 Do 3d, Do 20 in. pump Nails, 1 ps Red, 1 ps blew Duffields, the ballance will pay you as Soon as I Receive the Goods. In Case you ship them to N Y to Peter Vandervoort, if to Boston to Danl & W. Hubbard. I am Gentlemen, yrs &c.

N. Shaw Junr.

New London March 20th 1771

Dear Sir

I have shipt you by William Harris Junr. as by the Inclosed Bill of Lading Twenty Eight hogsheads of Melafses, the marks we have not been Particular in, but would have you take notice of them in the Accott of Sales. I think it would be best to Dispose of them as Soon as they Arive. I am now Loading Sheffield in a Small Schooner who will Sail tomorrow if the Wind Serves. Send me by Harris 1 m white Chapple Needles Sorted, ½ dozn small Sharp pointed Sifsars ye best Sort, 1 pack 4ct Pins, ½ dozn barlow Penknives, 20 boxis Spermacity Candles, 6 barrells milk bread, 10 barrels Lt packt Flower. In Case you have not already Shipt the Flower I wrote by Tinker, let it be Light Packt. I am Dr Sir Your humble Servt.

Nathl Shaw Junr.

P. S. let me know the Price of Coffee

To Mr Peter Vandervoort

New London March 20th 1771

Gentlemen
    I Receiv'd yours of ye 16th & 27th Ulto and have drawn a Bill on you for Six Hundred & fifty Dollars in favour of George Irish also one in favour of John Hertell for One hundred Dollars, which please to honour. Capt Chapman Arived here Yesterday After being Fifty Five Days at Sea, he tells me he was Six Days off your Cape Endeavouring to get in but was Oblig'd to bear away to the Eastward. In ſhort he was a meer Wreck. I have a Brigtn now out that Saild Fifteen Days before him & as yet have had no News from them. I ſhall Ship some Melaſses & Sugar for your Markett ſoon & am Gentlemen

                          Your humble Servt
                          Nathl Shaw Junr.

To Meſsrs Thos & Isaac Wharton.

New London March 22, 1771

Dear Sir
    This Serves Just to Cover a Bill of Lading for thirty one hogsheads and One Terse of Melaſses Shipt by the barer Capt Isaac Sheffield which I wish Safe to hand and a Good Markitt. You are to pay him Eight Shillings pr hogshead & Four Shillings pr Terse Freight, & his Custo house Charges in New York. I am Sir Your huml Servt

                          Nathl Shaw Junr.

To Mr Peter Vandervoort
Mercht In New York

To Mr Richard Downing Jennings   New London April 9th 1771
  Sir,
    This will be handed you by Capt. Melally who I have given Orders to Settle with you for the Cordage Shipt by him in February, 1770, which Cordage is now in my Store and it has not been in my Power to Dispose of it. I am very Sorry that it has happen'd so Unlucky in the Sale. I expect to make use of it on Board of a new Veſsell which I am now Building & will be Launched next Fall. I have Endeavour'd to Ship you some Goods to the Amo of it but could not get any Person to take them on Board. Notwithstanding there is so many of our New London Veſsells that come to St Eustatia it is almost imposible to Ship any Goods, as it is very Seldom they intend to go there when they leave this Port. I am Sir

                          Your humb. Servt.
                        Nathl Shaw Junr.

To Mesrs Thos. & Isaac Wharton　　　　　New London 10th April 1771
　Gentlemen,

　　　　I this Moment Receiv'd yours 23 Ulti. by Capt Watrous, with a Letter Inclosed from Capt Leeds, who I hope will be with you by the Time this comes to hand. When he Arrives I would have you Dispose of his Cargoe for the most you Can. When he Sail'd from this Port I gave him Orders to Return to Philadelphia and in Case Flour was in good Demand att Hispaniola, he was to take in a Load and Return without Coming to New London. I have Inclos'd a Letter for him, and would have you put on Bord such Goods as he Should think best, and Dispatch him as soon pofsible. I wrote you the 20th Ulto and Advised of my Drawing on you in favor of George Irish for Six hundred and Fifty Dollars. Since that I have taken the Bill back again as he did not have Occasion to make Use of it. A few Days ago the Briggtn I mentioned to you Arrived after a pafsage of Eighty Seven Days. I am now Loading Harris who will take on Board about Ninety hhds of Melafses & Sugar, for Philaa where I hope he will Arrive to good Markitts. Should be glad you would Advise me the price Current. I Really Expected you would have been able to have Sold the Indigo at 10/ however I beleive you got the best Price you could. Mrs Shaw Returns you her thanks for the China, which is not yet bro't on Shore but beleive it to be very good. I am Surpriz'd that Flour continues so high with you, it is only 17/ in N York. I am Gentlemen, Your very humble Servt

　　　　　　　　　　　　　　　　　　　　　　Nathl Shaw Junr.

To Capt. Leeds　　　　　　　　　　　　New London 10th April 1771
　Sir,

　　　　I was Sorry to hear of your bad Luck in Looseing your Horses, however we must make it up next Voyage. If Capt. Fousard & Betar think it best to take in a full Load of Flour & Return without Coming to New London I am Content; but I think the best Plan would be only to take in about two hundred Barrells and come to New London & take a Load of Horses, tell them I shall leave it intirely with them wch. to do. In Case you Return you'l take such a Cargoe as they think best, I suppose you'l take Boards on Deck & hoops Shaken Cask &c Sufficient for a Load of Melafses. I have wrote Mefsrs Whartons to supply you with such Articles as you want. Make all the Dispatch in your power, and make as little Charge as pofsible. Your Family are all well. I am Sir
Write me by the post.　　　　　　　Your huml Servt

　　　　　　　　　　　　　　　　　　　　　　Nathl Shaw Junr.

To Mefs^{rs} Hubbard & Greene   New London April 11, 1771
Merch^{ts} In Boston

Gentlemen, last Post I wrote you for some Fish and desird you to Inform me by the Return of the post the Price of Melaſses and Expected a Line from you but was Disapointed. I want Twenty hogsheads of Jamaica Fish very much and Should be Glad you would Send them by the first Opportunity. I am now Loading Hancok with Melaſses who Sails tomorrow or next with a Load of Melaſses for Boston to your Addreſs. I have drawn an Order on you in favour of Meſs^{rs} Theophulas & L Rogers for one hundred & thirty pounds Lawfull Money, as it is very Difficult to dispose of bills on Phil^a hear. I Mentioned to your W^m of drawing Bills in your favour for you to Dispose of and then to draw on you, for which he thinks one half pr C^t will be Equal to your trouble, as I Imagine your Connections in Phila^a are such that Bills pay. their will Readily Comand Cash. If you Agree to this Plan I Imagine I shall draw for a Considerable sum this Summer, as I Can dispose of Bills pay. in Boston much Easier, and very like many of them to People who want the money in your hands and will sute me better then to Run the Risque of the money from Phil^a. I have hear Inclos'd you a Bill on Meſs^{rs} Thomas & Isaac Wharton for Seven hundred Dollars pay. on Sight which dispose of and C^r my Acco^{tt}. I am Gentlemen,

Your hum^l Servt
N. Shaw Junr.

Dr Sir   New London April 12th– 1771

I have now Shipt on Board Capt. Edward Tinker the Bearer hereof 62 hogsheads of Melaſses & hope you'll Dispose of it att a good Price. Inclos'd is a Bill of Lading for Forty seven hogsheads Eight Terses of Melaſses for Acco^{tt} of Collⁿ Fitch which you are also to Dispose of for his Acco^{tt}. I Expected he would have wrote you, but there is no Letter come to hand. I have drawn two Orders on you in favour of John Perritt for fifty two pounds 7/ & one in favour of John Hertell for ten pounds which you'll please to pay—and if you can Dispose of the Melaſses so as to send me some Cash by Tinker should be very Glad. You'll Send me by Tinker as many Shaken Cask as you Can. I am Sir

Your humb^l Servt
Nathl Shaw Junr.

To Mr Peter Vandervoort

Gentlemen   New London April 12th 1771

I wrote you by Post the 10th Inst. I now Inclose you by the Bearer Capt. Willm Harris a Bill of Lading for Fifty five hogsheads & Eleven Teirces of Melaſses Six hogsheads and thirty three Barrells of Sugar, which

Dispose of for my Acco[tt]. The three barrells markt BN are of the best whites from S[t] Domingo, I sent them with a View to know what Sugars of that kind would sell for. I have Drawn an Order on you in fav[r] of Mefs[rs] Hubbards & Green for two hundred & sixty two pounds 10/ in order to Purchase some Fish In Case they Can get them so as to Answer, if not they will Return me the Order. I Receiv'd yours 2 Inst. & observe you'll send me the Acco[tt] Sales of the Sugar & Indigo with the Different marks by the first Opportunity. Should be glad you'll send me as much Cash as you can Conveniently by Harris. I am Gentlemen, Your humb[l] Serv[t]

Nath[l] Shaw Jun[r].

To Mefs[rs] Thomas & Isaac Wharton

To Mefs[rs] Andrew Oliver Esq[r]   New London 17th April, 1771
Arnold Welles Esq[r]

Gentlemen,

We Receiv'd yours 30th Ult[o] Relating to our Acco[tt] with M[r] John Spooner deceas'd wherin you make Objections to Several Articles Charg'd in our Acco[tts].

First Relative to a pipe of Wine we Shipt him in July 1760 by Christian Higgins, Said pipe was in his Hands att the Time the C[o] Acco[tts] was Settled. Afterwards he took it to his own Acco[tt] and we Imagine he made use of it. The Price sett down was by his Directions, we have a Bill of Lading for it.

The next is three Lottery Ticketts. Nath[l] Shaw Jun[r] was one of the Managers of the Light house Lottery and sent him twenty four Ticketts to Dispose of & he Return'd them only keeping three to himself w[ch] were Blanks. The 20/ Charg'd for going to Stonington was by M[r] Olivers Desire, who wrote us that he would pay the Expence. We Advis'd him off it & desir'd him to pay it to M[r] Spooner.

The Musketts he Shipt us to Dispose of for his Acco[tt], we have his Letter—we have his Letter to Dispose of the Reasons for what they would fetch as he had a Large Quantity by him & att the same time he Charg'd Hugh Ledlie only 30/ & am very Certain we lost money by them Even att that Price—after paying y[e] Freight from Boston—on the whole, the Matter is so Clear to us that there is not the least Room for a Dispute & we would rather Suffer than have any.

As to the Sugars we never had any Acco[tt] Sales so Cannot tell what they Sold for, and beleive if we Settle and Allow one half of the £22.5.8 we Really beleive it will be the nearest Method to do Justice to both Sides. We are Gentlemen, Your most Obed[t] hum[l] Serv[ts]

Nath[l] Shaw Jun[r].

Dear Sir   New London 17th April 1771

  Send me by the first Opportunity for New London three hundred Bushells of Salt. Have nothing further to add but am Sir

          Your humble Servt
          Nathl Shaw Junr.

To Mr Peter Vandervoort

Gentlemen   New London 17th April, 1771

  I wrote you by Willm Harris who Saild from this port laſt Sunday, with a Cargoe of Melaſses & Sugar. Since which I have nothing further to add, only that I would have you send me One hundred Barrells of Good Flour. I am Gentlemen   Your humble Servt
          Nathl Shaw Junr.

To Meſs^{rs} Thomas & Isaac Wharton

To Meſs^{rs} Hubbards & Green New London 17th April, 1771

  Gentlemen, I Receiv'd yours of the 8th & 9th and 15th by post and observe you have Shipt me the Fish I wrote you for. This by Capt. Hancock who has on Board as by the Inclosed Bill Lading Thirty Six hogsheads of Melaſses which Dispose of for my Acco^{tt}. Please to send me as many Jamaica Fish (if to be Bo't, if not, of the same kind as the others you Shipt) as Hancock can take on board in hogsheads, & half hh^{ds}. You'll Observe I have paid Hancock ye Freight but you must let them have as much Money as will pay his Port Charges, if he can't do without it.

  You must C^r my Acco^{tt} for only the Money you Receiv'd of Erving, as I would not have you call on him again—and when you let me know the Ballance I will pay it, I am Gentlemen   Your Humb^l Servt
          Nathl Shaw Junr.

To Meſs^{rs} Thomas & Isaac Wharton New London May 7th, 1771
Merchants In Philadelphia

  Gentlemen, This by Capt Jones in the Schooner *Pompey* with Sixty Three hogsheads, Sixteen Terses and Seven Barrels of Melaſses, One hogshead & Twelve barrels of Sugar which I wish Safe to hand, and would have you dispose of them to the best Advantage, and In Case you Can dispose of the Schooner for Two hundred pounds Sell her, Otherwise putt as many boards in her as will ballase her and Dispatch her for New London as Soon as you Can. I am very much Supriz'd att the Great Price of Flower, I wanted some very much, butt it will not do to give that Price for it. Capt Leeds Arived hear last Fryday with a Cargoe Cheifly Sugars which are very Good. If they should be in Demand att Philadelphia, I will Ship them to you, att Preſent shall putt them in Store.

I hope Harris is Arived by this. In Case you do not Sell the Schooner if you Can Sell the Cargoe for Cash would have you send me as much as you Can by Jones. If their Should be any Alteration in the Price of Melaſses be so Good as to Advise me of it, I am Gentlemen

Your huml Servt
Nathl Shaw Junr.

To Mr Peter Vandervoort New London May 7th 1771
Mercht In New York

Sir, the barer Capt Jones in the Schooner *Pompey* has on Board Sixty three hogsheads Sixteen Terses and Seven Barrels of Melaſses, One hogshead and Twelve barrels of Sugar, if you Can Dispose of the Melaſses att One Shilling and Nine pence pr Gallon sell it, if not, I have order'd him to Philadelphia. If you Sell the Cargoe, I would have you Sell the Veſsell also if you Can Git Two hundred pounds for her. If you Sell the Cargoe & do not Sell the Veſsell Send me One hundred barrels of best Super fine flower. I am Loading Wm Harris Junr with Melaſses and shall send him to N York if I find the markitts sute. Send me Four Sett braſses for Desks with Locks. Your huml Servt.

Nathl Shaw Junr.

To Meſsrs Hubbards & Greene New London May 9th 1771
Merchants In Boston

Gentlemen, I Received yours by Capt Hancok Inclosing the Invoice and Bill of Lading for the Fish Amo to £201.14.11. I have hear Incloſs'd you a Bill on Meſsrs Thomas & Isaac Wharton for one hundred pounds Phila Currency, and have drawn on you in Favour of Charles Eldrige Junr for Fifty pounds Lawfull money att Ten days Sight. Should be glad you would send me the Accott Sales of the Melaſses by the first Oppertunity.

I have a Quantity of Best St Domingo Brown Sugars Just Arived. Should be Glad you would let me know the Price they will sell for in Boston. I am Gentlemen. Your huml Servt

Nathl Shaw Junr.

To Mr Peter Vandervoort New London May 10th 1771
Merchant In New York

Sir, The barer Wm Harris Junr has Twenty Six hogsheads of Melaſses on Board, which dispose of for my Accott. I wrote you by Jones who Saild in my Schooner for New York to dispose of Veſsell and Cargoe, In Case you Could git 1/9 for the Melaſses, Otherwise to Send her to Phila. The hundred barrels of Fine Flower I wrote for In Case the Schooner goes to Philadelphia, you must send by Harris, also Twelve Terses of Bread, you'l Find this Melaſses to be as Good as any that has Come to Markitt this Year. I wrote you by Powers in whom went Paſsenger Capt Betere with some Sugars, and I have a Quantity by me of the same kind, and if you Can Sell it att 50/ or upwards I will send it down to you in Small Quantitys, but if you Cannot git that Price for it, you must Clear out Ten hogsheads Five Terses and Twenty barrels in Harris for Philadelphia for I must ship them to raise a little Cash, I am Dr Sir Your hum. Servent

N. Shaw Junr.

To Meſs. Tho. & Isaac Whartons New London May 14, 1771
Merch^t In Philadelphia

 Inclosed is a bill of lading for 45 hhd^s & 9 teirces of Melaſses, and Ten hhd^s of Sugar by Capt Powers, in the Schooner *Hawk*, which dispose of for my Account. I wrote you the 7th Instant by Capt Jones in the Schooner *Pompy* with a Cargo of Melaſses, which I ordered to you in case it would not sell for 1/9 in N. Y. Since that I have not heard from him. The 9th Inst. I drew a Bill on you in favour of Meſs. Hubbards & Green for £100 pay. in five days; which please to pay. Their is only two hogsheads of Sugar cleared out, and you must get the Remainder on shore in the best manner you can. I have put 19 bags Coffee on board which is cleared out as Cocoa, you must manage that in the best manner you can. Send me one hundred bar. fine flower; I should choose them about $1\frac{3}{4}$ C^t w^t as many of those kind of Boards, as Capt Clay brot me in the Brigg *Thames* as Powers can take in. I am now Loading Tinker with Melaſses and about 20 hhd of Sugar, and if I find when the post comes in that your marketts are better then at N. Y. I shall send him to Phil^a. If you can send me any Cash by Powers should be Glad, I am Gentlemen Your Hum. Servent

N. S. Junr.

To Mr Peter Vandervoort New London May 14th 1771
Merch^t In New York

 Sir, the barer Wm Rogers has on Board Four Terses Seven Long barrels & Four Comon Barrels of Good Muscovado Sugar and thirty One Casks of Coffee which dispose of for my Acco^{tt}. I am now Loading Tinker with Melaſses & Sugar and hope you'l be Able to git 1/9 for the Melaſses, otherwise Tinker will go to Phil^a. I hope Powers got Safe to hand and that you Sold his Sugars for a Good price, I think they are very good. If they turn out well, I shall send down what I have, but dont you think the Pitcher will go to the well once too often.

 I want 100 hams of Bacon and 6 or 8 Casks of Bristol bear. Let me know in your next what they Can be bought for. You must Continue takeing the Shaken Casks from the Distillers. I am Sir Your hum^l Servt.

N Shaw Junr.

To Meſsʳˢ Thomas & Isaac Wharton   New London May 15, 1771
Merchᵗˢ In Philᵃ.

    Gentlemen, This is Just to desire you'l Send me Either by Powers or Jones One hundred barrels of fine flower Abᵒ 1¾ wᵗ & Two Ton of Iron. I hope Harris is Saild for N L

Your humˡ Servᵗ.
Nathˡ Shaw Junʳ.

To Meſsʳˢ Hubbards & Greene   New London 16ᵗʰ 1771
  Gentlemen,

    I Received yours by Post 13ᵗʰ Inst. and Observe you have sent the Accoᵗᵗ Sales of the Melaſses by Mʳ Lothrop but have not Received them (I suppose Wᵐ will bring yᵉ mail this afternoon). If you can purchase me a Load of Merchantable Fine Boards to be Deliver'd here for thirty six Shillings or under I would have you send me a Load & I will pay the Cash on the Delivery. You Desire to know what is become of Capt. Saltonstall. Yesterday I Received a Letter from our Friend at Amsterdam advising that Capt. Saltonstall had made severall Attempts to get the Brigg off but to no purpose and that he had at last determined to strip her & sell at Vendue. The 2ᵈ March, that the Season was so severe that they had not been able to bring the Sugars to Markett, but hoped soon to have them, they being all safe on Board the Lighters which took them out. I believe we shall have Charge enough. He says there is no Veſsell Coming this way so I imagine the Effects will come by way of Sᵗ Eustatia.
    I am Gentlemen

Your Humble Servᵗ
Nathˡ Shaw Junʳ.

To Mʳ Uriah Rogers   New London May 16ᵗʰ 1771
  Sir

    I Received yours 9ᵗʰ Inst. and Conclude to take the Fish, and would have you send them Along as soon as poſsible. They must be in good Order. I am

Your humble Servᵗ
Nathˡ Shaw Junʳ.

To Meſsʳˢ Thos. & Isaac Wharton   New London May 17ᵗʰ 1771
  Gentlemen,

    I have by the bearer Capt. Edwᵈ Tinker in the Sloop *Sally*, Shipt you seventy four hogsheads of Melaſses, and thirteen hogsheads Sugar, which dispose of for my Accoᵗᵗ. The Sugar is in Melaſses Hogsheads & you must Land them in the Safetest manner you can, for I Could not Clear them out. I Receiv'd yours 7ᵗʰ Inst. by post and Observe Harris has not then Arrived, but as the Wind has been favourable Since, I Imagine he is

Arrived. You must send me Fifty barrells Fine Flower by the bearer Capt. Tinker. I hope Jones in y^e *Pompey* & Powers in the *Hawk* are both safe Arrived. I am Gentlemen, Your humb^{le} Servt

Nathl Shaw Junr.

P S. As I have a Partner in this Cargoe, I should be very Glad if you could Close ye Acco^{tt} Sales & send ye Ballance by Tinker.

To Mr Peter Vandervoort New London May 17th 1771
Merchant In New York

Sir, Capt Betere Just now Arived from New York but have no Letters, he tells me that Harris has 100 Barrels flower for me. Should be Glad you would Send me thirty more Super Fine by the barer Edwd Tinker J^r. I am Sir Your hum^l Servt.

N Shaw Junr.

To Mr Uriah Rogers New London May 20, 1771

Sir, I wrote you ye 16 Ins. y^t I concluded to take your Fish, and would have you send them soon as poſsible. Mr Sam. Booth of Sterling was over here yesterday w^t bony-fish, or as he called them Menhadon & says y^t there is no other fish catched on Long Island. If yours are of this sort they will not do. I thought they were Herren. If they are Herren & in good order, Barrels full gauge I will take them; if they are not Herren I cannot take them. I am Sir Your Hum. Serv.

N S. Junr.

To Mr Peter Vandervoort New London May 20 1771

S^r, Capt Wm Harris Junr the bearer has on Board thirteen hogsheads of Sugar Markt N S & two Ditto Markt I B and two I L which dispose of for the Moast they will fetch. I Received yours 16th Ins^t Inclosing Mr Laws Note which I will acco^{tt} for as you Mention. Mr Goddard I have not had an oppertunity to Preſsent your order to. Send me Ten Terses Bread. I am Sir Your hum^l Servt

Nathl Shaw Junr.

To Meſs^{rs} Thomas & Isaac Wharton New London May 29th 1771
Merch^{ts} In Phil^a

Gentlemen, I wrote you by Tinker 17 Ins^t who Saild the next day & hope he is by this Arived Safe. Since Capt Harris Arived and I Received yours 14th Ins^t Inclosing Acco^{tt} Sales of the Sugar & Indigo Shipt you by Wm Harris Junr & those shipt by Mr Vandervoort all which I find to be Right, also the Cash & Flower by Harris.

Send me an Anvil with a Steel Face of the same Fashion of the One sent me before, and Exchange the One Sent by the Sloop who brot Mumfords Sugars for Another of the fame kind, as it was not a Good one. I hope you'l be Able to git 21d for the Melafses.

N Shaw Junr.

To Mefsrs Thomas & Isaac Wharton   New London June 12th 1771
Philadelphia

    Gentlemen, I Received yours 27th and 29th Ulto. by the Captains Jones and Powers who both Arived Safe with the Goods you shipt, one Cask &c all Right. I Observe what you mention in Regard to the Peoples Ventures on Board ye Vefsell and am Sensible its a disadvantage in the Sale of ye Cargoe and Intend for the future to Either Purchase it of them or oblige them to take it out. I also take notice that you would have what Sugars I Send to Phila Regularly Clear'd out but must observe to you that it Cannot be done for we Cannot Clear them out unlefs they were Enter'd & the dutys Paid. I think Powers did not manage the Matter Right. He Should Landed only two Casks at a time and left no more be in Sight. I hope you have had no Difficulty in Landing Tinkers Cargoe. If Melafses Should Rise any I shall Send another Vefsell with Sixty or Seventy hogsheads and should want to Send About Twenty or Thirty hogsheads Sugar if you thought it might be done with little or no Risque. Matters of this kind are Daly Practis'd in Boston & New York for In Short brown Sugars will not bear to pay dutys on.

    I Received a Line from your Friend Relative to a Saddle horfe which I Shewed to a Person who I Employ to purchase horfses, and desird him to purchase one that he thought would answer that Description and he Gave for Answer that he knew of none that would Suit Except one that I had Just putt on board Capt Leeds. I then orderd him taken out, he is a Black horse of Fifteen hands high, paces and Trots Easy, wants neither whip nor Spurr, Abo Five Years Old and I beleive would Suit your Friend very well—if the Price is not too much, the Lowest he can be deliverd in Phila for will be One hundred Dollars. I have putt him in Pasture and have Shipt Another horse in his Room, if you would have me Send him let me know in your next, Otherwise I Shall Ship him by the first Vefsell to the West Indias. Our Friend Vandervoort Just now wrote me that Tinker had Arived and that you had putt his Cargoe in Store, I Suppose the Occasion was that it would not fetch 21d. How Ever I hope it will not be long before its Sold. I am Gentlemen, Your Huml Servt.

N Shaw Junr.

To Mr Peter Vandervoort   New London June 17, 1771
Mercht In New York

    Sir, I have by the barer Wm Rogers Shipt you Five hhds and One Terse of Coffee which dispose of for my Accott and Send me Twelve Keggs butter bread, 8 Casks Ship bread, 1 hhd bristol bear, Six boxis

Spermacity Candles & 1 Small Neat Hadleys Quadrant. I shall Send you by Wm Harris Junr who will Sail in a day or two Ten or Twelve hogsheads of Sugar.

I forgot to Mention that Hugh Ledlie has paid me thirteen pounds 9/5 on your Acco^{tt} and Twenty Four pounds 8/1 on Acco^{tt} of Samuel Broome & Co. Should be Glad you will pay them that Sum & take their Receits for Ledlie & Charge to my Acco^{tt}. I am Sir, Your hum^l Servt

Nathl Shaw Junr.

P. S. I have Shipt ye Above Ten hogsheads of Sugar by Wm Rogers.

N. S.

To Mr Saml Mifflin   New London June 25th 1771
Merch^t In Philadelphia

Sir, I Received yours 11th Inst. Inclosing a Protested Bill of Exch^{ge} for Fifty Pounds Sterling, drawn by Saml Grotton in favour of Jabez Huntington. Agreable to your Request I Demanded Payment of Mr Huntngton, who gave for Answer, that he would not pay ye said Bill, and that he never had any thing to do with it. I suppose y^t Thos Fanning who is one of the Indorsers of the Bill Sign'd Huntingtons name on the back of it, for I know its not Huntingtons hand writing. I shall wait the Return of the Post to know your farther Orders about it, but think the best Method of getting ye Money would be to let it rest untill Fanning returns from ye West Indies which will be in about Six weeks & then Arrest him for the Money. Unlefs you think best to Send to the West Indias. Fanning is a Man of Interest & there is no danger of Looseing it. In this Colony Ten p C^t Damages is allowed and Six p C^t Interest. I am Sir

Your humb^l Servt

Nathl Shaw Junr.

To Mefs^{rs} Read & Yates   New London June 30, 1771
Merch^{ts} In New York

Gentlemen, I Received yours 24th Ins. and now inclose you the Acco^t of what I supply'd Capt Hay Am^o to Four pounds 14/3½, L Money for which have taken his order on you and sent it to my friend Peter Vandevoort which please to pay & 1/ for postage, Capt Hay sail'd ye 23^d with a fair wind & hope he will arrive safe. I advised him to take his corn out in order to seperate it from the damaged, but he did not & I believe it will be the means of damaging the greatest part. He left some staves which I now ship you as by the Inclosed bill of Lading and am Gentlemen y^r Hum Servt

N. S. Junr.

To Mr Saml Mifflin   New London Aug 1st 1771
  Sir

     I Received yours 9th Ult^o & have now to Inform you that Fanning is Arrived from ye West Indies, and he Says that he will not pay the Bill (for this Reason) that ye Bill has been detain'd so long since the Protest, that the Drawer is now become unable to pay. We have no Court untill November next. If you think best to put it in Suite you must send me a Power. I beleive he disputes ye matter only to put off the payment I am Sir Your humble Servt

                                              Nathl Shaw Junr.

To Mr George Erving   New London Aug 8, 1771
  Dear Sir

     I have here Inclosed you a Bill on Mefs^rs Thos & Isaac Wharton Mercht^s in Phila. for Sixty Six pounds Seventeen Shillings & 6. that Currency which with the Six pounds nine Shillings & 11¾ due me in Acco^tt L. Money make fixty pounds L. Money & Should be glad you would Inclose me an Order on Richd Law Esqr from your Father, it being Mr Laws Desire. I expect Capt. Harris from Norwich to Call this Week for the Six Casks & the Remainder shall Ship by the next Opportunity. I am Sir

                       Your very humble Servt.

                                       Nathl Shaw Junr.

To Mefs^rs Thos. & Isaac Wharton   New London 14th Aug. 1771
Mercht^s In Phila.

     Gentlemen, I Received yours by Capt. Chadwick, and am very sorry to hear that the Horse did not sute your Friend. I was Inform'd that he went from New York to Phil^a without being Shod which I am Sensible must be a great Damage to him. Capt. Chapple the Person who Carry'd him to New York tells me that the Horse ran away from the Post, and was running about the Streets on full Speed for half a Day which am certain must hurt his feet. Mr Logan has desir'd me to get him one more and I will Endeavour to get him one this Fall and send to Phil^a by Water. In Case your Markitt is any better for Melafses, I have a Quantity of Sugars now on hand but am at a Lofs how to get them to you. I drew an Order on you in fav^r of George Erving for Sixty six pounds seventeen fhillings & six pence which please to Honour. I am Gentlemen, Your humb^l Servt

                                       Nathl Shaw Junr.

To Mr Peter Vandervoort   New London Aug. 14, 1771
Mercht In N. York

Dear Sir, Inclosed is a Bill of Exchange for 800 Dollars drew by Nathan Palmer on Meſs^{rs} Grant & Fine att 7 M^o Sight. Should be glad you would get it accepted & let me know if you think they are Gentlemen that will be punctual in payment &c. Send me by the first Boat 4 Reams paper & one bar. Sheething Nails, I want them immediately & Ten bar. Tarr. Y^{rs}

N S Junr.

To Mr George Erving, Merch^t In Boston   New London August 15th 1771
    Sir,
    I Receiv'd yours 12th Inst. and in Regard to the Bill on Phil^a if you Cannot dispose of it without an Abatement of One pr C^t I must allow it. I expect Harris down the River this Day and shall then Ship as you Order'd. I am Your humb^{le} Servt

Nathl Shaw Junr.

To Mr John Erving   New London August 15th 1771
Merch^t In Boston
    Sir
    Mr Law Informs me that you wrote him to make out a Deed of the Land on Mamacock, and att the same time to Collect the Rent due from McKneil which must be some Mistake, as I wrote you that I would give One hundred and Fifty pounds for it In Case you would make over the Lease to me and Mr Law says that he wrote you the same and I Sincerely think there is no Person in this Town that would give so much for it by Thirty Pounds—and if you'll send up the Deed to Mr Law & Orders to give me the Lease, I will pay you the Hundred & Fifty pounds Immediately. Mr Law tells me that it would be best for you to make out the Deed and Inclose it to him. I have Desir'd your Son George to pay you Sixty pounds and take your Order on Mr Law for it. I am Sir Your humb^{le} Servt

Nathl Shaw Junr.

New London August 15th 1771
    Dear Sir
    I have Shipt by the Bearer Capt. Wm Harris Fifty Six hogsheads thirty three Terces & Ten barrels of Melaſses which I beleive you will find to be very Good & would have you dispose of it on the best Terms

you can. The freight you are to pay Harris will be for every 125 Gallons of Melaſses Five ſhill[gs] Lawful Money. I Observe you have paid the Money to Beekman. I want some Money paid in Boston, Should be glad you would get me two Bills pay. there for One hundred pounds Lawfull Money Each. I wrote you Yesterday by the post & am Sir

Your humb[le] Serv[t]
Nath[l] Shaw Jun[r].

To M[r] Peter Vandervoort
Merch[t] New York

To M[r] Peter Vandervoort   New London Sept. 11th 1771
D[r] Sir

Tomorrow Capt. Chappell Sails in the Schooner *Hawk* for New York & has on Board 120 Casks of Melaſses which you are to Dispose off for my Acco[tt]. I shall want 120 barrels of Flower about 1¾ C[t] w[t] by the Return of Chappell. I Rec[d] yours Relative to Grant & Fines Accept[ce] of the Bills drawn by Palmer, and they must pay the Dollars when they become due if I want them, Otherwise Connect[t] Bills may Answer of which I shall Advise you in Time. I am Sir Your humb[le] Serv[t]

Nath[l] Shaw Jun[r].

P S. If John Chapman is Arriv'd with you sell his Cargoe if you can get 1/9½, Otherwise Store it. N. S.

1 Braſs knocker, 1 Gal Pott, q[t] d[o], 2 lb Tea, p[s] Red Base & 1 Black Smiths Vise.

To M[r] George Erving   New London Sept 19th 1771
Merch[t] in Boston

Dear Sir, Inclos'd is a Bill of Lading for 6 hh[ds] of Cocoa Shipt by Wait Warner y[e] 7th Instant which I inclos'd to you the next Post & desir'd my Boy to put it in the Post Office, but Meeting M[r] Miller in y[e] Street he gave it him & he put it in his Pockitt & forgot to put it in y[e] Mail & Yesterday he Return'd it to me. I hope he is Arriv'd safe. I Yesterday Shipt y[e] Remainder by Harris as by y[e] Inclos'd Bill of Lading & last Evening he Saild with a good Wind. I hope he will also Arrive safe. I did not let Either of them know y[e] Contents. I am Sir Your very humb[le] Serv[t]

Nath[l] Shaw Jun[r].

P S. I intend to Order your Father paym[t] for y[e] Land in a few Days. N. S.

To Mefsrs Hubbards & Green   New London Sept. 19th 1771
Gentlemen

Inclos'd is a Bill of Lading for twenty hhds Sugar Shipt by Jeremiah Harris & I would have you Dispose of it on as Good Terms as you Can. If you Obtain a good Price I shall ship more. Let me know by the next Post what you think they will Sell for and let me know how Bills of Excha are. I am Gentlemen Your humbl Servt

Nathl Shaw Junr.

To Mr Geo. Erving   New London Octo 23, 1771
Mercht In Boston

Dear Sir, I now Inclose you a Bill of Exchange on Mefsrs Thos & Isaac Wharton, Merchts In Philada for £187.10/ Currency which is Equal to £150. L. M. & should be glad you would pay ye sum to your father John Erving Esqr & desire him to let Mr Law know that he is Received the money, as I have not taken the deed from Mr Law as yet.

I Observe what you mention in regard to the Plan of remitting home ye Spanyards Cash, but their is more Smoke then Fire, they have but very little Cash, and Intend to purchase a ship that I have now on ye Stocks which I Suppose will take ye whole, however if any thing should be wanted from your way that I could help you in, you may depend on my calling on you. The expences on ye Goods you may pay to Mefsrs Hubbards & Green. I here inclose some Letters from ye Spanish Gentlemen & should be Glad you would forward them to some part of Europe that you think best & you'l oblige Your hum. Servt

Nathl Shaw Junr.

To Mefsrs Hubbards & Greene   New London Novr 7th 1771
Merchts in Boston

Gentlemen, I wrote you the 4th Inst. by Mr Manuel, a Spanish Gentlemen who has left Cash in my hands to the Amount of Three Thousand pound Lawful Money in Order to purchase Fish in Case they are to be bought so as he thinks they will Answer at Cadiz, and thinking it might be of Service to you to have the Purchasing of them I gave him a Letter to your House & I hope you will use him in such a Manner as that he will have no Reason to Complain. In Case You purchase for him, you'll let me know in what Manner I shall pay you the Money and fhall Immediately comply with it. I Recd yours 3d Inst. wherein I find that Bills on Cadiz are not to be had, which I am very Sorry for as Mr Francisco, a Gentleman with Mr Manuel has left Six hundred Dollars with me to be paid for a Bill which I expected you could have purchas'd & on that Accott I gave him a Line to you. Pofsible a Bill on London might Answer for him (if one Pay. at Cadiz cannot be Obtained) of which you'l be so good as to Advise with him & let me know what I must do with his Cash, they Sail'd from here the 5th Inst. for Newport & Intended to take Paſsage from there to Providence & so in ye Coach to Boston & Suppose they will be with you by the time this Comes to hand. Last Evening Dr Moffatt Return'd the Order I Drew on you for twenty pounds which I was a little Surpriz'd at as I Desir'd Wm to mention to you the Occasion of my Drawing it & at the same time I gave him an Order on Peter Vandervoort in New York for £26.13.4 Yk Currcy which is just Equal to £20. L My. I beg you'l pay the twenty pounds to John Moffatt & take his Recpt on Accott of Thomas Moffatt. I expect to hear from you by the Return of the Post & am Gentlemen Your humble Servt

               Nathl Shaw Junr.

Manuel de Valladaxes
Dr Franco Machin

To Mr Peter Vandervoort   New London Novr 22d 1771
Mercht New York
 Dr Sir

  I have here Inclos'd you our Bond to Mr Ludlow for Six hundred pounds & also a Deed for the Wharf & Warehouse for him to Sign which forward to me by the first Opportunity. Tell your Quaker Friends that they have not Offer'd half the Vallue of the Campeachy Wood. I Expect you'l Manage the Affair of the Boat Just as if it were your own. Chappell is now Loading with Melaſses by him I ſhall want three hundred Barrells of Common Flour, would have you Engage them if its Scarce. I beleive Sugars will Sell before the Winter is out & think it best to let them Remain in Store untill you have an Offer for them that will do at leaſt 48/. I want About the Vallue of hundred Joanesis to go to the West Indias. Should be glad you would Get me that Sum to come by Chappell & would Rather have them Under than Overweight.

To Mr Peter Vandervoort   New London Nov 26 1771
Merchent in New York

  I wrote you a few days agoe by Wm Harris. I have now by Ed Chappell ship'd 49 hhds & 3 Teirces Melaſses marked S.D. and 16 hhds mark'd And 10 hhds Rum which dispose of for my Account. Let the sales of ye 16 hhds Melaſses be in a seperate Accot as Mr Pomeroy is concerned in them. Send me 100 bar. fine flower & as much common Flower as Chappell can bring, Twelve Casks ship bread, 1 bar. Milk bread & 2 Ct Loaf Sugar. Send me as many Shaken Casks as you can git. Send me 6 yds Ravens Duck by the first Boat for I want it to make use of Immediatly. You must send Beterre a Good Telescope Glaſs of ye Same kind he bot when he was in N York & four barl Apples.

To Mr Peter Vandervoort   New London Dec. 4, 1771
Merchent In New York

    I Received yours by Wm Harris Junr with the Coals. Chappell has made severall attempts to proceed on his Paſsage to New York, but by Contrary winds obliged to return. He has on 65 hhd^s & 3 Teirces Melaſses & Ten hh^{ds} West India Rum, and I have wrote for 320 bar. Comon flower & 20 Teirces Bread which I would have you get ready to ship soon as he arrives for I have a Veſsell now waiting only for the flower. Send me a good Telescope by the first opportunity of ye same kind Butlar bought when in New York

---

To Meſs^{rs} Tho. & Isaac Wharton   New London Dec. 4, 1771
Merchents in Philadelphia

    Gentlemen, I Received yours by Jeremiah Harris Inclosing Acco^t Sales of the Severall Cargos shipt you last Sumer, which have Examined and find Right. Also inclosing an order on Meſs^{rs} Hubbards & Green for £200. When Harris arrived Mr Hubbard came to Town and I mentioned to him that I had an Order on them for £200 and that you had desired me to call on them for the ballance of what you had Shipt by Harris for their Acco^t and he gave me for answer that you had shipt the flower contrary to Order, and that he would not pay either the order, or the ballance, but would deliver me the flower to the amount of the ballance of what their Flex Seed sold for, which have received & gave them a receipt for; which you'l charge me in Acco^t & for the order of £200.
    I Received yours by the last Post Relative to Flex Seed—it is all purchased in this Town and mostly ship'd. I gave Mr Hubbard for the flower ye Prime Cost & 2½ pr C^t Commiſsions & you must Charge them no more, I am &c

                                                                             N S Junr.

To Meſs^{rs} Hubbards & Greene   New London Decr 27th 1771
Mercht^s In Boston

    Gentlemen, I Rec^d yours Novr 11th wherein you Inform me that you have Supply'd Mr Valladoris with One hundred & thirty two pounds Seventeen ſhillings Lawfull Money & taken his Receipt for the Same. This Gentleman has Alter'd his Plan of Purchasing a Veſsell att Boston & is to pay me the Money that you Advanc^t him here, and ſhould be Glad you would Inclose me his Receit by the Return of the Post and Charge me in Acco^{tt} for the Am^o of it. I hope by this you have dispos'd of the Sugars, as I am Inform'd they are in Demand. I am Gentlemen Your humb^{le} Servt

                                                       Nathl Shaw Junr.

To Mr Thomas Brattle　　　　　　　　New London Decr 27th 1771
Mercht in Boston

　　Dear Sir, Next Week I expect a Brigg from Cape Francois with One hundred Hogsheads of Melaſses & About as much Brown Sugars of the best Quality, and if I can Send the Brigg directly to Boston without Entering here, and the Marketts Sute I will send her. If that should be the Case, how much Sugar & Melaſses do you think I must the Dutys for & what Commiſs^ns will you Charge me, 2½ I think is Enough & no Person Charges me more. Let me know by the Return of the Post & the Price of Sugars & Melaſses. I am Sir Your Humb^le Servt

　　　　　　　　　　　　　　　　　　　　Nathl Shaw Junr.

To Mr Peter Vandervoort　　　　　　　New London Jan. 1. 1772
Merchent In N. York

　　Dear Sir I received your Several favours 16th, 18th & 24th Ulto. and observe you have come to an Agreement with Mr Apthrop for Chews house, and that Mr Chew is to leave it in a Month or Six weeks which I hope will be the Case, but I fear he will continue in it longer unleſs I advance £8 or £10 towards geting him another house and If I do I think Mr Apthrop should deduct it out of the Price as it will be for his Interest for him to leave it soon, as I shall pay him the money as Soon as I Receive it or alow him Interest. I Shall Rather pay the Money if I have a Vessell arrive that I hourly expect with a Cargoe of Melaſses.

　　I Received the Deed from Mr Ludlow and do now acknowledge that the Bond you Signed with me to him was wholly for my Use and that I will pay the money and Save you harmleſs from S^d Bond.

　　Am very sorry to hear times grow so bad I Scarsely know what an honest man Can do, I wonder what method those Gentry took to open ye Doors of ye Seller where they Seiz'd ye Tea. I dont Imagine they could open doors here.

　　I have settled matters with the owners of the Goods that Shipt by Chappell. Inclosed is an order drawn on you by Meſ^rs Whartons for Sixty pounds Phil^a Currency which C^r my Acco^t for and if you can send me any Connecticut money by the bearer should be Glad. Inclosed is a small Memorandum from Thos Allen which send & charge to my Acco^t. also one Looking Glaſs £10 Price & one of £8 & a Copper Coffee pott with a Cok to draw. Tinker has two hhd Melaſses on Board which Sell on my Acco^t.

To Mr Peter Vandervoort　　　　　　　New London Feb^ry 6th 1772
Mercht In New York

　　Dear Sir, Yours by Tinker of the 30th Ulto. Covering Several Acco^tts Sale of Sugar Melaſses Indigo &c I Rec^d and have Examined & find them all Right. Also the ſeverall Articles you Shipt me. I am now in Poſsesion of the House that was Mr Chews & have here Incloſ'd you a Deed for Mr Apthorp to Sign and would have you pay him out of the Money

that is in your hands as Soon as you Pofsibly Can. I Suppose you'll have
Enough when you Receive the Money from Grant & Fine for the Order
which I think is Due next Month & for the Sugars that are already Sold.
I suppose Mr Apthorp will want me to pay Interest until you are in Cash
but that will be unreasonable for I shall advance Mr Chew at least twenty
pounds to Enable him to move out of the House, which he could not have
done until warm Weather which would have been just the fame to M^r
Apthorp as to wait untill ye time for the Money and I think when you let
him know these Matters he Can have no Objection to waiting untill you
Receive the Money from those Persons for the Sugar you have Sold.
However I have just Mentioned those things to you & would have you do
the best with him you Can. I fhould be very Glad to have the Deed by the
first Opportunity. I Observe what you Say in Regard to Mr Pomeroy,
he is now at Hartford but expect him here in a few Days and will then
Settle the Affair with him about the Melafses as you Desire. Chappell is
still here & I beleive it is as well for I imagine as soon as the Weather
Moderates West India Goods will be in more Demand and I intend he
shall unlade his Melafses at N. York & then take in Sugars & Proceed to
Phila. unlefs you Can Sell them at four or five & forty Shillings pr C^t.
I am Sir Your hble. Servt.

Nathl Shaw Junr.

P. S. let me know the Am^o Premium Charge &c on ye Schooner *True Blue*,
tell ye Underwriters she is Arrived & I expect her home in Ten Days. N. S.

To Mr Peter Vandervoort   New London 22^d Feb. 1772
Merch^t in New York

Dear Sir
      The bearer Edward Chapple in ye Sloop *Sally* has on Board for
my Acco^t thirty one hogsheads and two barrells of Sugar and Fifty Nine
hogsheads & two Teirces of Melafses wch Dispose of for my Acco^t. In
Case the Sugars you have on hand do not Readily Sell I would have you
Ship them to Phil^a by the first Opportunity to Mefs^rs Whartons. I hope
by the Time Chapple Arrives you will be Return'd and beleive you had very
bad Riding & Especially pafsing Bridges &c as the last Sudden warm
weather has Carried all before it. I am Sir Your humb^le Servt.

Nathl Shaw Junr.

To Mefs^rs Hubbards & Green   N
Merchents In Boston

      Gentlemen, I have drawn two orders on you in favour of Eb.
Ledyard for £50 Each, pay^a at ten days Sight which I beg you'l pay out of
the N^t Proceeds of the Sugar I shipt you by Harris. Your Hum. Servt.
New London March 9, 1772   N. Shaw J^r.

To Mefsrs Hubbards & Green　　　　New London April 27, 1772
Merchents In Boston

  Gentlemen, I have hear Inclosed you the Order you sent me on Esqr Leffingwell for £113.1.3¾ which he has not paid, I have now drawn on you in favour Mr Abraham Booth Chapman for Ninty Five pounds Seventeen shillings & 8d L Money which I hope you'l honour & pay. I am Gentlemen Your Hum Servt.

                N. Shaw Junr.

To Mr Peter Vandervoort　　　　New London April 28th 1772
Mercht New York

 Dear Sir

  Chappell Sailed from hence Abo ten Days ago for New York & since have not heard from him. I hope he is Arrived safe and to good Marketts. I have now by Wm Harris Shipt Twenty two hogsheads fourteen Teirces & Seven Barrells of Melafses wch please to Dispose of if you can get 1/8 or more pr Gallon. If not Store it if you think best. Send me half Ton of Iron. I am Sir Your humble Servt.

                Nathl Shaw Junr.

Send me one ps Irish Linen Abo 4/ pr yd. If you can purchase a Cargoe of Shingles to Be delivered hear for 8 Gallons Melafses pr Thousand send me one.

To Mr Peter Vandervoort　　　　New London May 12th 1772
Mercht in New York

 Dear Sir

  Inclos'd is a Letter for my Friend Mefsrs Lane Son & Frazier which I would have you Forward by the first Opportunity for London & let me know in your next by what Vefsell you Send it. I am Sir

            Your humble Servt.
            Nathl Shaw Junr.

To Mefsrs Lane Son & Frazier　　　　New London May 12th 1772
Merchts in London

 Gentlemen

  Inclos'd is a Bill of Lading for One Hundred & Twenty Five Casks of brown Sugar and two Casks of Melafses shipt to your Addrefs by the Sloop *Dove*, John Chapman Master, who I Expect will Sail from this for London in a few Days, and I would have you Get me Fifteen hundred Pound Sterling Insur'd on the Said Goods. I have a Vefsell, Jo^s Powers Master wch Sail'd from this Port for Gibralter in January last. Since that I have not heard from him, I gave him Orders to send you a Bill of Exch^{ge} to the Am^o of the Note of Hand I gave to Jno for the first Payment of the Land I purchased from him. Shall write you by the *Dove* & am Gentlemen

             Your humble Servt.

               Nathl Shaw Junr.

To Mefs^{rs} Tho. & Isaac Wharton   New London May 13, 1772
Merch^{ts} In Philadelphia

  Gentlemen, I have by the bearer Capt Edward Chappell in the Sloop *Sally* Shipt a Cargoe of Melafses, which please to dispose of for my Acco^t. I Received a Letter from our friend Vandervoort that he had Shipt you Ten hogsheads more of my Sugars, and hope by this you have sold them. I would have you Send me as much Cash as you can collect for the Sugars, and also this Cargoe, and send me by the return of Chappell and you will oblige, Gentlemen Your Humble Servent.

               N. Shaw Junr.

To Mefs^{rs} Hubbards & Greene   New London May 14th 1772
Merch^{ts} In Boston

  Gentlemen, Inclos'd is a Letter for Mefs^{rs} Lane Son & Frazier Merchants In London which Please to forward by the first Vefsell & let me know by whom & when they Sail.

               N. Shaw Junr.

To Mefs^{rs} Lane, Son & Frazier   New London May 15th 1772
Merch^{ts} in London

  Gentlemen

  The forgoeing is a Copy of what I wrote you by way of Boston & New York & this will be handed to you by Capt. Chapman who has a Cargoe on Board as by the Inclosed Bill of Lading also two Baggs of Coffee & one Bag of Cotton Wool all which I would have you Dispose of to the best Advantage for my Acco^t. Our Trade to the Foreign Islands has of late Increas'd so much that those Articles are not in Demand here which is the Occasion of my Shipping to your Markett and In Case it Turns to Advantage we Shall send three or four Vefsells Annually. I beg you'll write me by the first Opportunity, and let me know the Price Current of those Articles, with the Duties & Charges that are on them from America. I would have you Dispatch the Sloop as soon as Pofsible & send me 3 bar. Sheething, 3 of 10^d, 2 of 20^d Nails, 20 p^s Rufsia Duck, Five Ton of Hemp, a large Scale Beam for to weigh hh^d Sugar, a good Silver Watch, 2 p^s Irish Linen, 2/6 p^r y^d, a Good Spy Glafs of the best kind, 2 doz^n white knit thread Hose, a p^s of Kersey four yards Scarlet Cloth at 18/ p^r y^d. I imagine it will be Difficult to get a freight back to America in a fingle deck Vefsell & if that should be the Case, I would Chuse to Purchase A Load of Salt and would have you Advise Chapman where to get it and furnish him with Cash to the Am^o of About One Thousand Pounds Pay. at Thirty Days Sight & hope by the Time they are Presented for Payment you will be in Cash for the Cargoe.

To Mr James Flint New London June 6th 1772
Merch^t in Windham

Sir

There is a Ballance due to me in Acco^t for which Should be Glad you would let me have some Good Shipping Oxen. I now want a Cargoe & let me know by the first Opportunity how many you will let me have & You'll Oblige Sir Your humble Servt.

Nathl Shaw Junr.

To Mr John Ripley New London June 6th 1772
Merch^t in Windham

Sir

I want to Ship a Cargoe of good Oxen. Let me know how many you will let me have on Acco^t as there is a Ballance due to me & is been since Septemb^r last. If you Cannot Supply me with Cattle Should be Glad you would Send me the money and you'l Oblige Your humble Servt.

Nathl Shaw Junr.

To Mr John Ripley N London June 13, 1772
Merchent in Windham

I want you to let me have as many shipping Oxen as to ballance our Acco^t and would have you send them down to N L next week. Let them be rather larger then smaller then the common Size, and if you and I cannot agree about a price I will leave it to any person who is a Judge. If you want a few Casks of Reasons I can Supply you. I am Sir y^r Hum Servt.

N. Shaw Junr.

To Mr Thomas Griffiths New London June 20th 1772
Mercht in Bristol

Sir

    I have here Inclosed you a Bill of Exchange on Meſs^{rs} Lane Son & Frazier for Sixty three pounds Fifteen ſhillings & Six pence Sterling which Credit my Acco^t for when Received the Contents. I am Sir

                            Your humble Servt
                            Nathl Shaw Junr.

To Meſs^{rs} Lane Son & Frazier New London June 20th 1772
Mercht^s in London

Gentlemen

    Inclosed is a Letter for a Spanish Merchant in London, it being from a Spanish Captain of a Frigate Laden with Sugars, which Came into this port, by Distreſs and has Apply'd to me for Aſsistance &c. It being of much Consequence to the Concern'd have only to Add that you'l much Oblige me if you Can Deliver it to him, as the Captain has Orders from his Owner at Cadiz to Apply to this Gentleman for Directions. I hope Capt. Chapman in the Sloop *Dove* has Safe Arrived by this. I have drawn a Bill of Exchange at thirty days Sight for One hundred pounds Sterling on you in fav^r of Wheeler Coit also for Sixty pounds in fav^r James Eldrige both ye 11th Ins^t and have this day drawn on you in favor of Thomas Griffiths for Sixty three pounds 15/6 Sterl^g which I hope you'l honour & am Gentlemen

                            Your humble Servt
                            Nathl Shaw Junr.

To Mr Peter Vandervoort New London June 20th 1772
Mercht in New York

Dear Sir

    I Received yours by Chappell & I aſsure you that Meſs^{rs} Whartons Sold the whole of Chappells Cargoe of Melaſses @ 1/8½ and Remitted the Money by him all Except about Five hundred pounds which they have Desir'd me to draw for when ever it ſutes me. I never Order'd them to Ship me any Goods unleſs they had Effects of mine in their hands. Consequently never paid more then 2½ pr C^t. I Remember I gave Meſs^{rs} Hubbards & Greene an Order on them & they Charged them Five pr C^t for purchasing Flower, whether they paid it or not I cannot ſay. The Flower Powers Complained of was Branded Connecticut. I would have you Charge me thirteen pounds York Currency & C^r David Mumford that Sum also to the amount of 9C^t. 0^{qrs}. 17^{lb} of hemp at the lowest price it can be Bo't for in New York. I have drawn on you in fav^r of Jedediah Huntington for Fifty pounds York Currency. Send me by Tinker Six Barrells pitch & six Barrells Tarr. If you can pay for Hugh Ledlie

Seventeen pounds to Samuel Broome & C⁰. Twelve pounds Ten ſhillings to William Denninge. Eleven pounds five Shillings to George Folliot & C⁰ and Send me their Receits, I Should be Glad as I want to pay that Sum to Ledlie. I am Sir Your humble Servt.

Nathl Shaw Junr.

To Meſsrs Samuel Broome & C⁰.　　　New London June 30th 1772
Merchants In New York

Gentlemen, Inclos'd is a bill drawn on Meſsrs Thomas & Isaac Wharton by our N S pay. att Ten days Sight for three hundred and thirty four pounds 10/1 Phila Currency which is Equal to three hundred & Fifty Six pounds 16/1 York Currency for which Please to Cr our Accott. We Should have paid you before & had Shipt sum Sugars to Phila for that Purpose but they were Sold on Creditt. We are Gentlemen, your huml Servt.

Nathl Shaw Junr.

To Capt Hugh Ledlie　　　New London July 9th 1772
Mercht att Boston
To yᵉ Care Mr Grey

Sir, I Received yours 7th Instant and I now Agreable to Your Request Incloſe you a Sett of Bills of Exchange on Meſsrs Lane Son & Frazier, Merchts In London for Two hundred pounds Sterling, which I have Charg'd you for in Accott att thirty three and one third & Shall Expect you to Allow me the Interest from this date to the time you propose for payment and In Case they do not Suite you on those termes you may Send them back to me by the Return of the Poſt.

I observe what you Mention in Regard to Recomending you to my Friends in the Great Town. I would Readily Comply with your Request, but its now Fifteen Years Since I have had any dealings or Connections with any other Person but Meſsrs Hubbards & George Erving, the Former you are well Aquainted with and yᵉ Latter is now in London. HowEver I Imagine you will meet with no Difficulty in Getting as many Thousands as you Mention hundreds, I am Sir Your huml Servt.

Nathl Shaw Junr.

To Mr P. Vandervoort　　　New London Augst 2d 1772
Mercht in New York

Dear Sir

As soon as you Arrive in N York you must if poſsible procure me Gold to the Amount of Four Hundred half Joanesis to Come by the first Opportunity also Six Casks Ship Bread, I would have you get Eighty Pounds York Currency Insurance on Interest in the Sloop *Dove*, John Chapman Master from this to London & back to N L. with liberty to touch in att the Isle Man on her homeward bound Paſsage on his own Accot. also Two Hundred and Fifty pounds on the Schooner *True Blue*, William Packwood Master from N L to Martineco & liberty to go to Hispaniola & back to N L on my Accot. The *Dove* Sail'd the 17th May, the *True Blue* Sail'd ye 28th June. I shall Ship some Good Sugars & Indigo to you Imediately & if you think there is any Risque I would have you send up a Boat to Stop their Comeing down.

N S

To Meiſrs Thomas & Isaac Wharton   New London Novr 11th 1772
Merchants In Philadelphia

    I Received yours by Capt Chappell and by the Post Inclosing the Bills of Exchange to the Amo of Five hundred pounds Sterling. I Should have wrote you by the last Post but was att New Port on a very Disagreable Errand. A Brigg of mine from Guadalupe with Two hundred hogsheads of Melaſses, by Streſs of Weather was drove into New Port and the Custom House Officers Oblig'd him to Enter his Cargoe and the Stupid fellow Reported only Seventy hogsheads and they have made a Seizure of the Remainder. I have Sent a Petetion to the board of Commiſsioners att Boston praying that it might be Admitted to an Entry. How farr they will be prevaild on, time only will Discover. In Case its Condemn'd they flatter me that I Shall have it att About Seven pence Sterling pr Gallon. I Shall Return their next Week in Order to have the affair Settled, and Intend to Ship it from that Port to Phila. I observe in your last that the Sugars were still Unsold, which I am very Sorry for as att this time I am much in want of Cash and have taken three hundred pounds Sterling from Mr Stewart our Collector in Order to Carry with me to New Port and have given him Incouragement to git him Bills to the Amount of three hundred pounds Sterling on London wich you will Greatly oblige me in, if you will Git them for me and Inclose One bill for One hundred pound Sterling in the Inclos'd letter & Seal & forward it for London by the first Oppertunity and Send me the other two hundred by the Poſt.
    I am Really Aſham'd that I Should be Oblig'd to Call on you in this Manner, but I am very Certain I Can Soon have Goods in your hands to Replace it, and Untill then I will Allow you the Interest Untill you are in Cash, and you will Greatly Oblige Your huml Servt

Nathl Shaw Junr.

To Mr Peter Vandervoort   New London Novr 11, 1772
Mercht In New York

    Dear Sir, I Received yours by Capt Fitch with the ship Bread. My last to you was by Capt Richards. Since that I have been to New Port once more on the Same Disagreable Errand as Formerly, by the Stupidity of Capt Melally who Came in their with two hundred hogsheads of Molaſses and made Report of only Seventy hogsheads. They have Seiz'd the

Remainder, and I am much afraid they will be Condem'd. I Returnd from their with the Brigg and the Melaſses that was Reported last Satturday and have Sent a Petition down to the Board of Commiſsioners, how farr it will avail I Cannot tell, but In Case its Condemn'd I Expect to make a Saveing in the Purchase. I have now Shipt by the barer Capt Chappell twenty Nine hogsheads & Seven Terses of Melaſses which Came out of the Brigg from Gaudalupe also thirty four hogsheads & three terses that Came in Capt Powers from Hispaniola which was first putt on board & is much Prefarable to the other and must be Sold Separate (for this Reason) I have Sold Roswell Saltonstall the Remainder of Powers Cargoe & am to have the Same price as you Git for this which is now on board. Their is Twenty five hh^{ds} of Sugar markt R P which I Should be Glad might be Sold as Soon as Poſsible as its not my own & want to Settle with the Concern'd as Soon as Poſsible also Seven hogsheads of Sugar and two hogsheads of Coffee markt N S and one hogshead of Coffee markt F F. I beleive it will be best to Ship the Coffee for Phil^a to Meſs^{rs} Whartons, but as you know the Price will leave it to you Either to Ship or Dispose of it att N York. Capt Powers is Return'd Safe, did not touch in att St Croix nor no other Place but Cape Francoise. You must Settle with the Underwriters for the Return premium. If the Price of Melaſses keeps up, I shall Load Chappell back as Soon as he Returns. I shall want sum Dollars to Carry with me to New Port. If you Can light of any Should be Glad if you will send them by Chappell, I have drawn two Orders on you Since my last by Richards. One in favour of Denison for Sixty four pounds and One in favour of Lawrence for Twelve pounds 8/6½.

Send me by Capt Chappell Twenty Casks of Ship Bread, One hundred barrels of flower of the Comon Quality but let it be Good, and Twenty Casks of New Rice.

To Mr Peter Vandervoort   New London Decem^r 12th 1772
Merch^t In New York

    Dear Sir, I wrote you last by post and I now have Shipt by Chappell Fifty Six hogsheads of Melaſses, Eight Terses & Four barrels markt S P twenty One hogsheads & one Terse D^o markt B M and Seven Terses Sugar which I would have you dispose of In Case you Can git 23^d pr Gallon or more, but if not I would have Chappell proceed on to Phil^a and if you Can Send the three Casks of Coffee by him I beleive it will Sell better their then with you, and then Send me the Twenty Casks of Rice and Fifty barrels of fine flower by the first Oppertunity. I have wrote Meſs^{rs} Whartons for Two Tons of hemp by Chappell and if he does not go to Phil^a you must Send it by him. I have drawn two orders on you in favour of Eleazer Pomeroy for Fifty pounds Each. If Capt Tinker wants a Trifle of Cash let him have it on my Acco^{tt}. The person who owns the Sugar I Shipt you last is very desirous that it Should be Sold Imediately. Send me Eight yards Green Cloth Rather finer than the Inclos'd Pattern, Ten boxis Candles, Six Casks Bristol Bear & one Fine White beaver hatt of a Middling Size.

To Mr Peter Vandervoort　　　　　　New London January 2^d 1773
Merchent in New York

　　Dear Sir, My last to you was by Edward Tinker Junr with Thirteen hogsheads Sugar and I hope he is safe arrived. Since that I received yours of the 31st Ult^o by Capt Chappell, and hope by this you have sold the remainder of his Cargoe. I observe you have sold Ten hogsheads of those Twenty six Chappell brought down. You must sell the remainder for what they will fetch and Ship the Am^o in Flower, by the first opportunity, as the owner intends to purchase a Vessell here & load for the West Indias. I believe I shall want three or four hundred barrels more, let me know in your next if their is not sum Chance of its being lower. I wrote Meſs^rs Whartons for a full Load for Chappell, and I now send him with a Load of Sugars and have only Clear'd out Seventeen hogsheads and think the best plan will be for him to enter at New York and apply for Liberty to take in those twenty Casks he brought down before, and git Certificates for abought Twenty more and go on to Phil^a or if you think their is no danger let him go on with his Clearence for the 17 hh^ds but am really afraid of the Consiquence and think it best to Clear out some more at N York. In Case Chappell cannot git up to Phil^a by reason of the Ice, I would have him return to N. York, and if you can not get 48/ pr C^t for his Sugars, I should be glad to have him Cleared out for Boston, and let him take out a new Register in his own name as I do not choose to have the Sloop go their with the old Register. I have been obliged to draw on you in favour of Wheeler Coit for Two hundred pounds. What will good West India Rum sell for, let me know in your Next.

To Meſs^rs Thomas & Isaac Whartons　　　New London January 4, 1773
Merchents In Philadelphia

　　Gentlemen, Yesterday I was surprised at the arrival of Capt Chappell who it seems after leaving New York two or three times for to proceed to Philad^a got discouraged, Landed his Cargoe in New York and came home. I have now put on board a Cargoe of Sugars, and hope he will arrive safe and to good markitts, I would have you dispatch her soon as possible & Load her with a Cargoe of Flower, and let as much of it be superfine as you can conveniently git. I have ordered Chappell to the West Indias and I immagine the Success of the Voyage depends much on his giting away soon. There is one hogshead Sugar on board that fell in the dock and is started in a Melasses hhd & Sixty Two hogsheads Sugar that I think is good, I would have you in the Acco^t Sales of this Sugar take notice of the Numbers and markes of the Casks. If their is any Rice that is new and good put Twenty Casks on board if it can be done without trouble, and as much lumber as he can Stow in the hold & on Deck, and any little matters he may want in fixing out let him have. Shall write you again by post.

To Mr Peter Vandervoort   New London Jan. 29, 1773
Merchent In New York

    I Received your Favour ye 22 Instant Inclosing my Acco^t Current Ballance in your favour Five hundred & Eighty four pounds 14/½ which I have Examined, and find all Right Except the last Eighty barrels of Flower you Sent which is not in the Acco^t. You have Charged £226.15/ for Eighty barrels of flower, 50 boxes Candles, 10 Teirces Bread & a quantity of Shaken Casks, and you will find ye Candles, Bread & Casks am^o to that Sum. I send this by Peter Rogers for three hundred barrels of flower, which you must send me, let him have as many as he Can take in and send the Remainder by sum other Boat, I want them very much, and I hope I shall not be obliged to call on you for any thing more untill I Send you a Cargoe of Melaſses, I must allow you interest untill you are in Cash, I beg you'l not Disapoint me for I have a Veſsell waiting for it. Send me Clinton Williams Note of hand that I sent you sum time agoe. If you can git the Insurance on Powers at Six pr C^t git one thousand pound York Currency on the Cargoe and Six hundred on ye Schooner *Thames* from this Port to the Medeterranen, to take Mules and go to the West Indias & return to N London on Acco^t of Gabriel Sestera & Co. and if the underwriters will not do it at that I will ſend to Phil^a. Your hum^l Servt

                                                        N Shaw Junr.

                                        New London Febuary 4th 1773

Gentlemen

    Our Friend Pomeroy tells that you Can purchase & Supply me with horſes on as good terms as any body, and if you will take one half in West India Goods down on the Delivery of the horſes the Remainder in Cash att Six months, I will write you when I Shall want them, and what kind of horſes will Sute. They will be wanted in the Spring and if you Cannot purchase them without sum Cash, I will Endavour to pay you part down. Let me hear from you by a Line & you will Oblige Your hum^l Servt

                                                        N. Shaw Junr.

To Meſs^rs Theodeus & John Weymans
    att Cambrige

To Mr Augustus Fitch   New London Feb^r 4, 1773
Joiner at Windsor

    Mr Eleazer Pomeroy tells me that he has given you a Plan for a House frame which you are to git and have made in the best manner Agreeable to his Directions and are to deliver it at Middletown in the month of May next Compleat, for which he is to give you £100 L M Payable in West India Goods. This Sir is just to lett you know that I will make you the payments according to his agreement & will receive the frame from you, and would have you send me a line & let me know what goods you want and I will ship them for your acco^t and let me know when I must be at Middletown to receive the Frame.

P. S. Desire Mr Belden to let me know how much I must give him for Sparrs of a proper length from 6 to 21 Inches. Your hum^l Servt

N Shaw Junr.

To Mr Peter Vandervoort   New London February 11th 1773
Merch^t In New York

    I Received yours 6th Instant and have Settled my Books Ballance in your Favour Seven hundred & Fifty Eight pounds 10/6½ York Money 29 January 1773 and you have now in your hands Fifty Three hogsheads & Nine barrels of Sugar & three hh^{ds} of Coffee, and believe you had better Ship it to Phil^a as Soon as Pofsible. I Received Williams Note but the Advertment & money to pay for Inserting it was not Inclos'd. Tuthill is not yet Arived. The Underwriters are too high, will not have any Insurance made on Capt Powers. I Observe what you Mention Relative to ye French Gentleman & beleive your Remark to be very Just. I do not Intend to putt my Interest in his hands. I am under much Concern about Capt Chappell. I am Sir Your very hum^l Servt

Nathl Shaw Junr.

To Mefs^{rs} Thomas & Isaac Wharton   New London July 2, 1773
Merchants In Philadelphia

    Yours 23 Ulto I Received and it gave me Joy to hear that Capt Foursard was on ye mending hand. I hope he will Soon be Able to Come to N. L. I observe you have Sixteen hogsheads of Chappells Cargoe on hand and I Really think that the price you have Offerd for them is very low, how Ever as you are the best Judges of the Markitt must leave it with you Either to dispose of them now or keep them longer. I am now ladin Chappell with sum very Good Sugars and West India Rum and Intend he Shall Sail in a few days for Phil^a. I shall want a Load of flower by his Return, about one half Common and the Other Super Fine. In your next let me know how bills of Exch^a are. I am Gentlemen Your hum^l Servt

Nathl Shaw Junr.

To Mr Peter Vandervoort   New London July 2, 1773
Merch^t In New York

    Sir, I Just now Returnd from Providence Court and have had the Satisfaction of getting a Judgment Against Mr Collecter for the Amount of my Melafses, and Shall be Oblig'd to go to Boston in about a fortnight to Prosecute my Appeal for the Rum before Judge Achmuty, and Imagine

I shall Succeed or I Afsure you I would not trouble my Self about the Matter. By the barer Peter Rogers I have Shipt Sixty barrels and Seven hogsheads of Sugar, wich I would have you turn into Cash as Soon as you Can. I wrote you att the time I Shipt the Coffee that Capt Ledyard was to be paid when you were in Cash for it and that was my Agreement with him. I hope the Price of Melafses will be up a little higher, I Expect sum in a few days, wich I Shall Ship you if it will fetch 21^d. Send me four Terses Ship bread. I am Sir Your hum^l Servt

Nathl Shaw Junr.

P. S. send the Inclos'd for the first Post. N.S.

To Mefs^{rs} Thomas & Isaac Wharton   New London July 7th 1773
Merchants In Philadelphia

    Gentlemen, I Received yours 24th Ult^o by Capt Francoise Inclosing the Acco^{tts} of Schooner *Pompey* and Sloop *Polly* wich have Examin'd and find all Right. I have now by the barer Capt Chappell Shipt thirty Nine hogsheads & Seven Terses of Melafses Forty Eight hogsheads and two Terses of Sugar, Eighteen hogsheads of Rum, three hogsheads of Coffee and three bails of Cotten all wich dispose of on the best terms you Can for the Interest of the Concern'd and send as much Flower as Chappell Can take on board, one half Merchantable and the other half Super Fine. Those Sugars and Cotten are Shipt to Purchase the Flower and you must not let them Interfear with the other Goods, they being the Property of another Person. Chappell has Orders to Purchase Severall Small articles for wich you must let him have Cash to pay for. I am Shipping sum more Melafses on Board Capt Powers who has sum Salt on Board and I Beleive I Shall give Orders for the Remainder of a Thousand Barrells of Flower Includ^g what you Ship by Chappell. I am Gentlemen, Your hum^l Servt

Nathl Shaw Junr.

Gentlemen   New London July 12, 1773

    I wrote you a few days Agoe by Capt Edward Chappell, who has a Cargoe on Board Consisting of Rum, Sugar and Melafses, wich Dispose of for my Acco^{tt}. I think if you Can git 20^d for it, it will be better then to Store it. Send me thirty Casks of Ship bread, One hundred barrels of Super Fine Flower and as many barrels of Merchantable Flower as Powers Can take on Board. Should be Glad you would Send me the Acco^{tt} Sales of the Sugar I Shipt in Chappell for I shall want to Settle with the Person who owns it. Let Capt Powers have Fifty Dollars on my Acco^{tt}. I wrote you this day that you must Acco^{tt} with Thos Wilson for the Neat Proceeds of the Eighteen hogsheads of Rum I Shipt by Edwd Chappell after deducting

10/ Phil^a Currency pr hh^d for the Freight, wich C^r my Acco^{tt} for. Capt Powers has on Board on my Acco^{tt} 30 hh^{ds} of Melaſses. I am Gentlemen, Your hum^l Servt

Nathl Shaw Junr.

To Meſs^{rs} Thos & Isaac Wharton
Merch^{ts} In Philadelphia

To Mr George Erving   New London July 22, 1773
Merch^t In Boston

    Sir, I Received yours of ye 19th Inſtant by the Post and Observe that Mr Aplin has forwarded the papers Relative to our Appeal to Mr Blowers, I am of your Opinion that it will be best to Engage Mr Adams on our Side & as I Certainly must be a Great Sufferer I would have you Engage him on the best termes you Can, am much Oblig'd to you for your kind Notice of the Station of those Pyrates. I Shall Endavour to let all our Friends know of it. I Expect a Cargoe of Melaſses in a Week or two, when it arives if I find your Markitt is the best Shall Ship it to you. Ebenezer Ledyard of this Town is In Debt to John Simson Forty or Fifty pounds, to Thomas Ruſsell About the Same Sum and to Oliver Wendell thirteen pounds. I should be Glad when you are in Cash for the Melaſses that you would pay Each of them their Demands Against him, and take their Receits. Ledyard tells me that sum of them were Purchasers of the Melaſses. I hope Soon to hear that the Day is fixt for our Tryall, untill then I am Dr Sir

Your hum^l Servt
Nathl Shaw Junr.

To Meſs^{rs} Thomas & Isaac Wharton   New London July 27th 1773
Merchants In Philadelphia

    Gentlemen, When I was att New Port I Purchasd a Negro Woman from Mrs Battar and gave an Order on you for One hundred and thirty Dollars, and I did not Advise you of it for I Expected it would have been Return'd to me as I have a Demand on her Deceasd Husbands Estate for Fifty pounds York Currency. Since that I Suppose she has gone to Phil^a to Live. I have now Inclos'd you an Order on her for Fifty pounds York Currency, wich she Advisd me by a letter that she would pay when Received C^r my Acco^{tt}. I hope Chappell and Powers are both safe arived with you, and am Gentlemen

Your hum^l Servt
Nathl Shaw Junr.

248   CONNECTICUT'S NAVAL OFFICE AT NEW LONDON

To Mr Peter Vandervoort   New London July 27, 1773
Merch^t in New York

    Dear Sir, I Received yours 24th Instant Inclosing Acco^t Sales of the Sugars Shipt by P Rogers, have Examined them & find it Right. The Bills of Exchange I sold to Samuel Broome & Co an hour or two before I Rec^d yours or I should have sent them to you. Capt Wm Packwood in the Sloop *Black Joke* Sailed from this ye 8th Ins^t. I would have you git Eight hundred pounds Insurance on the Sloop & Cargoe, One half on Each out and home. His orders where to go first to Martineco, if he lik't the Marketts was to fill, otherwise Proceed to any other Island and load his Vefsell and Return to Philadelphia, New York or this Port, the Risque to Continue only to his getting into either of these Ports. If the Underwriters will take it att Five pr C^t will, if not, I will not have any made. I am Sir

                                    Your Hum^{le} Servt
                                        N. Shaw Junr.

P. S. the Insurance must be made on Acco^t
    of N. Shaw Junr & Co.

To Mefs^{rs} Thomas & I Wharton   New London August 11th 1773
Merchants In Philadelphia

    Gentlemen, I Received yours by Chappell and Powers, with the flowers wich Arived Safe and to Satisfaction. I now want Five hundred barrels of Super fine flower to Cont^a. About 1¾ N^t flower, I Shall Send a Vefsell from this to take it on board the latter End of Next Week and Should be Glad you would have it Ready to putt on board by the time she Arives. I Expect a Cargoe of Melafses from Hispaniola hourly. If it arives before this Vefsell Sails I will putt on board 100 hh^{ds}. If not, you must Purchase the flower, and I beleive it will not be long before I Shall Send you a Cargoe of Melafses. I am &c

                                        Nathl Shaw Junr.

To Mefs^{rs} Thos & Isaac Wharton   New London Aug. 20, 1773
Merchents In Philadel^a

    Gentlemen, I wrote you 11th Ins^t by Post that I Should want Five hundred barrels of Super fine Flower to Cont^a 1¾ C^t N^t. I now Send the Sloop *Dove*, John Chapman Master to take it on board and Should be glad you would dispatch him soon as Pofsible. He will want some ship Bread & a new mainsail, which furnish him with and other little matters he may want for the Vefsell. I Received yours 10th Ins^t and am much obliged to you for your kind advise Relative to Flower in France. I am of your opinion that very little will come from their to the West Indias, of Course ours will be in Demand. The affair at Bourdeaux I had advise of from Hispaniola. I detained this Vefsell sum days Expecting sum Melaíses to arrive, but have none. I believe I shall have One or two Cargoes into Phil^a soon. If you can obtain twenty pence pr Gallon would have you Sell them, unlefs you see a prospect of its Rising. Pomeroy writes me that Saltonstall arrived Safe and seems much Suprised that his Cargoe did not Guage more in Phil^a. What Premium must I pay on a Vefsell that Sails next week for Gibralter & is to try the Marketts in the West Indias, & load & Return to N London. I am Just setting out for Boston. Expect to be absent about a Fortnight. I am in hast Gentlemen Your Hum. Servt

N. Shaw Junr.

To Meſs^{rs} Thomas & Isaac Wharton   New Lond^n 15th Sepr 1773
Merch^{ts} In Philadelphia

    Gentlemen, I Received yours 31st Ulto Inclosing Dudley Saltonstalls Order on Thomas & Dav^d Mumford for Fifty Five half Joes wich David Mumford has Expected to pay att the House of Peter Vandervoort in New York. Mr Vandervoort who is now hear tells me that the Money has been in his hands sum time to pay this Order.

    Inclos'd is a letter for John Burnly, Merch^t Living in Cumberland County in Virginia also a Note of hand Against him for One hundred and Forty Four pounds Sixteen Shillings Sterling in favour of John Deshon. I Should be Glad you would git Payment for it and Remitt it me in a Bill of Exchange in London or the Cash.

    Yours of the 4th Ins^t is also before me and am much Glad to hear Capt Melally is Safe Arived and I hope you will Manage Matters so as not to pay Dutys for so many Gallons as we did in the last Cargoes. I observe you will send him along soon in Ballast. I hope you'l Soon Send Chapman on his Voyage, as much Depends on his Ariving Soon. I hope you have Sold all the Sugar by this. I have a Cargoe Just Arived & Shall want to git sum of them to your Markitt. I am &c

N. Shaw Junr.

To Meſs Whartons   New London Octo 8, 1773
    Gentlemen

    I Just now Returned from New Port were I have been on Bufsinefs for this Fortnight past, and find my brother (at the desire of Mr Stewart our Collecter) has wrote you to git a German Woman of about thirty years of age to afsist him in his house, he now further requests that you would now git him a young man about 18 or 20 years that is Sober, honest & good tempered, Active & healthy, and that is been Us'd to horfses, also a young Woman of the fame age to do work in the Kitchen. I should be very glad if you could git him three such Servents to fute him, for I really think him to be as good a man as any that belongs to the Revenue. His motive in sending to you for them, is that he has a great aversion to negroes & ye white Servents about here have too many Connections. If you can send them to Mr Vandervoort he will have opportunities daly for this place.

I expect Capt William Packwood in a Veſsell of mine will be at Philadelphia in a short time from Martineco with a Load of Melaſses. Its now 2/ York Currency, if you can't git that price for it or much as it sells for in N York I would have him come their. Inclosed is a Letter for him wich please to deliver. I observe you are largely in advance for me. I hope you'l soon be able to collect what is due for the Sugars and Melaſses. I shall be very much miſtaken if West India Goods are not in demand this fall then they have been for sum years Past. Let me know in your next how many Gallons Melaſses y^e *Nancy* Cargoe gauged.

To Mr Peter Vandervoort   New London Octo. 22, 1773
Merch^t in New York

I am obliged at last to send Capt Leeds in the Schooner for the four hundred barrels of flower. I really expected to have had a Veſsell arrived with Melaſses, so as to have Loaded the Schooner but am disapointed. I intend to send Capt Champlin down in the Brig *Mermaid* as soon as she arrives with his Cargoe, and will send down some Sugars when you think best to send them. I Rec^d yours ye 13th Inst. with the several small articals & Cash, the order in favour of Bulkly I expected you had paid before. I have for want of Cash or I ashure you I would not have drawn in favour of Ponderson for £100 & in fav^r Doc. Moffatt for £80 York Currency which I beg you will pay, and I am in hopes it will not be long before you are repaid. I should be glad you would let me know in your next how much you are in Cash for the Coffee Rogers Carried down, as Packwood was a part concerned in it, and I would pay him in Proportion to his interest. I Received a letter from Wm Packwood at St Lucia. He writes me that he shall Sail the first of this Month for N L and if the winds are to the Eastward he will go in to N York or Phil^a. I have wrote a letter to Phil^a that in case he arrives there to come immediately to N York, & when he arrives I would have you dispose of his Cargo which will be Melaſses Chiefly. I shall want Two hundred bar^l of the best quality of Common flour in about three weeks for to ship to Gibralter and should be glad to have it come either by Champlin or Packwood. If you can git any Permacity Candles or Oill at a price that Capt Fransway thinks will answer, I should be glad you would putt thirty boxes Candles & twenty barrels of Oill on board, and as many boards as they can putt on board. Leeds says he must have a new Fore Sail and Several small articals which let him have for the Veſsells use. I should be glad you would send me by the first opportunity One Ton of Iron Thirty bolts of Rousia Duck and two hundred of white Lead Ground in oils, the Duck I cannot pay for in leſs then three M^o at least, I shall want Two Anchors of Nine hundred and one of Six hundred. Git them ready to come in Champlin. I hope you will have matters Settled so that their will be little or no Risque in sending down Sugar.

In regard to the Tea that is expected from Great Britain, I pray heartly that the Colonies will not Suffer any to be landed but in case your Governer has any directions about the matter its my opinion you will not oppose him. The people with us seem determined not to purchase any that comes in that way. Pay Capt Leeds Twenty Two Pounds York Currency. I am Sir

Your hum^l Servt
Nathl Shaw Junr.

To Mr Peter Vandervoort   New London April 27, 1774
Merchent in New York

Dear Sir, Capt Joseph Powers in the Sloop *Hawk* Sailed from this Port ye 31st Ult^o for Guadalupe. Since that we have not heard from him. He goes Consigned to Mr Pomeroy who I suppose is at Point Pelve. Powers has directions when he arrives of the port to go in with his boat and then follow Pomeroys directions, and what part of ye Island he will order him to is uncertain, but I suppose it will be to come into some port in Guadalupe. I most think it will be into the point. Or Powers may go directly to Dominico & go over himself in some small craft and take his directions. I want to have Fifteen hundred pounds Insurance, One half on the Cargoe and half on the Vefsell from this Port to the Port that he Lands his Cargoe att. I will not give more then three or three & a half pr C^t. I believe I mentioned to you that Capt Lamb toucht in at St Estatia in his way to the Cape. I am Sir, Your Hum^{le} Servt.

N. Shaw Junr.

To Mr Joseph Durfee   New London May 5, 1774
Merch^t Newport

Sir, I received yours 25th Ulto. this day and if your Indigo is as good as the last I had from you, I will take a Cask, and pay you in good Pork (of this Colony) at three pound pr barrel. If this sutes, you may send it by Ingraham, or any opportunity & I will send the Pork on the return of the Vefsell y^t brings & write me by the return of ye Post.

Your Hum. Servt
N Shaw Junr.

To Mr Joseph Durfee   N London May 12, 1774
Merchent Newport

Sir, I rec^d yours 10 Ins^t and if you'l Send me the Pork [Indigo] I will send you the Pork. I will pay the freight of the Indigo & Risque it from Newport, you are to do the Same by the Pork.

To Meſsrs Tho & Isaac Wharton   N London May 12, 1774
Merchents in Philadelphia

  Gentlemen, The bearer Capt Edward Chappell has on board the Sloop *Sally* One hundred & Twenty two Casks Melaſses which dispose of for my Accot and let him have as much Money as you can conveniently send and dispatch him soon as poſsible. Inclosed is a memorandum for Several articals which please to send. I am Loading a Schooner wth Melaſses which will sail for Phil. in a few days & hope will arrive in time for to take ye advantage of ye present Markett.

                  N Shaw Junr.

To Meſsrs Thomas & Isaac Wharton   New London May 19th 1774
Merchts In Phila

  Gentlemen, I wrote you by Capt Chappell the 12th Inst who Saild for Phila last Sunday with 120 Casks of Melaſses on Board and hope he will Arive Safe. I now Send by the barer Capt Wm Harris Seventy Casks of Melaſses and hope you will be Able to git 22½ pr Gallon att least for their never was so Great a Scarsity of that Article in the West Indias as att this time. I have pd Harris the Frt.

                  N. Shaw Junr.

To Meſsrs Tho & Isaac Wharton   New London June 2, 1774
Merchents In Philadelphia

  Gentlemen, The bearer Wm Rogers in the Sloop *Black Joke* has on board One hundred & thirty four hogsheads Melaſses, which Sell for my Accot. There is forty hogsheads Markt B M which in your Accot Sales keep Seperate. The 94 hhds is in ye Bottom & I believe you will find to be better then those mark'd B M. The whole is extraordinary good quality, and I hope you'l git a good price for it. If you can Sell the Sloop, I would take One thousand Dollars for her rather then have her come back. I have wrote Peter Vandervoort to sell her as she goes by New York if he does he will advise you of it. If you can't sell her put some Empty Melaſses hogsheads on board to be filld with water for Ballast and send her back soon as you can. I am Gentlemen, Yr Hum. Servt.

To Mr Peter Vandervoort   N London June 2, 1774
Merchent In New York

  The bearer Wm Rogers has on board 94 hhds Melaſses mark'd S B I and 40 hhds markt B M & if it will sell for York Cury what it is in Phila that Cury I would have you sell it, if not let Rogers proceed to Phil^a. I have taken Nathan Douglaſs Note for the Am^o of your Acco^t pay. on Demand with Interest. He could not give any Security that I thought would do, he has a very pretty Sloop that is now at Casco Bay & Expect her hear soon, I will then attach her. Should be glad you would send me a Receipt for £10 on Acco^t And^r Huntington, on Acco^t Jed Huntington £30, on Acco^t of Cyrus Ponderson £11.10/, and pay Van Vlack & Son £30, Van Vlack & Kipp £30, & Danl Phoenix £21.1/ on Acco^t Eb Ponderson. I have also given him an order on you for Forty pounds, and In case the Sloop goes to Phil^a I will give you an Order on Meſs^{rs} Whartons for the Am^o of what you are in Advance for me, and if you Sell the Melaſses you must take up a Note of hand that C^s McEvers has against Wm Packwood as I have promised him should be paid out of this Cargo. There is £292.4/ L M due on Y^e Note with Six pr C^t Interest from 21st Jany 1773. If the Sloop goes to Phil^a tell McEvers I will send him a Bill on Meſs Whartons soon as she arrives. Do you sell the Sloop if you can git £400 Cur^y or more. If not put sum empty Melaſses hhd^s on board & let them putt Water in them for Ballace. If Ponderson does not order Salt sent him. Inclos'd is a Mem^o from Doc Moffatt, I beg you'l get it & send, for I aſsure you I am in a very bad way. Do you think their is much risque in sending down a few hhd ſugar or Can you get a Clearance for Philad^a (If she goes let Wharton know it as I have wrote them to Sell her). Rogers will leave her on his Return, the Inclos'd letter send along with him, but if you Sell, Inclose the letter back to me.

Meſs Thomas & Isaac Whartons   New London June 20, 1774
Merchents In Philadelphia

    Gentlemen, I Rece^d yours by post advising ye Sale of Harris's Cargoe of Melaſses. Should be glad you would in your Next let me know the am^o of Sales of two hhd that Harris left with you for John McKebbin, also Capt. Melallys, as I shall pay them here. Our friend Peter Vandervoort will forward you two Horſes wich Capt^t Melally chose out of a Cargoe that I just now Purchased. He thinks the Largest will sute T W and the Smallest Isaac. Mrs Shaw was very much displeased wth Chappell for not calling on Isaac at N Y & bringing him wth ye two Young Ladys to N L. I am Gent

                                                   Y^r hum Servt.

Meſs^{rs} Peter Vandervoort & Co.   N London June 30 1774
Merchents In New York

    Gentlemen, I Rec^d yours by E Tinker Junr with the Shaken Casks & I send this by Rogers Boat for thirty small bar flower Super fine & twenty boxes Spermacity Candles, which beg you'l send by her as soon as you can. Inclosed is a Bill I have drawn on Meſs Tho & Isa Wharton for £500 Phil^a Cur^y at 5 days sight. If you could sell it & send me the money you would Greatly oblige me. I every moment Expect three Vefsells with Melafses which shall Send to you soon as they arrive. What will Powder'd sugars sell for.

Mefs Tho & Isa Whartons N L June 30 1774
Merch^{ts} Phil^a

    Gent. I have not Rec^d any of your favours since ye 4 Ins^t. I hope by this you have disposed of the Remainder of Harris's Cargoe of Melafses, if the price keeps up I believe in a few days I shall send you some more. I hope the two horfes I sent to the care of Mr Vandervoort are come to hand. What will white powder'd sugars sell for. I have drawn on you at five days sight in fav^r Theo & Zeb Rogers for £128, also in favour of P Vandervoort for £500 & hope you will be in Cash for the Melafses to pay them.

Mefs Peter Vandervoort & Co N L July 6, 1774
Merchants New York

    Gentlemen, Please to pay Mefs Haviland & Farrington fifteen pound Seventeen shill & 6^d for & on Acco^t Saml Wheat & Thomas Pearsall £29.15.10 on acco^t s^d Wheat and send me their Receipts and also one box 7 by 9 Glafs.

Mefs P Vandervoort & Co New London July 13 1774
Mercht New York

    Gentlemen, I Rec^d yours by John Harris of ye 6th Ins. with Cash. This by Peter Rogers in the Sloop *Mackaronia* with Fifty hhd Melafses which sell for my Acco^t. I am Loading Job Rothbon also & hope you'l git 1/10 at Least. I have drawn in favour of Guy Richards & Son for £150 & in favour of Mefs Ledyard for £100. I observe what P V says in regard to Bills of Exch^a. Pomeroy writes me from Antigua that Capt Deshon had arrived att Dominica with 74 Mules & had them Sold. I hourly expect the am^o in Bills wich you shall have & will pay Mefs^{rs} Brooms the money for my Note, as soon as you can Collect the money for this Cargoe of Melafses, & would have you send me up my Note when you can pay it. The Seven hhd Melafses Ed Tinker Junr del^d you markt B M you must C^r my Acco^t & send me ye Acco^t of Sales, also send me fifty bolts Rusia Duck & Screws for 2 bedsteads as by the Inclosed mem^o. You may let the underwriters know that the *America* is safe Arrived.

The flower & Candles by P Rogers came safe to hand. Tell Mr Pagan his Schooner Saild this day with a good Wind in C^o w^t Capt Packwood, Peter has 5 Casks more on board then is Clear'd out. I suppose it will make no difficulty when I clear'd him out I did not expect that he had or could take so many on board. I am &c

---

Meſs P Vandervoort & Co   N L July 13, 1774
Merchents N York

  Gent. I have Shipt you by Peter Rogers 50 hh Melaſses by Richd Spink, 18 by Job Rothbone, 70 hhd^s and hope they will all arrive save. I this moment rec^d yours 12th Inst. & am glad to hear that Melaſses is in demand. I have drawn two orders on you in fav^r D Manwaring to the Am^o of £186. The bearer Keph Tinker has on board about twenty thousand Gal Melaſses in the Brig *Mermaid* wich you must dispose off on the best terms you can for my Interest. We have reported 150 hhd & 50 Teirces. I beg you will Cheat them much as you can of ye Duties.

 I Rec^d a Letter from Capt Deshon & find he has sold his cargoe of Mules (74) for 22^lb Ster^g pr head pay in 12 m^o w^t Interest, the greatest part to Mr Nelson who I know to be a man of Fortune & Character. The Season being so far advanced he could do no better. Deshon is now at Guadalupe Load^g w^t Sug^r & Melaſses so that I shall not have the Bills I expected. Soon as you can take up my Note to Meſs Broom & Co Inclose it to me. John Chapman Saild in C^o w^t Tinker & I hourly expect him. If Melaſses keeps up I will send him down.

 I think if you can get the papers & Trunk from Capt Cox the underwriters may be Sattisfied with ye Loſs of Capt Powers & I think they may pay ye money in 3 M^o of this, you'l take care & do ye needful. You mention that I must send proof of my Interest below decks, to the am^o of £750—unleſs I include the Stock on Deck I have not to that am^o. I always understood & Expected that if the Stock were drowned on Deck or thrown over, the underwriters would not have paid for them, but when their is a totall Loſs, what matter is it to them whether the Interest was on Deck or in the hold. I think they may as well Refuse paying for Stock when the Veſsell is taken by an Enemy. I take it that the very intent is that a person should not Insure more then his Interest. I am short two hundred pounds at least. I have Rec^d no advice from Meſs Whartons of their receiving ye horſes.   Y^rs &c

P S. Inclosed is a Bill drawn by Dan & Eliz^a Roberts of ye 10th June att Dominica att 60 Days Sight for 250 Spanish Mill'd Dollars on Robt Hinchman at Jamaica in fav^r John Easton. I beg you'l git it paid. Y^rs

                       N S.

256   CONNECTICUT'S NAVAL OFFICE AT NEW LONDON

To Meſsrs Peter Vandervoort & Co   New London Augst 23d 1774
Merchants In New York

  Gentlemen, I Received yours by Capt Melally, with Seven hundred and Five pounds 5/8 Currency. Am very Sorry you did not Send me a Thousand or Fifteen hundred Dollars, for I am in great want of them to pay the Custo House. The barer Peter Rogers has on Board 86 Casks of Melaſses and hope you'l git 1/9 pr Gallon for it att least. I am Loading Chappell who will Sail in a few days with a full Load of Melaſses, you must Send me sum Dollars. Mr Vandervoort is now att Hartford. I am Gentlemen, Your huml Servt

                 Nathl Shaw Junr.

To Mr James Gordon   New London, Sepr 7 1774
Mercht In George Town

  Sir, I Received yours 12th April by Capt Edward Wheelar with 80 barls Pitch and Two Small Casks of Indigo, the Pitch I have still on hand the Indigo I Sold on Cr att 4/6 to A Person who is to pay me the Cash the 1st of October Next. Good Indigo will always sell for One Dollar pr pound but this was of an Inferior Quality. The article of Pitch is a very Slow Sale in this Town & their being more Imported this Year than Can be made use of Severall persons have Shipt theirs to N York for a Markitt. How Ever as I have not Imported any, I shall make use of yours on my Own Veſsells and allow you York Price and Remitt the Amo with the Indigo as you Desir'd. Their is but very few Veſsells that are own'd in this Port Consequently the Demand for Naval Stores are but Small and when Ever any is shipt it would be best to have an Equal Quantity of Pitch Tarr and Turpentine.

  Rice and Indigo will allways Command an Imediate Sale, if Good, for Cash. This Indigo of yours I Could not Sell for Cash. I Recd yours 11th April and I now Inclose you a Certificate to Cancel the Bond you Gave for Wheelar. I am Sir Your very huml Servt.

                 Nathl Shaw Junr.

To Meſsrs Mercer & Schenk   New London Sepr 7 1774
Merchts In New York

  Gentlemen, I am favoured with yours of ye 31st Ulto and am very much oblig'd to A M for his kind Aſsistance to Capt Chappell.

  I have only 40 hhds Melaſses on hand that I Shall ship you, and if any Arives before the Brigg Sails I will make up the Remainder att the Price you Mention. Saltonstall tells me you Shall have Forty hogsheads of Rum, he has no more. I Cannot git him to take leſs then 1/9 L My. Shall have the Rum & Melaſses properly Stow'd, and git the Brigg away as Soon as Poſsible, am Sorry you did not Send up the Duck for ye Sales, ye Coursers in Particular. The Brigg of mine Sails this day, so that I have no Sails that will Sute yours, and you must Send sum from N York by the first Boat. Capt Smith has not been over, their is many things to be done wich I shall finish, and leave the Matter with you to Settle, as I know not the Agreement you made with him. I observe you'l Send two or £300 by Capt Chappell wich I hope will be in our paper Money or Silver, as their is a Lofs on half Joes unlefs they weigh 9^{dt}3^{grs}. Your Young Man writes you and has Inclos'd the Dementions of your Sparrs.

I Yesterday Rec^d ye News of one of my Vefsells being Lost with a Load of Lumber, att Soco River and am Sending of my Brigg to take out her Load, wich is the Reason that I Cannot Spare you the Sales.

N S

To Mefs^{rs} Mercer & Schenk   New London Sepr 20th 1774
Merch^{ts} In New York

    Gentlemen, this will be handed to you by Capt James Angell in your Brigg *Polly & Getty* with Forty hogsheads of N E Rum and thirty three hogsheads & Twelve Terses of Melafses all wich I wish may come safe to hand, also an Acco^t of Sundry disbursements on the Brig *Polly & Getty* Am^o to ——— and my Acco^t Ballance in my favour. I wrote you for some Bread & flower last week which should be glad you would send me by the first opportunity. I have endavour'd to draw a Bill on you, but their is no person I can light on that will take any. If you can send me the Money by Capt Angell it would much oblige me as I must pay for the Rum on her Return. I have Settled with all the people to this day. Their Wages for carrying the Brig to N York must refer you to Capt Angell, I would not detain the Brig on acco^t of the Sails therefore the Sailmaker takes pafsage in the Brig & will finish them. I have Supply'd you with sum small Duck and have taken an Equal Quantity of yours & will C^r your acc^t for the Difference by ye first opport^y. I will send you a copy of ye Severall Bills.

To Mefs^{rs} Peter Vandervoort & Co New London Octo 14, 1774
Merch^{ts} In New York

    Gentlemen, I Just this moment Returned from Newport & find Capt Wm Packwood is arrived & left his Vefsell & Cargo with you. If you have not already Sold his Cargo, I would have you putt it in store & Send the Sloop to N London for I am very Certain the price of Melafs^s must be much higher. I Rec^d a Letter from Mefs Whartons that it's quick at 22^d & in all probability will be higher. If you can git £300 Sell the Sloop. I would have you stop taking any more Casks from the Destillers for unlefs the times alter we had better do nothing then Import Melafses. I am Gentlemen

Your Hum^l Servt
N Shaw Junr.

To Meſrſ Thomas & Isaac Wharton   New London Octo. 15, 1774
Merchtſ In Philadelphia

    Gentlemen, I Received yours of the 1st & 8th Inst and am Glad to hear that West India Goods are on the Rise. I now Send you by Capt Chappell a Cargoe of very Good Melaſses and I hope you will be Able to git a Good Price for it. Send me One hundred and Fifty barrels of Super Fine Flower, and if you Can Collect any Dollars, I Should be Glad you would Send me near About the Ballance. If Melaſses Continues high I will Send Chappell back with another Cargoe. Capt Deshon wants to know when you are in Cash for his Bill. Have not to add but am Gentlemen, Your huml Servt

                                                        Nathl Shaw Junr.

Gentlemen,   New London October 26, 1774

    The first Wind the Schooner *Thames*, James Angell Master with about 110 hhd Melaſses which you may depend is of the very best quality will come to N Y to your addreſs & am in hopes you will be able to git 2/ pr G for it. She is to be Loaded with Square pine timber Albany Boards & sum good Shingles & the ballance must be in half Johanisis or dollars that are no defraud in Cutting but must be Reduced in a Nt maner to 9dwt. Shall write you more particular by Angell. Have not to add but am Gentlemen Yr Huml Servt

                                                        N Shaw Junr.

To Meſs Peter Vandervoort & Co
Mercht N York

To Meſs Thom & Isa Whartons   New London Octo. 26, 1774
Merchtſ In Philadelphia

    We wrote you by Capt Chappell who Sailed from this ten days agoe with a Cargoe of Melaſses, which was of the very best quality and hope ere this comes to hand he will arrive and to good Sales. Since that I have Recd yours of ye 15 Inst & observe you have Cr my Acot for Mr Rawsons order for Sixty Dollars. Mr Transhant has sent the Schooner *Thames* to N L with a Cargoe of Melaſses, & he complains much about the charge of your Commiſion and as I am one half concerned in the sd Schooner I think on the whole you had better make out the Accot & Charge at the Same rate as you have my Concerns and send me the Accot by the Return of the Post, as Capt Leeds will sail in a Fortnight for Hispaniola, and I want to Settle Accot with Mr Transchant for Leeds to Carry out with him. Capt Foursard says they did not Receive your Accot by Leeds.

N London Octo 27, 1774

Gent.
The foregoing is a Coppy of what I wrote you by ye post. This will be handed to you by Capt Angell & hope he will arrive safe & should be glad you would dispatch him for Hispaniola as soon as you can with Lumber & cash, and send me the Acco^t of Sails &c with Angell Bill Lading for what you put on Board to be delivered to Mon^r Tranchant, Merch^t at Logane. Next week Peter Rogers will come down, by him I shall want 150 bar of Super fine flour & 30 Cask of good Rice. If you could send me sum Cash by ye first oper^y should be very glad. Angell has a Horfe on board which be so good as to send to Mefs^{rs} Whartons. I am Gentlemen, Your Hum^l Servt

N Shaw Junr.

To Mefs Peter Vandervoort & Co
Merchants In New York

To Mefs^{rs} Mercer & Schenk   New London Octo 29, 1774
Merchents In New York

Gentlemen, I wrote you a few days agoe by Capt Chappell, Since that I have not Rec^d any of your favours. This is just to Inclose you my Acco^t Ballance in my favour £333.11.1½ L M^y which I have drawn on you for in favour of R Saltonstall the person whom I bought the Rum off, and make no doubt but you'l pay the order, I am Gentlemen, Your Hum^l Servt.

To Mefs P Vandervoort & Co New London Octo 29, 1774
Merch^{ts} In N York

Gent. I wrote you by the Schooner *Thames* who Sailed two days ago & make no doubt but they had a good Pafsage. The bearer Ros Saltonstall is to Receive £150 York Currency when you are in Cash for the Lofs of the Sloop *Hawk* & should be glad when you are in Cash to pay him that Sum & take his order on me for it. I have drawn on you in his favour for £86.4.2. Next Week Rogers will be down & call on you for 150 barrels flower & 30 Casks Rice & 20 Casks Ship Bread. I am Gent. Your hum Servt.

To Mr James Anderson   New Lond^n Novr 3, 1774
Merch^t In Boston

Sir, I Received yours 6th Sepr and would have Answerd it before but was not att home when it Came to hand. Mr Gordon Shipt me sum Indigo and Pitch and Desird the Neat Proceeds paid to you. The Indigo

I sold on C^r & am now in Cash for it. The Pitch is not Sold but will take it to my own Acco^{tt} wich will make a Ball in my hands of £88 L M^y in Bills of this Col^y. You may Either draw a Bill on me for that Sum or I Can give you a Bill Payable on Sight att Phil^a or New York or will Remitt as you Desire by the Return of the Post, shall Expect your answer. Untill then I am Sir Your hum^l Servt.

N Shaw Junr.

To P Vandervoort & Co N Lond. Nov. 9, 1774
Merch^{t}s N York

Gent. This by P Rogers in the *Maccarone* By whome I have sent you a Wedge of Gold weighing Ninty two ounces which I want the Value in Cash, our Connecticut Bills or Silver & beg you will send it me by Rogers on his Return. If you want to make any remittance to Great Britain you may send it to your Friend and acco^t with me for the neat proceeds in that case would have you git it insured, but the money to the Vallue of it must have by Rogers. Also send me 42 Cask Rice and the Nails I gave a Mem^o to Ledyard for, the 150 bar flour I wrote Meſs Whartons to Ship me by Capt Chappell. If any good Apples are come in send me ten barrels & twenty bar Tarr and one thousand weight of Deck nail Rods. If you have any oppor^y to ship any of that Coffee to Phil^a I think it would answere better then at N. Y. What Premium must I pay on the Ship *America* from this to Gibralter or the Straights to continue untill they find a suitable markett to dispose of her Cargoe. Let me know in your next also when you are in Cash for the Loſs of the Sloop *Hawk*. If Chadwick wants to the Am^o of £80 York Cur^y let him have it & take his order on me. Your hum^l Servt

N Shaw Junr.

To Meſs^{rs} Thos & Isaac Whartons   New London Nov 23, 1774
Merchents In Philadelphia

Gent. I Rec^d yours by the post Inclosing Acco^t Sales of the Schooner *Thames* Cargoe: Transhants Acco^{ts}, Letters &c which I have shewn to Mr Fousard and think I have made him easy on acco^t of the Charges of Commiſsion on the Cash as I think you had no orders to send any consequently where Liable in case of any accident. Inclosed is his order on you for £98.½ Currency ye ballance of said Acco^t which paſs to my C^r. Capt Chappell arrived here six days agoe with the flour and Bread, and agreeable to you will draw on you when I can have an opportunity it being attended with much difficulty to git any parson this way to take a bill. Should be glad you would purchase a Bill of Exchange of £100 Ster^g & inclose two Bills of ye Sett & send to Meſs^{rs} Hugh & Whitelock Druggest in London on Acco^t of Eliphalet Dyer and send me the third Bill with the Cost. I believe I shall send Chappell once more to Philad^a with a Load Melafses before the River Shuts up unlefs the Marketts in New York should be better then with you.

To Mefs^{rs} Mercer & Schank   New London Nov 23, 1774
Merchents In New York

    Gentlemen, I Received yours by Mr Saltonstall and I called on the Sail maker in regard to his Bill and I must confefs that I did not examine it as I should have done, for it was charged in York Money & I have charged you Lawful for it, which makes a great differance. The post just setting out or I would have sent you an order on Mefs Vandervoort & Co for it. I purchased

To Mefs^{rs} Peter Vandervoort & Co New London Nov 28, 1774
Merchents In New York

    Gent. I Rec^d yours by Rogers with the Casks of Rice. I find an error, difference in your favour the odds between £3.10/ York Currency & £3.10/ L M being in Ten Crown & half carried out £3.10/ York Cur^y. In the Nails you will find 10/ over last in the Cask 4^d Nails, and 10/ in adding up which makes 20/ in my favour. I hope to have a cargo of Melafses in a few days from Guadalupe. I shall send it down as soon as it arrives. I hope you are in Cash from the underwriters on ye *Hawk*. I want the money very much, I beg if you have any Opportunity you'l send me sum for I cannot do without. Peter Latemer is on his pafsage down.

                                 I am &c

To Mr Samuel Alcott   N Lond Dec. 8, 1774
Merchent at Hartford

    Sir, When you wrote Esqr Miller to call on me to underwrite on your Sloop I was informed that you had advice from N York that a Vefsell sailed from that Port (17 days after your Vefsell left this port) and discharged her Cargoe at Medeira & Loaded & sail'd from their, & your Vefsell had not arrived when they came away, which circumstance you did not Informe me of. Should be glad to know if it's true. I am Sir

                               Your Hum Servt
                               N Shaw Junr.

To Mefs^{rs} Peter Vandervoort & Co New London Dec. 13, 1774
Merchents In New York

    I Received yours by Capt Latimer with the Cash wich I find to be right, you do not mention wether you have Rece^d the Money from the underwriters of the Sloop *Hawk*. I want to pay John Myers sum money

Soon as you have Rec^d it. If you can draw on Mef^{rs} Whartons for Four hundred pound & forward that sum to me Should be much obliged to you, I have wrote them In case you draw to honour ye same. Am very Sorry the Brig *Nancy* does not arrive. I have drawn on you in fav^r of Mr Clements for £252.13.11 which beg you'l pay. I am Gent. Your Hum. Servt.

N. Shaw Junr.

N Lond Dec. 13, 1774

Gent.

I wrote you ye 23 Ult^o. Since then have not Received any of y^r fav^{rs}. If our Friend Peter Vandervoort & Co draw on you for about Four hundred pounds should be glad you would pay it and Charge to my acco^t. I am Gen.

Y^r Hum. Servt.
N Shaw

To Mefs Tho & Isaac Whartons
Merchents In Philadelphia

New London Decem^r 14th 1774

Dear Friend

In Consequence they Order we purchas'd Jacob Wineys Draft on John Whitmore Senr & Junr Esqr of London for £100 Sterlin & transmitted the Same on the Account of Eliphalet Dyarr to Hughs & Whitelock, Druggist in London. The 1st by the last Packitt & the 2^d by a Ship Directly from this Port, the third we now Inclose to the. We could not Purchase it under 67½ pr C^t & as we ware Oblig'd to Endorce it we trust thou'l have no objection to our Commifs^n of 2½ pr C^t thereon, making £171.13.9 to thy Debit. Endosing of bills is attended often with so much Risque & Lofs that we would not be in the Practice of it for a much Greater Consideration unlefs it were for Thy Self & a few Other of our Particular Friends whom we Shall be always Glad to Serve. Sir, Above is a Copy of what Our Friends Whartons wrote me this post & Inclos'd the Within Bill, for wich they have Charg'd me £171.13.9 wich in Lawfull Money is £137.7/ for wich Please to Send me your Note of hand on Interest. If you Could Conveniently Send me any Money it would not be Amifs. In Consequence of the Cannon being mov'd from the Fort att New Port to Providence, we Yesterday Remov'd ours into the Cuntry, but I Lement the Unhappy Situation we are in for want of Powder, we are universally without any, for our our Town Stock in this Town we have not a barrell and they know not ware to git any. I think if the Afembly is Cal'd they Should Imediately give an order in the Treasury for a Sum of Money Sufficient to Purchase 4 or 5 hundred barrells. If they would Employ me to git it, unlefs sum Accident, I think I Could have that Quantity hear in Ten weeks. Yesterday Col^n Huntington and Col^n Spencer were in Town and they both seem'd to be much in ye opinion of the Nefsesity of sending for it Imediately, if it Should take with the Assembly, your mentioning my Name will be Agreable as I have a Small Vessell in Readiness that I am Cartain is the fastest Sailor in the Colony, Can be Ready att a Days Warning. I am Sr Your hum Servt.

Nathl Shaw Junr.

To Mess Tho & Isaac Wharton   N Lond Dec 15, 1774
Merchents In Philada

    Gent. I Received yours 9th Inst. Inclosing Jacob Wineys Bill of Excha for £100 Sterg for which have Cr you Accot £171.18.9 Cury. As to the Money Recd on Accot of Bunleys Note hand Capt Deshon wants it very much and would be glad to have whatever part is collected, & should be glad you would Soon as you Receive it, Remitt to P. Vandervoort & Co for his Accot. I wrote you a few days agoe that if Vandervoort drew on you for my Accot to the amo of Four or Five hundred pounds, to Honour his Draft. Have not to add but am Gent. Your Hum Servt.

N. Shaw Junr.

Gentlemen   New London Decemr 15, 1774

    I wrote you Yesterday by Mr Clements, have only to add that I have drawn on you in favour of Sam Belden in Two Orders to the Amo of £248.8.5 pay 30 Days Sight and hope by that time you will be in Cash to pay them. You must Send me Eight or Nine Casks of powder by the first opper. If I Should want Four or Five hundred Casks do you think it may be had in St Eustatia or Curraso. Should be Glad you would Inquire and let me know in your Next. If you draw in Mess Whartons for Five hundred pounds on my Accot Your Bill will be honor'd. I am Your Hum. Servt

Nathl Shaw Junr.

To Mess. Peter Vandervoort & Co.

To Mr Thomas Bennett   New London Dec. 20, 1774
Mercht Granada

    Sir, I Reced your kind Letter of the 28th Octo Relative to the Protested Bill left with you by Capt Mitchall, and I now Inclose you a Power, & beg you'l git the Money from Either Eames or Deveron, and when in Cash Ship me Rum, by the first opportunity for this Port to the amount. If I can be of any Service to you this way, shall Readily do it, I am Sir,

Your Humle Servt
Nathl Shaw Junr.

By favour Capt Tracey.

Gentlemen, N London Decr 22, 1774

I Rec^d y^r fav^r 30th Aug & I really expected to have paid you the ballance of my Acco^t long before this time. I sent out Capt Deshon to the Meditarrenen with Cargo who was to purchase a Load of Mules & proceed to the West Indias, there sell for Bills & Remitt you, but being detained so long at Gibraltar that when he arrived in the West Indias Mules would not Sell for Cash & he was obliged to give 12 M^o C^r which disapointed me very much. John Lamb Sailed last Week on the Ship *America* for Gibralter. I gave him orders to putt Some Cash in Mefs^{rs} Robert Anderson & Co hands with orders to Remitt the same to you, also to desire you to make Insurance for my Acco^t on the Said Ship to wherever they Proceed for. You may rest Afsured that you will be paid both principal & Interest for what I am in y^r Debt and when that is acomplished Mr Lane must give me a Deed of those Lands, for untill that I cannot make Sale of them If I where disposed so that lett matters go as they will in America. The Land is still yours, untill I pay for it, which certainly shall be this summer. I am Gentlemen

Your Hum. Servt
N Shaw Junr.

To Mefs Lane Son & Fraser
Merchents In London

To Mefs P Vandervoort & Co   N Lond Dec. 29, 1774
Mercht^s In New York

Gent. Yours 19th Ins is now before me & am sorry to find that the underwriters on the *Hawk* have not paid you for I Really want ye Money. I wrote you by Capt Chappell & Rogers, hope they have both arrived & y^t you will be able to send me ye money for ye Draft on Mefs Whartons, also Negociate £800 Currency to be pd in Boston. I expect Pomeroy in a few days with a Load of Sugar from Guadalupe with sum Coffee which shall send down soon as it arrives unlefs you find the risque too great. Pomeroy writes me of ye 18th Nov y^t ye Sloop *Sally*, Ed Hulling Master was at the Mole Grand hear in Guadalupe & was to take in Sugars and Sail in Twelve days for this Port. I would have you git three hundred pounds Insurance on ye Vefsell & £700 on ye Cargo on Acco^t of N Shaw Junr & Co. The Sloop was waiting for the Guardacostas to be out of the way to have an Oppor^y to take in Sugars so that it is uncertain whether Pomeroy will be able to Ship any Goods or that the Vefsell will Sail for N L. He writes me to have the Insurance made Conditionally, that if she does not Sail to pay nothing, but the Charges, which is customery. Inclos'd is John Myers Rec^t for £63 in part pay for my Note wich is on 6 pr C^t Interest, as it was given in this Colony, but if he insists on 7 to pay him.

To Mefs Thos & Isaac Whartons N London Jany 15, 1775
Merchents In Philadelphia

 Gent. I Recd yrs by Capt Harris of ye 17 Ulto with 110 bar flouer Amo to £230.13.7 which I have put in store & if I can dispose of it shall take it to my own accot. Have also Recd yr 20th Inclosing a Bill of Ex for £147.1.6 Sterg on accot of John Burnleys Note of hand, and am much obliged to you for yr Trouble in the affair & would have you charge me the Amo of what Expences you have been at for Postage &c. I expected to have sent Chappell with a Load of Melafses to you before ye River shutt up, but the price at N Y being higher a ¼ Dollar have shipt to that markett. When any alteration in yrs be so kind as to advise me of it. I am Gent.

           Your Humle Servt

P. S. our friend Col Dyar says you must not charge the 2½ pr Ct on ye Bill you sent home on his accot.

To Mefs P Vandervoort & Co N Lond Jany 15, 1775
Merch N York

 I Recd yrs by *Macerone* wth ye Cash. This is just to let you know that I intend as soon as Chappell Returns that he will go on board ye *Macerone* for West India & will call on you for one hundred bar Super fine flouer & two hundred half Johannises which should be glad you would have Ready for him. Hope you have been able to get the 100 bar of pork at ye price I wrote for from Hartford last week. I am Gentlemen

           Yr Humle Servt.

         New London January 24th 1775
Gentlemen

 I Recieved your 13th by Capt Chappell also of the 18th by post came to hand. I have now by the Sloop *Macaroni* Shipt a Cargo of Melafses wich is very Good. Hope you'l git 2d/ for it. You must Certainly send me Two hundred half Joaneses and Fifty barrels of Super Fine Flower att least. I shall send the Sloop to the West Indias as Soon as she Returns, & beg you'l dispatch her as Soon as you Can. I Received a letter from Mefsrs Whartons that they hourly Expected your order on them for Four or Five hundred pounds and that the Money was Ready whenever it appeard, but that no Person would take the Charge of it this time of the Year. I have drawn on you in favour of Mefsrs Lothrops for Forty three pounds 11/1 in favour of I Pitton for one hundred pounds att thirty days Sight in favr of David Manwaring for One hundred & Fifty pounds & two orders in favr Wm Neilson to the amo One hundred & Fifty Pounds L in favour of Arther Jarvis for Twenty Five pounds 14/. I wrote you by the Post that I had sum Good Sugar & Coffee wich I will send down when you think they Can come Safe. What Premium must I pay on the *Macarone* Against the Danger of the Seas & Seizures from this to the West Indias with Liberty to go to Severall Ports untill we Can git our Cargoe. I Recd your order in favour of P V on R. Saltonstall for £150, have Cr his Accot for that Sum. I am Gentlemen, Your hum Servt

Nathel Shaw Junr.

P S. send me two Pieces of Ticklinburg. Have sent 35 hhds Melaſses.

To Meſsrs Peter Vandervoort & Co.

To Mr James Anderson   New London Feb 1, 1775
Merchent In Boston

    I Recd yours last Post of ye 22 Ulto and I now agreeable to your Request Incloſe you my Bill on Meſsrs Thos & Isaac Whartons Mercht in Philada for £110 Phila Currency at five days Sight which is equal to £88 L M on accot of Mr James Gordon. You'l let me know by the Return of the Post your Receiving the Inclos'd. I am in hast Sir yr Huml Servt.

To Meſs Thos & Isaac Whartons   New London Feb 1, 1775
Merchents In Philadelphia

    Gen. This day I recd a line from our friends P. Vandervoort & Co and find they have not been able to draw on you on my Accot. I have drawn on you in favour of Jas Anderson for £110 at five days Sight. I Recd yrs by ye post Inclosing Sales of the Melaſses Shipt by Chappell & find it right. Also the third Bill of Excha for Burnleys Debt. Melaſss now sells in N York at 2/ so that I Ship what I have come to markett. Have not to add but am &c.

To Mr Peter Vandervoort   New London Feb 13, 1775
Merchent New York

    Dear Sir, I Recd yrs Incloſing P Vandervoort & Co Accot Current with me ballance due the Co £359.17/9½, York Cury. I have examined the accot & find all Right Except £5.2/8 pd a Sailor on board the *Black Joke* Octo 15th which you have not charg'd, also 40/ over charg'd in flower & Oznabrigs ye 30th Ulto. The Invoice you sent me is £183.18/10, and you have charged £185.18/10. Rectify these mistakes & ye ballance will be £363.0.5½ which I have C^r you for in a New Acco^t and Charged the 2½ pr C^t for Settling the Lofs on Sloop *Hawk*. In the Acco^t of P V you charged me 2½ pr C^t for Settling y^e £1470 and Carried it out £33.15/, and its £36.15/, you'l alter that and let that acco^t Stand untill we have the am^o of ye Wedge of Gold. I drew an order on P V & Co in favour of Jabez Huntington 31st Jan. which I suppose had not come to hand when you Sent me the Acco^t. I have given C^r for this order in ye New Acco^t. I am &c.

To Mr Peter Mumford   New London Feb 15, 1775
In Newport

    I Rec^d y^{rs} by Capt Rufsell with Seventy boxes Candles which was 26 boxes more then I really wanted, however I have taken the whole agreeable to your Invoice Am^o to £270.11.10½ L M and I now as Mr Irish desired Inclose you three Orders on P Vandervoort, Merch^t N Y for £150 York Each wich is £270 L M and have given the bearer 11/10½ which ballances the 70 boxes. Will you take sum Coffee for the other Boxes that you have my Note for, and how much will you give me pr pound delivered at Providence. Let me know by the Return of the post. I am yours &c.

To Mr Phillip Dumarisque   New London March 15, 1775
Merchent In Boston

    A few days agoe our Mutual Friend Thomas Mumford shew me a Letter from you recomending to send a Vefsell to Cohafsett Rather then Salem with West India Goods for the Boston Markett. I have by the bearer James Angell in the Schooner *Thames* Shipt a Cargo of Brown Sugars Consisting of Sixty Seven hogsheads and two teirces, which Sell for my Acco^t. They Just now came in from Hispaniola, and I believe are of a good quality, we have not made any report at our Custom House and must leave the whole matter relative to the entry with you and paying the Duties, and would have you manage the matter so as to pay as little as pofsible for on that string my buifsinefs with you will turn, and if I find you can do better or as well as at any other Port, its very probable I shall send you Severall Cargoes during this Summer. Capt Angell will call on Mr Stephenson att Cohafsett as you desired for advise. I shall want Twenty hhd^s of Fish by the return of the Schooner, which must be Large and good and would have you Despatch her for N L soon as pofsible. If Capt Angell can git a Stick for a foremast he will call on you for the money. Their is four hhd^s & two teirces of Sugar on board Ma̧rkt 8 which is not so good as the Cargoe & must be sold Seperate which you will take notice of in Acco^t Sales.

Mr Ferrebault who is on board the Schooner as a French Capt has about one thousand w^t of Coffee which you will be so kind as to afsist in Landing &c. Have not to add but shall write you by the next post & am Sir,

Your Hum^l Servt.

To Mr Phillip Dumarisque   New London March 16, 1775
Merchent In Boston

    Sir, the foregoing is a Coppy of what I wrote you by Capt Angell who Sail'd this day with a Good Wind & hope he will arrive safe. I gave him orders to Sett his Jack at his foremast head that in case you had any fresh orders you may have an opportunity of conveying them on board before he comes to anchor. In about three weeks I expect another Cargoe of Sugars which I shall send round the same way, if I have pleasing Sales of this Cargoe. I shall want the pay soon and I make no doubt but you'l endeavour to get a good Price for them. I should be Glad you would git what little Freight you can (at the same time not detain the Vefsell). Give my Compliments to M^r T & D M & tell them any freight they will put on board will be so much saved to them. The Hubbards may have some freight. I hope you will be at Cohafsett so as to give Angell directions about Entering and to have no mistake or Difficulty, for I think I have had my share. Angell will Enter Just as you think will answere. Of this I must entirely leave with you and flatter myself you'l make all the saving you Can. Let me hear from you the return of the post, with the price Current, Politiks &c. I am Dr Sir Your Hum^l Servt.

To Mr Samuel Solly Wentworth   New London April 6th 1775
Merchant In Dominica

    Sir, by our Friend Capt John Deshon who was in a Vifsell of mine last Summer I find that you afsisted him in the Sale of his Cargo of Melas. and the Obligations were left in your hands, as by your Rec^t to the Amount of Twenty Five hundred & Seventy Seven pounds 8/5 and Acco^t in my favour. I should be Glad you would Collect the Money in Good Bills of Exchange pay in London. Should Choose the Persons bills who bought the Mules, Especially Mr Nelsons and hope you'l not take any but what will be paid with Honour. Of this you must be the best Judge and when you have Rec^d the Bills forward them to me by the first Oppor^y the Mules trade, and shall give my Captains Orders to Call att Dominica & if the Markitts there are Agreable shall give them Directions to Call on you to Dispose of their Cargoes. But as to trade for the future, the Whole Depends on the Brittish Parliament Repealing the American Acts. I have Sent you sum

of our News Papers by wich you'l see that we are Determin'd and Unanimous to Abide by the Resolutions of the Continental Congreſs. I am Sir.
Your hum. Servt.

Nathl Shaw Junr.

To Mr Eleazer Pomroy   New London April 6th 1775
Merchant in Guadalupe

Dear Sir, I Received a line from you at St Eustatia and find that you had Sold your Cargoe and was to Return back to Guadulupe, hope you'l make money by it. I Effected the Inſurance you wrote for in N York and now Intend to mention to the Underwriters that you did not Procede on the Voyage no further then St Eustatia and that I think it Reaſonable the Risque now must be from St Eustatia to New London when you Come home but I am much at a Loſs when to mention of my Opinion of your Returning. I Just now received a Line from your Brother Ralph. He writes me that he is Just Setting out for Mr Wheelocks Colledge. He is to be a Lawyer there and as the Courts are Just Comeing on he Intends to leave his Family and after the Court is Over Return to Hartford and bring them up. All your Friends are well. I hope You'l be able to Collect all the Debts that I have Demand. Ship the Effects in some of my Viſsels. The Jin you Shipt home was Seized at New Port and your Br^o Bot it at Vendue for 10/6 Ster^g pr Caſe and was Obliged to pay the freight. He has Shipt it to New York, its very slow sale. Nothing will Command Cash but Molas. and Powder. I am Sir your H S^t

Nathl Shaw Junr.

To Meſs Thomas & Isaac Whartons   New London Apr^l 8, 1775
Marchants in Philadelphia

I Rec^d y^r fav^{rs} by ye Post & observe y^t Melaſs is rather lower w^t you then it is in N York. I have had what I have shipt there this Winter past sold at 23^d 7 2/ pr G & when I find y^r markitts higher shall send there as to half Jo^s being Cur^t at 9^{wdt} w^t you it makes it difficult here but we must do as well as we can. I want fifteen Tons of Lead wich should be glad you'l purchase immediately & let me know the Am^o & I will send a Veſsell for it w^t sum sugar or Rum. I am Gen^t y^r Hum Servt.

To Mr Peter Vandervoort   New London April 8, 1775
Marchant New York

Dr Sir, I Rec^d y^{rs} by Spink w^t ye Tools & for Cutting tobacco, also by Dr Harris is 30 bar flour & aco^t Sales of Coffee & Sugar. I expect Pomeroy will come home sum time this summer & would have you propose to ye underwriters to take the same sum to y^t Veſsell that he comes in from St Estatia or from Guadalupe. I think thay may take it from y^r Letter as the Risque is not so great in ye Summer Season, but from St Estatia they can have no objection. Inclosed is a mem^o from Col Parsons for Sum triming Cloth & beg you'l be so kind as to git them & send by ye first opportunity. I think by ye best acc^t from England matters seem to draw near when ye longest sword must decide the controversy. I returned yesterday from Newport & Providence. I afsure you thay are very dilligent in getting in readinefs but I am much afraid that we have now a Sufficientcy of Powder. Have you any lately arrived or do you Expect any in. Let me know in y^r next & what its sold for. Inclosed is a letter for Mefs Whartons wich forward by the first post.

To Roger Sherman Esqr N Lond Apr 12, 1775
at New Haven

    Sir, Last Week Col Parsons called on me, and said that you desired I would write to my friend att Philad^a for Fifteen Tons of Lead. I have wrote by this post, and shall have an answere soon as it can return. I am Sir y^r Hum Servt.

To Mefs Tho & Isaac Whartons   N Lond Apr 12, 1775
Merchants In Philadelphia

    Gent. Yours of the 4th 7 8th Inst. I have Received & am glad to hear y^t Melafses is like to rise. I hope soon to have a Cargo arrive wch will send to your Port, and I am a little in hopes as the Wind is Easterly that sum of my Vefsells will call on you with a Cargo. If they do, dispatch them soon as you can. I wrote you a few days agoe to procure me Fifteen tons Lead. If you can ship it to this port or N York should be glad as I want it immediately. Peter Vandervoort will forward it. In regard to T W for sum time he has not been hear, the last Acco^t from him was at Granades, & his practice is not to go to one port more then once. He owes so much money here y^t I imagine he will not come home, but I expect hourly to hear of his Arrival at sum port on this Continant, & when I hear will Inform you.

                I am Gent. your Hum Servt.

To Mr Phillip Dumarisque   N Lond Apr 12, 1775
Merchent In Boston

    Dear Sir, By the Post I received yours of ye 9th Inst. and am glad to hear that you are so well as to go out again. And hope you will soon meet with a good Sale of ye Sugars. I shall want to pay about Six hundred pounds L Money ye 1st of next month and hope you'l be in Cash by that Time. I am very much of your Opinion that French Goods will Rise.

Let me know by the return of the Post the state of your Marketts, as I hourly expect several of my Vefsells. Angell arrived here last Sunday. It really seems that Great Britan &c. I am y^{rs} &c.

To Mr William Hart   N Lond Apr 12, 1775
Merch^t In Say Brook

    Sir, For the amount of what is the ballance between us send me sum common red Oak, hhd Staves that are good. I shall want them in Ten days. I am Sir, your Hum Servt.

Dear Sir,   New London April 25th 1775

    The Bearer in the Sloop *Macaronia* has on Board fifty One Hogsheads and Eleven Terses of Mollafses and four hogsheads of Cocoa which Despofe of for my Acco^t and hope you'l Save the Dutys in the Cocoa. I have Drawn on you in favour of James Tilley for One Hundred & Eighty Pounds York Currency pay Twenty Days. I want Five Hundred w^t of Powder, fifteen Hundred Flints and Eighteen Hundred weight of Lead and beg You'l be Careful in Shipping it in Some of the Small Boats. I Expect Capt Chapman in with a Load of Melafses Very Soon which I shall Send Immediately Down without Unloading. I hope you'l be Able to Send me four or five Hundred Pounds by Rogers and if there is Any Good Boards you may put as many On Board as he Can Conveniently Take and Six Casks of Ship Bread. We have no further News from the Eastward only that there is Thirty Thousand Provential Troops in the Neighbourhood of Boston, the Communication between the Town & Country Intirely Stop^d. and I believe its our Intention to keep it so. I think its now high time that all the Tory Party should be made to be Silent. Our Generall Afsembly Setts Tomorrow and I pray God Almighty to Direct them to Adopt Such Meafures as will be for the Interest of America. I am Dear Sir

                                Your Very Humble Servt
                                    Nath Shaw Junr.

To Mr Peter Vandervoort
Merch^t in N. York

                                    New London April 25th 1775
Madam

    Inclos^d is a letter I Received Yesterday from our Friend. I Sent up Eight Hogsheads of Sugar (I Rec^d by Capt Starr) by Capt Peter Rogers, Two hogsheads and the Box of Clarret by Capt Bunts. My Complim^{ts} to all Friends and am your very humble Servt.

                                    Nathl Shaw Junr.

To Mrs Mary Pomeroy

N. London April 26th 1775

Sir

By the Bearor Richard Spink I have Shipt Six hogsheads Sugar, Seven Hogsheads of Melasses and Two hogsheads of Old Antigua Rum which I would have you put in Store, and take Care of until I see you & You'l Oblige Your Humble Servt

Nathl Shaw Junr

To Mr Humphrey Lyon
at East Haddam

New London May 5th 1775

Gentlemen, I wrote you by Col^o Dyarr and Mr Dean (our Colony Deligates to the Continental Congress) Desireing you would let them have what Money they should have Occasion for to the Amount of Four or five Hundred Pounds. Since that I received your Favour by the Post and am Sorry to hear you Could not Procure the Lead, and Observe your Saying that Melasses was in Demand. I now Send George Champlin in the Brigg *Nancy* with a Cargoe Consisting of Two Hundred and Sixteen hogsheads, Twenty Six Terses and Four Barrels of which Thirteen hogsheads, five Terses and One Barrel is Ventures, the Remainder is Cargoe which may be more, if you can Send me Some Money in half Joes by Capt Chappell it will be Agreeable. I have now a Cargoe of Extr^a Good St Domingo Sugars in Store if they would Answer I would Send Chappell with a Load as Soon as he Returns, and if Melasses Keeps up Shall Ship More, Unless Prevented by the Confusion of the present Times. I can tell you no News. Our Troops in the Neighbourhood of Boston are in good Spirits and are forming Themselves into Order as fast as possible. When Anything Transpires from the Congress beg You'l be so kind as to Communicate it for I Really do not know what Plan to Follow, or what to Do with my Vessels. You must Send the Brigg Back in Ballast. Have not to add but am Gentlemen

Your Humble Servt
Nathl Shaw Junr.

To Messrs Thomas & Isaac Wharton
Merch^{ts} in Philadelphia

New London May 8th 1775

Gentlemen

I have Received from Peter Curtenius Treasurer To the Committee in New York One Hundred Barrells of Flower for the Poor in Boston. Should be glad you would Give me Directions in what Manner I shall Send it. He writes me that he Shall forward three Hundred and fifty pounds in Cash for the Same Use. I am Gentlemen. Your Humble Servt

Nathl Shaw Junr.

To The Select Men
   In Boston

New London May 8th 1775

Sir

I Received yours by Capt Harris Inclofeing his Receit for One Hundred Barrels of flower. I have this Day wrote to Boston for Directions what I shall do with it, Alfo advis'd them you would Send Some Cash which I will take Care of when it comes to Hand. I am Sr Your Humble Servt.

Nathl Shaw Junr

To Mr Peter Curtenius
   Treasurer To the Committe
    New York

New London May 15th 1775

Sir

I Received yours 11th Instant and you may Depend on my Supplying you with the Quantity of Powder you Mention, Vizt: Six Hundred half Barrels. I am now Getting a Vefsel in Readinefs and Intend she shall Sail in a few Days. I shall Call on you Next Week. I am Sir, Your humble Servt.

Nathl Shaw Junr.

To John Lawrence Esqr
   Treafurer

New London May 19th 1775

Sir

When you was here you was so kind as to tell me you would procure me Two Hundred Boxes of Spermacity Candles if I wanted them. I have now Determined to Ship that Quantity, and beg you'l be so good as to Get them on the best Terms You Can, and send them to me by the Bareor Richard Spink and you may depend on my Doing my Endeavour to make Good the Bargain you make for them and you'l Oblige Your hum: Servt

Nathanl Shaw Junr.

To Mr George Irish att
   New Port

New London May 31st 1775

Capt Handy

Sir I Received yours by Capt Keith and wish it was in my power to Give you a Bill pay in London for the Amount of my Note but at Prefst I Cannot Draw and I never Met with so much Difficulty to get hard Money

Since I have been in Trade, as I have within this two Months past. I have Considerable Large Quantities of West India Goods in Store both at Boston, N. York & Philadelphia but Cannot Raiſe a Shilling. I have our Paper Bills in my Desk, that I can give you for the Note at Any Time, but as you Mention takeing a Bill Pay in Philadelphia for Candles I am in hopes it may Suit you to take one for what I Owe you and I have Given Capt Keith a Bill for Four Hundred and Four Pounds Phil^a Currancy in your Fav^r pay at Five Days Sight on Meſs^{rs} Thos & Isaac Wharton which you will see Am^o to Rather More then the Note, as it may be Some Days before you Could Turn it. You may Depend on its meeting with Honour, and beg you'l be so kind as to take it, for in short the Times are such that I Scarcely know what to Do or what Plan to Perſue and hope when Ever Times are Settled we may have Further Concern that may be to our Mutual advantage. I am Sir Your Humble Servt

Nathl Shaw Junr

P S. if you Send the Bill to Phil^a I will Allow you the Interest on the Note until paid.

To Capt Charles Handy
    Merch^t In New Port

New London July 12th 1775

Gentlemen,

    Yesterday John Mackkibbin in the Sloop *Black Joke* with 10000 Gallons Melaſses, 15 Thouſand w^t of Coffee, 26 Thouſand of Sugar Sailed for Phila. Capt Chappell is on Board as a Pilote and I have given him Orders to take the Sugar and Coffee on Shore without paying the Dutys and if it Can be avoided not to pay any for the Melaſses for I think its time to lay that Matter Aſide for the Preſent. I beg you'l have your Store in Readineſs to Receive it. He Intends to leave the Veſsell at Gloſsister Point & Come up and advise you of her Arrival. If she Arrives and Can Discharge her Cargoe, take in Another and Clear out before the 20th of July Inst for Hispaniola, I would have you putt on Board Three Hundred Barrels of Super Fine Flower and Some long Staves for Sugar Casks & Sail for Hispaniola. If not, would have her Come home in Ballast, for I think it will not Anſwer to Give Bonds to be obliged to Sell in an English Island. If you can get her a freight should Rather take it then Return home in Ballast. I think it will be best for my Interest to Let the Goods Remain in Store until they will Sell for their Value. Inclosed is a Letter for Capt Mackibbin which please to Deliver. Shall write you Again by the Next Post, and Am Gentlemen Your Humble Servt

Nathl Shaw Junr.

To Meſs^{rs} Thomas & Isaac Wharton

New London July 12th 1775

Sir

I hope you will Arive Safe, and Land your Cargoe Agreeable to my Directions without Any Difficulty. I have Defired Meifrs Whartons to put on Board Three Hundred Barrels of Super Fine Flower and fill up the Sloop with Long Staves, if you Can make Out so as to Clear your Vefsell for Hispaniola at the Custom Houfe before the 20th Instant, for After that time I Suppofe no Vefsel Can Clear out for a Forreign Port. If you Can't Get Loaded by that Time you must Come home in Ballast unlefs you Can Get a freight to Some Port in the West Indies or if you Can Sell her for Three Hundred Pounds Phila Currency Sell her, if you Load for the West Indies do you Sail for Hispaniola & do the best you Can in the Sail of your Cargoe and Purchafe Gun Powder & Return as Soon as you Can. If that Article is not to be had Purchafe Brown Sugar and Coffee. Dont keep this Letter on Board for Fear of Accidents but burn it. I Imagin after the 20th of this Month you Cannot Clear out for N London if that should be the Cafe you may Come Home in Ballast without Clearing out and Get me Two Thousand feet of Good Long Yellow Pine Plank 2/2 Inch for the Brigg *Nancy* Deck. Have not to add but shall write you again by the Next Post if Nothing Extra Happens I am Sr

Yours &c
Nathl Shaw Junr

To Capt John Mackibbins

New London July 17, 1775

Sir,

I wrote you the 12th Instant, to which I Refer you. Since that I am Inform'd that there is a Large Quantity of Powder Arived at the Cape And I would have you in Cafe you Can Clear out go Directly for the Cape and when you Arrive there you may Very Eafily know wether you Can have Liberty to Trade there or not And if you Can Purchafe Powder to the Amount of Your Cargoe, and if you Cannot trade there you Can Agree for the Powder to be brought Down to the Mole if there is no Powder Purchafe Melafses, Sugar & Coffee and Make all the Dispatch in your Power so wish you a Good Voyage and Safe Return to your Friend & Owner.

Nathl Shaw Junr.

To Capt John Mackibbin

New London July 17th 1775

Gentlemen,

I wrote you the 12th Instant that Capt John Mackibbin in the Sloop *Black Joke* with a Cargo of Sugar, Melafses and Coffee and Sail'd for Phila. Hope by the time this Comes to Hand he may be Arived. Have Nothing more to add only hope you'l be Able to get the Sloop out or at least Clear'd out before the time Expires for Clearing Out to a Forreign Port. If it Cannot be Done, if you Can Conveniantly Send me Two Hundred half Joanesis by Chappell I should be Glad. I am Gentlemen, Your Humble Servant

Nathl Shaw Junr.

To Mefs^{rs} Thos & Isaac Wharton
Merch^{ts} in Philadelphia

New London Septem^r 18th 1775

Gentlemen

I Received yours 10th Ins^t Inclosing Invoice and Bill Lading for the Flower Shipt by Harris and Chapple, who are Arived Safe. Observe Capt Champlin is Arived from Leaganes but af he has no Property in his hands belonging to the Owners of the Schooner only the Vefsell I will not Meddle with her, the Cargoe I Advanc'd for them was About £1000, and I have Two Thousand pounds worth of Sugar their in Boston in Philip Dumaresque hands and I make no Doubt but I shall be able to git the Money Unllefs Dumarisq Should prove Dishonest. Capt Jon^a Leeds writes me that he Expects to Sail by ye 1st of this Month, and if he Calls on your Coast would have you give the Pilits such Order & Directions as you would were the Property your Own, for I think it best for all Vefsells from Forreign Ports to Git in were Ever they Can. I Expect also his Bro Wm Leeds from Guadalupe will Call on you & would have you give the Same Directions for him, he is in the Schooner *Pompey*, Jona^n is in a Large Schooner Cal'd the *Defiance* & if he gits in before the Schooner Champlin comes in leaves Phil^a & Leeds Afsures you they have not Shipt me the Whole of my Interest Exclusive of what I putt on Board of Capt Champlin, I would have her Attach'd for the Ballance if its more than £200 and Leeds Approves of it. But in Case he thinks they mean to be Honest I would not do it. I shall sett out tomorrow for the Camp att Roxbury and its more than Probable, I may Come to Phil^a on my Returns and hope I shall be Able to Procure Adams Letters wich I have never Seen.

Am very Sorry for the Accident to the Sugar & Coffee & dare say you'l do the best you Can with it, and as to the Article of Melafses am Certain it will Command a Good Price before Next Spring. I Expect you'l give me the Earliest advise of Either of my Vefsells Ariving. Both Leeds & Champlains Familys are well. I am Gentlemen. Your hum^l Servent

Nathaniel Shaw Junr.

To Mefs^{rs} Thomas & Isaac Wharton

To Mr Peter Vandervoort   New London Novr 23, 1775
Merch^t In New York

Sir, Send me by the first Oppertunity One hundred barrels of Super Fine Flower, Twenty Terses Bread, Ten Bolts Rufsia Duck and one Bolt Ticklinburg & you'l oblige.   Your hum^l Servt

Nathl Shaw Junr.

To Mr Nicholaſs Tracey   New London Decem^r 13, 1775
   att Newbury Port

      Sir, I Received yours 28th Ult^o Relative to sum Melaſses wich I Rec^d by Capt Stewart on Accot^t of Robert Tracey and was Shipt by Mr Saml Newall and as the Veſsell Could not Unlade her Cargoe in this Port for sum Reasons it was Carried to New York and Sold as pr Acco^{tt} Sales Inclos'd Ballance in your Favour £101.16.2 York Currency wich will be paid on Sight to his Order. Its attended with much Difficulty to Ship Provisions from this to your Port. I am Sir   Your hum^l Servt

                                                        N Shaw J^r

---

To Meſs Thos & Isaac Whartons   New London Decr 13, 1775
   Merch^{ts} In Philadelphia

      Gentlemen, Since I wrote you last by Capt Leeds in the Sloop *Polly* and Capt Chappell in the Sloop *Betsey* are both sail'd for Phil^a and my Friend Peter Vandervoort writes me that they arived in N York and would Sail from last Monday, so that I flatter my self they will arive by the time this comes to hand and make no Doubt but you will dispatch them with their Cargoes soon as poſsible, the method of Clearing out must leave to you. Inclosed is two Letters for them wich deliver, am Glad to hear West India Goods are on the Rise, as I have had them so long on hand immagine they will pay the extra. I have not heard from W Leeds in the Schooner *Pompy* Since I left Phil^a. Am much concern'd about him, if any Veſsell should arive from Guadalupe should be glad you would inquire of him. If you have any late News from Great Britain be so kind as to let me know, as I imagine the first we hear will be of great importance to this contry.

                 I am Gent.   Your Most Hum Servt
                                             N Shaw Junr.

                                        New London Decem^r 17th 1775
Sir

      Mr Ralph Pomeroy being determind to go into the Army, he Cal'd on me and desird I would take Charge of your Son, and have him putt to Board & School & to have him Cloath'd and as I have heard your Name Mentioned as a Person of Honour, I have Provided for him and Shall Continue to do so Untill I hear from you. I have drawn on you in favour of Wm Constant for One Thousand Livers, wich I make no doubt but you will pay, and hope when you have the Pleasure to see your Son will think the Money is not Ill Spent. Any Directions you give me Relative to him Shall be Observed and must Refer you to Mr Constant and am Sir Your hum^l Servt

                                               Nathl Shaw Junr

To Monseiur Giddiſs

CONNECTICUT'S NAVAL OFFICE AT NEW LONDON

New London, Decem[r] 17th 1775

Sir

M[r] Ralph Pomeroy came to this Town in Septem[r] last and desir'd me to Furnish your Br[o] with Lodging, Wearing Apparel, Schooling, Books &c for that he was Unable to keep him any longer by Reason of his Going into the Army att & near Boston Town. All Captains who have Saild in my Imploy have Mentioned your Name as A Person of Honour &c Wich has Induced me to take Care of him, and have Supply'd him with Cloathing and have putt him to School, and Board in a Good House and hope you will find that he will, when he Returns give you Good Satisfaction, and Occasion to Beleive that the Expence you have been att is not Ill Bestow'd. I have drawn a Bill on you in favour of W[m] Constant for One Thousand Livers wich I flatter my Self you will Honour, and let me know by the first Oppertunity how long you Intend he Shall Continue in this Cuntry. I have not to add, but must Referr you to M[r] Constant for Particulars, and am Sir Your very hum[l] Servt.

Nath[l] Shaw Jun[r].

To Monseiur Sargenton

To Meis[rs] Clark & Nightingale   New London Jan[y] 16th 1776
Merchants In Providence

Gentlemen, Please to deliver the Inclos'd letter to Governour Cook. Have also Inclos'd you an order on W[m] Fallman att Bedford for one hundred and Thirty Casks & Keggs of Gun Powder wich would have you Send for and deliver to him and Send me an Acco[tt] of the Expence & You'l oblige

Your hum[l] Serv[t]
Nath[l] Shaw Jun[r].

To Samuel Solly Wintworth Esq[r]   New London Jan[y] 16th 1776
Merchent In Domineco

Sir, I Received yours of y[e] 9th and 30th Nov[r] the Letter Inclosing Acco[t] Sales of Sixty Mules Imported in the Ship *America*, John Lamb Master Am[o] to thirteen hundred & seventy Seven pounds 16/1½ Sterling. And observe that you think the Risque is too Great to send me the Bills untill you here from me. If the Money is in good hands I am content to let it remain on Interest, untill I shall have occasion for it, & when that will be is uncertain as all our Trade is now at an end, & God knows wether we shall ever be in a Situation to Carry it on Again, no Bufsinefs now but preperation for Warr, Ravaging Villages, Burning of Towns &c. Inclos'd you have some of our last Papers. I am &c

N S

THE MERCANTILE LETTER BOOK 279

To Mr William Constant　　　　　New London Jan 16th 1776
Merchent In Guadalupe

　　　Inclosed is a Bill Lading for Nine thousand three hundred Staves, which please to dispose off for the most they will fetch. Capt Leeds is arrived after a paſsage of Sixty Six Days. I find your Brother has not paid him any of the money you left behind last Voyage, and he tells me that he imagines their will be plenty of Powder out to Guadalupe from France and I hope you will be able to get to the amount of all the Interest you have of mine in. In that case I shall expect you home very soon. Pray make all the Despatch in your power, for the Sooner you Come, the Danger will be the least, their is no Creusers now, nor I believe will be untill May Next and we shall want it very Soon. I ordered Capt Chappell to Martineco from Phila with flour, if you here of him and can let him know you have powder to Ship he will take it on Board and I aſsure you he is a very Safe Good man to Ship by. Melaſses is now very Scarse hear, if you are a mind to Load the Schooner I suppose the Old Ballance will pay one half of the Amount and do you advance the Remainder & let it be on your Joint Accot. But if powder is to be had plenty, lay out the whole in Powder & send the Schooner for a Load Salt. I have nothing further to say only make all the Despatch in your power. I am &c
　　　　　　　　　　　　　　　　　　　　　　　N S

To Meſsrs Thos & Isaac Wharton　　　New London March 5, 1776
Merchts In Phila

　　　Gentlemen, I Received yours 19th January, also of ye 16th, 21, & 24 Ulto and am much oblig'd to you for ye Intelligence, observe you have Charg'd Five pr Ct for Purchasing ye Flower Shipt on Board of Capt Leeds & Chappell wich is 2½ pr Ct more then I Expected, of this will say more about hereafter. I am very Glad to hear you have not Sold much of the Melaſses, I would have you let the whole of the Goods you have of mine Rest in the Stores Untill I Give directions for the Sale of them. Would have you in your Next Advise me the Qty of Each Article that is Unsold. Vandervoort is now Selling a Cargoe of Melaſses for me at 3/6 York Cy pr Gallon and as I Cannot do any thing with the Money, Imagine it as well for my Interest to let the Goods be in Store. The Reason that I have given no Direction about Pomeroy affair is that am waiting to hear sum News from his Bro in the West Indias. I am Gentlemen, Your huml Servt
　　　　　　　　　　　　　　　　　　　　　Nathl Shaw Junr.

To Mr John Brown　　　　　　　New London March 5, 1776
Providence

　　　Sir, I Received yours 16th Ulto by the Post with the Bundles of Money, and have Since deliver'd both to Coln Fanning as by the Inclos'd Receit. I am Sir Your very huml Servt
　　　　　　　　　　　　　　　　　　　　　Nathl Shaw Junr.

New London Apr 25, 1776

Sir

Inclosed is an Invoice of ye w^t & Size of Thirty four Cannon Rec^d from Admiral Hopkins, Ten of wich is landed at Groton, viz: 3 24 pounders & 2 18 & 5 12 d^o. The Remainder are at N L & are moastly fitted on carriages, he has landed a great quantity of Cannon Ball, and shall pick out those that are suitable. Mr Ledyard I suppose has Carrages already made for the Guns at Groton so that we shall have ye Cartriges, Ramers &c ready to pay a compliment to any of the British ships. Let them come soon as they please.

The Morters and Shells General Washington desir'd might be sent to N York & the Admiral has sent them. The Remainder of the Cannon are partly sent to N Port & Part on board the fleet which he wants to carry to N Port. I shew him the Resolve of Congrefs relative to there being deliv^d here but he says they cannot be taken out. I am &c.

The Nine pounders are but ordinary Guns, the others are all very good. Col Knox a Gen who Gen Washington desir'd to take a perticular view of this Harbour &c.

To The Honrble Jon^a Trumbull
    Govenour

To Admiral Hopkins   New London May 21st 1776
    Att Providence

Sir, Inclosd is an Acco^{tt} of what I have Advanct to the People belonging to the Fleet for Nefsesarys wich they Could not do without Amount^s to 18.15.11 also Fifty dollars wich I have Deliverd to Sarg^t Hamilton & John MackNeil 2^d Mate of y^e *Providence* to pay their Expences on the Road and wich Sum they are to Acco^{tt} with you for. I thought it best to send them of for they are now fitt to do Duty & they Cannot bear to be Idle.

I am Sir   Your hum^l Servt

                                 Nathl Shaw Junr.

To Admiral Hopkins   New London May 29, 1776
    Att Providence

Inclosed is an Acco^t of the Money I have advanced the people who sailed yesterday in y^e *Providence* £15.1.4 for Providence, hope will arrive safe. In the Acco^t sent you by Sarg^t Hambleton of what was advanced their people a pr trouses to Richd Owen was omitted, Robt Rich of y^e *Alfred* had a Blanket belonging to John Hannah deceased, Sam Farguson of y^e *Providence* & Sam Williams of the *Alfred* had each a pr shoes 7/ & sett out by Land to come on board at Providence, Will Stewart that sett out with Hambleton had a shirt that was omitted in that Accott 7/10. There is now Eighteen in the Hospittle the most of which will in a few days be able to sett out for Providence. I am Sir, Your Humble Servt

N Shaw Junr.

To Mr Peter Vandervoort   New London June 7th 1776
Mercht New York

    I Received your 3 Inst & observe the Contents. I believe Melaſses & Sugar will soon be up again and have sent you Fifty hogsheads of Melaſses which was shipt me from Hispaniola as by the Inclosed Bill Lading for which you are to pay freight one third of the proffetts & ten Livers pr hogshead from this to New York you'l see that we have agreed that the price of Melaſses here shall be estimated at three Livers. I have paid him in part of freight one hundred & fifty four Dollars & 1/3 which you must deduct. If it does not Sell quick put it in the Store after having it gaug'd so as to Settle with him for the freight. Capt Melally says that the Guagers in Generall wrong me out of a great deal of Money. He says that they made sum of the hhd 10, 15, & 20 Gallons short of what they guag'd and that he made them alter it. I imagine you do not over look them Enough or they would not presume to do it. If you can git Eighteen pence for the Coffee it will be best to dispose of it. If you can git any Buntin I would have you git the Flagg made Suitable for the fourt & send by the first opportunity. Observe you will endeavour to git me a permitt for the Sugars. Inclos'd is a Bill Lading for eleven hogsheads & five Teirces Melaſses belonging to Samuel Marther, Lyme which was shipt on the same terms & wich Marther desired might be sent to you. Mather has a Note hand of mine for One hundred & Sixty five pounds Lawful Money which I would have you pay when in Cash & you'l oblige   Your Huml Servt

N Shaw Junr.

To Admiral Hopkins   New London June 13, 1776
att Providence

    Sir, I Received yours of ye 5 Ins. and agreeable to your request I now Inclose you an Invoice of the Artillery & stores left in N L also an Accot of what has been sent to N York. You have also an Invoice of the Cargoe & Venturs that was on board the Prize Schooner *John & Joseph* and as to the Value of the Goods will submit it to yourself or any other Person you may Choose for I am determined that you shall not have any blame for delivering the Veſsell to me. I am Content to alow the highest price that Goods were Sold at in this Town at that time which I think no Reasonable man can object to, the Vefsell I will have apprized.

I observe what you say relative to my being appointed agent for the Congrefs, am surpriz'd that they have not sent me any Instructions, as I have not heard any thing of that matter from them. I give you Joy on the Succefs *Cabot*, hope you will have many more prizes before the Summer is out. The Gent. from Phil^a set out Yesterday to see his Honor the Govr with the Resolve of Congrefs for fourteen of the Largest Cannon, I suppose they will have no objection in ordering them Delivered. Inclos'd is an Acco^t of what I have advanced to the People belonging to the fleet since I wrote you last Am^o to £16.1.2 L M^y which I suppose you will want that it may be Charged their Acco^t. The prize Vefsells that you bro't into this Port are Libel'd, the Perticulars Refer you to the bearer Capt Saltonstall, the Bermudian Sloop, I suppose you'l give sum directions about, their is many Persons who want to Purchase her if they could have a price sett. I am Sir   Your Hum Servt.

N S

P S. Inclos'd is an Acco^t Relative to the powder you del^d me & a ballance due you of fifty four pounds & their is one barrel Damaged powder on hand.

To Frances Lewis Es^q New London June 19th 1776
att Philadelphia

Sir, I Received yours 11th Ins^t this day and have to Inform you that Capt Serley has so farr Recoverd his Health that he will Proceed in the Sloop as Soon as their is any Probability of Getting out. Att Prefs^t I think their is no Chance of Escaping the Men of Warr. Capt Kenedy also in the Ship is Still hear, they have made Several Attempts to git out, but have been drove back by the Men of Warr & am much of the mind they will not go out any more. I have Rec^d 70 barrels flower from Kenedy. Inclos'd is ye Numbers, let me know ye Price it Cost and I will desire my friends Thos & Isaac Wharton to pay you ye money. I have Rec^d a letter from Comadore Hopkins wherein he says that I was appointed by the Congrefs as their Agent for this Port desiring I would have the Prize Vefsells be bro^t into this Port to be Libel'd for Condemnation wich I have done and the Court is to be the Sixth of Next Month. Their is also a large Bermudian Sloop hear wich was taken by the Comadore to bring the Cannon in & Imagine is the Property of the Continent. In Case the Congrefs have appointed me to Act for them, I should be Glad to have directions how to Procede. I am in advance att least One Thousand pounds for Supplys to ye Fleet and Hospital in this Town. Their was 120 men Landed that were Sick and Wounded, twenty of wich are Since Dead, the Remainder are all Since Join'd the Fleet att Providence. I Suppose the occasion of my not hearing from the Congrefs Relative to those Matters has been through the hurry of Bufsinefs. I Should Esteem it as a favour you would Mention it to that Department were those Matters Rest wich will Oblige

Your Huml Servt.
Nathl Shaw Junr.

N	1		59	125	136	147	161
	3	27	60	126	137	148	175
	4	29	61	128	139	152	176
	5	39	64	129	140	153	180
	6	41	66	130	141	154	182
	8	47	116	131	142	156	183
	12	48	121	132	143	157	186
	15	50	122	133	144	158	187
	16	53	123	134	145	159	189
	27	58	124	135	146	160	189
							195

To Meſsrs Thos & Isaac Wharton   New London June 24, 1776
Merchents In Philadelphia

    Gentlemen, Yours by Capt Leeds of ye 17 Ins. with the Cash came safe to hand, also by Capt Jona Leeds covering Sales of the *Defiance* & *Sallys* Cargoes of Melaſses which have examined and find all right only One hhd Melaſses short in ye *Defiances* Cargo, being 228 Casks left in your hands & (which you mention in your Letter of having Recd) in Accot Sales is only 227 Casks. Am Glad the Sales is Compleated, could wish the Coffee & Sugar was as well Sold. The Bill I mentioned to have drawn in favr of Geo Irish I have herd nothing of, suppose it will soon be presented. Observe you'l send me Lord Chathams Speech & Letter, it will be a good opportunity by Commodore Hopkins or Capt Saltonstall. The Diaper Mrs Wharton wrote for is become a Scarse article, but it if can be obtained it shall be sent.

                                        I am Gen, &c

To Meſs John Wright Stanley & Co   New London June 24, 1776
Mercht Newburn N. C.

    Gentlemen, I wrote you 5th Ins. by Post, since that I have advanced to Capt Tinker to the Amo of £768.1/8 L M Dolars at 6/ which I beg you'l order paid to my Friends Meſsrs Thos & Isaac Wharton, Merchts in Phila. Capt Tinker sailed two days agoe, and hope he will arive safe. He has a parcel of the best Gunns I ever saw, & hope you will find your Accot in getting them, Every article of Warr is now extravagantly high, I could have had 25 pr Ct on the purchase of them. Beg you'l not disapoint me in ordering payment in Phila. I am Gent

                                         Yr Huml Servt.

To Admiral Hopkins New London June 25, 1776
at Providence

Sir, Since my last have advanced Richard Steward Sailor board

ye *Columbus*	£0.12.0
Joseph Crage Master of Armes *Alfred* . . .	0.14.0
Waller Spooner Midshipman	5.10.0
Gideon Whilfield ditto	4. 0.0
	10.16.0

besides which have paid for their board, viz: Spooner & Whilfield at ye rate 12/ pr Week. I forgot to mention that I have paid ye board of the other small officers while here. In behalf of Nathl Shaw Junr Your Most Huml Servt

T S

To Coln Eliphalet Dyarr New London June 28th 1776
att Lebanon

I Received yours of yesterdays date and in Regard to Capt Sneids Papers have to say that they are to be Exhibited to ye Court on the day of tryall in order to Condemn ye Vefsell wich will be ye 5th of Next Month. After that I will Send them up as you direct. Observe what you say as to the Five hund pounds Lawfull Money Recd from ye Treasurer on your Accott. It was Recd before I knew how much you would have occasion for att Phila and you have drawn on me for £570.10/ Phila Cury, Viz: in favr Mefsrs Whartons for £500 and in favour of Mefsrs Chriso & Chas Marshall for £70.10/ wich will leave a Ballance in your favour of Forty three pounds 12/ L Money wich I have given ye Treasurer Cr for but if you'l Settle the £500 I Recd from him I will ballance that Accott with the £43.12/, which I here Inclose by Capt Ely, a person who I think has the real good of his Country at heart & wish that he might be &c

Nathl Shaw Junr.

To Wm Sever Esqr New London July 1, 1776
at Kingston

Sir, the bearer Capt Adams shew me a paper from you impowering him to purchase a number of Gunns to arme one of your Provence Brigs. I had just now purchased fifteen Four & Six pounders a pr Swivels Shott &c as pr Invoice which he will deliver you Amounting to £907.9.2 which I intended for a Privateer, but Capt Adams has prevailed on me to let you have them, and that you might not be disapointed I have taken the Guns out of my Vefsell discharged my people &c and have agree'd to wait for the

Money untill he can go & Inform you & return here with it, and shall rest satisfied that he will comply with his promise. Indeed no other person should have them. I am Sir

$\qquad\qquad\qquad\qquad\qquad\qquad\qquad$ Your hum^l Servt.

To William Sever Esqr
or in his Absence to
Mefs^{rs} Watson & Spooner at Plymouth

To Govr Trumbull $\qquad\qquad\qquad$ New London July 18, 1776
Lebanon

$\qquad$Sir, The foregoing on y^e other Side is a Coppy of a Letter I Rec^d from Phil^a & if you Incline to find y^e acco^t of Powder Supply'd Genl Washington by the colony so as it can be sent forward next post I will Inclose it to the Committee, the ballance due to us for the powder I delivered in Phil^a will be about 6500 w^t. Must you have an Acco^t of the powder Ball & Flints delivered by me to Col Parfons Reg^t last year, or has he given you an Acco^t of it. I am Sir

$\qquad\qquad\qquad\qquad\qquad\qquad\qquad$ Your Hum Servt

To His Excellency Gen Washington $\qquad$ New London, July 22, 1776
$\qquad$New York

$\qquad$Sir, I wrote you 18 Ins by Capt Tinker in a Gally belonging to this Colony & forwarded three Cases Arms & one Bar & 1 Keg Flints by direction of Dan Tillinghast & Clark & Nightingale and I now by the bearer John Keeny have sent Two cases of Arms & one Chest & bar Con^a Arms Flints & Cutlafses as pr Invoice Inclosed, hope they will arrive safe. I am Sir

$\qquad\qquad\qquad\qquad\qquad\qquad\qquad$ Y^{rs} &c

To George Clepner Esqr $\qquad\qquad\qquad$ New London July 31, 1776
Chairman of y^e Com^{tte} Safety
In Philadelphia

$\qquad$Gentlemen, I Received yours of the 4th Ins. and Should with pleasure have complied with your Request in Sending the Cannon, but at present am Informed that they are not to be sent immediately. Soon as they are to be delivered me you may depend I shall loose no time in sending them on to Phil^a. I am gentlemen your ob^t & Hum^l Servt.

$\qquad\qquad\qquad\qquad\qquad\qquad\qquad$ N S

To Robt Morris Esqr Chairman　　　　New London, July 31, 1776
of the Secret Committe in Phila
　Gentlemen,

　　　　I Received yours of the 8th Ins. and agreeable to your Request I apply'd to Gov. Trumbull to know the Quantity of Powder Supply'd his Excellency Gen. Washington, but as yet they have not furnished me with ye Accot. Since that I have had thirteen thousand five hundred wt more arrived from Port Au Prince and all Safe landed in this Town which makes a ballance as by the Inclosed accot in my hands after paying the Colony for the powder you Recd of theirs in Phila from Mefsrs Whartons 7950lb which will keep in Store to be delivered to your order, and hope soon to have some more arive. Yrs &c.

　　　　Agreeabl to your orders of the 15Ins. I now Inclose you the Apprizement of the Cannon Stores &c delivered me by Commodore Hopkins Amo to £4765.4.10 L M. You'l observe the Shells & Morters were sent to N Y to General Washington & Six of the heavy Canon wt 15.8.0, 6 & twenty four Wheels wt 19.3.9 to Phila. Last Sunday a Ship sent in as a prize by Capt Bidle in the *Andrea Doria* Ran on the Rocks near Fishers Island (being Chased by a British Ship of warr) & Imediately a number of arm'd men from Stonington went on board & as they say prevented the man of Warr from Destroying her, the next day Capt Hinman in the *Cabot* went to their afsistance & has saved & brot into this Port 90 hhd Rum & about 7 hhd Sugar, the Remainder of her Cargoe is lost, it consisted of about 200 hhd Sugar & 95 of Rum bound from Jamica to London. The *Cabot* has been lying here in this port ever since Commodore Hopkins sett out from Phila with a fine brave Crew waiting only for Orders &c.

To The Hon. John Hancock
President of the General
Congrefs at Philadelphia

To His Hon Jona Trumbull Esqr　　　　New London Augst 7, 1776
　Lebanon

　　　　Sir, We Recd yours Relative to the Inlisting and Incouraging of the Inhabitants to inlist, in order for the imediate filling up of the Several Cos &c. The bearer Capt Deshon can fully Inform you how farr this Town has been drain'd of men already, so that their is Scarsly Sufficency of hands left to get in the Harvest, and have had a Meeting of the Select men Justices Committees &c and it was Judg'd not best to warn a meeting of the Inhabitants, as Capt Deshon has been at unwaried pains to go to all the Compys in the Town & has already Inlisted many as can pofsible leave their homes. He has a plan that we think will git him sum men & be no detriment to the Service which he will communicate. We have purchased the Bermudians Sloop for the Colony at £2710.15/6 Phil^a Cur^y which was the very lowest price we could git & their was severall people from Providence who would give the Same, Viz: what She Cost. We shall fitt her out soon as pofsible agreeable to your Directions. Their is no public Magezien for powder in this Town, it's now deposited in Severall Stores, which really gives sum uneasinefs. Quere would it not be best to have one Built in a proper place at ye public expence. I am Sir Your Hum Servt

N Shaw Junr.

To Capt Saml Alcott   New London Aug. 10, 1776
Hartford.

    Inclosed is Robert Knights Receipt for some Cordage & Sail Cloth which is intended for the Vefsells fittting on the Lake & must be immediately sent of for Albany to the Care of Philip Van Renslear Store Keeper. It would be best to have the waggon that carries the Sail Cloth Covered. It was purchased here by Capt Leonard Van Beuren, who I Suppose will be with you by the time this boat gits up. He will leave a draft with you for the amount of my Bill on Jon^a Trumbull Esqr pay Master General & beg you will desire him to make the draft pay to you & send it to Albany by the Wagoner or some safe hand & let me know when you receive it. I would not have given you this trouble but know the Service requires it. I am &c.

N Shaw Junr.

N B. Pay the fr^t £3. y^e storekeeper will pay y^e Cartage.
    30 bolts Duck @ £6 .   . £180.
    Fr^t   3
                   £183.

To Mr Barnabas Dean   N London Sepr 5th, 1776
Merch^t In Wethersfield

    Sir, The Marine Committee at Philadelphia wrote of y^e 22^d Ul$_t$o that the Secrett Committee had given you orders to deliver me what Articles you had imported on Continent Acco^t. Should be glad you would forward them to me soon as you can, as I want to make use of them, and any matters you want for the Ship, if wanted before she comes Round you can keep, and any other Articles you want let me know of it & will Indeavour to supply you. I am Sir

Y^{rs} &c.

To Mr Jer^e Wadsworth   New London Sepr 10th 1776
Merch^t att Stanford

    Sir, Agreable to your directions I have Sent Fifteen hogsheads of N E Rum for Mr Trumbull by the Barer Frances Harris as by the Inclos'd Bill of Lading & Invoice, hope it will come Safe to hand. Shall forward the Remainder as fast as I Can. In Case of any Danger up Sound, you must Imediately Send of a Boat or two by water to Speak with the Vefsells in the Sound, that they may meet with. I Shall Send to Mr Trumbull for Money when I have a Good Oppertunity. I am Sir, Your hum^l Servt

                                            Nathl Shaw Junr.

To Mr Frances Lewis   New London Sepr 11, 1776
Merch^t Philadelphia

    Sir, Yours 24th Ult^o came to hand last Post, & I find that I can purchase Seed to put on board Capt Kenedy in the Room of ye Flower, consequently shall sell the flour which begins to take damage. Kenedy says that he can take on board three hundred hhd. A few days agoe Capt Alex Exceen in the Brig *Friendship* arrived here from the Southside of Longsland, being drove out by the Tories, having left most of his Cargo on Shore, and is now waiting here for your orders, he has Six or Seven hundred bus Salt on board. I think its best to discharge the Vefsell & put the Cargo in Store. All the Melitia in this Colony being order'd to N Y makes it very difficult to get any work done, but imagine by the next Week Kenedy will begin to Load. I am Sir Your Hum Servt

                                            N Shaw Junr.

To The Hon^{bl} Jon^a Trumbull Esqr   New London, Sepr 12, 1776
Govr of ye State of Connecticut

    Sir, Agreeable to Col Huntingtons directions I have sent to New Haven for the Stores, Riging &c belonging to ye old Brig *Defence* & the Vefsell is Returned with only the two masts, one of which is been Cut & not fit to go in her again, and riging only sufficent for ye Shrouds to her foremast, with her main & fore stay, these being so much shorter of what we expected, I thought best to advise you of it before I begin to work on her & shall wait your further orders. My Bomb Brig is Cleaned Rigged and already to take Guns on board & Capable of Carrying Twelve four pounders, with a Good Suit of Sails, & is at your Service, if you incline to have her for the Use of this State I will take ye old Brig in part pay^t. I am Sir Your Hum^{le} Servt.

                                            N Shaw Junr.

To Joseph Trumbull Esqr New London Sepr 25th, 1776
at N Y
Dear Sir,
         Col Lippet of the Second Regiment of Continental Troops Rais'd by ye State of Rhode Island came to this Town with his Reg^t from that State going to N York & finding no Commifsary here to supply him he apply'd to the Govenour of this State for afsistance & ye Govr wrote me a Letter & Desired I would furnish him with Provisions &c which I have supply'd him with & four hundred pound in Cash for which I have taken his Rec^t & for which he must acco^t with you & have sent his bagage on by Water as their is frequently Troops coming through this Town & no person to afsist them, I beg you will in your next let me know if I am right in Supplying them & how I am to be paid. I am Sir
                                                Your Hum^l Servt.

───────────

To Mr Barnebus Dean   New London Sepr 26, 1776
Merch^t at Wethersfield
         I Rec^d yours 23^d Inst. this moment & observe what you say about Iron, am sorry I cannot have it as my Vefsell will be delay'd unlefs I can procure it. Note your wanting many articles for the Ship as stores of every kind are Scarse, I think you had better git as many of the articles you shall want in the River before the Ship comes round, and we will then endeavour to make up the Remainder here. The anchor you mention may be had, also two of a lefs Size that will answere if you want. I know not how we shall git the Cables unlefs sum of our Crusing Vefsells should bring in some large Ships, in that case we can strip them & take their Stores. If you'l Send me the Receipts for the Continental Goods at Providence I will send a Boat to bring them Round. As to underwriting I confefs I am too much of a Coward to Venture. I have orders to purchase all the Cloth that is Suitable for Tents that is to be bought, can you let me know if their is any to be had with you & what number of yards, I would purchase tow Cloth if I can get nothing better. I am Sir Your Hum^le Servt.

───────────

To Frances Lewis Esqr   N Lond Octo 2, 1776
Merch^t Philadelphia
         Sir, I Rec^d y^rs 21st Ulto & Immediately communicated ye Contents of ye Letter to Capt Exeen & he gave for An^s that he will clean his Vefsell, take his Salt on board & come immediately to Phil^a. The last of Kenedys Flex Seed is to be deliv^d by agreement ye 1st Nov & he will then Sail. You'l send him his orders by that time, he expects to be able to take in to ye Am^o of Three C^t Casks, I am Sir, Your Hum^le Servt.
                                                Nathl Shaw Junr.

To Robt Morris Esqr N Lond Octo 2, 1776
Chairman of ye Sec. Com^{tte}

    Gen. Y^{rs} of ye 5th Ulto came to hand last Post & agreeable to your Directions have made inquiry for Duck & Cloth Suitable for Tents, & am sorry to say their is not a pease to be purchased in this State. I Suppose Mr Dean has advisd you of his Sending me one hundred & one Bolts of Ruſsia Duck and Fifty bolts of Oznabrigs, have made use of a few bolts for the Navy. This Moment a Fine Ship from Jamaica with 400 hh^{ds} of Sugar and 100 hh^{ds} Rum & sum Cotten was sent in hear by Capt Harding belonging to this State, she Saild in C^o with Two hund^d Sail & Harding was in Pursuit of the Fleet. Imagine our Crusers will alter the Course of many of them. I am Gentlemen, Your hum^l Servt.

                                                         N Shaw Junr.

To Daniel Tillinghast Esqr N Lond Octo 7, 1776
Continental Agent at Providence

    I Just now rec^d a Letter from the Com^{tte} at Phil^a desiring I would consult with you Relative to Furnishing Gen Washington with Six hundred Tents between us, beg you would let me know by the Return of the Post how many you can furnish & I will endeavour to make up the remainder.
    I have forwarded the two parcels of Tents you sent by the way of Norwich. I am Sir

                                                         Your Hum^{le} Servt.

To Robert Morris Esqr New London Octo 8, 1776
Chairman of ye Committe
att Philadelphia

    Gentlemen, I wrote you 2 Ins^t. Since which have Received yours of ye 20th Ult^o and as I find the Army is in Great want of Tents, I have orderd the Tent Maker to Imediately make up what Duck I have on hand and have wrote to Esqr Tillinghast to see what Number he Can furnish ye Army with. He has already sent to my Care Two hun^d. & forty one Tents which I have sent on in Small Boats and make no doubt of their getting safe to Biram. Shall forward the Remainder as Soon as Poſsible. I am Gentlemen, Your hum^l Servt

                                                      Nathl Shaw Junr.

                                                New London Nov 14, 1776
Gentlemen

    Last evening I Return'd from Hartford & was surprized to find that Capt Kenedy in a ship fitted out by order of the Continental Congreſs for France, was by Capt Hardings order stopt & not suffered to depart, the men belonging to the ship have quitted her, and if this is done by your order I think its best that sum person should be directed what to do with the Ship as she is very valuable Vefsell and Capt Kenedy seems not to be a mind to have any further to do with her. My last Letters from Phil^a from Philip Levingston & Frances Lewis are dated the 14 Octo, they were then very desirous that the Ship should sail Immediately.

Inclosed is a letter I Just Received from Mr Morris by which you will See that I have a Quantity of Powder Just arived at Maryland. This powder was shipt by a Gentleman at Martineco who Capt Packwood left Effects with last Spring to purchase it on Acco^t of our State & the Sloop *Macaroni* was to have returned to Martineco in order to take it on board but unfortunately was taken on her outward bound pafsage, which has been the occasion of its not coming to hand Sooner. If you are disposed to take the money for it should be glad you would give me directions. I have about Eight thousand w^t of Continental Powder now in store that might be exchanged & I daly expect more, if you had rather take powder this Landed in Maryland is about thirteen thousand w^t. I shall write an Answer soon as I have your orders. I Suppose their will be about Six Thousand of the above that will belong to us and the Remainder to the Continent.

N Shaw Junr.

To Gov Trumbull & Councel
                        By Miner
  State Connecticut

To Daniel Tillinghast Esqr New London Nov. 16, 1776
Continental Agent att Providence

     Sir, I Rec^d a letter from the Marine Com^{tte} at Phil^a desiring I would send them an Acco^t of their part of all the Prizes brot into this Port &c, every three months. I suppose you have or will soon Receive the same directions, you would much oblige me if you would let me know the Com^s you charge on the Continents part, also on ye peoples share, and whether you charge Storage of Goods that are Landed before the time of Sail. I have sent forward all ye Tents & Marques that you have sent to my care, Viz: 533 Tents & 29 Marques, & emmagine they are all got safe to head quarters. What prices do you alow for making & who finds the line & twine, as I am to pay the same that you give. The boards you desired me to procure I expect hourly from the Country & will send them soon as they arive. Should have answered yours before this but have been absent at New Haven. I have sent 101 Tents to his Excellence the Genl, so that imagine they will not be in want of that article besides Twenty more which Col Richmond left with me. The Continental ship that was built in this State is now ready to sale, wants only Two Large Cables & where we shall git them I cannot tell unlefs you take them from sum of the Large Prize ships that are brot into your State. Should be glad you would consult with the Admiral about the matter for I think if we had them we should soon be in readinefs for a cruse. I am Sir

Your Hum^l Servt.

To Frances Lewis & Hartford Novr 23^d 1776
Philip Levingston Esq^rs
Philadelphia

    Gentlemen, I Received yours 18th Ult° Inclosing a Letter to Capt Thos Kennedy, also directions &c Relative to the Distination of his Voyage, at the time your favour came to hand Capt Kennedy was Loaded & ready to proceed on his Voyage & agreeable to your directions I fill'd up the Bills Lading, and Inclosed them as you desired to your friends at Havre De Grace in France, and being obliged to go into the Country, I wish'd Capt Kennedy a Good Voyage, & sett out on my Journey but on my return (which was in a Week) I was Suppriz'd to find Capt Kennedy still in port, and the ship detained by Capt Seth Harding of an arm'd Brig belonging to this State, I emmediately sent an Exprefs to his Honor the Govenour to know if it was by his order that the Ship was detained but received no answere, and as the Govenour & Council where setting in this Town I came up here to see if the Ship might proceed on her Voyage, and Last evening I waited on them, and at their request I am desired to keep the Ship in Port untill I receive your further orders for her Sailing, as they think you will consent to have her unladen at N L, when you receive the inclosed depositions of Sundry persons in N L which was sent to his Honour by ye N L Committee setting forth the great difficulty there is in getting out to Sea without falling into the hands of our enimies and further that the Govr & Council think that in case part of the British Troops should make an excursion to the Eastward, the article of Wheat would be much wanted here being none & is now at a Dollar pr bus^l. As to what is said in one of the depositions reflecting on Capt Kennedys Conduct being not friendly &c I must in Justice to his Character say that I believe him to be as Good a man as could be imployed in the buifsinefs you was pleased to Honor him with. True it is that the greatest part of his Ships Crew were persons that have been brought into America by our Crusing Vefsells (having only four persons besides himself but was in that Situation on board) it being impofsible to get any other, as to the men of Warr Crusing of the Harbour at the time Kenedy was to Sail, these where four at anchor of Gardiners Island, and our intention was to have sailed through Fishers Island Sound, and into the Vinyard & over the Sholes, as the day before a Ship taken by the *Cabot* was brot into N L that way, by an excellent pilot who I ingag'd to take charge of Kenedy, and it was his opinion that he could carry him out, thus I have mentioned the Facts, and the Ship will be detained untill I here from you again which I hope will be Soon, as I think the Wheat is been too long already on board & begins to take damage, and were it mine I would rather sell then ship it & Load the Ship with Flex Seed, but must Say that their is no seamen to be had only such as are taken in Brittish Ships. The Risque of having such people you must be Sensible is worthy of consideration, those that Kennedy employed were as Good of the kind as could be had & seemed much averse to be taken by any of the

Brittish ships & what is in their favour in my opinion they refus'd taking their months advance before sailing, choosing rather to have it on their arrival in France. I emmagine I can dispose of the Sead on Board for near the first Cost if you determine to give up the Voyage.

I have not to add but am Gentlemen

Your Obed^t Hum^l Servt

To Robert Morris Esqr Hartford, Novr 23, 1776
Chairman of ye Secret Com^{ttee}
at Philadelphia
   Gent

Yours 5th Ins^t came to hand inclosing a Letter from Mefs^{rs} Sergenton & Constant by which I find they have shipt me 133 bar^l & 20 Kegs powder Cont^a about thirteen thousand weight and observe you have given orders to receive it, as I have no particular Acco^t from those Gent. I cannot tell how much is on Continental Acco^t or how much on Acco^t of this State, as their was money left in the hands of those Gent. belonging to both to be invested in powder, and Suppose that our Interest may be near equal, and they write me that one of them will be soon in Phil^a when that matter will be settled, in the mean time our council of Safety say that you may have the whole, and either pay them 5/4 L M pr lb or give me orders to let them have their part out of the powder I have in my hands belonging & imported for your Acco^t. You'l please to give Directions to have it weighed & let me know your determination. I am Gentlemen

Your Hum^l Servt.

To Joseph Trumbull Esqr N London Decr 7, 1776
Com^s General

Dear Sir, I Rece^d yours 29th Ult^o and observe what you say about Mr Cable, have engaged one hundred Teirces of Bread of him for the Navy and am very sorry to here that he has Rais'd the price of flour, however shall wright him about the matter and shall take care how I employ such Fellows for the future. As to the pork I purchase have given exprefs orders that they give no more then what you do. Their is a Continental Prize now in this Port with about Sixty Punchions Jamica Rum London proof. The Sale comes on next Monday, the last that was sold at Norwich was at Ten shillings, our state have pafs'd an Act that we must not sell at more then 6/ pr gal. I should be glad you would take the whole and give the Customery price 10/ which will settle the matter and I believe will give universal Satisfaction to all concern'd, otherwise I must keep it untill I hear from the merine Com^{tte} at Phil^a. I have orders to Remitt what money I have of theirs to Phil^a and they have desired that I would procure Bills from you or sum other Person that is Imploy'd in the Public way, soon as I can compleat the Sales of this Cargoe Should be glad to git a Bill from you to the Am° of what I may have in my hands. I have had a Small Vefsell Loaded with Twenty five hhd N E Rum for you this three Weeks, but the Men of Warr are been so much in the Sound that I dare not send it along. Yesterday there was about Sixty Sail of Ships Sail'd through the Race, after Lying two days under Black Point which alarm'd us in this Town (not a Little) all the Melitia this Side the River was order'd down to this Town, and I afsure you they came in very full. We sent a Boat out to Dog the Fleet and they this moment Return'd & say that they saild between Block Island & the main and doubled round Point Judith, so that undoubtedly they are gone to Newport. I believe the Sound will be pretty clear and shall send what N E Rum I have as fast as I could ship it, what Salt I have shall deliver Wadsworth whenever he Sends unlefs the people break open the store which I afsure you they threaten. The expedition to Long Island under ye command of Col Richmond, I Supplyed with shipping &c by order of our Govr. How & by whom am I to be paid should be glad of your advice. Please to forward the Inclosed by the first post for Phil^a as it is of Consiquence that I have an answere directly. Pray if you can spare the time let us know how matters go on the other side of the River, for we have had no news that can be relied on Since the taking of Fort Lee.

I am &c.

To Mefs^{rs} Frances Lewis &   New London, Decr 7, 1776
    Philip Levingston Esq^{rs}

Gentlemen, I wrote you 23^d Ult° advising of the Ship *Mary* being in this Port, Since that I have not Received any of your favours. Have now to informe you that this day there came out an Order from ye Govr & Council of this State to have the Cargo unloaded & sent up to Norwich to the Mills with orders to have it Ground & made into Bread. I Suppose the reason for this is that Wheat is become a very Scarse Article this Way and the great probability of a move being made of by the Brittish Troops to Newport, for this Two days past we hourly expected a Vifsell from them in this Town, a Large Fleet of between Sixty & Seventy Sail of Ships lay at Anchor Just back of our light house, & yesterday Saild to the Eastward, we sent out a Boat to Watch their motions and they Returned & say the whole fleet Sailed between Block Island & the main, and Doubled round Point Judith so that undoubtedly they are gone into Newport. Expect soon to have your directions Relative to the Ship for I believe now she will not be able to get out this port by reason of the Men of Warr which are Crusing of this Harbour for this Ten Days past. If you approve of it I can git the Commifsⁿ Bills for the Am° of the Cargoe Pay in Phil^a. I am &c

To Mefs[rs] Levingston & Turnbull   New London Jan[y] 26, 1777
att Boston
   Gentlemen

      Yours of the 21st Ins by the bearer came to hand when I was out of Town Inclosing a Letter from the Secrett Committee desiring me to afsist you with Cash &c. I have now by the bearer sent you Ten thousand Dollars, I should have sent you more but I was directed to Remitt Bills drawn by the Commifsary General, & I have for that purpose putt all the Money of the Continents that was in my hands, in his Custody, but nevertheless have sent you the above some for fear you may be disapointed, as I know that its Difficult to obtain money this way for Bills payable to the Southward. You'l please to forward me a Bill for the Ten thousand Dollars by the first Conveyance, hope I may have the pleasure of seeing you in N London on your return &c. Am Gentlemen
                                        Your Hum[l] Serv[t].

To Commodore Hopkins   New London Jan[y] 27, 1777
Providence

      I Received yours 20th Ins[t] and have ever Since been endeavouring to furnish you with an Acco[t] of Whatt Interest you may have on Acco[t] of the Prizes that have been sent into this State in my hands but I find that I cannot with any exactnefs do it, by Reason of the Rum not being Sold, not in Cash for the Stores from New Providence, neither am I furnished with the number of persons who have lost their Limbs in the Service as I suppose these are to be reimburs'd before any Division is made. I really wish I could know the names of the Ships Crews who are to receive the prize money that is in my hands for I want to pay them, knowing that the Service Suffers for want of this Division. I have two hundred pounds in M[r] Tillinghasts hands which I shall for Soon as I can find what more is in your favour. Untill them, I am Sir   Your Hum[l] Serv[t].
N. B. by the bearer M[r] Lyon, have sent you 1000 Dollars.

To Robert Morris Esq[r]   New London Feb 4th 1777
Chairman of the Secret Committee
Philad[a]

      Sir, Inclosed is a Coppy of what I wrote you in Answere to yours of the 5th Nov[r] Relative to the Powder. Since that I have not received any of your Orders. I Just now was Informed by a person from Hispaniola that Cap[t] Geo Champlin in the Brig *Nancy* belonging to me had sailed from that port with Ten tons of Powder & three hundred Musketts and that he designed to fall in to the Southward. In case he has arived, this being on the Continent Acco[t] you can give directions for the disposal of it. Yours of the 4th Decr by Mefs Ab^r Levengston & Wm Turnbull was sent me from Boston last Week desiring I would furnish them with as Much Money as I could conveniently Spare at that time. I had advanced the Com^s Genl much more money then I had in my hands but that they should not be Disapointed I sent them Ten thousand Dollars, and shall Send you there Bills as Soon as it comes to hand.

I am Sir, Your very hum^l Servt

To Robert Morris Esqr   New London Feb 4, 1777
Chairman of the Secret
Committee Phil^a

Sir, I Received yours 14th Ulto. and observe the Contents and relative to the ship *Mary* Capt Kennedy, she is now laid up and her Cargo all Landed. I have by Govenour Trumbulls order delivered the Wheat to the Commifsary General, all except a few bushels to the Neady Inhabitants and sum I have ordered to be made into ship Bread, for the Supplying of any of our Continental Fleet that may want. I shall git the Commifsarys Bills for the Am^o of what he has received, and as to Loading the Ship or sending her to the Southward its impracticable, for his Majestys Friggates have intirely shutt up this Harbour so that its impofsible to git out without falling into their hands. This day a prize Schooner was run on shore by the *Niger* Friggate & her Station of our Light House so that we must give over thinking of getting Kennedy out, untill we can oblige those Gentry to remove. I wrote Mr Alsop & Inclosed you have his advice and I think with him that if he ye owner Receives his freight he cannot have any objection to Receiving his Ship in N London. Capt Kennedy intends in a few days to sett out for Phil^a & to him must refer you. Agreeable to your orders I had all the Stores Commodore Hopkins brot from New Providence apprized and Sent you the am^o. The people who were in that expedition want there prize money, should be glad you would let me know whether I am to pay them out of the Continent share of Prizes now in my hands. Inclosed is a List of Prizes that is been brot into this State since the Commencement of this Warr, and shall continue to advise you of all that comes in. I have and shall continue to supply Capt Saltonstall with what money he may want to get his ship out, at present she is in Connecticut River and am fearful we shall meet with Difficulty in gitting her out as she draws so much water, it must be a very extraordinary tide to get her over the Barr, and in case she lies any time on the barr, as the British Ships are Continually pafsing they may take that opportunity to Destroy her. However you may depend that the greatest prudence will be observed. The Sale of the prize Ship *Clarendon* taken by the *Cabot* is not compleated, soon as it can be effected shall send the Acco^t. Your favour by Mr Rose & Mr Eveleigh of Carolina is not yet come to hand, you may depend that I shall render them all the service in my Power.

THE MERCANTILE LETTER BOOK 297

This moment a person came in and says that the prize Schooner I mentioned being drove on shore by the *Niger*, proves to be a Prize belonging to an Armed Vefsell of mine, Laden with beef pork, butter bread & flour, she is 150 tons burthen we have got on those 800 Firkens of butter, 100 Casks Bread. Last Night, the Friggate sent her Boats to burn her, they boarded her & sett her on fire in the Cabbin but our people fired on them so smartly they were obliged to quit her and tumbull into their Boats, drove of with the wind not daring to stand up to row &c &c. The *Niger* Still Continues to cruse of this Harbour &c &c. I am Sir your very Huml Servt.

To Jona Trumbull Esqr Govr   New London Feb 20, 1777
State Connecticut.

     Sir, I Recd yours Relative to Mr Chew, and on my letting him know that he could not be permitted to carry his Servants or effects he chose to Return without his Family. I have sent for Capt Smith to exchange for Capt Palmer. I suppose Gen. Perfons has given you a history of the discovery we made of the Correspondence carried on from our neck on board the Man of Warr, Capt Palmer says that when he considers himself exchanged (and not a prisoner) he shall make much greater discovery of the pernicious doings of our internal enemies. I am now largely in advance for this State for Supplys to the Vefsells, Fort & Barracks, and shall make out the accot in a few days Soon as I can get Coit Supply'd. I want a Bill for Twenty five thousand Dollars payable in Phila or Baltimore which will I immagine sute better then the Cash, should be glad you would send me one for that Sum by the bearer, and if by my Accot there should not be so much due to me you can give an Order on me for the ballance. Inclosed is a coppy of Letter from Capt Hinman, If you will let him have the Guns I will send them immediately, as the rodes are now very Good. Coit has Landed Sir out of the *Oliver Cromwell*, has his Ship Clean'd and taking on Board fast as pofsible. Inclosed is sum News Papers which I immagine you have not seen.

To The Honbl Jona Trumbull Esqr   New London Feb 27, 1777
Gov State Connecticut

     Sir, Yours 21st Inclosing a Bill for twenty five thousand Dollars upon the President of Congrefs I Received. Since that am favoured with yours 24th Ins. Relative to the Prisoners. They may be sent emmediately to this Town and I will have them taken care of at the Harbours mouth near the Light House where we keep a Guard, and will there take them on board. The person who brings them should have Orders not to come into the Town but to Let me know of his coming so as I may send him a guide to conduct them directly to their quarters. As to Pig Iron, Capt Coit has taken in all his on Board & he cannot leave any as the Ship requires the

Whole, there is not any in this Town but what is intended for the Ship *Trumbull*. Capt Niles Landed what he had on board the *Spy*, but am Inform'd that Christ^o Leffingwell has purchased it. I am Sir Your very hum^l Servt.

To Mr John Wright Stanley   New London Mar 13, 1777
Merch^t Newbern N Carolina

Dear Sir, This moment I had Intelligenge that Capt Wm Powers had got within your Barr in a Brig that was a Prize to my Sloop *American Revenue*, Samuel Champlin Commander. This is to desire you would do the Needful in having the Vefsell Libled, Condemned & Sold &c and shall Order the Am^o of the neat proceeds convay'd to this place in the Safest manner either by a Bill or in Continental Bills. I should think it would be best to Lodge the Money with the President of the Continental Congrefs & take an order for our Treasurer to give his Note with four pr C^t Interest for use of the Continental States, but of this I shall write you more fully when I here from you. I have desired Powers In Case he can git a small Vefsell that will Sail fast to apply to you to purchase her & Load with naval Stores for N London and for him to come home with her. Capt Stev Tinkers family is well &c. I am Sir

                                                  Your Hum^l Servt.

To Capt Will Powers,   N Lond Mar 13, 1777

Sir, I this moment was informed by Capt Thos Willson that he came out from Newburn ye 21st Feb^r and saw you in a Brig prize from the *American Revenue* going in. I have wrote to Mr Stanley to Afsist you & do every thing needful towards desposing of the prize. This harbour is very difficult to get in as their is Men of Warr Crusing from Fishers I^s hommack up to Plum I^s. Capt Leeds in the Prize Schooner got in far as Gardiners I^s but was chased by a man of Warr on Naregansett Beach &c. Stanton & Palmer is boath arrived. If you come home by Water Run for Watch hill Reef & go into Stonington. Naval Stores are in great demand especially Tarr, if you can get a Small Vefsell cheap that will Sail fast you may apply to Mr Stanley & desire him to purchase her on my Acco^t & Load with naval Stores & would have you come home with her. I hope to hear from you soon & am Sir

                                                  Y^r Hum^l Servt.

To Thos & Isaac Wharton   N Lond Apr 26, 1777
    Gen.

Your favour of the 17th Ult^o I Rec^d this Week & should have wrote before but have Just returned from Boston, Mrs Wharton may have One doz of the Stockings if they sute her. I expect Wm Powers or Mr Rogers from Newbern in North Carolina to call on you in a few days & would have you send the remainder by them. I Expect they will have a draft on the Continental Treasury for a considerable sum of Money, and should be glad you would afsist them in gitting a draft on the Continental Loan Office in this State for the amount of the Money they May receive in Phil^a as it will save the risque of bringing the money, and you may add to the said Draft as much as you Judge may be the ballance of our Acco^t & also the Cash belonging to Constant, who arrived hear last Week but Mon^s Fransway we have no Acco^t of. I am Genl your Hum^{le} Servt.

N S J^r

To Thos & Isaac Whartons
Merch^t Philadelphia

To Capt Edward Tinker   New London Apr^l 26, 1777
Newbern North Carolina

I Rec^d yours 4th of Mar. and observe the advise you gave Capt Powers relative to his prize, and I now thank you for it, as it is just my mind about the matter. Would have you see that there is no wrong done to the concern'd, and after the whole is sold I would have Bills purchas'd on the Continental Treasury at Phil^a and have them sent along with Rogers as Soon as pofsiable and would have you purchase a fast Sailing Small Sloop and Load with Tarr and send Mr Powers with her to N L. Hope you will be able to send Rogers off with ye Bills Soon, as I am fearfull the enemy may git pofsifsion of Phil^a and the risque of gitting to N England more hazardous every day. Rogers will call on my friends Thos & Isaac Wharton who will afsist him in the negotiating the Bills and gitting other Bills on the Continental Loan Office in this State. I wrote Mr Stanley much to this purpose but as he is out of Town shall expect you will do every thing in your power for the good of the Concerned. Your Father has been Sick this Winter but is gitting better. I am Sir your hum^l Servt.
P. S. If you want to send any money this way you can include it in the same draft & I will pay him the Money.

To Mefs^{rs} Wm Powers & Wm Rogers   New London Apr. 26, 1777
att Newbern North Carolina

Gent, I Received your several Letters, and am glad to hear that you are safe arived at Newbern with your Prize. I wrote to Mr Stanley to do the needful buifsinefs and observe by your Letters that he is abroad, and that you will be very carefull to see that there is no embazelment of the Cargo or Stores &c and that every thing be sold to the best advantage, and for the Am^o I would have you get a Bill on the Continental Treasury at Phil^a & let Rogers proceed home as soon as pofsiable, in Phil^a he can git a Bill on the Continental Loan Office in this State for the whole Am^o. I have wrote Mefs^{rs} Thos & Isaac Wharton to Afsist you in gitting it. I wrote Mr Stanley to git a small Vefsell & load her with tarr & for Mr Powers to come home in her, as that article is much wanted here. I could wish that plan might be prosecuted & Rogers come by Land with the Bills. Capt Champlin is got into Bedford with the Sloop, has taken no other prize. I have wrote Capt Tinker by this Post. All Friends are well & am Genl

Your Hum^l Servt.

To Capt Elisha Hinman   New London May 20, 1777
att Boston

    Sir, I Should be glad you would send me up the 4 Guns you mention for Capt Chew who I am fitting out upon the Acco^t of ye Continent. I imagine if you send them on to Providence to the care of Mr Asa Waterman their, the Carts returning to Norwich almost every day. I have not to add but am &c.

To John Bradford Esqr New London May 20, 1777
Cont^l Ag^t Boston

    Sir, I rec^d yours of ye 14 Ult^o & should wrote you before but have been out of Town. I shall Supply Capt Modie with whatever he may have occasion for in this State. I am fitting out a Brig here on Acco^t of the Continent for Capt Sam Chew & want a quantity of Cordage and should be glad you would let me know by the return of next post if it can be had in Boston. Shall also want some four pound Cannon, I was at Bedford some time since and saw a number there that came out of the ship *Millish*. If I can have them pray let me know. I am &c.

To Samuel Broom   New London June 23, 1777
Wethersfield

    Dear Sir, Your fav^r 19 Inst. I Rec^d & observe the contents. I really am of ye opinion in regard to the purchase of ye Sloop *Montgomery* & think she will answere to send on the Voyage to Europe better then the Brig and consent to the purchase of her & to be concerned in one fifth, but Insted of the Brig going to Virginia I would have her fitted out as a Privateer, there is not a better Vefsell on the Continent. I have Six cannon Six pounder^s which added to what the Sloop has will be almost enough & make no doubt but I can git the remainder. Capt Thos Kennedy will go master of the Sloop and a better man cannot be had. I this moment sent John Hartell into the Jersey to purchase sum Iron to finish the Ship, I gave him money to get it, but I suppose it cannot be got unlefs we pay West India goods in part. I sent for Eight Tons, and I should be glad you would write John Hartell Under cover to Harey Kipp of New Windsor and let him know how much West India Goods you can let him have and the price, that he may know how to engage the Iron. Let me hear from you soon. I am Sir Your Huml Servt.

N Shaw Junr.

To Jere Wadsworth Esqr 　　　　　New London July 5, 1777
at Hartford

Since I saw you at Hartford, I sent up & your man sent me Ten Thousand Dollars. I imagine by this you have had directions from Mr Trumbull to let me have the ballance of my Accot and as I am every day advancing, would have you send me Loan Office Notes for the Amo of Ten thousand pounds (one thousand in each note) by the bearer Capt Deshon. What price do you give for West or N E Rum. I am &c.

To Daniel Tillinghast Esqr 　　　　　New London July 6, 1777
Providence

Sir, I am directed by the Marine Comte to fitt out an armed Brig to be commanded by the bearer Saml Chew Esqr & have almost compleated the Buifsinefs. There will be several articles wanting that cannot be had in this State and Capt Chew comes on purpose to git them, I beg you would afsist him with what articles that he wants for the purpose & have them sent forward soon as pofsiable that there might not be no delay in the Brigs Sailing. I am ordered to draw Bills for the fitting out the Brig on the Comte and can either give you a Bill for the amo of what you supply or you can charge it in your Accot. I am Sir Your Huml Servt.

To John Bradford Esqr 　　　　　New London July 6, 1777
Conta Agent Boston

Sir, I am directed by the Marine Comte to fitt out, and arm a Brig to be commanded by the bearer Saml Chew Esqr and have almost compleated the Businefs. There will be several articles wanting that cannot be had in this State and Capt Chew comes himself on Purpose to git them. I beg you would afsist him with articles that he wants for the purpose and have them sent forward soon as pofsible that there might be no delay in the Brigs Sailing. I am ordered to draw Bills for the fitting out the Brig on the Committee and can either give you a Bill for the Amo of what you supply or you can Charge it in your Accot. I shall want one hundred Musketts more then what is wanted for the Brig, for the Continental Ship *Trumbull*, which now lys in Connecticut River & is almost ready to Sail, if you have any belonging to the States, would have you send them also Pistols & hangers. This Frigate is to carry Twenty Six, Six pounders & has every thing ready and nearly compleated, except those articles, hope you will send them as the Service requires it. My Bro. wrote you that Capt Moodie was taken and carried into N York, since that have rec^d a Letter from his Mate, the Four pound cannon came safe to hand from Bedford. I am &c.

                                                        New London July 24th 1777

Gentlemen,

      Yours of ye 17th Ult^o by Capt Chew came to hand (and as I Expected) you Consider that I was not Authoriz'd by your former orders to buy a Brigt^n Eight Months after without first Consulting you on that head.

The Case was Just this, I was Determin'd that so Good a Man as Capt Chew should not Remain UnEmploy'd, and if you would not let him have a Vefsell, I would let him have one on my own Acco^{tt}. If you had Refus'd to take the Brigg it would have been no Determ^t to me. On the Briggt^n Sailing shall furnish you with the Acco^{tts} &c. I shall have her Ready to Sail in a few days. With advise of His Excellency Goven^r Trumbull, I have fitted out the Continent^l Sloop *Scuyler*, Under the Command of David Hawley who has his Station att or Near Norwalk, and have the Satisfaction to observe to you that I think he has Exerted himself to the Utmoast in distresing the Enemys Coasting Vefsells from Long Island to N York & has taken and bro^t into Port Five Sloops and One Schooner Laden with Wood, Provisions &c. No Great Value to the Contin^t but a Determent to the Enemy.

Mr Ellery of N Port and Mr Whipple of N Hampshire on their Return home from Congrefs mentioned to me that you was Inform'd I had a Sum of Money in Martineco, & that you wanted it & to give me Continent^l Bills hear. I have a ship that Saild from this Port on Decem^r 1774, John Lamb master with a Valuable Cargoe, and have had no Remittance from him Since, and Suppose he has the Interest now with him and Expect he is att Martineco, but have Received no Letters from him, therefore am att a Lofs to know the Sum he has or in what Situation. Should be Glad to know if your Agent att Martineco has given you any more Information about it, so as I may draw for the Money. I have no objection to letting you have the Whole or part of it, and Indeed would give you the Prefference Provided you give the Curr^t Exch^a.

To Jere Wadsworth Esqr New London Augst 27, 1777
at Hartford

      Sir, Capt Wm Tryon acquaints me that Wm Green of the Sloop *Industery* had shipped by him 12 hhd^s Six Teirces Rum, 134 bags Coffee on Acco^t & Risque of the United States with orders to deliver them to the Cont^l Ag^t of the first State he should arrive at. Having arrived in this

State, suppose they may be wanted by the Army, have tho't it best that they should be lodged at Hartford, and have accordingly given him orders to deliver them into your care. You'l please to receive them & write to Capt Green or to his owners at Greenwich (Capt Tryon can acquanint you who they by) respecting them. In behalf of Nathl Shaw Junr Cont^l Ag^t I am Sir Your Hum^l Servt. Thos Shaw.

To Joseph Trumbull Esqr New London Novr 23, 1777
Lebanon

    Dear Sir, I have now returned to N L after a very Sevear fitt of Sickne∫s, am hardly able to do Busine∫s, but am oblig'd to it by the Continual calling on me for money, for this reason have sent Doc Noliott to desire you would send me about Twelve thousand pounds; there is more then that Sum due to me, which you will be sensible of when we reckon, and in about Ten days or a fortnight I hope I shall be able to see you at any place you shall appoint but I really wish to have the pleasure of seeing you here at N L. Pray what do you intend to do with the Beef & Pork I have on hand, am afraid of its taking damage for I do not know whether Wadsworth has made use of that up the River, as I have been absent so long, and have some at N L. Have Herd the Wheat you ordered to Joshua Huntington has taken damage, have repact the provisions. Yours &c.

To the Hon Marine Committee of Congre∫s   New London Novr 24, 1777
Gentlemen

    I wrote you the 24th July that by Govenour Trumbulls Advice I had fitted out the Sloop *Scuiler* belonging to the United States, under the Command of Capt Hawley. He shipt his hands for a term of time which has Expird and has bro^t the Sloop into this Port with all her Stores and Deliver'd her up & chooses not to go in her any more finding that he Ranks only as a L^t & being a Capt on y^e *Lake* &c. Yesterday I Received a Line from General Parsons & he writes me that he is Requested by General Putnam to Desire that I would Imediately send the Sloop with all her Warlike Stores in C^o with an Arm'd Schooner belonging to this State (which Goven^r Trumbull has Consented should also go with them) up the Sound as farr as Fairfield or Norwalk, they both Sail this Evening. Y^e *Scuiler,* the Barer Lt Carr late of y^e *Cabbott* takes Charge of her. His Character I Suppose is best known with you. I mention to him that it was more than Probable you would Give him the Command of her, and I Really think that if the Sloop was to Cruse in the Sound this Winter (In Case ye Enemy keep Po∫sesion of N York) would be of much Service to us in Di∫tresing the Enemys Coasting Ve∫sells. Since the purchasing & fitting out of the Briggt^n *Re∫istance* & Supplys for the Ship *Trumbull*

I am in Adv^a largely for ye Contin^t and Expecting the Honb^{le} Board of Commifsioners for ye N E States would have Power to Settle my Acco^{tts} I have Neglected applying to your Board, but att Preſs^t I can see no Proſpect of their doing any Buſineſs. I should be Glad to be Inform'd wether I must wait on you with my acco^{tts} before I can draw for any Money or wether I must Stay Untill the New Created Board Can do Buſineſs. If I may be Permitted to draw on you I shall not Exceed the Ballance, you may depend its now Twelve m^o Since I have been in Advance.

To General S. H. Parsons   New London Novr 24, 1777
   at Mareneck

     Dear Sir, I Rec^d yours 17th Ins^t & the Sloop *Schuyler* and *Spy* Sails to morrow morning & hope they will have a good paſsage, have sent all the Stores that where delivered me by Capt Hawley, and have the Command of her to the bearer Leiut Karr, who was a L^t on board the *Cabot*, and has been unfortunate, the particulars he can inform you, and immagine the Congreſs will Commission him to command her as they always make a Point to give those that have been in their employ the preferrence, I have just Return'd &c.

To the Continental Navy Board   New London Decr 19, 1777
   Eastern Department at Boston

     I Rec^d yours of ye 19th Ult^o and shall endeavour as far as I can to supply Capt Saltonstall with such stores as he may want for the Ship *Trumbull,* but at the same time must observe to you that almost every Article neceſsary for fitting out an Arm'd Veſsell are extreemly Scarce and very difficult to be obtained for the Money, but as there is no prospect of getting the Ship out this Season, shall be more at leisure to procure them. Capt Saltonstall calls on me for Money to pay his People & for other neceſsarys disbursements, beg I may be informed where I am to apply for it. I am Gentlemen Yours &c

---

To John Bradford Esqr New London Decr 30, 1777
   Boston

     Inclosed is a Bill Lading for a quantity of Warlike Stores from Martineco in the Brig *Josh Gimblel,* John Lamb Master which are for the use of the Continent & beg you will be so kind as to Receive them & have them stored in a place of safety Untill we can Receive further orders from the secrett Committee of Congreſs for their Disposal. Mr Bingham writes me " you will find more Gun Carriages then what are necefsary for the field peices on board having shipt seventeen Cannon to New Hampshire in a Bermudian Sloop which was not large Enough to Receive ye Carriages & the other apparatus, you will therefore please to advert to J. A. Langdon Esqr of Portsmouth to whome they are addrefs'd of their arrival. Inclosed is a Letter for Mr Langdon which please to forward the first opportunity & if he sends or gives any Directions you will please to deliver them, he paying you the Freight & Charges. I am &c.

To John Landing Esqr [Langdon]   N London Decr 30, 1777
Portsmouth

    I Rec^d a Letter from William Bingham Esqr at Martineco advising that he had shipt to my care sum gun Carriages, he mentions it in this manner, you will find more Gun Carriages then what are necefsary for the field peaces, on board having shipt seventeen Cannon to New Hampshire in a Bermudian Sloop which was not sufficiently large to Receive the Carriages & the other apparatus, you will therefore please to advert to John Langdon Esqr of Portsmouth to whome they are addrefs'd of their arrival.
    The above articles are arrived at Boston in the Brig *Irish Gimblet*, John Lamb Master & I have given orders to have the whole stored by John Bradford Esqr Con^t Ag^t & have Desired him to deliver to your order such of the Articles as are for you and the freight & charges you will Settle with him. I am &c.

To John Lamb   N London Decr 30, 1777
Boston

    I just now Rec^d a line from Capt John Billings of Norwich & he writes me that he came pafsinger with Capt Lamb, so by that I suppose that your Holinefs is arrived in Boston, and as we have rec^d no Letters from you, Cannot give any other directions in regard to the ships American affairs then Just this, if you have any goods on Acco^t of the Concerned you'l Store them with Col Josiah Waters and advise us, or may we not afsist you up to N L & in Regard to the Continental Stores I have given orders to John Bradford Esqr Continental Agent in Boston to Receive them. I am &c

---

To the Secrett Committee   New London Jany 5, 1778
of Congrefs

    Gentlemen, I Received a Letter from Wm Bingham Esqr from St Peters Martineco, advising of his shipping to my care Seventeen Brafs Field-pieces, shott, carriages, Powder &c by Capt Lamb, who is Safe arrived at Boston, and desires I would retain them in my hands untill I

Receive your further orders respecting them. I have given orders to have the whole delivered to John Bradford Esqr Con^{tl} Ag^t and suppose he has informed you of their arival & quantity of each of the other articles. Capt Lamb was to have customery freight should be glad to know what you alow for such Stores from Martineco.

I am &c.

New London Jany 5th, 1778

Gentlemen,

  Inclosed is a copy of what I wrote you ye 24th Novr. Since that I have not Received any of your favours. I suppose by this you have heard of ye total Lofs of the Sloop *Schuyler*, being drove on shore by a British ship. Having nothing further to add only the Ship *Trumbull* calls daily for Supplys & must be obliged to advance a Large Sum as the Seamens time Expires and must be paid off. Expect to have her out of the River this Spring Early. I am Genl Your Hum^l Servt.
P. S. Suppose that Mr Bradford has advised you of the Brig *Refistance* sending in a Prize.

To the Honb^l Marine Committee
of Congrefs

To Joseph Rufsell Junr New London January 6, 1778
Merch^t att Bedford

  I have sent the barer on purpose to git your account as I Cannot make up mine with the owners of the *Revenue* without it and should be Glad you would send me by the barer, the Ballance as I am Disapointed of the money from Col^n Griffing and am much putt to it for want. The New Courses & Top Sails of the *Rebecca* must be Apprizd and att foot I have Stated the Proportion of Money due to Each Vefsell for the *Rebecca*. I should be Glad that when you see Mr Millir you would Desire him to make out his Acco^{tt} and Send me and I will Send him mine, I did Intend to Come down to Bedford but am so Unwell that att Prefsent I dare not Think of it. I am Sir

Your hum^l Servt
Nathl Shaw Junr.

P. S. I hope you wont have a Vifsit from your New Port Neighbours but am much afraid of it. Sell the Beaf as soon as you have a Tolerable offer. N. S.

The Ship Sold for	£5750.0.0
The Men are to have one half	2875.0.0
Capt Perse had 33 Men whose part is	£ 988. 5.0
Capt Champlins had 63 Men whose part is	1886.15.0
	2875. 0.0
Capt Champlin had 12 Guns whose Share is	£1725.0.0
Capt Perse had 8 Guns whose share is	1150.0.0
	2875.0.0
Nathan Millir as Agent for Capt Perse is to Receive	
for the Crew	£ 988.5.0
for the Owners of Perses Sloop	1150.0.0
	2138.5.0
Nathl Shaw Junr as Agent for Capt Champlin is to	
Receive for the Crew	£1886.15.0
for the Owners	1725.00.0
	£3611.15.0

New London Jany 8, 1778

Sir,

  I Received your kind favour by the bearer M^r Roſs and am much obliged to you for the acquaintance of so worthy a person. By fitting out many of the Continental Veſsells I am largely in Advance and have been very unlucky in not having any of the Prizes coming into this Port, I expected Capt Chew in the *Resistance* those that he should take into this port, and in consiquence of that have not made Application for the Money. I beg you will let me know by a Line if this New Board, will have Power to Settle Acco^{ts} pay &c or whether I must be obliged to come to your State & you'l oblige Sir &c

To Robert Morris Esqr
Pennsylvania

To Dan Tillinghast Esqr New London Jany 20, 1778
Con^l Ag^t Providence

  I Rec^d a line from Mr Green Informing me that as soon as the 4^{lb} Shott were ready he would advise me y^t I might send for them. Since y^t I have not heard from you. I beg you'l let me know when I may send, as the Veſsell I want them for is almost ready to Sail. I also want Three Tons of Grape Shott & 5 doz Lathorns, I beg you would be so good as to procure them for me, as I know not where else to get them & you'l much oblige

           Your Hum^l Servt

To the Honble Mareane   New London Febuary 2, 1778
Committe of Congress

 Gentlemen, I wrote you 24th Nov^r & 5th of January last, Since that have not been favor'd with any Answer, the Continual Call on me for Money from the Ship *Trumbull*, for Provisions, Mens Wages, Stores &c for more than Twelve Months Past, purchasing and fitting out the Brigg *Refistance*, Saml Chew Command^r and no Prizes comeing into this Port, that in Short I have advanc't my own Money to so great Am^o that I am oblig'd to Send the barer Mr John Hertell on Purpose to Request that you would Send me att least Twenty Thousand Pounds Lawfull Money, which Sum I have drawn on you in his favor of this date, he will have Occasion to make use of Five Thousand Dollars before he Returns home, beg you will let him have that Sum in Continent^l Dollars, and the Remainder give him an order on Mr Lawrence the Treasurer of the Loan Office in this State. The Occasion of my not drawing you desir'd me of ye 10th Decem^r 1776 and ye 17th June Last was that I Really Expected that their would have been sum Prizes Sent in hear by the Continent^l Arm'd Vefsells, and In that Case the Money would have come into my hands, twelve months ago I paid all the Money in my hands belonging to the Contin^t to Mefs^rs Levingston & Turnbull, by your order & no Prize is come in since & Mr Dean who was to furnish the Ship *Trumbull* with what she wanted in the River has Sent Mr Jois the Rope maker to me for payment of Two Large Cables Am^o to One Thousand pounds, and Capt John Lamb who arived att Boston with a Large Quantity of Warlike Stores that was shipt to my Care by Mr Bingham att Martineco Consisting of Seventeen brafs Field peces, and Carriages, Shott, powder, Arms &c which I orderd Capt Lamb to Deliver to Mr Bradford the Continent^l Ag^t and last Week Capt Lamb Came up from Boston and Demands the freight from me as Bradford says he has no money and will not pay him, have also Rec^d orders from ye Commifsioners of the Navy Board in Boston to git a Quantity of Provisions in Readinefs for Publick use att this Port & have Cal'd on them for Money but Cant git any, and I make no doubt but we shall Soon have the Ship *Trumbull* out of the River and fitted out. I mention those Matters only that you might see the Nefsisty of my having the Money and Cannot git Supplys without it.

 We have a Report that Capt Chew in the *Refistance* since Sending in the Prize into Boston has been into Demarari River to Clean his Brigg and Since taken an Arm'd Schooner that was fitted out from Barbadoes, to Cruse on our trade, & that he has Mann'd her and keeps her to Cruse with him. It gives me Pleasure to hear of his Succefs, as the fitting of him out was a Plan of my own, & I hope he will Answer your Expectations. I am Gentlemen y^r hum^l Servt.

              Nathl Shaw Junr.

THE MERCANTILE LETTER BOOK 309

To The Secrett Committee   New London Febuary 2, 1778
of Congrefs

     Gentlemen, I wrote you ye 5th Ult^o that Capt Lamb had arived in Boston with a Quantity of Warlike Stores from Mr Bingham on Acco^{tt} of the Continent and that I had given Orders to Capt Bradford ye Con^{tl} Agent to Receive them. Capt Lamb has Cal'd on me for the freight and Demands Ten pr C^t on the Value of the Goods which I think is too much and of Course have not paid it, but have Agreed to leave the matter to Col^n Isaac Sears and any other Person of Character in trade in Boston to say what is the Customary price, and am to pay as they shall Say. I am Gentlemen y^r hum^l Servt

                                         Nathl Shaw Junr.

To Mr Patrick Moore   New London Febuary 26th 1778
Merch^t In St Pierres Martineco

     Sir, I Received your favour of ye 28th of Novr and 10th January last, the former by Capt Lamb, who Arived att Boston, and is fitting his Brigg for a Privateer, and Imagine by this he has her in great forwardnefs. I observe that he has left in your hands (att my disposal) Godfry Hutchinsons obligations to the Amount of Sixteen hundred pound Sterling, and that he has taken a Concern of 1/8 in the Sloop *Trumbull* (now the Brig^{tn} *Ranger*) for a Privateer for my Acco^{tt}. I hope she will have Succefs, and should be Glad you would Send me the Acco^{tts} of ye Charges, Prizes &c, when an oppertunity Prefsents. Samuel Champlin Command^r of the Privateer Sloop *American Revenue* will Deliver you this, and as the Vefsell belongs to me Should be Glad you would Supply him with such Stores as he may have Occasion for, and Charge the Am^o to my Acco^{tt} & Send me his Bill, have Given Capt Champlin orders In Case he takes any Prize, whose Cargoe may sute att St Pierres to Send her to your Addrefs, the N^t Proceeds of which would have Ly in your hands Untill further Orders, have also given Capt Jo^s Conkling in the arm'd Sloop *Revenge* a letter of Credit on you for Afsistance &c, and have Recomen'd to him to send such Prizes as may be Suitable for your Markitt to you, and would have you follow his Directions In Regard to the N^t Proceeds. Capt Lamb this moment came from Boston, and writes you by this Oppertunity, and Suppose he has Mentioned my purchasing One eighth of the Brigg. I am Sir Your hum^l Servt.

                                         Nathl Shaw Junr.

To Col Isaac Sears   New London Mar 24, 1778
Merch^t Boston

     Sir, I want to pay a Sum of Money to the bearer Capt John Lamb for freight & Stores, that he brought for Acco^t of the United States which I should be glad to pay him, but have advanced so much on the Acco^t of the public that I cannot do it without your Afsistance, and should be glad you would let him have two thousand pounds L M & charge to my acco^t. The Ship *Putnam* has all her Stores compleat, Provisions &c and I hope soon to have her out on a Cruse. I Imagine she will Am^o to Forty Fife Thousand Pounds. Pray be so good as to give me your opinion in regard to Dav^d Dixson, I sold him and Col Griffing 200 hhd Sugar last Augst to pay in two Mo Am^o to £20000, have only rec^d Seven. Should be glad you would let me know what Dixon is about and wether he will Leave Boston Soon. Y^{rs} &c

---

To John Bradford Esqr New London Mar 24, 1778
Cont^l Agent

    Sir, I Rec^d a letter from the Honb^l Board of Warr Directing me to send all the Warlike Stores in my hands to Springfield. I suppose they imagined that the Stores by Capt Lamb were del^d here as I have no others & suppose if you were to send those Stores to Springfield you would comply with those Orders. Perhaps you have Rec^d Similar Directions, be so kind as to let me know by return of the Post, &c.

To His Excellency Jon^a Trumbull   New London Mar 25, 1778
Governor of Connecticut

    Sir, Yours of ye 19th Ins came to hand by Mr Barrell who writes you by this opportunity and any Directions you give relative to the Clothing will be complyed with, there is boats that Daily pafs from this into Connecticut River & do not at present think there is any danger of falling into the Enemies hands. I have engaged of the French man all his Lead, Tent Cloth & Powder for the board of Warr, ye Board gave me directions to have it sent to Springfield, would you advise me to send it by Water to Hartford or otherwise by land. Agreeable by your directions by Major Putnam I have procured him the cordage he wanted, & shall send it on to the Westward in a few days. I have engaged the Frenchmans Salt for the State & Mr Colt one of the Continental Commifsarys wants for the public, if you consent to let him have it you'l write me, I expect to git it at or near five dollars a bus^l. I have advanced a large Sum of Money for the Continent, & have their Order on the Loan Office, but cant git any Bills, which obliges me to call on this State for what I am in advance & have sent my Brother on purpose for particulars must refer you to him. I am &c.

To Mr John Broom   N Lond Mar 25, 1778
Merch^t Hartford

    Dear Sir, I find the Ship *Putnam* will Am^o to at Least £45000 every article is purchased & hope soon to have her out on a Cruse. I want money & you must send me to the Am° of the above Sum or I must be obliged to stop for want of money, having advanced so much to the Public & the men concerned in the ship that I cannot proceed any further. I am &c.

To Col Samuel Broom   New London Mar 25, 1778
Merch^t Hartford

     Dear Sir, I have purchased every article, Stores, Provisions &c for the ship *Putnam* & the Brig *Nancy*, the ship will be at least £45000 & Brig £12000 & pofsible they will come higher but your part of those sums you must pay me & I want it very much for I have advanced largely & you have charged 100 pr C^t & more on the Stores. I gave you Directions to purchase which you should have put in at the prime Cost as the Money was then due to me, however if you & I think different we must leave it to indifferent persons. I have advanced so much for the public & the others Concerned in the Ship that I cannot go any further without you send me a supply of money.

To John Bradford Esqr New London March 29th 1778
Con^l Agent Boston

     Sir, Inclos'd is a Copy of a Certificate given by Col^n Sears and Col^n Waters of the Value of the freight bro^t by Capt Lamb, as I Agreed to leave the Matter of freight to those Gentlemen (being Mentioned Customary freight in the bill of Lading) I should be Glad to know if you furnisht them with the Quantity of Powder, Number of Arms, w^t of Lead Ball &c & I suspect they have given fr^t for a Larger Quantity then was bro^t for I Cannot Conceive that Sixty barrels of Powder should cont^a Seven Tons. I should be Glad you would Call on those Gentlemen & desire them to let you know by what Rule they were Govern'd by which should make the fr^t Am° to so high, if they have putt it att so much pr C^t I should be Glad to have the Estimation of the Value of the Several Articles & you Can furnish them with the Exact Quantity of Each. I wrote you ye 24th Ins^t & am Sir, Your hum^l Servt

                                           Nathl Shaw Junr.

To the Hon^{bl} Maj^r Genl Gates President   New London Mar 29, 1778
of ye Board of Warr in State of Pennsylvania

     Sir, I Received three Letters from your Board of the 27th Ult°, 3^d & 10th Ins^t Relative to Military Stores. Inclosed is an Acco^t of Sund'y Articles Shipt to my care by Mr Bingham at Martineco, which were Landed at Boston & delivered to Mr Bradford, Continental Agent. I have wrote him that it was your Orders, they should be sent to Springfield, & suppose you have wrote him to the Same purpose, there has been no Military Stores brot into this State for 12 M⁰ Past on Acco^t of the States and whenever any arrives shall give you the earliest notice. I have purchased Sixteen thousand yards of Canvas for Tents of the width of English Duck, and shall transport it to Springfield immediately with about One thousand w^t Lead which is all I can get, the Canvas is of Too good quality for Tents, but as you wrote so pressingly for it, I Judged we had better make the purchase then run the risque of wanting Tents. I shall as you desire call on His Excellency Governor Trumbull for the Am⁰. I can purchase Four thousand w^t of Powder at Two Dollars pr lb, but as it is so very high shall wait your further Orders before I buy it. Let me know in your next if its your desire that I shall purchase all the Tent Cloth, Arms & Amunition that is imported into this State on Private Acco^t. I shall send up to Springfield 5750 of powder imported by Thos Mumford on Acco^t of ye United States.

To Ezekiel Chevers Esqr New London Apr^l 2, 1778
at Spring-Field

    Sir, I have sent by Peter Rogers One hundred & Twenty five peices of Cloth for Tents, & Nine Roles of Sheet Lead by order of General Gates, who wrote me in the most earnest manner to forward such Things to Springfield but did not mention who they were to be delivered to. I should be glad you would direct Capt Rogers to the proper Perſon to Receive such things for Continental Use & you will not only oblige me but the Public. I am &c

To Meſs^{rs} Otis & Andrews New London April 2, 1778
Boston

    Gen. I Rec^d yours of ye 27 Ult⁰ in Regard to the Goods purchased by Mr Barrell. They are in my Store to be Delivered to your orders, there is no Continental Teams in this Town, and I cannot prevail on any person to Cart them at the stated price. I Should be Glad you would Give Directions to the Q^r Mr Genl in this State to Receive them, as I cannot think them safe in this Port. I am &c.

    New London, April 16th 1778
Sir

    Capt Michel the Command^r of the French Ship *Lyon* who lately arived in this Port from France, has been landing, and almoast Complleated the Sale of his Cargoe and is Preparing to go out on a Cruse, and this day a Recruting Officer, of the Continental Army Inlisted Several of his Men, and many more have a Disposition to leave him. The Captain says that unlefs your Excellency will Interfear in the Matter, he shall be Oblig'd to lay up his Ship, as he Cannot git any more hands, and as he is a Commifsioned Vefsell he thinks that his Men Cannot be taken from him and that Congrefs would not allow of it, as it would be the means of Discouraging any more Ships from Comeing here, should be Glad to know your Excellency's Opinion by the Return of the barer M[r] Brooks who Comes on purpose. This day Cap[t] Peter Griffin sent Six Prifoners hear that he had taken on Long Island belonging to a Fleet who are now att Shelter Island getting wood. They Consist of Twenty Five Sail Convay'd by a Frigate of Thirty Six and a Ship of Twenty Guns, and are to Return to New Port. I am Sir Your hum[l] Serv[t],

N Shaw Junr.

To Col[n] Josiah Waters   New London April 26th 1778
Merch[t] In Boston

    Sir, I Received your two Letters of y[e] 14th and 21st Ins[t] and in Regard to my Debt due from Col[n] Griffin and David Dickson, I Really begin to think its in a Dangerous Situation and I think I have Reason to beleive so for they have deceived me in Every Promise they have made of Payments. I have here Inclos'd you their acco[tts] by which you will See the Ballance in my favor is Eighteen Thousand Four hundred and thirty Six pounds 8/4 L Money, Reckoning the Interest to the 3 May also their Agreement and order for Delivering the Sugars & as they have Disapointed me so Often I hear Inclose you a Power of Attorney and would have you Imediately arrest Dickson. In Case he has not paid you Six Thousand pound and Can git Security to pay the Remainder in Next Month I would have you Act with Caution and keep the affair as Secrett as Pofsible and the Method would leave to your Discretion. Inclos'd is an acco[tt] of the last Money Rec[d] by which you will see the Mistake of £7.14. Pray forward the Surgeons Instruments as the Ship is Ready to Sail and write me by Every Oppertunity. Y[r] hum Serv[t]

N Shaw Jun[r].

P. S. If he pays Six Thousand pound & gives Security not to leave the Town Untill the Whole is paid, which must not Exceed One month you may withdraw the Writ. N. S.

The Honorable   New London May 4th 1778
The Continental Navy Board
att Boston

    Gentlemen, I have Purchas'd a Q[ty] of Duck and Cordage for the Continent[l] Friggate att Norwich and am largely in Advance for the Ship *Trumbull*. I have now an Oppertunity to dispose of a Bill on Congrefs for

Twenty Thousand pound Lawfull Money, and Shall Esteem it as a favor if you will draw in my favor for that Am⁰. I Intend in a few Weeks to wait on the board with my Acco^tts against the Marean Committe. Untill then I am Gentlemen

Your moast Obed^t hum^l Servt.

Nathl Shaw Junr.

To The Honorable   New London May 4th 1778
Maj^r General Gates
Pref^sed^t of the Board of Warr att York in Pensylvania State

    Sir, I wrote you the 29th of March last I had Purchas'd a Q^ty of Duck Agreable to your Orders and have sent it to Springfield with Eight hundred & Eighty One pounds of Lead att foot you have the Acco^tt Am⁰ to Nine Thousand One hund^d & forty Eight pounds 5/ Lawfull Money Equal to 30494 1/6 dollars which Sum I have drawn on you in favor of J^no Michel pay on Sight & beg you'l Honor it. I am Sir Your hum^l Servt.

Nathl Shaw Junr.

To Amosiah Joseline   New London Sepr 6, 1778
Falmouth Casco Bay

    Sir, Yours of the 24 Ulto by P. Darrow I Rec^d ye 4 Inst & it gave me pleasure to here from the *Putnam*, it being the first & only advice from her since she left N L. The Prize you brot in I am of your opinion that it is best for the Concerned to have her disposed of where she is then to risque her further. I therefore would have you proceed to the Sale of both Vefsell & Cargo Soon as pofsible & bring the N^t Proceeds in Cash to N London not doubting but you will take such methods for the sale as will be the most beneficial for the concern'd, as to the prisoners you brot into port you may dispose of them as you please, but take care you bring no Penalty on yourself by not complying with the Laws of the State you are in.

Y^rs &c

Write me by the Return of the Post ye Value of ye Vefsell & Cargoe.

To Col Josiah Waters   N London Sep^t 6, 1778
Merch^t Boston

    I have had but very llittle time to look over your Acco^t but I perseive you have charged £300 for your trouble of the dry goods in the general acco^t & then charged me in my private acco^t 2½ p^r C^t Com^s for what Goods I delivered Thompson, Col Norton & others. This by no means is right & cannot be allowed, tell Col Norton he must come here before I can settle with him as sum of his shares were purchased from Servents who had masters & who will not allow it, I shall want Eight of the Six pounders that Lamb sent in the prize for a Privateer, I am fitting out. My part of the wood on board the prize I shall want as I have about thirty tons of Cam Wood now on hand & want more to make up a Cargo. Indeed I should like to purchase the whole if it goes cheep, I should be glad to know the Quality & the price before it be sold. Will you be concerned with me. Tell Lamb if he is got in that I have Letters from his owner to fitt out for Virginia immediately

Y^{rs}

To Col Isaac Sears N Lond Sepr 19, 1778
Merch^t Boston

    I Received yours 4 Ins & before it came to hand I had wrote to Mr Joceline Prize master who came in the Brig to Falmouth to dispose of the Vefsell & Cargoe, as I take him to be a Prudent Good man, and make no doubt but he will give satisfaction to the Concerned, her Cargoe Consists of Salt & sum Bread, & if you Choose to take your part as being owner of one Eighth part of the *Putnam* you may do it, I have no objections. Capt Allan in the *Putnam* is arrived safe here from a Cruiz yesterday, he has taken Six prizes Viz: Four for NewfoundLand ye one that is in at Falmouth & a Brig from the Granadese with 150 hhd Rum, 10 hhd Sugar, 40 bar^l d^o & Sixty bags of Coffee. Capt Deshon just now came in & says that one of the Brigs is in at Boston, I hope the others will soon arrive. I am &c.

New London, Sepr 19, 1778

Dear Sir

    I Received yours 15 Ins by Capt Deshon and am glad to hear of another of the *Putnams* Prizes getting safe into port, & hope soon you'l advise me of some more getting in. The *Putnam* arrived here yesterday, has taken Six prizes, among them is one from the Granadoes with Rum, Sugar & the others much like the one in Boston.

    I am not determined about the Cargo, let me know the particulars in your next. Col Sears is owner of one Eighth of the *Putnam*, Mr Shettuck 1/32 & you must follow their directions so far & no father as to selling you any part of the Cargoe to Supply the Town I see no occasion for it. I think if you charge me a Commifsion, the Cargoe should be sold at the most it will fetch for the Concerned. As you have disapointed me about the Guns I will have nothing to do with them but will purchase others, neither will I be concerned with the Wood, and would have you proceed in the Sale of Vefsell & Cargoe. Capt Lamb will soon be in Boston & he will give directions about the Brig *Favourite*. Y^{rs} &c.

To Col Josiah Waters
Merch^t Boston

To Samuel Elliott Esqr 　　　　　　　New London Sepr 19, 1778
Boston

　　　The Ship *Oliver Cromwell* is come into this port with the Lofs of Sparrs & Sails. If you have any Duck on hand belonging to this State, I beg you would send up a Sufficient Quantity to make her a whole suit in Carts to Norwich to ye Care of Jabez Perkens. I am &c.

　　　　　　　　　　　　　　　　New London, November 15, 1778
Sir

　　　Yours by Capt Lamb with the Money Came safe to hand, and on examining the same I find the Bundle N° 6 to Contain only £1765.14 & the Paper Containing the Mem^o of the Money which I now inclose says £2421.10 which just leaves out the uper bundle marked on the head of the paper £655.16/ and you'l find this very same sum in the List of Money marked N° 11 which Cover I also inclose and in Bundle N° 21 from Col Sears for wood (a parcel missing Marked in the List £113.14/ which Cover I inclose for your inspection & I also find In Bundle N° 5 Rec^d of Saml Parkman a parcel marked £204.6/) a Counteft 5 Dollar Bill which I inclose, and I find a Small Bundle No number of £324. in your favour.

　　　　　　　　　　　　　　thus　£655.16.
　　　　　　　　　　　　　　　　　113.14.
　　　　　　　　　　　　　　　　　　1.10.
　　　　　　　　　　　　　　　　　―――――
　　　　　　　　　　　　　　　　　771. 3.0
　　　　　　　　　　　　　　　　　324.
　　　　　　　　　　　　　　　　―――――
　　　　　　　　　　　　Short　£447. 0.0
The Am^o of the List money (which I also inclose) by Lamb is
　　　　　　　　　　　　　　　　£20972.5.1
　　　　　　　　　　　　　　　　　　447.0.0
　　　　　　　　　　　　　　　　―――――――
　　　　　　　The exact Sum Rec^d　£20525.5.1

I have been very carefull in examining this Money and you may be easily convinfed of the mistake of the £655.16 as you may see that very sum in the List of Money N° 11, and also see the very same sum added in with the Bundle of Money N° 6. Send me by the first oppurtunity by Land to Norwich Fifteen bolts of Rusia or Stout English Duck, I want it for Imediate Use. Observe the *Favourite* is Lost. You'l Inform me what if Sav'd that I may give directions for the Disposal of it. Am Sorry if Tracy & Miller are to give a Bill on Mr Colt for the Rum that you did not send it me when I was att Hartford. Pray send it the first Oppertunity & let it be drawn payable with Interest from the time the Rum was Purchas'd. When I was att Boston, Mr Ervin offer'd me his house, Warf, store &c with his Hills Lott for Five Thousand Pound. If he Still Continued the Same mind you may pay him that sum and take a Deed, of this let me know in your Next. I have not Recev^d yours by Joselin. If Mr Hubbard Intends drawing on his Bro^r att Norwich send me the Bill. Yours of the 4th Ins^t I Received and Observe these words, Viz^t: Yours Busineſs I never ask'd or sough^t for. I am Sir, your humb^l Servt

Nathl Shaw

To Col^n Josiah Waters Esqr
Boston

To Mr Wm Patterson   New London Novr 22, 1778
  Philadelphia

     Sir, I Rec^d a Letter from our Friend Mr Moore ordering ye Brig *Favourite* to be sent to Virginia when she returned from a Cruise. Accordingly I communicated those orders to Capt Lamb who had ye Comm^d & in consiquence of those orders she was fitted to proceed on the Voyage and sailed from Boston last month and was run on shore at Cape Race where the Veſsell is intirely lost, I Just now hered that most of her Stores will be sav'd, shall inform Mr Moore by the first Opportunity. I am Sir, &c.

P. S. For particulars must refer you to Capt Lamb who transacted for the owners in the West Indias.

To Mr John Bragg   New London Nov 30, 1778
  New Haven

     Sir, I Received a letter from Mr Colt informing me that you had a quantity of Wheat & flour purchased in New York State and that in case I would procure a request from G. Trumbull to G. Clinton for Liberty to bring it into this State, that I might have it. I have just now obtained the needfull from G. Trumbull for ye am^o of Two hundred bar^l & shall want it soon as poſsible, as the State Ships are near Ready for Sailing. I would have part of the flour Bak'd into sea Bread at N Haven & part at Fairfield by Ge^o Cable, if you get any Wheat it will Suit Cable better then Flour as he has a Mill. I would have you consult with the bakers at N Haven what quantity they can Bake & how soon, Cable I know can bake very soon. The bearer Capt M Melally has an order on Mr Colt for a Sum of Money and in case he gits it will let you have much as you judge sufficent for the purchase, if Colt cannot pay the Money you may draw on me and your Bills will be paid, be so kind as to write me by every opport^y as I am in great to git the Ships out. If you can git 400 bar^l I shall want it.

To Col'n Josiah Waters   New London Decem'r 6th 1778
  Boston
Dear Sir

    Yours 2 Inst have Rec'd allso of ye 25th Ulto and Note the Contents. The Duck Is Not yet come to Hand, Neither is the Cask with the two Peaces of Jermin Serge. I am Suppriz'd that Mr Thomas Rusell should send the Bill of Sale to Carolina when Capt Allon desired it might be Returned to me, as I have Already Repaid him the Money. I must be Informed of this more Particular before I pay him any Money on Accott of the Putnam. Observe you Intend soon to Furnish me with a Gineral Accot (I wish you Would Com and Bring it your Self) also with what Is Saved of the *Favourite*, I shall Want my Self Part of the Guns & Stores (observe I Do Not give you any Orders Only for my Part). Bro Thoms is att Meeting and I Can Not send Mr Temples Note. If he Comes home Before the post Goes I will InClose it. I am Sr.

                    Your Humble Servent
                             Nathl Shaw

P. S. Inclosed is a Rect of John Temple Esqr for 477 dollars which you will please to Colect.

To Capt John Forbes   N Lond Decr 13, 1778
  Boston

    Sir, I Rec'd yrs 5th Ins. & am very glad to hear you have got your Vessell & Cargo Returned. In regard to ye Money I have advanced you, I had much rather have your bond on Interest, then have a Bill, & would have you settle the exchange with Col Waters, & give the bond for Sterling Money & when you arrive at Amsterdam, let Messrs Hoope & Co know that I have advanced that Sum, & that its very probable when these difficulty times are over, I shall draw on them for the Amo. Shall at all times be glad of a Line from you. I am &c.

To Mr John Forbes, Boston

To Col Josiah Waters   New London Decr 13, 1778
Merchent Boston

    Sir, Capt Forbes wrote me last post that his Vessell & Cargo was cleared and that he wanted to give me a Bill for the Amo of what money he had rec'd from you pay in Amsterdam, at present I do not want any money their, and had rather that you would Settle the Current of exchange and take his Bond on interest, or if he could sell his Bill & return the Money either of which would sute me, as I had only a mind to Serve him in this. I suppose about Six for one between this money & Sterling would be near the matter.

Yours of ye 9th Ins is come to hand and observe what is saved belonging to the Brig *Favourite,* also what particularly belongs to me. I shall want one p^r of the Brigs Six pound Cannon, all the rest of the Articles saved am content to have sold at public Vendue. Those articles of mine, let them rest in your hands untill further orders, Except the Bread, which Sell as I immagine is perishing—endeavour to exchange the Pork & Beef with Miller & Tracey and git me an order to Receive it Norwich. I shall deliver your Letter to Capt Lamb. He mentioned that Mr Moore had wrote you to act for him in regard to the *Favourite.* The *American Revenue* Sails next week, all her Officers are ingaged. The *Putnam's* officers go in her again, Consequently have no berth vacant. As to settling with the Owners of the Ship *Putnam,* I did not intend to have a Settlement in Boston, only to let you know who they were, that in case they wanted any Goods you might deliver them near the amount. As to Mr Babcock, I thought I had mentioned to you that he was 1/16 owner and as I have paid Capt Allon for Mr Rofes part of ye Ship & have not the Bill of Sale, I will Acco^t with him myself for his part of the prizes, therefore you'l forward the Acco^t Sales & of what you have paid the owners, that I may make a Settlement. Sell the Brig *Caroline* at Vendue and in case she does not Sell for what I sett her at, purchase her for my Acco^t and take care of her untill further orders. As to Dickson debt tell ye Gent^l who have orders to pay it, that I think the Settlement must be made in this Town, were they engaged to pay it, & if they mean to be Honest men, tell them in justice should pay me the difference between £20,000 in Certificates that draw Interest in France, and those that are now taken. I choose to have the Settlement of this affair myself. Has my Friend Jo^s Rufsell paid you any money on my acco^t.

I am &c.

To Col Isaac Sears N London Decr 23, 1778
Merch^t Boston

I Rec^d y^rs by post 16 Ul^o & as to ye Ship *Putnams* Sailing I intend to have her ready if pofsible in the next Month. We have been obliged to give her new Masts & Bowspreat & New Sails & Standing Riging. The Riging & Sails I had from you & Mr Broom are good for Nothing, I ordered some provisions from Boston for the Ship & it is lost on Cape Cod, have now purchased enough for the Cruise. Y^e Bread is to come from Norwalk, I wish the Ship had come into Boston, am satisfied she might be fitted for one half the Money there. I Expect it will take the prize that was sold to the Eastward & the Goods that was sold here to fitt her out again you shall have the acco^t in a few days. I wrote Col Waters to let you have your part of the Goods sold in Boston & the remainder will settle with you when I can finish the Acco^t of the charge of fitting out, as to the purchasing your part of the Ship, I would very readily do it but I have taken Mr Rofes part & Mr Brooms so that I own almost the whole which is too much in one bottom, I had rather sell you my part. As to ordering the prize to Boston that was at Falmouth, in case she had been lost, I emagine I should have been blamed by the concerned. There was no desert knives, I will furnish you with an Acco^t of all the Plate and in case you had rather have your part in anything else you may have it. Am determined to have no dispute with you about any thing. Yours &c.

To Patrick Moore   New London, January 3, 1779
att Martineco

      Sir, I Received your Several favours and Inclosing my acco^tts which I suppose if Right. I Expect by this you have Received the Money from Mr Hutchinson for his Notes in my favour, hope the Brigg Ranger is safe Arived with you & to good Markitt.

      I shewed your letter to Capt Lamb Respecting the Brigg *Favorites* going to Virginia which seem'd to Displease him very much as their had been so much money lay'd out to fix her for an Arm'd Vefsell and those Persons who Purchas'd from Capt Lamb Imagin'd they were Ill treated. How Ever as you was the Cheif Owner they were oblig'd to Submit to your orders, and as Admiral Byrons Squadron was Crusing in the Bay, it was Judg'd best to send her through the Vinyard Sound & to touch att this Port in her Way, but unfortunately the Pilot Run her on Shore att the Cape and have lost the Vefsell, Moast of her Stores are Saved. Col^n Josiah Waters, Merch^t In Boston has the whole Directions of the Brigg Ever Since she has been in America in Conjunction With Capt Lamb & to them must Refer you for the Acco^tts &c as I have had Nothing to do with her no further then being 1/8 Concern'd which I paid Capt Lamb for. The barer Capt Wm Leeds is in an Arm'd Sloop of mine Cal'd the *American Revenue,* and In Case he sends any Prizes into Martineco, I have Recomended his Sending them to your Care, and the Am^o of the Owners part you'l keep in your hands Untill further orders, and take Capt Leeds Directions Relative to the Peoples Share, and In Case he has Occafsion for any Supplies for the Sloop you'l Please to furnish him and take his bill on me for the Am^o. I am Sir

                                     Your hum^l Servt.
                                       Nathl Shaw

To Col Josiah Waters   New London Feb. 28, 1779
Merch^t Boston

      Dear Sir, I Rec^d y^rs by Capt Hinman & observe you have sent me sum Money which you say is near the Ballance Includ^g Sears's Ballance, what you can think by referring me to Col Sears I know not, I gave you Directions to let him have 1/16 of the Am^o of the Prizes you sold in Boston & Beckus was to have only his part. I have been once to Windham myself, & have only got £750. I beg for the future you would attend to my orders, and call on Col Sears for the Ballance, the Goods that was Sold here & at Casco Bay will not pay the fitting out of the *Putnam*, & soon as she sails will furnish Col Sears with the acco^{ts}. I am very much in want of Money that will pafs, I beg you will not send me any more of those Emifsions. You must sell the Rum you have on hand for the most it will fetch & dispatch Harris with as much Money as you can. I have sent him to Capt Deshon for a Commifsion for the *Putnam*, who waits for Nothing else. I beg you would forward the matter in the most expedecious manner & if they require any other Bonds you and Col Sears, or Mr Babcock can give them. As to the Collecters calling on you for my Tax, I think they may as well call on the Pope, you know I have not sold or bought any goods in Town of Boston this warr & the reason for Taxing me I cannot tell, am determined not to pay any, I am Sufficiently tax'd here for all the Trade I carry on. Inclosed is a Letter to Friend Jo^s Rufsell. I believe he will pay you sum money on my acco^t & tell the Person who is desired to Settle Dixons obligations, that they must send the money here and pay me the ballance as its on Interest & I suppose we shall soon have a Law in this State that all contracts shall be made good. In that case there will be many thousand due me & I shall insist on sum allowance more then the interest before I will settle it. Bro. Thomas writes you relative to the Money advanced the French Man. I hope you will get without any trouble. I have not to add but am Sir &c.

To Col Josiah Waters   N London Feb. 28, 1779

Dear Sir, I here inclose you Major Mersereaus Rec^t for Nathl Shaws Acco^t against the French Consul for £3319.10/2 & my Acco^t against the major for £460.2/ adjusted & settled in the manner the consul has requested by which you will see that he has promised to pay the money into your hands, this is to desire you to call on said Mersereau for payment of both the Acco^{ts} & on his refusal, I desire you to arrest him on my Acco^t for £460.2/, & to apply to the Consul for the payment of N Shaws Acco^t & on his refusal to have him arrested without any ceremony. Mersereau having my Acco^{ts} in his hands will make no difficulty, I have the copys here & can get the Committees to Sign them & send you. If you think best to acquaint the Honb^l John Holker Esqr French Consul before you arrest the Vice Consul you may & for that Reason also inclose you Daniel Bells Letter who ingages to pay or see the expences paid, and at the same time you may acquaint him that 113 French Prisoners were Landed here in the dead of Winter, Sick & naked on board a Flag Ship John Greely, Master who is now in Boston, whom we ordered round to Boston with these prisoners, but he refused to go with them & he might as well have knock'd them in the head, as to attempt it. We imprefsed a Large House, turn'd out ye family for them, kept up Nine large Fires night & day & could hardly keep them from freezing, being almost naked &c, &c.

Mersereau is to pay you about £37 on acco^t of Jo^s Holt, if he does send it up with mine &c. Inclosed is a Letter from ye Committee which adjusted his acco^t with the French Hospital & thro' mistake docked his Bill of £76 which sum they request may be paid by the Consul & for this reason I now inclose there Letter also, which if they refuse to pay, the Doc^r will be obliged to go down to Boston him Self.

Thos Shaw

To Col Josiah Waters   N Lond Mar 14, 1779
Merch^t Boston

    Dear Sir, I Rec^d Y^r 10 & 11th Ins. with the Cash by Mr Mumford, & observe that Col Sears has not pd you the whole of his Ballance, however next week if pofsible I will send him his acco^t of Expence in fitting out the *Putnam*. The Charges in my acco^t wth you y^t I think ought not to be charged are for Goods that I gave orders to be delivered or Reserved out of a Cargo that is put in y^r hands. Viz: the Commifs^n on ye Goods d^l Thompson & Col Norton, also the Rum & Coffee that I ordered reserved for me. I really expected you would been able to have sold the Rum for 16 or 17 Dol^rs. Dont sell any more for lefs then Seventeen untill you here further from me. Beg of you to urge the Frenchman to pay the money & also the Charge of Bringing it up. I am &c.

The Hon^bl Marine Com^tte   N Lond Mar 14, 1779
Eastern Department

    Genl. I Rec^d yours by the last Post giving directions to have the Schooner (that Capt Burk left here) sent to Philadelphia, I have desired a person to overhall her Stores & I find she is in a wretched Condition having neither Riging or Sails that is Sufficient expect a Four Sale & her Hull wants recalking &c.

We are in such a wretched state in this Town by reason of the Smallpox, Fever & Famine that in short I cannot carry my bufsinefs & am laying my own Vefsells as fast as they come in, for every necefsary of life is at such an extravagant price that whenever I imploy any person to do any thing they insist upon provisions which is not in my power to give them at present, Consiquently I cannot fit her out. I Rec^d the N Y News papers & find they have by their Privateers taken almost every Vefsell y^t has saild from the Southerd. Col Wadsworth ye Commifs G^l is in town & says y^t Congrefs are extreemly averse to letting Flour be exported & y^t in his opinion it would be much better to have a Vefsell Loaded at Phila^a (where there is many to be had) and sent to Boston & their dispose of her which would be much cheeper & lefs risque, if you are determined at all events to make a tryall to get Flour. My helth is such that I must leave ye town & go in the Country. I am &c.

To Col Josiah Waters   New London Apr¹ 25, 1779
Merchent in Boston

    I Rec^d yours by post 21st Ins^t and am sorry to find you have not Rec^d any money on my Acco^t. What is the reason the French Consul does not pay you the money I advanced for him. I want much to pay the order to Thos Ruſsell. Am surprized you did not mention the Rate Bills on France sell att, but as I am so desirous of paying M^r Ruſsell, I have here inclosed you Bills to the Am^o of Twenty Nine hundred & Forty dollars which would have you dispose of for the most you can git. Mr Mumford tells me that they go at Six & Six & half, must depend on your getting the highest Price. The *Putnam* has sent a Sloop of 8 Guns, a privateer from New York. Hope you'l send me the Bill Mr Rose drew on me by the Return of the Post.

  2 Setts Bills 1200 dol Each   2400 Returned by Mr Hogsdon Novr 21, 1779
  1 d^o   300
  8 d^o .   30   .   . 240 Returned
                         2940

To Col Josiah Waters   N Lond May 9, 1779
Merch^t Boston

    Yours by the post ye 6 Ins Inclosing M^r Ruſsells Rec^t for £7000.2/ came to hand, as to the bill of 300 Dollars you may have it at the Value. I sett out to morrow for Hartford & expect to be there during the setting of the Genl Aſsembly (I suppose four Weeks) will let you know when I return. Am in sum hopes of having a prize in at Boston. If that should happen will come and pay you a Visit. Y^{rs}.

To Mr Thomas Ruſsell   New London June 26, 1779
Merch^t In Boston
  Sir,

    Inclosed is an Acco^t with Alex^d Roſe ballance due him 450.19.3 & an order on Col Sears for it. The Ship was settled with Capt Allon.

To the Honble Richard Lee Esqr N Lond June 27, 1779
Chairman of the Marine Committee

    Sir, I have Rec^d a Letter from Meſs^{rs} John Wharton & Ja^s Reed of ye 7 Ins^t Acknowledging the Rec^t of mine ye 24th Ult^o inclosing an Acco^t Sales of the Ship *Nathl & Eliz^a* wherein they desire to know if that be all the Prizes sent into this State by y^e *And Doria,* To which I answere that, that was all the Prizes sent in here to my care or that I have the knowledge of excepting the Schooner *John & Joseph* which the *And Doria* took while she was in the Fleet & under the Command of Commodore Hopkins & I suppose the Captures part was to be sheered among the Whole Fleet. Let this be as it will, this retaken Vefsell is all, Acco^t Sales of which I now inclose.

Col Josiah Waters   New London June 29, 1779
Merch^t Boston

     Dear Sir, I Rec^d y^rs by Mr Latimer & w^t regard to the Prize *Snow Clinton,* I would have you take out all her Cargo into Store and divide it & deliver the one half to Capt N Saltonstall & Wolcott in behalf of the Ships Crew, and the owners part to ly in y^r hands untill further orders, as we do not choose to dispose of one Single article at present, for we had much rather our part of the goods should ly in Goods then in Money in these unstable times. The *Snow,* if you think best to sell her seperate from her Warrlike Stores you may, and dispose of the Warrlike Stores as you think will fetch most. I have wrote you already to sell the *Charming Nancy* and I would have you to fitt out the *Putnam* immediately on a Cruize & to give all the Officers an offer to go in her again, and if they will agree to enter with Spirit they may have Liberty to bring up their shares of dry Goods in the Ship & Land them here in this Port for the benefit of their families, provided that they agree that the Ship shall not be detained here by this. I know this is difficult but I think it can be done. If the officers conclude on this plan, the Ship must be fitted out with every thing necefsary for a three or four Months Cruize, so that she may have no excuse to ly here. If any of the officers do not choose to go in her from Boston you must get others appointed. As I cannot think of fitting her out here in the present Ill state of health of my Brother. If there is no Bread in the Prize you may Exchange provisions for it. I have wrote Capt Saltonstall on the Subject & dare say he will do every thing in his power to forward the fitting and maning the Ship. If they choose to Victual her for a Longer Cruize you may.

To Col Samuel Broom   New London Aug^st 15, 1779
Merchent Boston

     Dear Sir, Yours of ye 12 Inst is before me and observe you have Rec^d 25 p^s of the Duck & that you expect the other daily. Inclosed is an order for it, & Heathcoat Muirsons Note for Ten Lewe Doris, which Capt Niles let him have when in great distrefs & his Letter to Adam Babcock requesting him to pay the Same, I hope he will with honor as it was on his Credit that Niles let him have the Money. If he refuses to pay the hard money you will please to recover it from Niles as he had no orders to give away our money. I also inclose all the Acco^t I can get of Niles in which you will see that he has charged 3 pr C^t Primage, is it not too high. I wish you would shew this Acco^t to Mr Wills. The whole of ye Remainder was shipd in y^e *Spy* & one Bam, & he has Lost the Bills of Lading & Acco^t &c. I have Received the 192 Livers. Our part of the Duck we want for the *Putnam*.

Am^o of Ivory		6100
	Livers	
Am^o of Duck purchased . .	5038.15.9	
Com^s 5 pr C^t . . .	252.	
freight from Nantuckett .	48.	
Cash Lent Murison . .	240.	
Cash Rec^d	192.	
Primage 5 pr C^t on 6100 .	305.	
Ballance due . . .	24.4.3	6100.

To John W. Stanly   New London Octo 13, 1779
North Carolina

    Sir, Agreeable to your Letter of the Eleventh of June, I have this day Received of Capt Prince 1239 1/3 Dollars for and on your Acco^t.

Joseph Hews Esqr New London Octo 31, 1779
Philadelphia

    Sir, In my last of the 16 Ins^t I wrote you that I should forward the Money I had in my hands belonging to the Owners of the Schooner *Portious* or get Bills on Phil^a Since which I have Rec^d yours of the 12th Ins^t wherein you say that you shall leave the City sometime next month. I hope you will Receive this with the Inclosed Bill for 104662/3 Dollars on Robt Morris Esqr by Thos Mumford before you leave the City, and give me some directions who to Remit the Money or Bills in case I can procure them to, in Phil^a, If you should leave it before I can get the remainder of the Money out of Mr Larrabes hands. In settling with the persons whom I sold the Tobacco to, I find that I did not deduct the Tare, supposing it was taken out in the devision but find the devision was made without Respect to the Tare of the Cask. And also on delivering the Tarr & Turpentine find Ten bar Tarr & five bar^l Turpentine more which I have sold for £450. Y^{rs} &c.

                                                       Thos Shaw

Mr Joseph Rufsell Junr   N Lond Nov 14, 1779
Merchent Bofton

    Sir, I Recd yrs 11 Ins. & find yt my Camwood is partly removed to Boston. I did intend to have Loaded a Vefsell for Holland in the Spring but Since it is at Boston I would have you send for the Remainder and ship the whole to Amsterdam for my Accot on the best Terms you can and have the neat proceeds shipt in Jermin Steel and advise me, I am Sir, Your Huml Servt

                                                     N. S.

The Honbl Commifsioners of the   N Lond Jany 13, 1780
Admirality of the United States
  Philadelphia

    May it Please your Honors,
        In the Absence of Mr Nathl Shaw (who attends the Genl Afsembly of this State at Hartford) I received your Letter of ye 10th Ulto informing him of the defsolution of ye Merine Committee & the establishment of the Board of Admirality, and that he is to govern himself accordingly, and also that he is requested to transmit his Accotts up to the 31st Decr & inform your Honors what ballance may be in his hands, in order that you may draw for it,—which I shall lay before him on his return. Their has never been any Prizes of Consiquence brought into this State, and none since 1776. The ballance then in his hands he paid by order of the Marine Comtte to Mefsrs Levingston & Turnbull, which was Ten thousand dollars, and has their Bill for the Same. Since which he is in considerable advance, expecting some Prizes might be sent into this Port. I am in behalf of Nathl Shaw.

                     Your Honors Most Obt & Huml Servt.
                                   Thos Shaw.

                                       New London Mar 30, 1780

1 Continental Certificate in favr Thos Rufsell No 1528 dated Aprl 23, 1777 for		300 Dol.
2 Ditto in favour Christo Prince No. 3725 & 3726 Dated Sepr 17, 1777	400 Each	800.
3 ditto in favour Ditto Same Date No 3424, 25 & 26	300 Each	900.
1 ditto in favour Nathl Tracey No 1320 date Feby 6, 1778		600.
1 ditto in favour John Deshon No 5394 dated Feb 20, 1778		200.
		2800.

Sir, Inclosed is Eight Continental Certificates as pr the above List amo to 2800 Dollars taken out of your office at Boston, on which no Interest been paid. I beg you would be so kind as to get the Interest due in Bills of Exchange, & Inclose both Bills & Certificates to me by the First oppertunity & you'l oblige.

To Mr Alexan^{dr} Hogdon } Returned as by his Letter Apr^l 12, 1780.
Present

Mr Patrick Moore   New London Apr^l 12, 1780
Philadelphia

     Sir, Inclosed is Copy of a Letter I Rec^d from Capt John Lamb, with Continental Certificates of ye 18th May, 1779 to the Am^o of four thousand, four hundred dollars. I have often call'd upon him since I Rec^d your favour of ye 26th November last, but have not rec^d it before yesterday & agreeable to his desire sent him a Rec^t for the same for and on your Acco^t. In behalf of Nathl Shaw

                          Your Humble Servent
                               Thos Shaw

These Certificates are settled in acco^t with Mr Moore at Phil^a July 1st 1788 by Mefs^{rs} Wharton & Lewis in my behalf. T Shaw.

Col Josiah Waters   New London Feb 12, 1781
   Merch^t Boston

     Dr Sir, I take the Liberty to Inclose you Capt Babcocks Order and Rec^t for a Box Lemons for £400 which was the rate the Cargo Sold for. His not sending me the money as he therein promised, induced me to send it to Boston by M^r McCurdy. His failing, I am now obliged to trouble you with it, & as he is now come home, hope there will be no further delay & that he will pay it on presentation.

Col Josiah Waters   New London Mar 7, 1781
   Merch^t Boston

     Sir, I take the liberty to Inclose you Wm Shattucks Note for £533.10.10½ dated June 22^d 1779. I have wrote him on ye Subject & inclosed him my Acco^t ballance due him £101.2.10 which is to be indorsed & leaves a ballance on ye Note of £432.8.0½ which I have desired him to Settle with you by ye Scale of Depreciation & pay you ye current exchange with the Interest.

Also Adam Babcocks Acco^t ballance due me £107.8.6 Lawful Money, which I have desired him to pay you at ye Current exchange, when he was at N L he requested me to send my Acco^t to Boston, & he would Settle it. N. B. Mr Shattucks order on Thos Mumford is rec^d for his debt Mar 25, 1781.

New London April 20th 1781

Gentlemen

    I Rec^d the Steel & Linnen you shipt me by way of Boston. I now inclose you ye following Five Bills of Exchange viz: 2 Bills drawn by F. Hopkins Treas^r Loans on ye Commiſsioners at Paris & Countersign'd Wm Imly N° 118 & N° 119 date Feb^r 27, 1781. For Twelve hundred Dol. each in my favour, 1 Bill drawn by Bautint on Mon^s de Serilly Tresorier Paycear General des Depenses de le Guerre Paris N° 329 dated at New Port January 28, 1781 Pour 4936^{lb}.3.4 in favour of John Carter, 1 Ditto drawn by de Grarceliaus Major de l'Escadre on Monseiur Beaudart de St James Tresorier General de la Marine a Paris N° 545. dated New Port Feb^r 22, 1781 Pour £1500 tournois in favour Wadsworth et Carter. I d^o N° 329 ye Same date & Tenor as the 2 first for Six hundred Dollars. Which Bills I would have you Receive Payment for & Paſs to my Credit in Acco^t. I expect to send a Veſsell to your addreſs in the course of this Summer & shall then give you Directions how I would have the Proceeds disposed of. I send this to my Friend in Boston to Forward you by the first opportunity and am Gentlemen Your most Ob^t & Hum^l Servt.

                                                      Nathl Shaw

To Meſs^{rs} John De Neufville & Son
   Merchants in Amsterdam

New London Augst 15, 1781

    The foregoing is what I wrote you by way of Boston, Inclosed is a Bill of Lading for 40 barrels Turpentine & 15 hhd^s of Virginia Tobacco, which I have shipt by the bearer Capt Trowbridge in the Brig *Firebrand* which I hope will come safe to hand & a good markett. You'l Please to dispose of it for the most it will sell for, and after paying the freight & charges Credit my Acco^t with the N^t Proceeds. Inclosed is a Bill of exchange drawn by de Graueliaus Major de l'Escadre on Monseiur Boutin Trisorier General de la Marine a Paris dated New Port 20th July 1781 for Two thousand four hundred Tournois in favour Andre Carante N° 974 which Receive Payment for, and C^r my acco^t with the N^t Proceeds. Send me Fifty pounds Ster^g worth of Chany (such as you shipt Jere Plat) must leave it to you to send such as is neceſsary for House use. I am &c

                                                      Nathl Shaw

Meſs^{rs} John De Neufville & Son
   Merchants in Amsterdam

New London April 10, 1782

Gentlemen,

    My last to you was by Capt Trowbridge in the *Fire Brand* of ye 15 Augst last & Since have rec^d yours 30th Octo by which I find that she had arrived, hope you are in Cash for the Bills, Turpentine & Tobacco I shipt you by that opportunity. She has not yet arrived here. I now Inclose you one Bill of Exchange N⁰ 394 for Six hundred dollars dated Jany 28, 1782, one ditto for Twelve hundred dollars N⁰ 125 drawn by Wm Imlay on ye Commiſsioners of ye United States at Paris in my favour dated Feb 27, 1782 which would have you receive payment for and paſs to my C^r in Acco^t. Since I wrote you have been Visited by ye British Troops & they have destroyed ye Town Stores & Wharfs by which I have been a large Sufferer (more then Twelve thousand Sterling) at present I am not determined in what manner I shall order the ballance in your hands, but would have it Subject to any future order I may give. I am &c

N. S.

Meſs^{rs} John De Neufville & Son   (This Letter Returned)

New London April 10, 1782

Dear Sir,

Send me your Note of hand dated Feb^r 14th 1782 pay in Twelve Months for the Sum of Thirteen hundred & two dollars with Interest, agreeable to your promise for the Bills of Exchange I let you have when in Boston. Inclosed is a Letter for Meſs^{rs} John De Neufville & Son Merch^t In Amsterdam, which be so kind as to forward the first opportunity & let me know the Convayence.

P. S. Inclosed is Bills of Exchange to the am⁰ of one hundred & Eighty dollars which you may add to your Note, or Sell them for my acco^t. all in favour of Guy Rich^{ds} dated Jany 7, 1782.   I am Sir Your Humble Servent

Nathl Shaw

Col Josiah Waters
Merch^t Boston

New London April 25th 1782

O My dear friend

You have Doubtleſs heard the melencholy tiding of my brothers awful death. When this Town was destroyed & so many of my Dear friends reduced to extream poverty & Distreſs and others of them butchered in cool blood; it effected me deply; it wounded my very soul When my Dear Sister died of a putrid fever which she took from some Deſtreſsed priſoners she took in; it allmost overwhelm'd me; I thought it Imposible to meet with any thing to be compared with it. But O! the Death of my Brother is unconsolable. Friday (always called an unlucky Day) 12 Ins^t He with Melally, Capt Angel, Eb^r Way & Wm Clark sett out in His small Boat for the purpose of Shooting wild fowl; on their return^g off Leſter Rocks the Wind blowing fresh, he went to secure the musquet, one of which had gone off in the Morning on half Cock, & Now being Loaded & for fear of accident had the priming wiped out of the pan by one of the party and handed Him who took it by the muzzle and as he was putting it under the cuddy it went off full Loaded with Goofe Shott and Discharged all its fatal contents into his right side opposite to the diaphragm, carried away the Muscular parts, broke three of his ribs, wounded the right lobe of the liver & of the Lungs, & as the Charge thus pas'd thru his body & Clothes it wounded two of the party. One of them had seven shott picked out of his breast & some more yet to extract, another had three taken out of his forehead. This was four O'Clock, the wind extream high & a head the Boat in great Distrefs; Melally lay himself down on the ballast took the Dear Man in his arms after wrapping a Table Cloth round his mangled body to keep the Dredful wound from the cold; it was so seard with the blaze of the Explosion y^t it bleed but little. The rest covered him over with their Great Coats. At 5 O'Clock they made out to land him at a little House below the Light House. Soon as I heard of this fatal catastrophe I dispatched a Messenger after Doct^r Turner at Norwich one of the best surgeons in this Place & went down immediately to Him with what surgeons I could muster and found him in all the excruciating pains of expiring nature in a poor fishermans house that had been previously broken to peices & robb^d of everything by that savage banditte on the 6th Sep^t last that burnt this town. In ye time we had dres'd his wounds. I sent up for Bed & other comforts, we were all convinc'd he would not survive. He manifested a Desire to Die at home, I accordingly next morning took him up in the Bed & sett him gentle into a Large boat, & with another towed him up to town. O! what heart rending work to my poor aged mother, to me, to all to see him thus. Well may we cry out In the Midst of life we are in Death. After every humane effort being tried to reieve, to soften, & Molify the exquisite anguish of his wounds a mortification rendered all aborative And on Monday Morning 6 O'Clock being the 15th Ins^t heaven demanded its pledge. He Supported himself with Great fortitude & patience thru the whole Time; retained his sences to the last. He spoke of the emptinefs of this world & the Vanity of all its Glory. He Spoke much of the all Sufficiency of Jesus Christ and profesed his belief in him. Yes he declared he had a Discovery of the Gospel Plan of Salvation by Jesus Christ beyond what he even knew before and y^t he was perfectly resignd to the will of God, so that we do not mourn as they who mourn without hope. I blefs God for the unmerited grace & Goodnefs in the preserving his Scences & cuting off all hopes of recovery & Directing his Views immediatly by the Lamb of God. May you, may I, have this hope in us. He made his will & has appointed me his Executor. Nat & Chretia Woodbridge are the principles in it. It is surprizing that he should urge me at that time to Send you for a Pall & if you had sent it he no doubt would been the first to have want. You will send it up in the team that Mr Richards of this Town sends after some Goods that come in the *Firebrand.* The two Chests of China that came in the Same Brigg in Mefs^{rs} Jarvis & Russells Store belonging to the Deceased I think to have it sold as it will soon be in Demand. I inclose you the Invoice of it & you will let me know your Opinion what it will sell for. My Brother wrote you ye 10 Inst & Inclos'd a Letter for Mefs^{rs} John De Neufville & Son, Amsterdam to forward, if you have not done it I wish to have it Inclosed back to me as it contains Bills to the amount of 1800 dollars which I Shall choose to send in my own name & perhaps to have the effects come home in the Ship *Cato* now at this port which Sails in a few Days by Surrinam for Amsterdam. I observe yours of ye 15th Ins^t that you shall not mifs of sending the Bill of 1200 dollars to Amsterdam on my brothers acco^t. If you do not take it you will please to Send it me for the above reason. Observe you shall send the 180 Dollars by next Post, let it be in Gold.

Thos Shaw

Col^n Josiah Waters
Merch^t Boston

New London April 25th 1782

Dear Sir,

In my Brother Late excursion at Providence he fell in with one Gabriel Allen Sculp^t and engaged a p^r Tombstones I Suppose for his Lady and a Brother in Law, which I would defer at Present & request the favour of you because I think it agreeable to you to call on Mr Allen & know if it would not be best to have a Marble Monument in form of a Table supported with five Pillars on a floor of the Same to be erected over them, both him & his Lady as they are buried side by side with both their Epitaphs engraved, if you and Allen think it best, please to Send me your Opinion by return of the Next post & alfo how you would form the epitaphs to be place on our friends monument Leaving blank for age and Death which I will fill up & send to the engraver if agreable. I wifh you'd enquire if this find you at New Port & you are not going up soon if you could with Capt John Hopkins on this Subject it might do as well, but I Should choose to be pleased & particular in having something that was clever. For this reason I apply to you & if it should be a little time Delayed could dispence with it.

I am with esteem & friendship

Your most hum^l Servt
Thos Shaw

Mr Brattle

New London April 24th 1782

Sir,

Made his will, appointed me his Executor. I shall find myself involved in a multiplicity of perplexing Accounts among which will be the Appeals to Congrefs from Carolina & your State. When he went from Here Last to your Court he told me y^t ye post would bring on all his papers from Phil^a with regard to the Schooner *two Brothers* & would have me forward the Same to him & on the comeing in of the Post I found the Papers brought to be relitive to the Brig *Sally* w^c was the appeal from

N Carolina & Supposed he Sent for them to shew at your Court for some reasons. Since his return I have not heard him say anything about the paper or mention where they are. Neither do I know anything of the proceedings of the Schooner *two brothers* or the *Masters Hand*. I heard him enquiring when Col Dyer would sett out to Congrefs & Promised to see him in May at our Assembly to consult & Employ him in both these Cases at Congrefs. Col Dyer had the management of these cases at first, but the particular procefs & on what ground the Schooner *two Brothers* stands I am not able to Inform him or how it is to go to Congrefs or before what trybunal or whether their is a Court of Appeals &c. I could therefore wish you would write me all yt is nefefsary to communicate to Col Dyer that he might take it up properly & all ye Document papers & other matters in this Case & if you should have anything belonging to the Brigg *Sally'd* appeal, That is if it was yours & my brothers opinion to go forward with it. I find a Number of papers concerning the Schooner *Two Brothers* Deposition &c but I am most profoundly Ignorent of this whole Long intricate tryal. I Shall relly upon you to afsist me herein & of you letting me Know what has been Done & what is still to be Done so as it may go forward without mistake & your advice in still carrying it on perhaps on the Death of my brother what is done must all Drop & Stanton & Noice prich a New. If so whether it would not be best to try to settle it with them by leaving it to good Men or let them go over all the Ground again. If I know anything of the matter I think they are greatly mistaken, the whole amo Sales of ye Schooner was only about £2000 Continental Money then, & that every afsistant was paid but them two, it must be impofsible I think for them to recover.

Your Most Huml Servt
Thos Shaw

Bousa Helms Esqr

To Col Josiah Waters   New London May 2d 1782.
Merchent Boston

    Sir, I recd yr letter of ye 28th Ulto & ye £43.18/ for ye Bills of 180 dol, ye pall & ye Letter directed to Mefsrs De Neufville & Son. As ye post came in late last night & goes out early this morning, I have not examined into the calculation, or into the nature of your not complying with your Rect of ye 14 Feb. exprefsing "1302 dol at 5 livers tournois pr dol—or in case I take them to my own Accot I am to give sd Shaw my Note therefore payable in Sps Mill'd dol. in 12 Mo wt Interest annually"— And your Letter 15th April, "I will take the Bills for 1302 dol.—I shall send my note for the Bills." The deceased understood it thus in his letter to you of ye 10th Ulto. If you send me your note it must be in my Name. Observe you will make inquiry into the demand & price of the Chiny. Yrs &c.

T Shaw

Mr John Wright Stanly   New London May 8th 1782
Mercht Philadelphia

    Sir, you have doubtlefs heard the affecting death of my dear brother Nathl Shaw from a wound he recd by ye accedental discharge of a Muskett the 15th April last. I observe in your letter of ye 16 Febr last you mention a Sum of Contl Money sent on to Ed Tinker wc he refused to receive & Stephen Tinker left in the hands of my late Brother, which money after some little time was for your interest invested in the Loan office perhaps two or three months after. I have spoke Mr Tinker on the Subject but he still refuses to receive the Certificates. A Continental Certificate of abought that date & that sum will be subject to your order. &c.

                                             Your Hum Servt
                                                 Thos Shaw

                                        New London May 8th 1782

    Gentm, I am Sorry to Inform you of the Death of my Brother Nathl Shaw who died on the 15th April of a wound he received from the Accidental Discharge of a Musket, Since which I have received your favour of the 20th Octr 1781 by the *Fire Brand* with the Cheeney & the Several Inclosiers, Vizt. the Accot of Sales of the Tobacco & Turpentine & the Invoice of Cheeny together with the amount of the Bills which you have received payment for all pafsed to his Credit. This is to Inform you that in my Brothers last Will & Testament he has appointed me his sole Executor. The amount of his Credit in your Hands you will please to pafs to my Credit and hold the Same to my Disposal, as the Times are so Precarious I shall not Venture to Order out any Goods and as it is uncertain when I shall have an oppertunity to draw it out of your hands, perhaps you could hold it on Interest until I can Draw or Order Goods, the Bearer Mr Richards a Friend & Neighbour of Mine has a Small Bill to Negotiate for me & to Purchase the Amount in Goods which he thinks will be of most advantage and Ship on my Account for Boston One Half in the *Cato* and the other in the Brig *Minerva*. Any Civilitys you render him will be highly Esteemed by

                      Gentlemen
                      Your Most Obedt & Huml Servt
                                 Thos Shaw
Mefsrs John De Neufville & Son

                                        New London May 8th 1782
Gentlemen,

    The Above is what I wrote you this day by Mr Nathl Richards in the Ship *Cato*. After Confirming the Same would Inform you that I have Sent by him Two Bills for 1800 Dollars and are Indorsed over to you by my late Brother for fear of being Taken and as Mr Richards with the first sett may Miscarry I have taken the Liberty to Inclose you the second sett Viz^t. One for 600 Dollars Dated January 28th 1782 and the other for 1200 Dollars Drawn by Wm Imlay on the Commissioners of the United States of America at Paris in favour of Nathl Shaw which in Case of Mr Richards Miscarriage you will Negotiate and remitt in Goods to the Amount of the Nett Proceeds in this Vessel who is Bound to Boston, in fine & Coarse Linnen Ravens Duck & Rousia or the One Half of the Amount in some other safe Vessell that's Bound to Boston on the best Terms you can, paying the Freight there, but if the first Sett Arrives safe this is of no Effect. I am with Esteem Gentlemen

Your Most Obed^t Hum^l Servt.
Thos Shaw

Messrs J De Neufville & Son

New London May 14, 1782

Sir, I rec^d y^r Letter of ye 19th Ult^o calling upon my bro^r N S for a Settlement w^t ye Secret Com^tte. This is to inform you y^t he died ye 15th Apr^l last of a wound he rec^d from ye accedental discharge of a Muskett. By his last Will & Text. he has appointed me his Sole Exc. It is my wish to have this & all other of his Acco^ts w^t ye public settled soon as possible. It is unhappy y^t they ly in such a way that I cannot settle them w^t any degree of accuracy. The day ye enemy was at this place Mr Shaw was out of Town & his Books & Papers were huddled away by his Servents; except one chest w^c was left for a team y^t was sent for but was taken by ye enemy, by w^c means it was left & was burned in his office. The approach of ye enemy was so quick y^t it was w^t ye greatest difficulty y^t any of his B & P were saved. But however ye acco^ts may be made out from what Books & Papers y^t are saved if any Gentleman of y^r appointment might attend w^t me & were any documents are wanting to make inquiry & get what proof he can, we may be able to draw them out. I have always understood from the deceased y^t he was in advance for ye Contit. I will give every assistance in my power to have these intricate & complicated Acco^ts settled & to give every paper & Book of Mr Shaws to examination. I am with ye greatest esteem & respect &c.

P. S. Our delegates in Congress can recomend some good man in this State or Town if you should think it best to save ye trouble & expense of a Gentleman from Phild^a or what way or method you shall think best I will endeavour to comply with to the best of my ability. Y^rs

T. S.

To Robert Morris Esqr
Financier &c. Phild^a

New London May 15, 1782

Sir,

I Rec^d yours of the 11th Ins^t Inclosing your Note hand for the Bills £372 in favour of my late Brother & accordingly inclose you your Receipt to him for the 1302 Dollars, which I am satisfied with. Make no doubt you will do your best with the Cheeny & must leave it to your judgment to dispose of it in setts or otherwise as for the advance I should think it would command 4 for 1. If you should have an opportunity from Boston to Amsterdam & Martineco or Guadalupa let me know as I want to forward Letters of consiquence to me & especially to the Latter place. Y^{rs} &c.

T Shaw

Col Josiah Waters
Merchent Boston.

New London June 14th 1782

Gentlemen

Inclosed is Copies of Letters I wrote you by Nathl Richards in the Ship *Cato* and Brig *Minerva* by Suranam. I now take the Liberty to draw on you for One hundred pounds Sterling in favour of Daniel Deſhon, which you will please to pay and Charge to

Si^r You^r Hum^{le} Servt.
Thomas Shaw

Meſs^{rs} John De Neufville & Son

New London July 16, 1782

Gentlemen, Inclosed is Copies of my Letters to you of the 8th May w^t ye 3^d Sett of Bills therein refered to, & also of ye 14 June. I have also Wrote you in fav^r of Meſs Parſons & Marther for Fifty pounds Sterling each in case they should be under the necefsity of drawing. I have drew a Bill on you in fav^r of Christ^o Deshon for £20 Ster^g. This will be delivered you by Capt Will Worttles of ye Brig *Thetas* whom I understand is recomended to your House in whose fav^r I have drew on you for £900 Ster^g in Three Bills of £300 each of this date, all w^c you will please to pay & charge to me. For your certain Security of the Transfer of my late Brothers Credit to me, I now Inclose you ye Judge of Probates Certificate of my being Executor &c.

You will please to advise me of these Several payments & of the remaining Ballance. I am with the greatest esteem

Gentlemen
Your Most Hum^{le} Servt
T Shaw

Meſs Jno De Neufville & Son
Merchents Amsterdam

New London July 24, 1782

Sir,
    I wrote you the 8th May last in An^s to yours of the 16 Feb & observed y^t Ed Tinker had refused to receive the 704 Dollars tendered him by Stephen Sepr 16, 1777 & y^t he left it in my late brothers hands who sometime after invested it in the Loan office & y^t Mr Tinker still refuses to take the Certificates, & also y^t a Certificate of about this Time & Sum would be subject to your order, to which I have received no answere. Y^r &c.

                                                                       T. Shaw

John Wright Stanly
Merch^t Philadelphia
(Settled as by his Letter indorsed, on file 14 July, 1786.)
(See Mr Stanly Letter March 12, 1778, on file.)

Mr Rouse Halm Esqr New London July 23, 1783
South Kingstown
  Sir,
    Inclosed is Charles Chadwicks Note to my late Brother Nathl Shaw Junr for £51.1.9 Dated Sepr 16, 1773 on Interest payable one Year 10 Years Interest £33.1, who is now in Newport please to attach &c. Y^{rs} &c

                                                   T Shaw Ex^r &c.

(This Note returned & finally Settled.)

                Settlement with John Wright Stanly.
Decr 31, 1777 4 Years Interest Rec^d in Bills .   .   50.13.0
                      discount 5.13.0
                                                      45. 0.0

Decr 31, 1782 1 Years Interest . £12.13.3
                    discount .   .   6.13.3 .   .   6. 0.0

704 Dollars £211.4^s/; @4^s/, ...   42. 4.0

(The above give Steph Tinker March 24, 1786.)   £ 93. 4.0

Paid Wm Shepherd my order on Isaac Wharton   } . . 35. 9.4
    for 118¾ Dollars
Paid him 1 Continental Certificate for 1000 Dollars⎫ 57.14.8
    with 5 Years Interest indorsed dated Feb 27, 1778 ⎬
    as by his Rec^t on the back of Stanlys Letter on ⎪
    bill July 14, 1786.   ⎭   93. 4.0

Captains Mentioned in the Mercantile Letter Book (1765-1783) of Nathaniel Shaw, Jr., Merchant

Some of these Captains sailed vessels owned by Nathaniel Shaw, Jr., others sailed their own vessels and still others sailed for their employers, all, however, carrying cargoes and merchandise for Nathaniel Shaw, Jr.

―――― Adams
Samuel Alcott
Thomas Allon
James Angell

―――― Babcock
Abijah Beebe (or Bebee)
―――― Betere
―――― Bidle
William Billings
―――― Bunts
―――― Burk
―――― Bushnell

―――― Chadwick
―――― Champion
George Champlin
Samuel Champlin
John Chapman
Edward Chappell
Sam Chew
Stephen Clay
Nathaniel Coit
―――― Cox

John Degine
Daniel Deshon
John Deshon

―――― Ely
―――― Erving
Alex Exceen

―――― Ferrebault
―――― Fitch
John Forbes
―――― Foursard
―――― Francoise

John Greely
William Green
Peter Griffin

William Hancock
Charles Handy
Seth Harding
William Harris
William Harris, Jr.
Jesse Harlow
―――― Havens
David Hawley
―――― Hay
Samuel Hern
―――― Hicks
Elisha Hinman
John Hopkins
Ed Hulling

Amasa Jones

―――― Keith
―――― Kelly
Thomas Kennedy
George Kidd

John Lamb
Joseph Latham
Peter Latimer
John Leak
―――― Ledyard
Jonathan Leeds
William Leeds
Hugh Leslie (Ledlie)

Alexander Mackdugale
John Mackibbin
Michael Melally
―――― Michel
―――― Mitchell
―――― Modie (Moodie)
Nathan Moore
David Mumford
Robeson Mumford

―――― Niles

―――― Packer
Joseph Packwood
William Packwood
―――― Palmer
―――― Peirce
Joseph Powers
William Powers
Christopher Prince

Job Rathbone
―――― Read
Nathaniel Richards
John Rogers
Peter Rogers
William Rogers
Thomas Russell

Nathaniel Saltonstall
John Shackmaple
―――― Seabury
―――― Serley
Isaac Sheffield
―――― Smith
―――― Sneids
Richard Spink
―――― Stewart

James Tilley
Edward Tinker
Edward Tinker, Jr
Keph Tinker
Stephen Tinker
Nathaniel Tracey
―――― Trowbridge
William Tryon

Leonard Van Bueren

Jed Waterman
―――― Watrous
Edward Wheelar
Thomas Willson
―――― Wolcott
Will Worttles

BIBLIOGRAPHY

Beck, Alverda S. *Esek Hopkins' Letter Book*, Rhode Island Historical Society, Providence, 1932.
Blake, S. Leroy. *Later History of the First Church of Christ*, New London, 1900.
Caulkins, Frances M. *History of New London, Connecticut*, New London (reprint), 1895.
Caulkins, Frances M. *History of Norwich, Connecticut*, Hartford, 1864.
Caulkins, Frances M. Manuscript *Necrology of New London, Connecticut, 1652-1867*, Library of the New London County Historical Society, New London.
Caulkins, Frances M. Unpublished manuscripts, Library of the New London County Historical Society, New London.
Collier, Thomas S. *Records and Papers of the New London County Historical Society*, New London, 1890.
Gorton, Elizabeth, editor. *Records and Papers of the New London County Historical Society*, New London.
Hempstead, Joshua. *Diary of Joshua Hempstead*, New London County Historical Society, New London, 1901.
Hoadley, Charles J. *Records of the State of Connecticut*, 2 vols., State of Connecticut, Hartford, 1894-1895.
Huntington Papers, Collections of Connecticut Historical Society, Vol. 20, Hartford, 1923.
Johnston, Henry P. *Nathan Hale, 1776*, Privately printed by Henry P. Johnston, New York, 1901.
Johnston, Henry P. *Nathan Hale, 1776*, New Haven, 1914.
Journals of the Continental Congress. Washington, D. C., Vols. 3, 4, 5, 7, 10, 11, 12, 1904-1928.
Lathrop, Cornelia Penfield. *Black Rock, Seaport of Old Fairfield*, New Haven, 1930.
McClellan, Major Edwin N. *History of the United States Marine Corps*, 1st edition, 1st revision, Washington, D. C., 1932.
Middlebrook, Louis F. *Maritime Connecticut During the American Revolution*, 2 vols., Essex Institute, Salem, Mass., 1925.
Paullin, ———. *Out Letters of the Continental Marine Committee*, Vol. 2, Library of Congress, Washington, D. C.
Perkins, Mary E. *Chronicles of a Connecticut Farm*, Privately printed by Mr. and Mrs. Alfred Mitchell, New London, 1905.
Rogers, Ernest E. *Sesquicentennial of the Battle of Groton Heights and the Burning of New London*, State of Connecticut, Hartford, 1931.
Root, Mary Philotheta, editor. *Chapter Sketches, Connecticut Daughters of the American Revolution*, New Haven, 1901.
Shaw Collection of unpublished manuscripts, Library of the New London County Historical Society, New London.
Shaw Collection of unpublished manuscripts, Yale University Library, New Haven.
Starr, William H. *Repository*, Vol. I, No. 40, New London, 1858.
Trumbull, J. Hammond. *Colonial Records of Connecticut*, State of Connecticut, Vol. I, Hartford, 1850.
Trumbull Papers—unpublished manuscripts, Connecticut State Library, Hartford.

INDEX OF NAMES

Index of Vessels, Page 356

Aborn, Samuel, 44.
Achmuty, Judge, 245.
Adams, ———, 128, 247.
  Alexander P., 126.
  Captain, 284, 337.
  John, 111.
  Samuel, 23.
Akerson, Richard, naval prisoner, 33.
Alcott, Samuel, 261.
  Samuel, Captain, 287, 337.
Allen, David, 79, 83.
  David, Jr., 83.
  Eurastus, Ship *Putnam*, 61.
  Ezra, Ship *Putnam*, 60.
  F. L., Mayor, 144.
  Fanny, 11.
  Gabriel, 331.
  Sarah Shaw, 83.
Allon, Allan, Allyn, Thomas, Captain, Ship *Putnam*, 54-55, 57, 59, 135, 180, 315, 318-319, 323, 337.
Allyn, Robert, 29.
Alpin, ———, 247.
Alsop, ———, 296.
  John, 180.
  Richard, 175.
Anderson, James, 259, 266.
  Robert & Co., 264.
Andrews, ———, 312.
Angell, Angel, James, Captain, 9, 257-259, 267-268, 329, 337.
Anthony, Lemuel, naval prisoner, 33.
Apthrop, ———, 234, 235.
Arbouthnot, Admiral, 103.
Armstrong, B. A., 156.
Arnold, Benedict, Brigadier General, xvi, xvii, 5, 22, 24, 29-30, 56, 120-124, 128, 136, 165, 167.
  Rhodes, 1st Lieutenant, 45.
Arwin, Thomas, 48, 52.
Athell, Athill, James, 205, 216.

Atkins, Silas, naval prisoner, 33.
Averil, Thomas, Ship *Putnam*, 60.
Avery, Peter, 29.
  William, 29.

Babbit, William, Ship *Putnam*, 59.
Babcock, ———, 319, 321.
  Adam, 324, 327.
  Captain, 327, 337.
  Henry, Colonel, 107.
  Joshua, Dr., 107.
  Stephen, 109.
  William, Ship *Putnam*, 61.
Badet, ———, 144.
Baker, Christopher, naval prisoner, 33.
  Nathaniel, naval prisoner, 33.
Baldwin, Nathan, quartermaster, Ship *Putnam*, 60.
Bancroft, Thomas, Ship *Putnam*, 60.
Barlow, Thomas, 203.
Barnes, ———, 144.
Barr, John, Ship *Putnam*, 61.
Barrell, ———, 310, 312.
  Theodore, 143-144.
Barrett, John, 190.
Barrett, John & Sons, 196, 199, 205, 210.
Bassett, ———, 144.
Battar, Mrs., 247.
Bautint, Boutin, ———, 328.
Baxter, John, Ship *Putnam*, 60.
Beach, Bache, Backe, Beache, ———, 171.
  Theophalict, Theophylact, 177, 179, 180, 206, 210.
Beck, Mrs. Alverda S., xvii, 16, 111, 130.
Beckus, ———, 202, 320.
Beebe, Bebee, Abijah, Captain, 174-175, 178, 180, 191, 337.
  Walter, 11.

340   CONNECTICUT'S NAVAL OFFICE AT NEW LONDON

Beekman, ———, 230.
  Michael, naval prisoner, 33.
Belcher, Nathan, 151.
Belden, ———, 245.
  Sam, 263.
Belding, ———, 185.
Bell, Daniel, 321.
  Hugh, 51.
Benell, Jeptha, Ship *Putnam*, 59.
Benjamin, Mary Eddye, 153.
Bennett, Thomas, 263.
Bernard, Paris, Ship *Putnam*, 60.
Berry, Benjamin, naval prisoner, 33.
  Thomas, Ship *Putnam*, 60.
Betar, Betere, Captain, 218, 223, 225, 337.
Biddle, Bidle, Captain, 97, 113, 126-127, 286, 337.
  Nicholas, Commander Brig *Andrea Doria*, 38, 45.
Bill, Ephraim, 2d Lieutenant of Marines, 40.
  Frederic, 153, 156, 161.
  Ledyard, 152.
Billings, ———, 144.
  Henry, 111, 115.
  John, Captain, 305.
  William, Captain, 180, 198, 211, 337.
Bingham, ———, 304, 308-309, 311.
  Family, 77.
  Hiram, xvii.
  William, 305.
Birch, Samuel, Brigadier General, 31.
Blakency, ———, 211.
Blowers, ———, 247.
Bolles, John, armourer, Ship *Putnam*, 60.
  John R., 145.
Booth, ———, 180.
  Sam, 225.
Bostwick, ———, 86.
Bouget, Stephen Joseph, 34.
Boulton, William, boatswain's mate, Ship *Putnam*, 60.
Bowel, Benjamin, Ship *Putnam*, 60.
Bowtriy, Thomas, quartermaster, Ship *Putnam*, 60.
Boylston, Boylstone, 170, 197.

Bradford, John, Continental Agent, 35-36, 38, 300-301, 304-306, 308-311.
  John, Captain, 17.
  Joseph, 27.
Bragg, John, 317, 320.
Brainerd and Armstrong Co., 153.
Brandegee, Augustus, 155, 156.
Brattle, ———, 331.
  Thomas, 234.
Braynard, Daniel, 206.
Breed, John, Jr., 109.
Brewster, Darius, Ship *Putnam*, 60.
  John, Ship *Putnam*, 61.
Brinsmaid, Ensign, 86.
Brooks, ———, 313.
  Jonathan, 55.
Brookway, Enoch, Ship *Putnam*, 60.
Broom, Broome, ———, 254, 255, 319, 320.
  John, 121-122, 310.
  Samuel, 227, 300.
  Samuel, Colonel, 311, 324.
Broome, Samuel & Co., 240, 248.
Brown, Browne, ———, 25, 144.
  Cabeb, 109.
  George T., 164.
  John, 39-44, 279.
  John Howard, 51.
  Montfort, Governor, 48, 52, 126.
  William, 27, 105-106.
Bruce, Peter Henry, 53.
Bruster, Joshua, naval prisoner, 32.
Bulkeley, Charles, Captain, 125, 126, 129, 130, 135.
  Charles, midshipman, 46.
  Leonard H., 125, 130.
  Peter, 129.
Bulkly, ———, 250.
Bullock, Benjamin, naval prisoner, 33.
Bunley, Burnly, ———, 263, 265.
  John, 249, 266.
Bunner, Mrs. Alice, 134.
Bunts, Captain, 271, 337.
Burbeck, General, 75, 137, 158.
Burgoyne, General, 127.
Burk, Captain, 322, 337.
Burney, Luther, Ship *Putnam*, 59.
Burroughs, Ezekiel, 3d Lieutenant, 46.

INDEX OF NAMES 341

Burton, Thomas, 15.
Bushnell, Captain, 206, 337.
Butler, Paul, naval prisoner, 33.
  Timothy, Ship *Putnam*, 59.
Byles, Rev. Marther, Jr., 198.
Byron, Admiral, 320.

Cable, ———, 293.
  George, 317.
Cane, Alexander, Captain, 128.
Canfield, Hezekiah, Ship *Putnam*, 60.
Carante, Andre, 328.
Card, Henry, Ship *Putnam*, 60.
Carew, Eliphalet, 109.
Carigal, Don Juan de, 53.
Carr, Karr, Lieutenant, 303, 304.
Carter, ———, 328.
  John, 328.
Castaignet, ———, 15.
Catlin, Thomas, Ship *Putnam*, 59.
Caulkins, Frances M., 3, 16, 20-26, 57, 88.
  Joanna Burnham Perkins, 84.
  John, Ship *Putnam*, 60.
Chace, Samuel, 105.
Chadwick, Captain, 228, 260, 337.
  Charles, 196, 336.
Chamberlain, Governor, 156.
Champion, Captain, 196.
Champlin, Captain, 250-251, 276, 307.
  George, Captain, 272, 295, 337.
  Oliver, 135.
  Samuel, Captain, 298, 300, 309, 337.
  Samuel, Jr., Ship *Putnam*, 61.
  William, Ship *Putnam*, 60.
Channing, 118.
Chapman, Sergeant, 86.
  Abraham Booth, 236.
  John, Captain, 86, 215, 217, 230, 236-240, 248, 255, 271, 337.
Chapell, Cornelia W., 156.
  Richard H., Mrs., 157.
Chappell, Chapple, Captain, 215, 228, 230, 232-236, 239, 241-243, 245, 247, 248, 253, 256-261, 264-266, 272, 274, 276, 277, 279.
  Alfred H., 155.
Chappell, Edward, Captain, 87, 232-233, 235, 237, 246, 252, 337.

Chappell, Ezra, 143.
  William, naval prisoner, 32.
Charles II, King, 1.
Charley, William, Ship *Putnam*, 60.
Charrier, ———, 7.
Chatfield, John, Prize Master, Ship *Putnam*, 59.
Chatham, Lord, 283.
Chesebrou, Cheesebrough, Nathaniel, 109.
Chevers, Ezekiel, 312.
Chew, ———, 172, 177, 184, 187, 207, 210-211, 234-235, 297.
  J. Lawrence, 154.
  Samuel, Captain, 34, 37, 300-302, 307-308, 337.
Church, John, 206.
  Singleton, 202.
  Timothy, Ship *Putnam*, 60.
Clark, Clarke, Captain, 126.
  Dr., 117.
  John, naval prisoner, 32.
  Reuben, Ship *Putnam*, 60.
  Thomas A., 151.
  William, 9, 11, 329.
Clark & Nightingale, 27, 95, 96, 105-106, 278, 285.
Clarkson, ———, 31.
  Livinus, Continental Agent, 36.
Clay, John, prisoner, 34.
  Stephen, Captain, 199-201, 223, 337.
Clements, ———, 262-263.
Clepner, George, 285.
Clinton, David, Ship *Putnam*, 59.
  G., 317.
Cobb, Ebenezer, 109.
Cobham, William, 202.
Codnir, James, naval prisoner, 32.
Coffin, ———, 183.
Coit, ———, 297.
  F. & H., 144.
  Grace, 79.
  James, 84.
  Jonathan, 84.
  Joshua, 11.
  Nathaniel, 1st Lieutenant, Ship *Putnam*, 59.

342   CONNECTICUT'S NAVAL OFFICE AT NEW LONDON

Coit, Nathaniel, Captain, 88, 194, 297, 337.
  Robert, 135, 144, 153, 155.
  W. B., 155-156.
  Wheeler, 239, 243.
  William, 187, 189.
Collier, Thomas S., 152.
Collins, James, naval prisoner, 33.
Colt, ———, 310, 316-317.
Conkling, Daniel, Ship *Putnam*, 60.
  Joseph, Captain, 309.
Connor, John, 183.
Constant, ———, 277-278, 293, 299.
  William, 7, 277-279.
Cook, Cooke, Governor, 105, 278.
Cooper, William, Ship *Putnam*, 60.
Copely, Elihu, Ship *Putnam*, 60.
Corkins, Ebenezer, Ship *Putnam*, 59.
Cornell, ———, 144.
  Samuel, 195.
Corts, Henry, 184.
Cowlins, Daniel, 109.
Cox, Captain, 255, 337.
  Samuel, naval prisoner, 33.
Crage, Joseph, 284.
Crary, Jonathan, 109.
  Peter, 109.
Craw, Philip, naval prisoner, 32.
  Samuel, naval prisoner, 32.
Crowell, Brazilla, naval prisoner, 33.
Cuffs, ———, Cook on Ship *Putnam*, 60.
Cunningham, 173, 175, 177, 181, 183-184, 187.
Currier, John, naval prisoner, 33.
Curtenius, Peter, 272, 273.
Cushing, Jonathan, naval prisoner, 32.

Dacres, Captain, 127.
Dagget, Samuel, naval prisoner, 33.
Daly, John, 203.
Danforth, Rev. J. Romeyn, 164.
Daniels, Hon. Josephus, 146-147.
Danielson, John, Ship *Putnam*, 59.
Darra, Peter, Ship *Putnam*, 61.
Darrow, Moses, 144.
  P., 314.
Dart, M. Wilson, 155.

Davis, Reuben, Ship *Putnam*, 59.
  Stephen, Ship *Putnam*, 60.
Dean, Deane, ———, 272, 290.
  Barnabas, 35, 287, 289.
  Christopher, Ship *Putnam*, 61, 109.
  Jabez, 109.
  James, 109.
  John, 109.
  John, Jr., 109.
  Silas, 35.
Deangelis, Paschal, Ship *Putnam*, 60.
Degine, John, Captain, 196, 208, 337.
  Grarceliaus de, Graueliaus de, Major, 328.
Delcasse, ———, 7.
Denison, Dennison, ———, 243.
  George, 68.
  Joseph, 109.
  William, Ship *Putnam*, 59.
Denninge, William, 240.
Dennis, Oliver Hillard, 109.
Depeister, James, 187.
Desbrosses, Eliass, 169.
Deshields, Christopher, 2d mate, Ship *Putnam*, 59.
Deshon, Captain, 58, 172, 254-255, 258, 263-264, 286, 301, 315, 321.
  Christopher, 335.
  Daniel, Captain, 335, 337.
  John, Captain, 23, 249, 268, 326, 337.
Des Moulins, ———, 7.
Deveaux, Andrew, Colonel, 53.
Deveron, ———, 263.
Devisone, Mrs. Ann, 179, 181, 185, 190, 193, 202.
Dickson, Dixon, Dixson, ———, 319, 321.
  David, 310, 313.
Dies, John, 202.
Dorsius, John, Continental Agent, 36.
Douglas, Douglass, Emma, 151.
  Jonathan, 68.
  Nathan, 55, 206, 253.
Dousset, ———, 15.
Dowe, Jesse, Steward on Ship *Putnam*, 59.
Dudley, Miles, Ship *Putnam*, 61.
Dumarisque, Phillip, 267-268, 270, 276.

INDEX OF NAMES

Dunmore, Lord, 51, 53.
Durfee, Joseph, 251.
Dyer, Dyar, Dyarr, ———, 265.
  Eliphalet, Colonel, 261-262, 272, 284, 332.
  Nathaniel, Ship *Putnam*, 61.

Eames, ———, 263.
Earle, Ralph, 84, 158.
Easton, John, 255.
Eddy, Samuel, 111, 119.
Edgar, Thomas, Ship *Putnam*, 59.
Edgerton, Frederick W., xvii.
Edmunds, John, Ship *Putnam*, 60.
Elderkin, ———, 54.
  Joshua, 196.
Eldridge, Eldrige, Charles, 205.
  Charles, Jr., 222.
  Daniel, Prize Master, Ship *Putnam*, 59.
  James, 239.
  Thomas, Ship *Putnam*, 61.
Ellery, ———, 302.
Elliot, Elliott, Charles, Ship *Putnam*, 60.
  Henry, Ship *Putnam*, 61.
  John, Ship *Putnam*, 61.
  Samuel, 316.
Ellis, Daniel, 191.
  Jonathan, naval prisoner, 33.
  Richard, Continental Agent, 17, 35-36.
Ely, Captain, 284, 337.
Ensign, David, Ship *Putnam*, 60.
Epictetus, 150.
Erving, Ervin, Erwin, ———, 221, 228, 316.
  Captain, 205, 337.
  George, 204, 213, 214, 228-231, 240, 247.
  John, 229, 231.
Erving, John & George, merchants, 205, 209.
Estaing, Count de, 58.
Eveleigh, ———, 296.
Everts, James, Ship *Putnam*, 60.
Exceen, Exeen, Alex, Captain, 288-289, 337.

Fairchild, Lewis, Ship *Putnam*, 61.
Fairfield, John, naval prisoner, 33.
Falconer, Nathaniel, 35.
Fallman, William, 278.
Fanning, ———, 228.
  Colonel, 279.
  Gilbert, 109.
  John, 46.
  Thomas, 227.
Fargo, Samuel, Ship *Putnam*, 60.
Ferguson, Sam, 280.
Farrington, ———, 254.
Fellows, Joseph, 109.
Felton, Thomas, naval prisoner, 33.
Ferrebault, Captain, 268, 337.
Fines, ———, 230.
Fitch, ———, 219.
  Augustus, 244.
  Captain, 241, 337.
  Helen R., 126.
Fitzpatrick, Lieutenant, Ship *Alfred*, 48.
Flagler, H. M., 53.
Fleet, Captain, 61.
Flint, James, 238.
Folliot, George & Co., 240.
Follmer, L. D., Lieutenant, 164.
Forbes, John, Captain, 318, 337.
Forsey, ———, 181, 185-187, 189.
Forsyth, ———, 144.
Foster, John, 186, 192.
  La Fayette S., 151-152.
Foursard, Captain, 218, 245, 260, 337.
Francisco, ———, 231.
Francoise, Fransway, Captain, 246, 250, 299, 337.
Franklin, Dr., 128.
Frasier, Fraser, Frazier, 198, 236, 237, 239, 240, 264.
French, ———, 144.
Frink, ———, 144.
  David, 144.
  Ephraim, 144.
Frisby, Samuel, Ship *Putnam*, 60.
Fry, Robert, naval prisoner, 32.
Fuller, Simeon, 86.

Gaignard, Pierre, 7.
Gardner, Commander, 145.
  Thomas, naval prisoner, 32.
Gates, Major General, 311-312, 314.
Gibs, Lemuel, 86.
Gibson, John, 21.
  Rogir, 212.
Giddiss, ———, 277.
Gilbert, Jesse, Ship *Putnam*, 59.
Gill, John, naval prisoner, 33.
Glison, John, Ship *Putnam*, 59.
Goban, ———, 7.
Godard, George S., xvii.
Goddard, ———, 191, 225.
  Ebenezer, Jr., steward, Ship *Putnam*, 59.
  George W., 153.
  Thomas, carpenter's yeoman, Ship *Putnam*, 60.
Gooding, Samuel, naval prisoner, 33.
Gordon, James, 256, 259, 266.
Gorton, ———, 144.
  Elizabeth, v, xvii, 66, 116, 118, 158, 162.
Grant & Fines, 230.
Grass, Jonas, naval prisoner, 33.
Graves, Admiral, 103.
Gray, Jonathan, 109.
Greely, John, Captain, 321, 337.
Green & Boylstone, 170, 197.
Green, Greene, ———, 219-224, 231, 233, 235-237, 239-240, 268, 307.
  Elisha, naval prisoner, 32.
  F., 105.
  General, 89-90, 95, 158.
  Thomas, 27.
  Timothy, 29, 31.
  William, Captain, 302-303, 337.
Gregg, Cunningham & Co., 173, 175, 177, 181, 183-184, 187.
Griffin, Griffing, Colonel, 306, 310, 313.
  James N., Ship *Putnam*, 60.
  Peter, Captain, 313, 337.
  Samuel, Colonel, 120-121.
Griffiths, Thomas, 239.
Griffiths & Thomas, 216.
Griswold, B., 119.

Griswold, Charles, 81.
  Ellinor Shaw, 78, 82, 84, 156.
  Family, 77.
  James, 82.
  Mary Ann, 81.
  Mary Perkins, 78, 79.
  Theodora, 82.
Grotton, Samuel, 227.
Guard, Elisha, naval prisoner, 32.
Guest, George, 156.
Gurrish, Paul, naval prisoner, 32.
Gwinn, John, Ship *Putnam*, 60.

Hacker, Hackers, Captain, 114, 126.
Hadley, ———, 227.
Hale, Edward Everett, 5.
  Ensign, 86.
  Nathan, xv, 27, 75-76, 85-86, 158, 165.
Hall, Latham, 109.
Hallam, John, 135, 143.
Halm, Rouse, 336.
Hamilton, Hambleton, ———, 136.
  Alexander, 142.
  Lieutenant, 127, 128.
  Sergeant, 280, 281.
Hamilton, Powers & Co., 144.
Hammond, Isach, Ship *Putnam*, 60.
Hamsdill, Joseph, naval prisoner, 32.
Hancock, Captain, 178, 180, 184, 203, 219, 221, 222.
  John, 18, 47, 48, 72, 110, 286.
  William, Captain, 190, 337.
Handy, Charles, Captain, 273, 274, 337.
Hannah, John, 280.
Harding, Seth, Captain, 17, 19, 87, 290, 292, 337.
Harlow, Jesse, Captain, 196, 197, 337.
Harnet, Cornelius, Continental Agent, 17, 36.
Harris, Captain, 9, 58, 190, 194, 198, 199, 215, 218, 224, 228, 233, 235, 253, 254, 265, 269, 273, 276, 321.
  Daniel, 132, 133.
  Family, 132.
  Francis, 288.
  Grace, 11.
  Jeremiah, 231, 233.

INDEX OF NAMES

Harris, John, 254.
  Joseph, 29, 133.
  Joseph, Col., 77.
  Joseph, Jr., 29, 31.
  Lucretia, 132, 133.
  Lucy Tinker, 133.
  Temperance, 77, 79.
  Thomas, 203.
  William, Captain, 191, 200-201, 203, 212-214, 219-221, 229-230, 232, 236, 252, 337.
  William, Jr., 215-216, 222-223, 225, 227, 233, 337.
Harrison, Captain, 128.
  Peleg D., 131.
  Theodore, Ship *Putnam*, 60.
Hart, William, 271.
Harvey, John, Ship *Putnam*, 60.
Harwood, P. LeRoy, 145.
Harzen, Captain, 126.
Haskins, Samuel, Ship *Putnam*, 59.
Hatch, Elnathan, Prize Master, Ship *Putnam*, 59.
Haven, Anna W., 82.
  Elizabeth L., 82.
  Family, 77.
  Henry P., 82, 151.
  Mrs., 151.
Havens, ———, 144.
  Captain, 175, 337.
Haviland & Farrington, 254.
Hawley, David, Captain, 302-304, 337.
Hay, Captain, 227, 337.
Hayes, 170.
Hazlehurst, Isaac, 211.
Heffern, Stephen, Ship *Putnam*, 60.
Helme, ———, 177.
Helme & Channing, 118.
Helms, Bousa, 332.
Hempstead, Joshua, 68, 69, 133.
Hern, Samuel, Captain, 195, 196, 212, 337.
Hersted, Hoysted, 1st Lieutenant, 45.
Hertell, Hartell, Herltell, John, 38, 109, 178, 202, 203, 217, 219, 300, 308.
Hibbard, Learned, 151.

Hicks, Captain, 186, 337.
Higgins, Christian, 220.
  Edwin W., 145.
Hillard, John, 109.
  Oliver, 109.
Hillhouse, William, 23.
Hinchman, Robert, 255.
Hinman, ———, 3.
  Elisha, Captain, 46, 87, 115, 126, 127, 286, 297, 300, 320, 337.
Hobart, Daniel, 109.
  Eliphalet, 109.
  Eliphalet 2d, 109.
Hobron, ———, 144.
Hogdon, Alexander, 327.
Hogsdon, ———, 323.
Holker, John, 321.
Hollingsworth & Richardson, 112.
Holt, ———, 144.
Hood & Clarkson, 31.
Hoope & Co., 318.
Hopkins, Esek, 16, 20, 34, 37, 45, 47-53, 76, 89, 111-119, 126, 158, 166, 280-284, 286, 295-296, 324.
  F., 328.
  John, Captain, 126, 331, 337.
  John Burrows, Captain, 45.
Howard, Nathaniel, schooner *Happy Return*, 87.
Howel, George, 108.
Hubbard, ———, 86, 205, 317.
  Daniel & W., 216.
  John, Ship *Putnam*, 60.
  N., 102.
Hubbard & Greene, 219-224, 231, 233, 235-237, 239-240, 268.
Hubbs, Joseph Cook, Ship *Putnam*, 61.
Hugh & Whitelock, 260, 262.
Hughs, Joseph, 325.
Hulling, Ed., Captain, 264, 337.
Huntington, Andrew, 253.
  Colonel, 262, 288.
  Ebenezer, General, 75, 137, 158.
  Jabez, 227, 267.
  Jedediah, 212, 239, 253.
  Jedediah, Colonel, 26, 136.
  J. M. & Co., 144.
  Joshua, 303.

Huntington, Madam, 136, 141, 142.
  Samuel, 20, 64, 65, 167.
Hurlbut, Hurlbutt, Captain, 94, 98, 102.
Hurley, John P., 53.
Hutchinson, ———, 320.
  Godfry, 309.
Hyde, Amasa, Ship *Putnam*, 61.
  Jedediah, Captain of Marines, Ship *Putnam*, 59.
  Solomon, Ship *Putnam*, 60.

Imlay, William, 329.
Ingraham, ———, 251.
Irish, ———, 267.
  George, 213, 217, 273, 283.
Irving, ———, 88.
  Joseph, 184.
Isaac, ———, 253.

Jackson, James, naval prisoner, 33.
  Margaret, 77.
James, Benjamin, naval prisoner, 32.
Jarvis, ———, naval prisoner, 33.
  Arthur, 266.
Jarvis & Russell, 330.
Jenks, H. O., 164.
Jennings, Richard Downing, 217.
Jocelin, Joceline, Josceline, Joseline, ———, 315, 317.
  Amaziah, Amosiah, Prize Master, Ship *Putnam*, 57, 59, 314.
Johnson, ———, 151.
  Isaac, 151.
  Joel, Ship *Putnam*, 61.
Johnston, Henry P., Prof., xv.
Jois, ———, 308.
Jones, Amasa, Captain, 179, 182, 185, 190, 192, 193, 221-226, 337.
  Azariah, Master *Pompey*, 86.
  Cato, Ship *Putnam*, 60.
  John Paul, 45, 126, 127.
  William, 137, 138.
Joy, Joshua, naval prisoner, 32.
Judah, ———, 203.
Judd, Rev., 75, 136.

Kee, Richard, 185, 198.
Keeney, John, 28, 285.
Keith, Captain, 273, 274, 337.
Kelly, Captain, 188, 337.
Kennedy, Kenedy, Captain, 282, 288-292, 337.
  Thomas, Captain, 21, 296, 300.
Keogh, Andrew, xvii.
Kettletass, Peter, 173, 175, 176, 182, 183, 185, 194.
Kidd, George, Captain, 172, 185, 337.
Kimball, C., 144.
King, Absolom, 68.
  Thomas, Captain, 97.
Kipp, ———, 253.
  Harey, 300.
Knight, Robert, 287.
Knox, Colonel, 280.
  D. W., Captain, U. S. N. (Ret.), 50.
  General, 95.
Koenig, Paul, Captain, 148.

Lafayette, Marquis de, 70, 71, 75, 76, 89, 135-139, 158, 160, 168.
Lamb, John, Captain, 251, 264, 278, 302, 304-306, 308-311, 315-317, 319, 320, 327, 337.
Landon, Cesar, Ship *Putnam*, 61.
Lane, ———, 198, 264.
Lane & Booth, 180.
Lane, Son & Frazier (Frasier, Fraser), 198, 236, 237, 239, 240, 264.
Langdon, Landing, John, Continental Agent, 17, 35, 36, 39, 305.
Larrabee, Larrabe, ———, 325.
  Adam A., 137.
Latham, David, 174.
  Joseph, Captain, 190, 191, 212, 337.
Lathrop, Azariah, 109.
  Joshua, Ship *Putnam*, 59.
Latimer, Latemer, Lattemore, ———, 86, 261, 324, 327.
  Peter, Captain, 169, 170, 182-184, 186, 189-191, 194, 212.

INDEX OF NAMES 347

Law, ———, 176, 180, 202, 211, 229, 231, 225.
  Richard, 23, 135, 228.
Lawrence, ———, 144, 212, 242.
  John, 21, 27, 273, 308.
  Sebastian D., 153, 154, 156, 157.
  William, 27.
Leak, John, Captain, 206, 208, 337.
Learned, ———, 144.
  Bela Peck, Major, 154.
  Walter, 153, 155, 157.
Ledlie, Hugh, Captain, 172, 220, 227, 239, 240, 337.
Ledyard, ———, 30.
  Ebenezer, 29, 205, 235, 247.
  William, Captain, 28, 109, 205, 211, 246, 260, 280, 337.
Lee, Frederick, 137, 138.
  Richard, 323.
Leeds, Captain, schooner *Pompey*, 207, 218, 221, 226, 250, 251, 258, 276, 277, 279, 283, 298, 337.
  Jonathan, Captain, 276, 283, 337.
  William, Captain, 276, 277, 320, 337.
Leffingwell, ———, 174, 236.
  Christopher, 298.
Leonard, Cornelia, 81.
Levingston, Philip, 291, 292, 294.
Levington & Turnbull, 295, 296, 308, 326.
Levingworth, ———, 86.
Lewis, ———, 327.
  Francis, 43, 282, 288, 289, 291, 292, 294.
Lincoln, President, 67, 151.
Lines, H. Wales, 153.
Lippet, Colonel, 289.
Logan, ———, 228.
Longfellow, ———, 69.
Loring, Joseph, Commissary General of Prisoners, 29-30.
Lothrop, ———, 224, 265.
Ludlow, ———, 186, 232, 234.
  Gabriel, 187, 189, 209.
Lux, William, Continental Agent, 17, 36.
Lyon, Humphrey, 272, 295.
Lyon, Samuel, 111, 114, 116.

Machin, Francisco, Dr., 232.
Mack Neil, John, 280.
Mackdugale, Alexander, Captain, 187, 188, 337.
Mackibbin, Mackkibbin, John, Captain, 274, 275, 337.
Maclear, Edgar Stanton, 51.
Magant, John, 29.
Mahan, Bryan F., 147, 148.
Malby, Lieutenant, 126.
Malcom, Malcolm, William, 172, 185, 188.
Manly, Captain, 58.
  Joseph, Ship *Putnam*, 60.
Manney, ———, 183.
Mannsell, John, Major, 202.
  Lieutenant Colonel, 202.
Manny, Margaret, 131.
Mansfield, Amos, Ship *Putnam*, 60.
  John, Ship *Putnam*, 60.
Manuel, 231.
Manwaring, Manwering, David, 206, 255, 266.
Marsh, ———, 183.
Marshall, Christopher & Charles, 284.
Marston, Daniel, naval prisoner, 32.
Marther, ———, 335.
  Samuel, 281.
Mase, ———, 7.
Mason, Amos Lawrence, M.D., 153.
  John, Ship *Putnam*, 61, 152.
  Lewis D., M.D., 153, 159.
Mather, Mathers, John, Ship *Putnam*, 61.
  John P. C., 151.
  Lois, 80.
Mathew, Robert, naval prisoner, 33.
McBride, William, Steward's mate, Ship *Putnam*, 60.
McCandless, Captain, 130, 131.
McClellan, ———, 64.
  L., 11.
  Samuel, Jr., 34.
McClure, Mathew, Ship *Putnam*, 60.
McCurdy, ———, 327.
  Charles J., 151.
  Richard, 135.

M'Dougall, 2d Lieutenant, 46.
Mc Evers, C., 253.
Mc Ewen, Rev., 75, 136.
Mc Ginley, John, 153, 155.
Mc Kebbin, John, 253.
Mc Kneil, ———, 229.
Mc Lean, Ex-Governor, 155.
Mc Mullins, James, Ship *Putnam*, 61.
Medcalf, Samuel, naval prisoner, 32.
Melally, Michael, Captain, 9, 11, 54, 86, 87, 217, 241, 249, 253, 256, 281, 317, 329, 330, 337.
Mercer, Captain George, 88.
Mercer & Schenk, 256, 257, 259, 261.
Mersereau, Major, 321, 322.
Meyer, ———, 143.
Michel, Captain, 312, 337.
   John, 314.
Middlebrook, Louis F., xvii, 49, 55, 130, 131.
Mifflin, Samuel, 227, 228.
Miller, ———, 230, 261, 306, 316.
   Amasa, 24.
   Jeremiah, 134, 141.
   Justin, Ship *Putnam*, 60.
Miller & Tracey, 319.
Millir, Nathan, 307.
   Mrs., 175.
   Timothy, 175.
   William, 86, 170, 174.
Mills, Drake, Ship *Putnam*, 60.
Milzard, George, naval prisoner, 32.
Miner, ———, 291.
   Ephraim, 109.
Minor, Mrs. George Maynard, 163, 164.
Mitchel, John, Captain, 21.
Mitchell, Alfred, 157.
   Captain, 263, 337.
   Family, 77.
Modie, Moodie, Captain, 300, 302, 337.
Moffatt, Dr., 232, 250, 253.
   John, 232.
   Thomas, 232.
Montagu, Duke of, 53.
Moore, ———, 317, 319.
   Doctor, 169.
   Mrs., 170.

Moore, Nathan, Captain, 170, 183, 184, 186, 337.
   Patrick, 309, 320, 327.
Morgan, ———, 179, 203.
   Theophilus, 174, 201.
Morris, Robert, 21, 286, 290, 291, 293, 295, 296, 307, 325, 334.
Morrison, Amos, Ship *Putnam*, 60.
Moylan, John, 95.
Mumford, ———, 12, 172, 226, 322, 323.
   David, 109, 239, 249.
   David, Captain, 174, 202, 237.
   Elizabeth, 80.
   Family, 77.
   Giles, 41, 109.
   Mary, 80, 81.
   Peter, 267.
   Robeson, Captain, 174, 337.
   Theop., 109.
   Thomas, 23, 41, 43, 115, 249, 267, 312, 325, 327.
Murison, ———, 325.
Murray, Jesse, quartermaster, Ship *Putnam*, 60.
Myers, John R., 181, 182, 184, 185, 188, 189, 192-196, 198, 208, 261, 264.

Nasin, William, Ship *Putnam*, 60.
Neadham, Elias, Ship *Putnam*, 61.
   John, Ship *Putnam*, 60.
   John, Jr., Ship *Putnam*, 60.
Negroe, Joseph Colly, Ship *Putnam*, 60.
Neilson, William, 266.
Nelson, ———, 255, 268.
Nesbit, John Maxwell, Continental Agent, 17, 36.
Neufville, John de & Son, 12, 14, 328-330, 332-335.
Nevins, Family, 77.
   Misses, xvii.
Newall, Samuel, 277.
Newcomb, Frederic S., 153.
Newcome, Daniel, Ship *Putnam*, 61.
Nicholas, Captain, 47, 51.
Nicholson, Captain, 39.

INDEX OF NAMES 349

Nightingale, 27, 95, 96, 105, 106, 278, 285.
Niles, Captain, 127, 298, 324, 325, 337.
Nixon, John, Continental Agent, 17, 36.
Noliott, Doctor, 303 (Should be Wolcott).
North, William, General, 75, 136, 137, 158.
Norton, Colonel, 314, 322.
  Elnathan, Ship *Putnam*, 59.
  Milatiah, Sailmaker, Ship *Putnam*, 60.
Nourse, Joseph, 21.
Noyes, Noice, ———, 117, 332.
Nugans, Peter, Ship *Putnam*, 60.

O'Brien, Michael, Ship *Putnam*, 60.
Oliver, Andrew, 174, 220.
  Isaac, Ship *Putnam*, 60.
  Richard & Thomas, 205, 216.
Olney, Joseph, 2d Lieutenant, 46.
Om Manney & Marsh, 183.
Osborn, Colonel N. G., 155.
Otis & Andrews, 312.
Owen, Richard, 280.

Packer, Captain, 181, 337.
  Thomas, 182.
Packwood, Captain, 26, 123, 177, 179-180, 190, 192, 194-195, 199, 207, 210, 212, 255, 291.
  Joseph, 29, 86, 87, 109, 122.
  Joseph, Captain, 173-176, 186, 189, 196, 203, 206, 210, 212, 337.
  Joseph & William, 170, 172, 174, 194, 195.
  Mrs., 171.
  William, 86.
  William, Captain, 176, 193, 199, 212, 241, 248, 250, 253, 257, 337.
Pagan, ———, 255.
Page, Joseph, 109.
Pagy, Thomas, Ship *Putnam*, 59.
Palankey, Commander of privateer, 26.
Palmer, ———, 230.
  Andrew, 109.
  Asa, 109.
  Captain, 297, 298, 337.

Palmer, Elisha, 157.
  F. L., 156, 157.
  George S., 152, 157.
  Howard, v, xvii.
  Moses, Master of Arms, Ship *Putnam*, 60.
  Nathan, 109, 229.
  Nathan, Jr., 109.
Parkman, Samuel, 316.
Parsons, Colonel, 270, 285.
  General S. H., 297, 303, 304.
  James, Ship *Putnam*, 61.
  Thomas, Ship *Putnam*, 61.
Parsons & Marther, 335.
Patterson, William, 317.
Paullin, ———, 16, 34, 49, 165.
Pearsall, Thomas, 254.
Peck, John, Ship *Putnam*, 60.
  Joseph, Ship *Putnam*, 60.
Peirce, Perse, Captain, 173, 198, 307, 337.
Pemberton, Jeremiah, 34.
Pendleton, Amos, Ship *Putnam*, 61.
  John, Ship *Putnam*, 61.
Pennington & Sons, 180.
Perkins, ———, 143, 144, 202.
  Benjamin Richards, Major, 67, 78, 81, 82, 84.
  Elias, Judge, 25, 67, 71, 75, 78, 80, 81, 84, 85, 90, 135-137, 139, 144.
  Elias, Jr., 81.
  Ellen, 82.
  Ellen Elizabeth, 81.
  Ellen Richards, 84.
  Family, 66, 76.
  Francis A., 82.
  Henry Coit, 81.
  Jabez, 316.
  Jane Richards, xvi, 22, 23, 57, 66, 67, 78, 82, 84, 85, 116, 118, 156, 158, 167.
  Jonathan Coit, 82.
  Joseph, 81, 119.
  Lucretia, 25.
  Lucretia Woodbridge, 81, 84.
  Mary Richards, 78, 82.
  Nathaniel Shaw, Dr., 21, 57, 66, 67, 69, 78, 80, 81, 84, 85.

Perkins, Nathaniel Shaw, Jr., xiii, 21, 81, 84, 85, 95, 135, 139.
  Oliver Ellsworth, 81.
  Thomas Shaw, 81.
  Thomas W., 82.
  W. Lewis, M.D., 82.
  William, naval prisoner, 33.
  William W., 67, 78, 82, 84.
Perritt, ———, 180.
  John, 219.
Perry, Madam, 136.
Perry & Hayes, 170.
Phillips, Daniel L., 161.
Phips, sailing master, 126.
Phoenix, Daniel, 253.
Pickering, Colonel, 128.
Picket, ———, 68.
Pierson, William, 1st Lieutenant, Ship *Aurora*, naval prisoner, 32.
Pike, Arnos, naval prisoner, 32.
Pinkham, Captain, 58.
Pitcher, Jonathan, 1st Lieutenant, 45.
Pitkin, Colonel, 54.
Plat, Jere, 328.
Platt, Graham L., 164.
Pomeroy, ———, 212, 232, 235, 244, 249, 251, 254, 264, 279.
  Eleazer, 216, 242, 244, 269.
  Mary, 271.
  Ralph, 269, 277, 278.
Ponderson, ———, 250.
  Cyrus, 253.
  Eb, 253.
Pool, David, boatswain, Ship *Putnam*, 59.
Potter, Richard, Master, Ship *Putnam*, 59.
  William, 151, 178.
Pouquet, ———, 7.
Powers, ———, 144, 192, 223.
  Captain, 223-226, 239, 242, 244-248, 255, 298, 299.
  Joseph, Captain, 237, 251, 337.
  William, Captain, 87, 89, 298, 299, 337.
Pratt, ———, 138.
  Anne S., xvii.
  Bela L., 155, 156.

Prentice, A. F., 144.
Prentis, ———, 144.
Prince, Captain, 61.
  Christopher, Captain, 325, 326, 337.
Pringle, Captain, 127.
Putnam, General, 303.
  Major, 310.

Randal, David, 109.
Ranson, Ransom, Captain, 136, 137.
  Henry, Ship *Putnam*, 60.
Rawson, ———, 258.
Rathbone, Rothbon, Rothbone, Job, Captain, 254, 255, 337.
Rathbun, Wait, 109.
Raymond, John, Colonel, 89.
Read, Captain, 210, 337.
Read & Yates, 227.
Reed, James, 323.
Remsen, Peter, 172.
Rich, Elisha, naval prisoner, 32.
  Robert, 280.
Richards, Benjamin, Captain, 80, 84.
  Captain, 241.
  Ellen, 80.
  Guy, 28, 206, 329, 330, 333.
  Guy, Jr., 29, 31.
  Guy & Son, 254.
  Nathaniel, Captain, 333-335, 337.
  P., Lieutenant, 127, 128.
  Peter, Midshipman, 46, 126.
Richardson, 112.
  James, 197.
Richmond, Colonel, 291, 294.
Ridfield, Frederick, Surgeon's mate, Ship *Putnam*, 60.
Ripley, Alice Adams, 27.
  John, 59, 238.
Roberts, Dan & Elizabeth, 255.
Robertson, Patrick, 202, 206.
Robins, Roger, Ship *Putnam*, 59.
Robinson, ———, 191, 194, 203.
  P., 212.
Rodney, Admiral, 103.
Rogers, Captain, 172, 206, 208, 250, 253, 259, 261, 264, 271, 298, 299, 312.
  E. Gorton, 148.

INDEX OF NAMES 351

Rogers, Ernest E., i, v, xvii, 50, 52, 55, 76, 139, 150, 152, 153, 162-165, 168.
Fanny Gorton, Mrs. Ernest E., iii, 162.
Harris, 11.
James, 32, 160.
John, Captain, 169, 337.
John, seaman, naval prisoner, 32.
Josiah, Captain, 9, 79, 86, 133.
Josiah, Jr., son of Captain Josiah, and stepson of Nathaniel Shaw, Jr., 9, 79, 133.
Lucretia Harris, 9, 78, 79, 133.
Peter, Captain, 11, 244, 246, 248, 254-256, 259, 260, 271, 312, 337.
Peter, Jr., 11.
Theophilus & L., 219.
Theo & Zeb, 254.
Thomas, Ship *Putnam*, 60.
Uriah, 224, 225.
William, Captain, 11, 206, 211, 223, 227, 252, 299, 300, 337.
Woodes, Captain, 52.
Rose, ———, 296, 319, 320, 323.
Alexander, 323.
Gideon, seaman, naval prisoner, 33.
Ross, ———, 307.
R. M., Lieutenant, 164.
William, naval prisoner, 33.
Rosseter, John Cotton, 109.
Rossiter, Timothy, Surgeon, Ship *Putnam*, 59.
Roundy, Uriah, Ship *Putnam*, 60.
Rowlee, 86.
Russell, Joseph, 115, 319, 321, 326.
Joseph, Jr., 306.
Samuel, seaman, naval prisoner, 32.
Thomas, 247, 318, 323, 326.
Thomas, Captain, 267, 337.
———, 330.
Ruth, John, seaman, naval prisoner, 32.

Sabens, Cesar, Ship *Putnam*, 61.
Sage, Elias, Ship *Putnam*, 61.
Salmon, John, Ship *Putnam*, 61.
Saltonstall, ———, Captain, 113, 171, 174, 215, 224, 249, 256, 261, 282, 283, 296, 304.

Saltonstall, Dudley, Captain, 24, 45, 46, 126, 249.
Gurdon, Governor, 56, 141.
Gurdon, Judge, 10, 143.
Joseph L., Ship *Putnam*, 61.
Nathaniel, 1st Lieutenant, 59, Later Captain, 55, 56, 58, 59, 64, 65, 86, 125, 199, 204, 324, 337.
Roswell, 213, 215, 242, 259, 266.
Winthrop, Justice of Peace, 29, 31.
Sampson, Alexander, naval prisoner, 32.
Sanger, ———, Engineer, 145.
Sargenton, ———, 278.
Saunders, Jonathan, naval prisoner, 33.
Schank, Schenk, 256, 257, 259, 261.
Scott, Malcolm M., Mayor, 164, 165.
Scranton, Noah, Captain of Hold, Ship *Putnam*, 59.
Seabury, Benjamin, 2d Lieutenant, 46.
Captain, 171, 337.
Sears, Isaac, Colonel, 57, 309, 311, 315, 316, 319-323.
Sergenton & Constant, 293.
Serilly, Monsieur de, 328.
Serley, Captain, 282, 337.
Setchel, Jonathan, boatswain's mate, Ship *Putnam*, 60.
Sever, William, 284, 285.
Seymour, Sinclair, Captain, 48.
Shackmaple, John, Captain, 180, 189, 192, 193, 337.
Shapley, Adam, 109.
Shattuck, William, 327.
Shaw, Daniel, 10, 11, 79.
Family, 8, 57, 66, 72, 75-77, 168.
John, 80.
Joseph, 80.
Lucretia, 71, 73, 74, 166.
Lucretia Harris Rogers, 78, 83, 84, 132.
Mary (Polly), 77, 80.
Mrs., 171, 218, 253.
Nathaniel, Jr., Continental Agent, i, xiii, xvi, xvii, 6-11, 14, 16-31, 34-44, 47, 48, 54-59, 61, 64, 65, 72-75, 77-79, 83, 86, 88, 90-106, 110-116, 119-123, 125, 132-134, 137,

Shaw, Nathaniel, Jr., continued.
  141, 143, 158, 164-167, 169, 170, 172-241, 244-249, 251, 252, 255-264, 266, 269, 271-285, 287-291, 299, 301, 303, 306-309, 311, 313, 314, 317, 318, 320, 321, 326-329, 333, 334, 336.
  Nathaniel, Sr., Captain, 68, 69, 74, 77 (his father), 79, 82, 83, 89, 167.
  Samuel, naval prisoner, 33.
  Sarah, 79.
  Temperance, 10, 68, 71, 74, 82-84.
  Thomas, 7, 9-13, 15, 21, 25, 34, 44, 71, 78, 79, 83-85, 95, 96, 106, 109, 111, 116-119, 143, 169, 175, 183, 197, 205, 284, 303, 318, 321, 322, 325-327, 331-336.
  William, 80.
Shearman, Thomas, naval prisoner, 33.
Sheffield, Isaac, Captain, 217, 337.
  John, Carpenter's mate, Ship *Putnam*, 60.
  Steors, 109.
Sheldon, Colonel, 102.
Shelly, Reuben, Ship *Putnam*, 61.
Shepherd, William, 336.
Sherebrook, ———, 178.
Sherman, Roger, 270.
Shettuck, ———, 315.
Shipman, ———, 86.
  Mrs. Leander K., 164.
Shirley, Governor, 88, 89.
  William, General, 51.
Simot, Patrick, Ship *Putnam*, 60.
Simson, John, 247.
Slaid, Thomas, 184.
  William, 184.
Slater, William A., 153.
Slattery, Thomas, Clerk, Ship *Putnam*, 59.
Slaves of Nathaniel Shaw, Jr., 11.
  Cosar [Cesar], 11.
  Prince, Negro
  Selah, 11.
  Woman [no name], 247.
Sloakum, Christopher, naval prisoner, 33.

Small, Henry, naval prisoner, 33.
Smally, Thomas, naval prisoner, 33.
Smith, ———, 144, 183.
  Agrippa, Ship *Putnam*, 59.
  Burrel, Ship *Putnam*, 60.
  C., 144.
  Captain, 257, 297, 337.
  H. B., 144.
  Jesse, Ship *Putnam*, 60.
  Joseph, Ship *Putnam*, 60.
  Joseph, 2d, 145.
  Lemuel, Ship *Putnam*, 60.
  Robert, 1st mate, Ship *Putnam*, 59.
  Robert, Continental Agent, 17, 36.
  Samuel, Ship *Putnam*, 60.
  Samuel, Jr., Ship *Putnam*, 60.
  Sylvanus, quartermaster, Ship *Putnam*, 60.
Sneids, Captain, 284, 337.
Spears, ———, 111.
Spencer, Colonel, 262.
  John, Prize Master, Ship *Putnam*, 59.
  Obadiah, Prize Master, Ship *Putnam*, 59.
Spink, ———, 269.
  Richard, Captain, 272, 273, 337.
Spooner, ———, 285.
  John, 175, 183, 220.
  Waller, 284.
Spooner & Whilfield, 284.
Sproat, David, Commissary General, 30, 33.
Squibb, Joseph, Ship *Putnam*, 59.
Squire, Joshua, Ship *Putnam*, 60.
Stanley, Stanly, John Wright & Co., 283, 298, 299, 325, 333, 336.
Stansbury, 1st Lieutenant, 45.
Stanton, ———, 298.
  Andrew, 109.
  Enoch, 109.
  Lebulon, 109.
  Phineas, Prize Master, Ship *Putnam*, 59.
  Robert, 109.
  Thomas, Ship *Putnam*, 61.
Stanton & Noyes, 117, Noice, 332.
Staplin, Edward, Ship *Putnam*, 60.

INDEX OF NAMES

Stark, ———, 50.
Starr, ———, 144.
  Daniel, Captain, 126.
States, Peter, 109.
Stedman, John W., 151.
Stephens, John, Ship *Putnam*, 59.
Stephenson, ———, 267.
Sterling, Lord, 52.
Steuben, Baron, 136.
Steward, Richard, 284.
Stewart, ———, 170, 175, 204, 210, 241, 249.
  Captain, 88, 277, 337.
  Duncan, 140, 174.
Stimson, Stephen, schooner *Endeavor*, 87.
St. James, Monsieur Beaudart de, 328.
Stocken, Timothy, Ship *Putnam*, 60.
Stoddard, Elisha, naval prisoner, 32.
  John, 204.
Stone, William, Ship *Putnam*, 61.
Stringham, ———, Commander, 145.
Strong, George C., 153.
Stuart, ———, xv.
Sullivan, ———, 195, 198.
  John, 185.
Swieft, ———, 195.

Tallmage, William, 86.
Tanner, Ebenezer, Ship *Putnam*, 59.
Tantiquigin, John, Ship *Putnam*, 60.
Target, Edward, naval prisoner, 32.
Taylor, Robert, naval prisoner, 33.
Tazewell, John, Continental Agent, 17. 36.
Temple, John, 318.
Terrill, Thomas, naval prisoner, 33.
Texier, ———, 7, 15.
Thibbin, John W., Captain, 26.
Thompson, Thomson, ———, 197, 314, 322.
  Captain, 127.
  Charles, 65.
Tibbals, Joseph, Ship *Putnam*, 59.
Tiffidy, Ephraim, Ship *Putnam*, 60.
Tilley, Tiley, Captain, 209.
  James, Captain, 271, 337.

Tillinghast, Daniel, Continental Agent, 16, 17, 27, 28, 35, 36, 39, 95-97, 106, 116, 285, 290, 291, 295, 301, 307.
Tinker, ———, 53.
  Captain, 173, 177, 195, 208, 211, 213, 214, 216, 219, 223, 225, 226, 234, 242, 255, 283, 285, 300.
  Edward, Captain, 176, 188, 190, 201, 207, 219, 224, 225, 299, 333, 336, 337.
  Edward, Jr., Captain, 243, 253, 254, 337.
  George F., Mayor, 153.
  Jehiel, Captain, 96.
  John, 133.
  Keph, Captain, 255, 337.
  Lucy, 133.
  Stephen, Captain, 87, 298, 333, 336, 337.
Tobin, Thomas, naval prisoner, 33.
Tod, John, naval prisoner, 32.
Tompkins, Benjamin, naval prisoner, 32.
Torrey, Michael, Ship *Putnam*, 60.
Tracey, Captain, 263.
  Nathaniel, Captain, 326, 337.
  Nicholass, 277.
  Robert, 277.
Tracy, 316.
Transhant, Transchant, Tranchant, ———, 258, 259, 260.
Trott, John P., 35.
Trowbridge, ———, Captain, 328, 337.
Trumbull, Governor, 8, 19-21, 26, 44, 48, 58, 72, 76, 85, 95, 96, 98, 106, 109, 112, 154, 158, 280, 285-288, 291, 296, 297, 301-303, 310, 312, 317.
  Joseph, 289, 293, 303.
Truxton, Captain, 120.
  Thomas, 122-124.
Tryon, Governor, 5.
  William, Captain, 302, 303, 337.
Tubbs, Stephen, Ship *Putnam*, 61.
Turnbull, 295, 296, 308, 326.
Turner, Dr., 330.
  Thomas, 15.

Tuttle, ———, 86.
Twigg, Daniel, Ship *Putnam*, 60.
Tyack, William, Ship *Putnam*, 60.
Tyler, ———, 86.
  John, Brigadier General, 29, 30.

Unkas, Daniel, Ship *Putnam*, 59.

Valladaxes, Manuel de, 232.
Valladoris, ———, 223.
Van Brundt, Commander, 145.
Van Bueren, Leonard, Captain, 287, 337.
Vandervoort, John, Ship *Putnam*, 61.
Vandervoort, Peter & Co., 86, 170, 176, 178, 180, 182, 183, 186-192, 194, 195, 198, 201-203, 206, 208, 209, 211, 212, 215-217, 219, 221-223, 225-230, 232-237, 239-245, 248-267, 269-271, 276, 277, 279, 281.
Van Renslear, Philip, 287.
Van Vlack & Kipp, 253.
Van Vlack & Son, 253.
Van Vleck, Henry, 188.
Van Zant, Vanzantz, Jacobus, Continental Agent, 17, 36.
Vaughan, Daniel, 3d Lieutenant, 46.
Vincent, Captain, 127.
  Joseph, 109.

Wadsworth, ———, 291, 303.
  Colonel, 322.
Jeremiah, 288, 301, 302.
Wadsworth and Carter, 328.
Wait, John T., 151.
  Marvin, 11, 109.
Waldo, Captain, 61.
Wales, ———, 54.
Wall, James, Ship *Putnam*, 60.
  John, Ship *Putnam*, 60.
Wallace, ———, Commander, schooner *Hawke*, 48.
Ward, Flora, 145.
  John L., Captain, 145.
Ware, Charles B., 153.
Warner, Elisha, 2d Lieutenant, 46.
  Seth, 3d Lieutenant, Ship *Putnam*, 59.

Warner, Wait, 230.
Warren, ———, 143.
Warricks, Gourdin, Ship *Putnam*, 59.
Washington, George, General, 6, 19, 23, 27, 28, 34, 39, 68, 70-72, 74, 75, 88-97, 105, 106, 111, 137, 139, 141, 142, 158, 165, 166, 168, 280, 285, 286, 290.
Waterman, Asa, 300.
  Jed, Captain, 171, 172, 199, 337.
  John, Ship *Putnam*, 60.
Waters, Josiah, Colonel, 305, 311, 313-315, 317-324, 327, 329, 331, 332, 335.
  Josiah, Jr., Colonel, 10, 12, 13, 55, 61, 62.
Watrous, Captain, 218, 337.
  John R., Dr., 75, 137.
Watson, James, 142.
Watson & Spooner, 285.
Wattles, John, 211.
Way, ———, 183, 184.
  Ebenezer, 9, 137, 138, 329.
Weatherhead, John, 203.
Weaver, Thomas, 2d Lieutenant, 46, 47, 51.
Webb, Colonel, 86.
  Constant, Ship *Putnam*, 60.
  Joel, Lieutenant of Marines, Ship *Putnam*, 59.
Webster, Captain, 97.
Welch, Captain, 127, 128.
Wells, David A., 152.
  John Edwin, Dr., v, xvii.
Wendell, Oliver, 247.
Wentworth, Wintworth, Samuel Solly, 268, 278.
Werden, ———, 170.
Wereat, John, Continental Agent, 36.
Westcott, Abram, 109.
Wetmore, Fanny S., 159.
Weymans, Theodeus & John, 244.
Whaley, Jonathan, Ship *Putnam*, 60.
Wharton, Isaac, 336.
  James, 131.
  Mrs., 283, 298.
  Thomas, 191.
Wharton, John, & James Reed, 323.

INDEX OF NAMES

Wharton & Lewis, 327.
Wharton, Thomas & Isaac, 86, 194, 199-203, 207, 213, 215-226, 228, 231, 233-235, 237, 239-243, 245-249, 252-255, 257-260, 262-266, 269, 270, 272, 274-277, 279, 282-284, 286, 298, 299.
Wheat, Samuel, & Thomas Pearsall, 254.
Wheelar, Edward, Captain, 256, 337.
Wheeler, Joseph, Ship *Putnam*, 60.
 Nathaniel, 86.
 Richard A., 151, 153.
Wheelock, ———, 269.
Whilfield, Gideon, 284.
Whipple, ———, 302.
 Abraham, Captain, 45.
 Amy, 11.
 Captain, 115, 126.
 Christopher, Captain, Brig *Marianne*, naval prisoner, 32.
White, John, naval prisoner, 32.
 John, Ship *Putnam*, 60.
Whitelock, ———, 260, 262.
Whitmore, John, 262.
Whyat, Daniel, naval prisoner, 32.
Wiatherlike, George, Ship *Putnam*, 60.
Wilkinson, ———, 95.
Willard, Julius, carpenter's mate, Ship *Putnam*, 60.
 S. G., 151.
Williams, ———, 115, 144, 245.
 Benjamin, Ship *Putnam*, 60.
 Charles Augustus, 152.
 Clinton, 244.
 Family, 77.
 Joshua, 109.
 Sam, 280.
 Thomas, 81.
 W., 143.
 William, 29.
Williams & Havens, 24.
Williby, Samuel, Ship *Putnam*, 59.

Willis, Abel, Prize Master, Brig *Marianne*, naval prisoner, 32.
 Frederick, naval prisoner, 32.
 William, Master Schooner *Mifflin*, 32.
Wills, ———, 325.
Willson, ———, 203.
 Thomas, Captain, 298, 337.
Wilson, ———, 180.
 Lieutenant of *Cabot*, 48.
 Thomas, 246.
Winey, Jacob, 262, 263.
Winthrop, Family, 154.
 John, Governor of Massachusetts, 154.
 John the Younger, Governor of Connecticut, 1, 2, 153-155, 160.
Wolcott, Captain, 324, 337.
 Simon, Dr., 11, 26, 91, 96, 97, Noliott, 303 (should be Wolcott).
Woodbridge, Chretia [Lucretia], 330.
 Ephraim, Rev., 77, 80, 83.
 Family, 77.
 Lucretia Shaw, 10, 11, 78, 80.
 Mary Shaw (Mrs. Ephraim), 71, 83, 84.
 Nathaniel, 330.
 Nathaniel Shaw, 10, 11, 79, 80.
 Sarah, 80.
Woodward, Asa, Ship *Putnam*, 60.
 Ashbel, 151.
 Joshua, naval prisoner, 33.
Worttles, Will, Captain, 335, 337.
Wren, ———, 127.
Wright, Charles, Ship *Putnam*, 61.
 Gilbert, 109.
Wyllys, George, 19.

Y ates, ———, 227.
Young, James, Gunner's mate, Ship *Putnam*, 60.
 William, Ship *Putnam*, 60.

INDEX OF VESSELS

Index of Names, Page 339

Active, privateer, 125.
Alfred, ship, 45-48, 51, 126, 127, 129-131, 166, 280, 284.
America, brig, 50.
  ship, 87, 105, 254, 260, 264, 278.
American, sloop, 87.
American Revenue, sloop, 298, 306, 309, 319, 320.
Andrea Doria, And Doria, Andrew Doria, continental brig, 38, 45, 46, 51, 97, 106, 286, 324.
Andrian, brig, 126.
Ariadne, ship, 127.
Aurora, ship, 32.

Bedford, 105.
Betsey, brig, 181.
  sloop, 87, 277.
Black Joke, sloop, 87, 248, 252, 266, 274, 275.
Bourbon, frigate, 41.
Bridgett, sloop, 200, 201.

Cabot, continental brig, 45-48, 51, 87, 126, 282, 286, 292, 296, 303, 304.
Caesar, schooner, 87.
Caroline, brig, 319.
Cato, ship, 331, 333, 335.
Ceres, sloop of war, 127.
Clarendon, 296.
Clinton, snow, 324.
Columbus, 45, 46, 48, 51, 115, 126, 284.
Commerce, sloop, 87.
Confederacy, 42, 43.
Constitution, frigate, 142.
Crane, galley, 50.
Culloden, ship, 105.
Cumberland, 58.
Cygnett, Cygnet, man of war, 171, 180.

Deane, frigate, 39.
Defence, brig, 87, 288.
  ship, 50.
Defiance, schooner, 87, 276, 283.
Delight, schooner, 87.
Deutchland, undersea freighter, 148.
Disco, brigantine, 87.
Dove, sloop, 87, 189, 193, 195, 196, 208, 236, 237, 239-241, 248.

Eliot, brig (afterwards Polly), 87.
Elizabeth Freeman, sloop, 87.
Endeavor, schooner, 87.

Fair Play, brig, 58.
Favourite, brig, 87, 315-320.
Fire Brand, Firebrand, 13, 328, 330, 333.
Flora, whaling ship, 145.
Fly, despatch vessel, 47, 48, 51.
Friendship, brig, 288.

General Putnam, Putnam, New London privateer, 54-58, 310, 311, 314, 315, 318, 319, 321-325.
Glasgow, man of war, 48, 126.
Groton Packett, sloop, 87.
Guilford, sloop, 50, 87.

Hannah, ship, 24.
Hannah & Molly, schooner, 87.
Happy Return, schooner, 87.
Hawk, Hawke, schooner, 48, 87, 215, 223, 225, 259-261, 264, 267.
  sloop, 251.
Hope, brig, 30.
Hornet, 47, 48, 51.

INDEX OF VESSELS

Industery, sloop, 302.
Industry, schooner, 87.
Irish Gimblet, Josh Gimblel, brig, 304, 305.

John, sloop, xvii, 122, 124.
John & Joseph, schooner, 281, 324.

La Isan Teresa, prize ship, 86.
Lark, schooner, 87, 216.
Le Despencer, 55, 64.
Liberty, sloop, 205, 210.
Little John, brig, 214.
  brigantine, 87.
Lively, sloop, 87.
Lucretia, brig, 171, 176, 185, 188, 189, 193, 196, 208.
  brigantine, 86.
  sloop, 87.
Lucy, schooner, 86.
Lyon, 312.

Macaroni, Macarone, Macaronia, Maccarone, Macerone, Mackaronia, sloop, 87, 254, 260, 265, 266, 271, 291.
Marianne, brig, 32, 87.
Mars, ship, Letter of Marque, 125.
Marshall, brig, 128.
Mary, 294, 296.
Masters Hand, 332.
Mermaid, brig, 87, 250, 255.
Mifflin, Mefflen, Flag of Truce schooner, 30, 32, 50, 87.
Millish, 300.
Minerva, brig, 333, 335.
  brigantine, 50.
  privateer, 24.
Montgomery, 300.

Nancy, brig, 199, 204, 212, 250, 262, 272, 275, 311, 324.
  brigantine, 87.
  sloop, 58, 86, 189, 193.
Nathaniel & Eliza, 323.

Navarre, Letter of Marque, brigantine, 30.
Neptune, schooner, 87.
New Defence, galley, 50.
New Pompey, 87.
Niger, frigate, 296, 297.

Old Defence, brigantine, 50.
Oliver Cromwell, ship, 50, 297, 316.

Peace, cartel, 28.
Penguin, Pinguin, cartel, 28.
Polacca, Polacre, three-masted Mediterranean vessel. Prize to the Deane, 39, 40.
Polly, sloop, 87, 246, 277.
Polly & Getty, brig, 87, 257.
Pompey, Pompy, schooner, 87, 207, 221, 222, 223, 225, 246, 276, 277.
Portious, 325.
Providence, 51, 280.
  sloop, 87, 126.
Putnam, see General Putnam.

Queen of France, private sloop of Nathaniel Shaw, Jr., 8, 11, 29, 30.
  cartel sloop, 30, 31.
  flag sloop, 31.

Raleigh, ship, 127.
Randolph, 127.
Ranger, brigantine, 309.
  ship, 127.
Rebecca, 306.
Resistance, brig, 37.
  brigantine, 303, 306-308.
Retaliation, prison ship, 44.
Revenge, sloop, 309.
Roadney, Rodney, sloop, 173, 174, 175.
Rose, man of war, 126.

Sally, brig, 331, 332.
  sloop, 87, 207, 224, 235, 237, 252, 264, 283.

Schuyler, Scuiler, Scuyler, sloop, 50, 302-304, 306.
Shark, galley, 50.
Speedwell, sloop, 86.
Spy, ship, 50, 298, 304, 325.
Success, sloop, afterwards *John*, 124.

Thames, brig, 199, 200, 201, 203, 212, 223.
  brigantine, 87.
  schooner, 244, 258, 259, 260, 267.
  sloop, 87.
Thetas, brig, 335.
Thomas, sloop, 87.

Three Sisters, schooner, 87.
True Blue, schooner, 87, 235, 241.
Trumbull, sloop, 298, 301, 303, 304, 306, 308, 309, 313.
Two Brothers, schooner, 331, 332.

Wasp, 47, 48, 51.
Whiting, galley, 50.
William, sloop, 87.

Yarmouth, ship, 64 guns, 127.
Young Cromwell, Cromwel, schooner, 34.

www.ingramcontent.com/pod-product-compliance
Lightning Source LLC
Chambersburg PA
CBHW051623230426
43669CB00013B/2160